Surviving College: Laying the Foundations for a Moral Life

www.FortifyingFamiliesofFaith.com

First edition
May 2011

Published by:
Fortifying Families of Faith
2161 Upper St. Dennis Road
St. Paul, MN 55116

Cover designed by Joan Czaia, Daystar Design
Book layout by Traditions Communications

Library of Congress Control Number: 2011922078

ISBN: 978-0-9827080-5-7

Printed in the United States of America.

Surviving College:
Laying the Foundations
for a Moral Life

By Linda Kracht

TABLE OF CONTENTS

Index of Appendices

Surviving College:
Laying the Foundations
for a Moral Life

By Linda Kracht

INTRODUCTION

"To live without regret" is a popular motto for high school yearbooks. This motto is either an idealistic or matter-of-fact philosophy to hold on to, depending on the underlying motivations. Consider how this motto could suit both hedonist and saint while producing drastically different outcomes. "To live without regret" infers that one will either live so as to not *require* repentance or apology — or to live but never give apology or experience repentance. The saint living by the "to live without regret" motto would strive to live without committing any type of transgression (sin of commission or sin of omission) or wrongdoing; ironically, true saints would be the first persons to admit or acknowledge personal sin and therefore they are less likely to hold onto such philosophies. The hedonist adopting this motto would eventually cause much damage to the world around him or her. Why? Because to live without inhibitions fails to civilize natural selfish tendencies.

This book will not try to teach you "to live without regret" but will attempt to teach you to be always mindful of words, actions, thoughts, or misdeeds that *can never be taken back.* These are sometimes characterized as the "spent arrow, the spoken word and the lost opportunity".[1] They represent the actions, words, and thoughts that de-civilize or disaffect your wellness.

The civilized society

A civilized society exhibits complexity as it strives to most excellently integrate its citizenry's needs, wants, desires, privileges, and rights. An advancing civilized society improves upon its innovation, growth, and knowledge and understanding of the sciences and related technologies in order to better serve humanity — not the other way around. Civilized societies are clearly dependent on an orderly and timely maturation of its many members. Members of a civilized society share camaraderie, concern, and respect for fellow neighbors. Key virtues are in play within civilized societies including self discipline, personal responsibility, good work ethic, and many others which will be discussed in subsequent chapters. In other words, civilized societies must operate as moral communities in order to advance the rights and freedoms of its people — orderly and protectively.

Civil societies must first reject *enslavement* of any type. Next, civilized nations must strive to uphold the dignity of every person joining, exiting, or contributing to their society. They are best equipped to do so when together they acknowledge and uphold the common belief that all people are created by the same Intelligent Design (God). Civilized societies must hold to the principle that justice for all must be equally but blindly meted out.

Stable, wholesome families are the cornerstone of a civil society; it is from these families that future members of the society will descend. These new members will provide the social and human capital resources necessary for growth (gross domestic product). Children from wholesome families will mature into tomorrow's productive adults, parents, and citizens. Civil societies recognize the uniquely important roles of marriage and parenthood.

Collectively, civilized societies bless their Creator for the gifts bestowed upon the members and the nations, gifts that include Truth, Wisdom, Knowledge, Peace, Love, and Freedom.

By contrast, uncivilized societies are socially or culturally undeveloped and they remain that way or become that way for a variety of reasons. These nations disregard the true rights and freedoms of various members. They show a lack of regard for fellow members. Their justice is not *blindfolded* against prejudices towards individual members. Barbarian societies have little interest in advancing themselves into a civilized culture with orderly governance balanced by moral laws and just reasoning. They lack spiritual depth beyond their own fabrications. Their members are aggressive and they elevate self preservation and self-interests above their neighbors' needs. The men become predators within their own society. Women and children are at the mercy of the predators' appetites or considerations. People's personal dignity and worth are generally undervalued. Lack of civilization allows and accepts vice.

It can be argued that there is a bit of barbarianism within every nation. We saw this barbarism recently after Haiti was hit by a 7.0 magnitude earthquake on January 12, 2010. This devastating earthquake brought out the best examples of amity and the worst examples of barbarianism and enmity. Civilizing agents provided blessings to disaffected people via disaster relief, organization, law enforcement, governance and hope. By contrast, the uncivilized agents plundered, raped, killed, rioted, and took personal advantage of the disaster.

Recently a New York resident tried to help a woman being attacked by another man. The scuffle felled the Good Samaritan; he lay bleeding from stab wounds on the sidewalk. Over the course of an hour more than twenty people were caught on camera passing by without concern or even calling 9-1-1. Finally, an hour later, one person phoned the police who arrived too late. The Good Samaritan – Hugo Alfredo Tale-Yax – had already died. These and other similar incidents are symptomatic of a society that is moving away from civility and amity.[2]

An uncivilized culture

The college culture can be either a civilized or an uncivilized frontier for young people. The primary purpose and mission of a college is noble as it tries to advance knowledge, thought, science, and society. Yet, many college students face increased personal risk due to a college culture that resists governance, oversight, hope, and virtuous living. This lack of civility is even expected and encouraged by some older adults who look the other way. Ironically, the instability of the

3

moral culture has led many college students to believe that universities do not even have the **right** to try and instill character, prepare them for a democratic society, or create communities conducive to learning.[3] Consequently, most of today's religious and secular colleges are not the moral communities many students and parents expect. Even more surprising and disappointing is the fact that **most** Catholic colleges are no longer considered to be communities of high moral standards and principles; in fact they evidence a similar coarsening of values and culture as secular institutions. Many students attending Catholic colleges do not even realize they are attending a *religiously-affiliated institution*. Caution: If students think they will have an automatic reprieve from uncivilized cultural influences while attending a Catholic college, they are seriously mistaken. It seems strange that the greater society permits the continued erosion of civility and moral living at any college.

But barbarism or lack of civility does not have to describe you and your friends. College can offer a myriad of benefits to students who attend these institutions of higher education for the right reasons while simultaneously ordering their maturation properly and on a timely basis. You probably already recognize that the advanced coursework is not what makes college life so difficult. No, the difficulties of college come about because students are thrust into a less *civilized culture* at a time in their lives when they are not **100 percent** convinced of who they are, their purpose in life, or where they are headed. Essentially, the typical college culture positions many students for failure as it juxtaposes the desire to fit in with the desire to find oneself, or the desire to succeed independent of fitting in. The culture will ask the college student to make many decisions that affect life, well-being, and health without arming them with objective knowledge, truth, virtue, personal goals, or advantages. The decisions and choices are even more difficult at this time of life because college students have a case of limited life experience, knowledge, maturity, and *stage fright*. Many students get through this stage by **giving in** to the desire to fit in according to the uncivil parts of the culture.

Society in general provides many mixed messages confusing many people including your age group — the Millennials. The 2010

Marist/KofC Poll[+] reveals that your peers hold inconsistent and often contradictory beliefs about morality, religion, spirituality, abortion, cohabitation, marital infidelity, medical testing on animals, gambling, out of wedlock births, economic decisions, same sex unions, spirituality, moral choices, and more. The poll results show that moral confusion reigns among college students affecting their decisions and therefore their lives. The results will be highlighted in upcoming chapters.

Your future outcome *is* affected by the choices and decisions that you make now. Please think twice before wasting your energy on things that can never be taken back. Do not spend useless arrows, speak hurtful words, or waste golden opportunities or time.

Maturation

Your path forward can go many different directions. You can merge quickly into the mainstream college culture, or you can travel by way of a completely different but parallel path. The path you choose and the decisions made will make your college experience frustrating or fulfilling. The path will determine your success or failure, the degree of that success, or the degree of that failure. While college students will eventually *emerge* into society as a full-fledged adult, not all will mature in a timely or properly-formed fashion. Achieving both the diploma and appropriate maturity will require that you work at *civilizing* immature tendencies and selfish interests. Remember that maturation is partially defined as being in the state of self mastery.

The total sum of our acquired virtues, talents, knowledge, wisdom, and faith should approximate our chronological age. In other words, all college graduates should be objectively and subjectively more virtuous, talented, knowledgeable, wise, and faithful than they were before entering college. If not, they will have actually receded from acquiring genuine **personal freedom** and its accompanying blessing.

We have been forewarned that it is "to the kindly influence of Christianity that we owe that degree of civil freedom and political and social happiness which mankind now enjoys. In proportion as the genuine effects of Christianity are diminished in any nation, either through unbelief or the corruption of its doctrines or the neglect of its institutions; in the same proportion will the people of that nation recede from the blessings of genuine freedoms and approximate the miseries of complete despotism. All efforts to destroy the foundations of our holy religion ultimately tend to the subversion also of our political freedom and happiness. Whenever the pillars of Christianity shall be overthrown our present forms of government and all the blessings which flow from them must fall with them."[5] Lack of progress toward civility and maturity only serves to hamper freedoms and social happiness.

Choices made become critical to the formation of future lifestyles. We make choices based on knowledge; however we may still remain misinformed or under-informed because of the avenues or routes to knowledge that we take. A person committing serious sin must know that an action is wrong, know the seriousness of the matter, and freely choose to commit the act. Similarly, a person avoiding serious sin knows the same things about the offense but chooses not to commit the sin for the same reasons just listed. Both deliberate decisions affect these people's future choices which, when repeated, turn into a way of life – a lifestyle. Everyone is capable of developing a virtuous lifestyle; similarly we are all capable of developing a hedonistic, narcissistic or wild lifestyle. It's about free choice.

In this book you will see how "living on the edge" contrasts sharply with living soundly while in college. Future chapters will reveal the significance of having long and short term goals as you begin transitioning into the adult world. Goal setting will be discussed in chapter two. You will soon see why this book focuses a great deal of attention to all of the wellness factors or markers for the entire self including religious, social, psychological, personal, and health components.

You live in a culture that spawns a lot of decoys to try and get your attention. These decoys are discussed in later chapters as well. Decoys are capable of forming lifestyles; they can also produce calamity or catastrophe. Chapters eight and nine discuss the various calamities that result from decoys. Finally, the book will end with discussions about two types of vocations, marriage and the religious life — one will be your ultimate calling. Long and short term goals will help prepare you to live out your vocation most excellently.

Advanced training for the rest of your life

College students are in a constant state of training – physical, mental, social, spiritual, psychological, emotional. This training will help you acquire higher levels of critical thinking skills, personal virtue, spiritual depth, financial independence, emotional stability, maturity, wisdom, and the ability to recognize truth. This training should be positive; when negative it does not help you progress toward healthy adulthood.

Many of you train physically and mentally with great regularity simply through your participation in a variety of sports teams, military ROTC programs, vigorous academic coursework, social organizations, and more. Some of you vigorously train to improve your personal health and fitness. We all realize that in order to attain higher and higher levels of physical fitness we need to regiment our physical bodies to balanced but successively more difficult conditioning. No person can tell himself, "tomorrow I am going to run 24 miles," or "tomorrow I am going to go in the ring and box with the best fighter," unless he or she has first prepared for the ordeal. Training is important and necessary; while getting in shape is neither easy nor fun, it is necessary before being qualified or capable of achieving the next level of performance. Olympians train for years to be the best at their sport and we all admire their devotion, ability, and strength. Their physical efforts are memorable and laudable. For the rest of us, just staying at "average" still requires effort and attention in order to stay active and healthy.

College students are in training to become more intellectually fit. This training may also not be very easy or fun as it demands your attention, devotion, and understanding about new constructs, principles, and theories.

The connection between physical fitness and weight and strength training and intellectual fitness with academic vigor is immediate and obvious. Ask yourself why it can be so difficult to appreciate the importance and need for additional training in order to improve upon spiritual fitness, mental and emotional fitness, and social and lifestyle fitness. By the way, how and whether we train to be fit in these additional areas helps prepare (or not prepare) us for the many other challenges that will eventually come our way in marriage, managing and assuming responsibility (for ourselves and others), helping the poor and needy, providing positive (or negative) social capital in our communities, etc. One day, you will all ponder your past – which is today's present time. You will wonder whether today's *vocational* training was effective or ineffective, progressive or regressive, positive or negative, helpful or hurtful, enough or not enough? Joy, success, happiness, and peace will be dependent on how excellently (or miserably) we lived out our life's vocation. The positive states of life make it easier to assess the degree by which we have spent arrows, lost opportunities, or miss-spoke words.

The way I see it, college students aren't opposed to the development of **virtues** because even physical and intellectual fitness training requires the development of specific human virtues such as self control and self discipline. But why do so many students experience so many personal, social, mental, emotional, and spiritual problems growing up? It is principally because many in your age group have yet to understand that "their body is like an artist's expressive medium that is not a **shapeless** raw material or immaterial but is a work of art **in waiting.**" You are waiting to be **drawn out** of the marble, the colors, or the musical notes **by God's handiwork**. You are an **image and likeness that is to be designed after the Creator** in order to co-create beauty that can be shared with the rest of the world.[6] Any denial of the need to be drawn out or be part and parcel of God's design and handwork only serves to oppose *much needed, advanced training* for life, love, and wisdom.

Furthermore, the progress made toward spiritual and human virtue is much more abstract than the achievement of physical or academic fitness. Many of us fail to appreciate the spiritual progress that we make simply because the results are not necessarily obvious. In fact, acquiring a deeper spirituality may even take us into a desert in which we fail to feel God's presence. After founding the Missionaries of Charity, Mother Teresa felt that her spiritual life became painfully dry, dark, and lonely. She rarely felt God's presence in contrast to earlier years which had provided her with a close relationship with Him. She felt tortured by this ongoing feeling of spiritual loneliness and dryness.[7] Theologians suggest that our inability to perceive Christ's presence does not mean he isn't there; rather the spiritual dryness can become the means by which we carry out even greater works for God (as evidenced by Mother Teresa's – and others – efforts). When used in this way, it is actually a gift from God Himself.

Therefore, it is imperative to recognize the evidence of God's handiwork as you advance in knowledge and understanding. Furthermore, this evidence is needed in all dimensions of your life including the psychological, personal, social, and cognitive dimensions. Taking and making the time to train in the areas of life and love will impact your future joy and success as a wife or husband, father or mother, employee, fellow citizen, neighbor, and daughter or son of God. Many of these advanced courses won't be found online or in college texts – rather they will come about through obedience to the church, reading and listening to those who have lived successful, joy-filled vocations in either single, religious or married lives, and by actively pursuing the acquisition of virtue. This fitness training will also require your participation in advanced religious instruction, Bible Studies, evening seminars, marriage seminars, pre-marriage seminars, etc.

Vocations

We are all created by God for a purpose whether we recognize it or not. Some of you are called to find that purpose in married life; others will be called to find that purpose in religious life; others still will be called to find purpose in single life. Your calling or *vocation* is the means by which you will allow yourself to be **drawn out of the** expressive medium that is you — *a work in progress.* Your drawing out by God's handiwork will be fruitful, joyful, and bring beauty to the rest of the world. Susan Pitman of the Archdiocese of St. Paul and Minneapolis explains further: "all of us can realize God's love more fully when we follow the vocation He designed for us. It is when young people find and follow God's designed path forward, they will find the most happiness possible in this life."[8]

Vocations and their paths of discovery will be different for each person and therefore it is necessary to discern for yourself what it is for you. Only when we keep our lives centered on God do we allow Him to draw us out to discern and discover our vocation – our path forward. If we are not moving closer to God we will be moving away from His guiding hand. Our unique vocation should remind us how we are each designed for a very special purpose.

Until you discover your God-given vocation, your search will likely be frustrating, seemingly endless or dangerous. It is a mistake to stumble into a vocation as often happens in marriage more so than religious life. The religious life requires more formation than entering the married life. Also it is important not to follow your friends into their vocations; rather, it is important for you to allow God to *draw you out.*

The term vocation has several classic definitions. A secular understanding of vocation is that it is somebody's job, work or profession – especially those *that require special types of commitment and education* including physicians, lawyers, engineers, or therapists. A second understanding of the word is closer to the definition pertinent to this section of the book. Vocation is the special feeling or calling that allows a person to follow Christ more closely. It is a *specific type* of work that is chosen by God. Vocations allow us to witness to a Christian life; it aims to order temporal things according to God; it allows us to inform our "world" about the power of the Gospel; it allows us to commit ourselves to the evangelical counsels appropriate for our particular state in life.[9] Thus, vocation means being called as a witness for God regardless of our state in life: married, religious, or single.

Oftentimes, vocation is the term applied to those entering the priesthood or a religious order. It is through marriage, however, that *most* of us will walk into our vocation. This vocation entails being a holy spouse first, a parent secondarily, and an employee thirdly.

Research suggests that college students desire to have, and need help in sorting through, the myriad of ways to navigate mainstream college culture so they can discover their God-given purpose and vocation in life and find happiness. In fact, college students are generally the first to acknowledge they have not yet reached adulthood and have a long way to go before being able to contribute significantly to a large, complex society. Furthermore, most college students readily acknowledge they are easily influenced by peers. These pages hope to influence you as well. Each chapter will ask you to consider short term and long term goals for each of the areas of wellness presented in the book. Each area will present its own unique set of challenges as you work through, and attend to, your goals.

History tells us...

You may presume that society – and its subcultures – will continue to advance naturally along a civilized path once begun regardless of personal choices or decisions made by its members. In fact, many people fail to appreciate the importance and essential nature that each person plays in advancing their own culture. History shows us that this natural advance is not always guaranteed. Instead, ongoing attention and effort to "put on" virtue — collective and individual — is what advances a civil society. In fact, the founding fathers believed that virtue was the foremost civilizing factor that advanced culture. Let's take a brief look at earlier perspectives.

In 1788, George Washington wrote in a letter to Benjamin Lincoln: "no one can rejoice more than I do at every step the people of this great country take to preserve the Union, establish good order and government and to render the nation happy at home and respectable abroad. Wondrously strange then and much to be regretted indeed would it be, were we to neglect the means, and to depart from the road which Providence has pointed us, so plainly; I cannot believe it will ever come to pass. The Great Governor of the Universe has led us too long and too far on the road to happiness and glory, to forsake us in the midst of it. By folly and improper conduct, proceeding from a variety of causes we may now and then get bewildered; but I hope and trust that there is good sense and virtue enough left to recover the right path before we shall be entirely lost."[10]

Clearly, G. Washington believed that our future was dependent on good sense and virtue of all the people.

Earlier, John Adams had expressed similar beliefs when he wrote:

"It may be the will of Heaven that America will suffer calamities still more wasting and distresses yet more dreadful. If this is to be the case, it will have this good effect at least: it will inspire us with many virtues, which we have not, and correct many errors, follies, and vices which threaten to disturb, dishonor, and destroy us. The furnace of affliction produces refinement, in states as well as individuals. And the new governments we are assuming, in every part, will require purification from our vices, and an augmentation of our virtues or there will be no blessings... But I must submit all my hopes and fears to an overruling Providence; in which unfashionable as the faith may be, I firmly believe."[11]

Jedediah Morse warned that *"as the genuine effects of Christianity are diminished in any nation, either through unbelief or the corruption of its doctrines or the neglect of its institutions, in that same proportion will the people of that nation recede from the blessings of genuine freedoms and approximate the miseries of complete despotism.[12]*

These several historical figures teach us that civilizations advance when they have collective virtue and faith. Together we have seen how this collective virtue and faith helped eradicate unjust slavery laws, instilled civil rights for women and minorities, worked to educate all populations of society, and overturned other unjust laws. The civil rights movement alone proves our need to rely on God's Wisdom and Justice in order to resolve conflict and execute righteous laws. Humans are notably fallible and often misinterpret His truth, therefore, we need God in order to get it right. As a Christian nation, the United States continues to be a beacon for other nations around the world who do little to feed their hungry, clothe their naked, or give comfort to the sick. But Faith, Hope, and Trust are necessary for continuing our advancement of civility. No society should presume that its civilization naturally continues to advance the greater good of its citizens when its various members and sub-cultures (including ones of higher learning) do not also pay attention to their spiritual development and virtue to ward off vice.

Conclusion

Know that today is the beginning of the rest of your life. You are the captain of your own ship. You will steer yourself into your future; that is your responsibility. But know that Someone still needs to provide the wind for your sails. Without God's energy you can easily run adrift or hit the doldrums. But when, why, and where you plan to sail is completely your choice. As you continue, remember the three things in life that can never be taken back: the spent arrow, the spoken word, and lost opportunity. Think about your spent arrows, spoken words and lost opportunities going forward. Minimize the energy spent on the things you cannot retrieve.

Her poem

Blessed Mother Teresa of Calcutta (1910-1997) composed the following short poem entitled Life. Read it first and then turn to the Appendix for Chapter One to answer the questions with regard to each line of this poem.

Life

Life is an opportunity, benefit from it.

Life is beauty, admire it.

Life is bliss, taste it.

Life is a dream, realize it.

Life is a challenge, meet it.

Life is a duty, complete it

Life is a game, play it.

Life is a promise, fulfill it.

Life is a sorrow, overcome it.

Life is a song, sing it.

Life is a struggle, accept it.

Life is a tragedy, confront it.

Life is an adventure, dare it.

Life is luck, make it.

Life is too precious, do not destroy it.

Life is life, fight for it.

Reflection Questions:

1. What are your thoughts after reading the Introduction?

2. List questions you would like to discuss with your group or class.

Chapter One

GOING TO COLLEGE

Parents want their children to have the opportunity to go to college; therefore 95 percent of freshmen high school students intend to do just that. Through their high school years, however, their ambition disappears, especially for a disproportionate number of male and minority students. "Between 12 percent and 34 percent of students can't even think about going to college because they will not have finished high school (or earned a diploma); 15 percent to 50 percent of minority students do not graduate with a high school diploma."[1] Clearly, academic success and college goals evaporate for many students due to changing personal, social, and economic circumstances.

For most students, the goal of going to college is still possible, but that *goal* has to be fine-tuned and expanded beyond simply *wanting* to go to college. Parents and other adults must help college-bound students set post secondary education goals broader than simply getting into a college. Mission statements for universities provide students with lofty reasons to go to college. They include being dedicated to the advancement of learning and the search for truth; to the sharing of this knowledge through education for a diverse community; the pursuit of research, learning, and study among student and faculty; the cultivation of a lifelong love for learning among students and professors; the acquisition of increased knowledge; the application of increased knowledge of the various life sciences, social sciences, ecological sciences, agricultural sciences, and engineering to improve and save lives; the promotion of wise stewardship of the earth's natural resources among its graduates; the development of future financial, social, political, and religious leaders for companies, communities, states, and nations; the advancement of critical thinking skills; the advancement of all good literature, arts and sciences; and development of safer and healthier communities; to generate, disseminate and preserve knowledge and to bring that knowledge to bear on the worlds' great challenges.[2] When college students adopt these same reasons, their goal of going to college is worthwhile. Acquisition of critical thinking skills and the advancement of knowledge and understanding should be the expected goals and outcomes for every college-bound student.

Attaining a higher education and degree is expected to help advance the economic, social, technological, artistic, moral, and spiritual condition of society. Quality higher education is therefore perceived to be a necessity for an advancing and healthy society. College education provides unique opportunities whereby students can readily soak up opinion, influence, instruction, and attitude; in essence your college experience will *reform you* — with your cooperation. College will refine and influence your brain and your body as you continue to mature and grow. It will also give you the opportunity to influence and instruct others. Or will it?

The college dream – expecting success

Going to college is still the dream – and reality – for a majority of high school students. Parents are happy when their students hold on to the goal of attending college, have successful college careers, and graduate with degrees that promise to improve their adulthood *social status and personal success*. Today a much higher percentage of high school students (67 percent) attend college after high school compared to earlier generations (49 percent went to college in 1972).[3] However, the actual graduation rate is quite dismal as you shall soon discover.

Like freshman high school students, college freshmen expect success. Both age groups bring refreshing idealism and hope to their peers. Unfortunately hopes and idealistic attitudes vanish too quickly among both groups. Recently, a professor at the Carlson School of Business at the University of Minnesota asked his business class what they thought was the average graduation rate for incoming college freshmen. Most of the students thought that at least 90 percent of incoming college students graduate from college. Little did they realize that less than 36 percent of their peers actually earn a post-secondary degree within four years (eight semesters). This number rises to 58 percent when examining graduation rates for a six-year stint in college.[4] It is also important to know that while only 12 percent of college students expect to switch majors, the vast majority (65 percent – 85 percent[5]) of them actually change their primary field of study at some point *after* declaring their original major. Also, while only 2 percent of students expect to fail a course, a much larger number of students actually fail class or two: 16 percent. One percent of students polled expected to drop out of college, but nearly half of those polled failed to graduate. Furthermore, students who attend private universities take longer to graduate than students who attend public institutions. Also, fewer students (8 percent) expect to take longer than four years to graduate even though in reality more than 65 percent of private university students (who do graduate) and 55 percent of public university students took at least six years to graduate! This means a whole lot of students aren't graduating from college until they are at least twenty-four years old! It also means a lot of extra money is being spent on securing a degree that could have been earned in less time.

Low graduation rates and lengthy, unproductive under-graduate college stints are costly and often caused by a loss, or lack, of students' vision, planning, commitment, or focus. Some degree programs actually involve semester or yearlong internships. While these co-op experiences delay graduation dates, they do not increase the number of semesters — ideally eight — spent in college. These co-operative education programs provide students with positive, practical, and unique and paid on-the-job work experience prior to graduation; they are highly recommended even if they delay your graduation date. Companies participating in such programs often look to hire the best co-op students after graduation. It is a win-win for students and employers; the students had a chance to get to know the company and the job while earning significant amounts of money and the company was able to assess students' work ethics and abilities prior to hiring them permanently.

College bound and in-college students need to know why going to college is important and they must internalize these reasons when going to college. They must prepare for college by setting and having appropriate goals and plans. They also need encouragement to stick to these plans even when immersed in a culture that is not very supportive. Success is yours to be had when you put real life goals into play. And, it is important to remember that solid, higher learning does indeed help advance civilization when directed toward good.

Why is college so difficult?

You should know that the socio-cultural decoys — not only academics — make college more difficult for many students. Experts suggest that your generation – the Millennials — are high performers. This means you all have high potential for success. But your peer group is also considered "high maintenance" due to having been pampered, coddled, and programmed through a slew of activities since you were toddlers.[6] This helps explain why many of your peers face personal difficulties when fending for themselves in a less-civil, less-directed environment. It also explains why many of your peers pursue and advance less civil, less-directed environments. Yes, it is the case that many will have difficulty navigating mainstream college culture.

It is expected that children and adolescents are "self-focused" due to their state in life which is in constant flux for a variety of reasons. Therefore, they are also expected to (under normal conditions) answer to parents, teachers, siblings, and other authority figures in order to minimize negative consequences resulting from this lack of broader perspective. Nearly all children and adolescents live at home with at least one parent with household rules and standards to follow. All of these children will be considered fully-fledged adults before the age of thirty – ready or not. By this time an "entire new web of commitments has been established. In between, there are few ties that entail daily obligations and commitments to others."[7] This is where college students fit in between adulthood and high school with few ties that entail daily obligations and commitment to others. And that's problematic.

What about college students? Are they adults or emerging adults? Jeffrey Jensen Arnett, author of the *Emerging Adulthood*, suggests that college students are emerging into adulthood with five common characteristics: The emerging adult frequently questions his or her own identity; they feel there is a lot of instability in their life; theirs is a self-focused age although the focus on career and jobs begin to focus more sharply than other areas; it is the age of feeling in between adolescence and adulthood; and, it is the age of possibilities where hopes flourish and they believe they have unparalleled opportunity to transform their lives for the better.[8] Many other sociologists also tag college-age students as emerging adults. Curiously, college students have few ties that entail daily obligations and commitments to others.[9] Lacking meaningful commitments and few obligations — including *dedication* to school, friendships, studies, jobs, physical well being, and religion and future relationships and responsibilities can explain why many students suffer from a loss of focus, confusion, and personal difficulties while living within the college culture.

College students must learn to set aside extra-ordinary self focus (self-centeredness, high maintenance characteristics, selfish demands, personality flaws) while growing "other focused" characteristics. Furthermore, personal and academic goals must be owned, achieved, and determined by each student; they must not be someone else's dreams and goals. More importantly, students must set personal goals that support academic, social, spiritual, emotional, mental, and psychological, physical, and economic success. Successful students learn to avoid the common pitfalls of college culture which include: denial of consequences from risk taking; declining physical fitness; declining emotional health; increased stress; fear of failure; concerns about relationships; and sexual violence.[10] Students who are not successful in college frequently fall into one or more of the common pitfalls listed above.

Many new college students rapidly lose their more familiar moral compass when they hit mainstream college culture. This loss creates tension within. Other new students may feel like a *fish out of water* in the new surroundings.

Many do not like feeling *in-between* adolescence and adulthood; this unsettling feeling can also challenge a student's resolve and commitment to success. College students exercise free choice and decision-making that falls somewhere between maturity and immaturity. Students can feel as if they are taking steps back and forth toward and away from maturity.

Experts suggest that it is natural to feel "in-between" as long as both the relevant past and expected future are still within a frame of reference.[11] In other words, feeling in between should be uncomfortable enough to make you yearn for tomorrow yet comfortable enough that you enjoy today without getting stuck here. Thus, it is natural to have shifting plans; it is perfectly acceptable to change from Plan A to Plan B, provided the revisions are thoughtful, natural, wholesome, and productive consequences of your exploration.[12] This state of being in-between can also be exciting and productive when explorations are undertaken with purpose and thoughtfulness.

This in-between state of life can leave you feeling energized, adaptable, and hopeful. The opportunities before you are staggering and exciting. You may occasionally suffer from conflicting feelings; one minute you will be excited while later you may feel discontentment or boredom. You will discover your abilities and your Achilles Heel. You will face challenges and rewards, stability and uncertainty; fear and courage; confusion and understanding; incivility and regard for others. All of these will either propel you, or interrupt your progress, toward adulthood. Together, these conflicting feelings and challenges will help you discover who you are, why you were made, and where your life is headed *if you pay attention to the outcomes and consequences of your actions.* In short, this is the time to undertake Big, Hairy, Audacious Goals (known in strategic planning sessions as BHAG's) checked against real life.

Your college explorations do not have to be fraught with high risk, danger or rationalizations (lost opportunities, mis-spoken words or spent arrows)! Instead, you have the opportunity to become the game changer for future generations to come.

Who is at risk?

Male students, in particular, have a higher risk for failing in college because they have more *"agility* problems when it comes to adjusting to campus living. They often lack organizational skills, prioritization, time management, and successful study habits and methods. Concrete goals are more elusive for young male students."[13] Thus, it is especially important that young college men create and stick to realistic, wholesome goals when pursuing higher educational levels.

Prolonged periods of selfishness and self centeredness do not advance maturation; self-focused students can get stuck in high maintenance modes or undertake behaviors that are highly exploitative, dangerous, or risky. These pathways seldom provide students with clear answers about who they really are. Risky behaviors do not allow progress or success — they essentially slow down one's progress toward maturity.

Academic challenges

It would be naïve to presume that college only serves up socio-cultural challenges; college can also serve up stiff academic challenges. Academics definitely increase student's stress levels. Increasing stress levels can cause some students to lose their focus or commitment for school. It is important to realize that many of students arrive at college academically unprepared due to a variety of reasons. Let's examine a few of them.

Today, universities admit students that come from more diverse backgrounds than ever before; many of these students – particularly first generation college students - are not wholly prepared for what lies ahead for them.[14] Standards of admission have changed in part due to affirmative action programs and fighting over a dwindling supply of the college bound student populations. Increased enrollment is the No. 1 way to increase revenues. But even relaxed admission standards or affirmative action programs do not doom students to academic failure.

It is also true that too many college students coast through high school. This has been shown to be academically costly for many students once they reach college. Students drift through high school academics for a myriad of reasons, including personal distractions and low academic expectations from instructors, self or parents. Less rigorous high school curriculums can cause some students to drift through high school. Regardless of the reasons, drifting through high school generally makes it that much more difficult to acclimate to the rigor of college academia. In fact, studies show that the intensity of the student's high school curriculum influences whether a student earns a college degree. "The academic intensity factor tops other factors including family income, high school grades, ethnicity, and test scores — ACT or SAT."[15]

While these *pre-conditions* make it more difficult to overcome academic failure, they should not preclude any college student's success. Today's students *are capable students;* they can adapt. Some students will simply have to work that much harder, or seek extra tutoring from professors and/or teaching assistants, in order to adapt to the academic rigor. They will have to want to *work* for their grades. Others discover they need to learn and apply new, appropriate time management skills. It is true that one's chances for academic success increase when students are strongly motivated to succeed, free from financial worries and difficulties, have supportive family and friends, know what they plan to pursue, and how they plan to pursue it. Conversely, students who fail to work toward concrete goals while in college often leave the same institution as unprepared as when they came.

Looking ahead

Preparing for tomorrow's future will help bring it to fruition. Unfortunately, college students are often only encouraged to think ahead in terms of career, jobs, and financial rewards. These goals are important but other matters are equally importantly including long range personal goals pertaining to the discovery of one's vocation — marriage, religious life, or singlehood. Short-sighted goals that foster self centered discoveries, materialism, consumerism or anti-family attitudes, work against finding your vocation or higher calling.

In the past, a person was considered to be an adult when they got married and/or had children. Today, the defining moment of having reached adulthood has been postponed; in fact many sociologists consider college students to be emerging into adulthood even after the age of twenty-six. This helps explain why legislation has been proposed allowing dependent children – up to the age of twenty-six – to stay on their parents' medical plans.

Today, the general markers defining adulthood include the following. A person is considered to be an adult when they make a single big purchase such as a home or car; attain "financial independence" or assume full responsibility for their personal actions. Adulthood also is attained when a person is able to shoulder the responsibility for the *actions of others* under his/her professional and personal line of duties. It is also generally marked with the willingness and desire to marry and to have children. Adults should be able to make independent decisions that are fruitful, virtuous, and wholesome for those within their "bubble" including dependents, spouses, neighbors, fellow employees, subordinates, and others. Adulthood is marked by personal *stability* benefiting all those within the adults' sphere of influence. Adulthood is not the time to wait to be handed a silver platter. Adults work to be successful. Adulthood is marked by changing the focus from self to a focus on others. Adulthood is also marked by aligning real life with the ideal life; today's idealism should be merging with tomorrow's realities. Ongoing explorations still take place but full-fledged, caring adults are generally more interested in looking out for those in their care than undertaking explorations that put these loved ones at risk, whether financially, psychologically, socially, or physically. Finally, adulthood is marked by stability. Yet even adults change and grow. For example, a thirty year old will normally have different dreams and goals than when he or she reaches the age of sixty or ninety. All people, regardless of age, should set goals that help them *grow* personally, emotionally, spiritually, and physically *according to the sum of their years.* Henry W. Longfellow wrote: "Age is opportunity no less than youth itself — though in another dress."

College can be your springboard into adulthood, career, marriage, family life, and successes or failures. So jump off the springboard with intact goals and plans and with your eyes wide open.

Reflection Questions:

1. Why did you pick the college you are attending? Is it a good fit? Why?

2. What challenges do you face today?

3. Why are you in college?

4. What are your plans after college?

ATTENTION TO SUCCESS BY SETTING GOALS

Throughout this book we will discuss the impact community living has on individual lives. Interestingly, the U.S. Department of Health and Human Services (HHS) draws a close link between the two. They say: *Individual health and community health—the health of the community in which individuals live, work, and play are interrelated. Community health is profoundly affected by the collective beliefs, attitudes, and behaviors of everyone who lives in the community.* This statement is very pertinent for the chapters ahead.

Definition of wellness

Too often, the definition of personal wellness is very narrowly defined to be an **outcome** pertaining only to our physical state. Narrow definitions fail to account for the fact that humans are multi-faceted creatures; we *are only as well* as the overall balance of our different parts that make us whole. It is widely acknowledged that each human person has a spiritual dimension, a mental and emotional (psychological) dimension, a physical dimension, an intellectual dimension, a social dimension and a career/academic dimension. The state of a person's health is also connected to the general state of health of one's community. Furthermore, wellness includes a well-balanced belief system, attitude, and behavior. The balance of all these components is as necessary to maintain wellness.

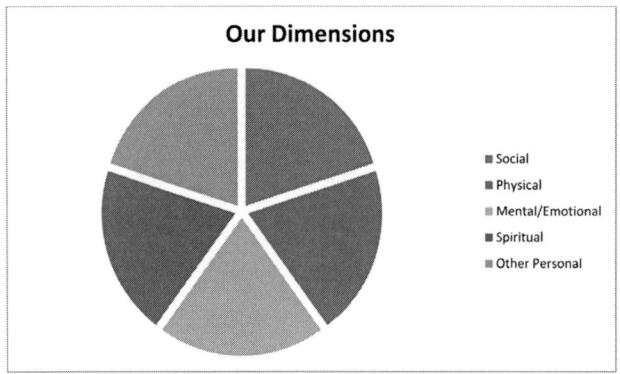

The Six Components of Self: Emotional & Mental, Social, Physical, Spiritual, Career, and Intellectual

The balance of our emotional, mental, social, physical, and spiritual dimensions is delicate — just as is the design of earth. When we pollute the earth we know there will be disastrous ecological effects. You probably recognize just how special planet earth is since it is the only planet capable of supporting human life. Our earth maintains temperatures that support life in part because of plate tectonics. But this isn't all. We are the perfect distance from the sun. If we were closer to the sun, or farther away, the result would be disastrous. The earth's design is perfect for holding the air and water necessary to maintain life – again not too much and not too little. When the earth experiences environmental changes due to the human hand, scientists worry that this perfect balance will be lost, and the consequences will endanger human life.

In the pages ahead, you will see that *polluting* (to make something impure or unclean by introducing chemicals, waste products, or damaging substances) your mental, physical, social, psychological, emotional dimensions will negatively impact your overall wellness. Just as there is only one earth, you only have one body to live in. Maintaining balance to ensure your personal wellness is important.

The World Health Organization (WHO) defines health as the "state of complete physical, mental, and social wellbeing and not merely the absence of disease and infirmity."[1] Unlike the HHS definition, the WHO definition seems to dismiss any link between health and spiritual wellness. However, Dr. Halbert Dunn[2] insists that wellness is: "an integrated method of functioning that is oriented toward maximizing the potential of which the individual is capable. It requires that the individual maintain a continuum of balance and purposeful direction with the environment in which he/she functions; it includes body, mind and spirit."[3]

Colleges and wellness

Today's colleges seem to be in the business of promoting wellness; this is readily apparent when visiting state-funded campuses that boast about their state of the art health/physical fitness facilities. The college fitness centers employ "analytical tools and techniques that assess and measure the wellness of student groups." These assessments measure and compare the wellness of first-year students to older students; some colleges compare their first-year students to first-year students from other universities or to national averages. They run these assessments in order to identify *behaviors* that impair students' wellness. These determinations can then be used to develop "wellness promotion strategies."

Unfortunately, all researchers face the difficulty of framing their studies in ways that allow them to find conclusive *physical* evidence linking student *behaviors* and some physical, spiritual, mental, or social *illness*. When studies fail to conclusively link behaviors to illness — other than physical for example — too often the researchers faultily assume there is no link and all is well. College faculty and students thereby avoid confronting the reality that a person's wellness is made up of inter-dependencies between their emotional, mental, social, physical, spiritual, and intellectual states. Furthermore, goals for each state must be addressed in order to facilitate true personal wellness.

Setting goals

Students must create and implement short and long term goals that are expansive, reasonable, focused, personal, and realistic. Student's goals must be their own. College is not the time to merely swap out parental goals for peer goals; following some other person's dreams and goals is not the way to figure out your own set of dreams or goals. The author recalls the warnings of an Army colonel who advised parents to stay out of the students' decision to attend or not attend one of the military academies. He said that this decision was clearly one that belonged to the incoming students. A high percentage of military academy dropouts tend to be students coerced by their parents into applying and accepting a position at one of the academies. The same inference can be made with regard to picking career paths, college majors, or colleges.

But success is yours when you order your dreams and goals around real life. Consider the following fable. Once upon a time there was a little boy who yearned to see the circus. Up to now, he could only *imagine* the glitter, the death defying acts, the loud music, the animal roars, barks, and squeaks and the tantalizing smell of cotton candy, popcorn and fresh-roasted peanuts. One day, the little boy heard that the circus was coming to town so he relentlessly begged his mother to go. She acquiesced to his pleas with the condition that he cleaned his room first. He promptly obeyed her request and set to work. Finally circus day arrived and the little boy happily marched off holding fast to his dollar bills. When he neared the coliseum, he suddenly came upon a parade of clowns, elephants, lions and tigers, bears, and acrobatic artists practicing their jumps and twists. The boy was spellbound by the passing events. As the last clown passed by, the boy gave him the money he had been clutching for he assumed that he had just witnessed the Big Show. As the crowd began to move once again in the direction of the coliseum, the little boy realized that he had only seen the pre-show! Without any more money, the little boy sadly walked home knowing that he had missed the real deal!

College students can miss the real deal when they follow goals and dreams that are not their own. They can also miss out on the real deal when they take personal risks that unhinge their physical, spiritual, emotional, academic, and career goals.

The human brain is very good at sorting and racking and stacking information; it *likes* objective (and subjective) order! The human brain helps us sort things out and to stay on track through ordered planning and thinking. The organization is stored as memory. Our brains like it when we get organized.

Lack of goals

Too many college students fail to establish appropriate goals during college for each of the various aspects of their person. When that happens, students tend to follow the crowd. Consider the admission of this coed who basically accepts others' goals as her own. "You stick 36,000 students who are basically between the ages of 18 and 25 together, without parents. They are on their own for the first time; they're all going to school. When you shove all these people in a small area, I think it's gonna (sic) develop a culture of its own, and I think that would be the weekend ritual of getting dressed up and going out and getting blitzed or going dancing or finding a guy to sleep with. Not everybody does it, but a lot of people do, it's kind of more acceptable."[4]

Another coed demonstrates similar herd instincts when he states: "You are supposed to drink and you're supposed to listen to the Dave Matthews Band... It's just the rule in college."[5]

College years pass by very quickly and quite expensively. You will have to make many important decisions as you begin to assume and take charge of your life. College will give you more free time than you ever dreamed possible. This opens the door to either spending an incredible amount of "lost" opportunity or taking advantage of gained opportunity. Essentially, nobody will be looking out for you when you are in college with the exception of close family and friends. However, even these relationships can be squandered with spent arrows, far flung words, or lost opportunities. It will be up to you to productively set the *whats* and *hows* of your real life. Thousands of seconds of lost opportunity can be frittered away each week, increasing personal stress and frustration. You will have to make many decisions on a daily basis. Some of these decisions may seem trivial while others could be life altering.

It is important to think about how each component of your life affects your overall goals. You are living in a difficult environment. For one, you are probably living in a communal environment that is completely different from your previous family home/living arrangements and unlike any future living arrangements you will encounter. Some people have difficulty setting goals in such situations. Nevertheless, it is important to do so in order to avoid getting caught up in or lost in the crowd as happened to the two coeds quoted earlier. Communal living has its ups and downs; it definitely can be challenging to set goals and stick to them because of the many influences, influencers and distractions.

It is important to keep your goals at the forefront to offset interruptions and demands that will surely come your way. Even best laid plans need reviewing and updating in order to keep your path moving forward, realistically and practically. Don't push off setting goals until another day or year. This *Scarlett O'Hara practice* doesn't usually work out very well. Finally, not everything will turn out just as we expect or hope. Sometimes real life collides with the ideal life and the two must be aligned realistically. You live in the real world and your future must be determined by you, not your Avatar.

Goals need to be specific; they are not merely notions that pop in and out of your head. Goals should be realistic, prioritized, and time-dated. It will be important to review your goals and plans frequently and it may become necessary to revise them after each semester in order to keep them pertinent.

You will be asked to compose specific goals and plans after reading the entire book. As you go through the chapters, begin to jot down thoughts, pre-goals and plans that pertain to the information discussed in each chapter. It should be easier to assemble final goals and plans after you have finished reading the entire book.

Appendix Two contains a worksheet that allows you to compare your ideal life versus your real life. (Ideal Life vs. Real Life Worksheet). This will determine how far apart, or close together, the two are. After finishing the text and completing the Ideal Life vs. Real Life Worksheet, locate the **Goals Worksheet** in Appendix 2 and follow the instructions.

Take heart – setting goals puts you on the fast track to accomplish your dreams. Successful people set goals and stick to their plans no matter the environment in which they live.

Idea	Short Term Goal or Plan?	Long Term Goal or Plan?	Real Life or Ideal Life?

Reflection Questions:

1. Have you ever made a list of goals and plans for the short and long term? Have they helped you achieve goals?

2. List the areas you plan to work goals for here.

3. Have you met students who follow everyone else's dreams except their own? What do you advise them to do?

My Thoughts

Write down everything that you might be interested in at the moment here. Also write down some quick-start ideas that will be helpful in setting goals and plans after finishing the book.

Chapter Two: Setting Goals

Write down goals that come immediately to mind for each of the components in your life. Prepare a final goal sheet after you have finished reading the book; compare your final goals with this one. Any differences?

Dimension	Short Term Goal - Ideal Life	Long Term Goal - Ideal Life	Short Term Goal - Real Life	Long Term Goal - Real Life
Spiritual				
Mental				
Physical				
Social				
Emotional				
Financial				
Intellectual				
Career				

Final Goal Plan

Priority	Dimension	S-T Goal, Merge Ideal & Real Life	LT Goal, Merge Ideal & Real Life	Date-Expect Completion	Date-Actual Completion
	Spiritual				
	Mental				
	Physical				
	Social				
	Emotional				
	Financial				
	Intellectual				
	Career				

Chapter Three

Social Wellness Implications

The next four chapters will examine the different facets that make up *you*. Looking at each separately will help you come up with goals in each area.

Social wellness is much more subjective than physical wellness but the essence of it is captured when describing a person's capacity and ability for having healthy social interactions, effective interpersonal connections, good friendships, quality communication, and positive relationships. In essence, social wellness is secured when a person is able to interact harmoniously with other people in and outside of their social community. This person readily provides positive social capital to his or her social community. Social wellness also enables people to work well for and with others.

Social capital

Social capital provides residents with benefits proportional to the extent of the collective involvement of the members living within the "community." Positive social capital is necessary for creating a common sense of well being – normally a highly-prized community characteristic.

Unless one lives as a hermit, we are all (even college students) members of a community, which is part of a city that is incorporated in a state, which is part of a union of states that forms a nation. In other words, we are all linked with a large network of people who collectively provide positive or negative social influences. Individuals provide varying degrees of influence in proportion to their level of influence, ability, and degree of involvement or activity in *community* matters.

Each social community — large or small city, town, or rural community – is made up of people who form natural *social bonds* in part because they share proximate space while networking and interacting with each other. Smaller social communities often form within the bubble of the larger social community. For example, members of a local church form a specific social community that is within the bubble of the larger community. Community members share the use of libraries, police services, shopping malls, and schools, and more. They hope to share an even more important purpose – peaceful coexistence and camaraderie.

Together, community members work to better their "village." For example, they may decide to remodel a neighborhood pool so it has better access and is more appealing for residents of that community. The community project will require hours of designing, planning, and execution. Community members also look out for each other; they need to care about one another's well being and feel like they really are their *brother's keeper.* Most are expected to live by the *Golden Rule.* (This will be discussed in a later chapter.) Community members expect to benefit from belonging to society just as they should expect to *give back* to the social network. Social capital is the collective intangible benefit generated for and by each member; it is obtained primarily through positive networking and interactions with others. Positive, shared interactions form communal bonds which become the bi-directional goals of healthy social communities. Shared interactions increase communal bonds motivating members to have even more social interactions/networks that forge deeper community roots and bonds. The overall strength of community networks provides the *social capital* for the social community.[1] Positive social capital energizes the community; in essence, it is a civilizing force. Positive social capital can be an effective *game changer* for communities.

Essentially, social capital is the sum total of the virtues of the community members. Stable communities develop more positive social capital than unstable collections of people; in turn, strong families provide necessary stability for the community. They also produce children who are "equipped to promote and serve a truly humane social order"[2] within communities.

College campuses are also social communities composed of a variety of smaller social units within the main structure. The smaller social units include the hundreds of different types of university-sponsored clubs, organizations, and associations including athletic teams and clubs, social sororities and fraternities, academic departments, church groups, political clubs, dormitory communities, academic communities, and more.

It is widely recognized that *social capital* is lower in college communities than larger communities with stable populations and close connections. College students come and go very quickly compared to residential communities. Nevertheless, it is important that students and faculty feel good about the campus social capital. All students and faculty deserve to feel safe, secure, productive, and satisfied with relationships within the college community.

Like the greater communities, a college community forms positive social capital in proportion to the collective good and virtue of its members. Therefore it is important that colleges enroll students "equipped to promote and serve a truly humane social order."[3] These types of students naturally look out for each other, strive to live by the Golden Rule, work on building up their own personal virtue, and contribute positively to friendships within the college community. Like other social communities, it is important that students share and have positive interactions with peers in order to bond with them. Positive social bonds motivate students to get involved in activities and social networks. Collectively, students generate positive social capital when they are socially well adjusted. Social capital is also a civilizing force on campus; social capital can prove to be the *game changer* in many students' lives. Conversely, students who experience negative social interactions form fewer positive social networks. This can lead to social isolation, illness, increased stress, or the adoption of risky behaviors. In essence, negative social capital serves to unravel civility and decency. In fact, negative social capital is a negative game changer enticing risky, barbaric behavior. Students can become ill equipped to "promote and serve a truly humane social order" when accepting of negative social behaviors as the way of life.[4]

College social communities are knit together by people who share mutual experiences and activities such as living in close proximity with each other, going to classes together, using the same on-campus amenities, forming friendships and relationships, and socializing together. College students automatically (or should) share a common purpose: securing a college degree, meeting others, and sharing experiences, albeit temporary. Finally, students share a common pathway — the university system and culture. People who share common purpose and environments will form unique social bonds depending on the frequency and intensity of the interactions. Unfortunately, social bonds can induce some students to assume risky behaviors when it is perceived that the negative activity is standard college behavior. Herein is the rub for college students. It is always important to fit in and be accepted and welcomed by peers. However, college students may need to form smaller, social units within the larger culture in order to find positive camaraderie, friendship, and support that also allows them to work productively toward their social, academic, spiritual, mental, and emotional goals.

Your social goals

Social goals to consider as you move through this chapter should include your expected graduation time-frame, academic major, and types of personal social interactions and networks that positively help you discover your true identity, bring balance your life, make college enjoyable and encourage you to meet academic challenges.

Be a game changer

Tangible and intangible benefits are generated within social communities – even at college. Positive social capital is essentially the collective virtue of the members; however, you learn to be compassionate for others by first adopting personal virtue.

Students have a real opportunity to be the game changer in other students' lives by what they say, how they live, how they act and by what they profess. Our actions impact other people in ways few of us sometimes realize. Relationships work for or against persons. Unhealthy relationships undermine *personal wellness and balance.*

Negative social relationships and activities are closely tied to typical college culture. These can be detrimental to students' social well being. Many students begin college well adjusted but over time end up unhappy or drop out of school. Too many students naively assume that experimenting with the wilder side of college culture will not disaffect their social well being. They are wrong. All behaviors – good and bad – have consequences for individuals and collective social communities. Our social well being is dependent on good behavior and positive living.

College students are thrown into one of the most challenging and seemingly *uncivilized* living environments when they *go to college*. Normally, people choose where they live and with whom, unless, that is, they join the military or go to college. Most colleges require that students live on campus for at least the first two years. Consequently, living arrangements become odd pairings of eighteen to twenty-four year olds. Collectively, college students share common deficiencies including lack of life experience, knowledge and maturity. Most have undeveloped or weak personal identities and life philosophies. College students live in less positive social environments because the system lacks rules, supervision, guidance and accountability. College students answer to few — if any — people in collective living environments. And so it is understandable why parents and administrators worry for their students' civility and safety. Clearly, many negative consequences can erupt in a *no-rules* environment.

My life feels so *different*

Most students tour their college of choice long before enrolling yet few live there for even a day prior to freshman orientation. Pre-arranged college tours allow parents and students to visit academic departments, see classrooms, discuss financial aid, and maybe get into one dorm — but only on one floor and probably only in one preselected room. Students' lives remain cloaked in mystery to visitors. As a result, many new students experience shock and awe – positive and negative – when they move to college. Students are most often surprised by the *socio-cultural* differences between college and high school. Students' personal and social well being can be temporarily thrown off balance by these new social settings.

Dormitories are dense living arrangements that are quite dissimilar from students' private bedrooms or bedroom/bath suites back home.[5] Dorm living requires students to navigate intimately among strangers. Dorm life also feels very different because parents, siblings, and friends are now miles away. One hundred years ago, and more, colleges adopted *In Loco Parentis* (surrogate parents) to keep close watch over students living away from home. These colleges created gender-specific dorms, curfews, gender restrictions after hours, and dorm mothers to help keep watch over students. *In Loco Parentis* arrangements didn't change until the defiant 1960s. After that, students asserted their consumer, academic and personal rights and freedoms. Students demanded that universities remove personal and social restrictions. As a result, *In Loco Parentis* rules and restrictions disappeared along with others.[6] Today's campuses have few restrictions, rules and regulations with regard to living arrangements. In fact, the rules that do exist frequently pertain only to property and/or property damage.

Students continue to wield a lot of influence about collective living arrangements as they complain about primitive community showers and shared bedroom spaces. Colleges acquiesce to these demands by building apartment-style living facilities on campus.

Campus life also feels very different because college student have significantly **less structured time** compared to high school. Most high school students spend at least six hours per day in classrooms

(30 hours per week) and additional hours per day at athletic practice, music or debate practice, or engaged in other activities. Many high school students also work part time or do household chores during the week. These students also have to study each evening; however, studies show that very few students are seriously overburdened with homework each night.[7] On the other hand, college students live in close proximity to classrooms, spend few minutes walking to class, and spend far less time per day in structured lectures or classroom activities compared to elementary or secondary school students. Academic loads feel lighter even though they are not.[8] College students are advised to spend two to three hours studying per credit hour per week. This means students are expected to study three-to-six hours per day (24-42 hrs/wk). Research consistently shows that college students spend significantly less time than the study guide rule of thumb.[9] In fact, a national survey of college students found that only 13 percent of full time four year college freshmen study 25 or more hours per week. Nearly half (41 percent) of the fulltime students study only 10 hours (or less) per week.[10] College provides students with a whole lot of extra non-structured hours but serious students soon discover they need this time to meet the rigors and challenges of college coursework. These students also realize that time management skills are vital for success. Many college students also shoulder part time work. As an aside, it is important that college students limit their part time paid work responsibilities to less than twenty hours per week for good reasons. College students' main job is to go to school and excellently attend to that duty. The majority of college students are basically free to schedule or do whatever they want and however they want. Responsible students fill this time constructively; less responsible students waste time, opportunity and money. The college athlete, and the part time student, however, face different scenarios.

Sociologists maintain that lack of familiarity or understanding of new social customs, culture, and relationships can cause college freshman to lose the social balance required for maintaining wellness.[11] This suggests that college students are at increased risk – at least temporarily – when they relocate to colleges where unfamiliarity is the name of the game. This "relocation effect" in essence causes a temporary loss of well being as students find themselves crammed into small dorm rooms and large auditorium classes without familiar companionship.

New college students coming from small, rural regions or towns may feel *overwhelmed* by sudden urbanization. Cross country students may feel beleaguered by the unfamiliarity of the new town or region or local culture. Students moving from large urban areas to small town communities may feel stifled by the loss of the hustle, bustle, and opportunities afforded by big city living. The relocation effect causes some students to withdraw (at least temporarily). This can lead to social isolation. Social scientists caution that this effect is especially true for students coming from rare ethnic or religious groups. The relocation effectively removes students from reliable and important social supports generating insecurity and a loss of general well being until new supports fall into place or old supports are re-confirmed. These losses – even if only temporary – leave students feeling stressed, depressed, or anxious.[12] Depression, anxiety, and stress are linked to increases in reckless student behaviors including violence, binge or heavy drinking, sexual experimentation, and substance abuse. Mental health issues increase in proportion to the degree of social isolation.

Your college town may feel different. College towns tend to look and feel younger than cities or towns that are not home to colleges. College towns may even have a different slant — politically and socially —than a person's hometown. College towns cater to college students to secure new businesses. Consequently, college towns value young peoples' consumer spending power. Some business establishments (in college towns) bend rules to increase their revenues – especially with regard to alcohol sales and gambling.

Finally, you may *feel different* because you are getting physically ill. Chances are high that you will get sick in college during the flu season due to the dense living conditions. Close living arrangements are notorious for spreading serious infectious disease and illnesses. We will see in future chapters how infections, use of drugs, and drinking all increase as a result of living in close proximity to your peers.

The collective living experience on campus

Student consumer power has helped to usher in modernized campuses that feature state of the art academic and physical fitness facilities and wireless classrooms and dormitories and other fabulous conveniences. Students can now listen to recorded lectures remotely. Today's colleges feature facilities and amenities unimaginable decades ago. College students have convenient amenities including internet access; technology centers; attractive dining halls that provide a variety of healthy food options; on-campus fitness centers equipped with the gamut of equipment, classes, and massage; shopping areas; banking facilities; classy bookstores; fancy sports arenas; attractive kiosks; and comfortable WiFi lounges.

Despite updated facilities, college administrators continue to look for ways to optimize the campus' *social capital* using "thirty-year-old research to influence today's student housing construction because there haven't been newer inquiries into these matters."[13] The hoped for optimization should improve safety and security while enhancing student learning, maximizing student interaction and networking, and ensuring that students have multiple positive social experiences. Ironically, electronic technologies offset these optimization attempts when they lure students back into their private spaces to spend excessive amounts of time alone while playing with game systems or using online technologies. "Even the perfect architectural design still can't make students leave their rooms if they don't want to."[14]

Dormitories

Colleges offer a variety of different types of living arrangements: suite style dorms, coed dorms, same sex dorms, learning community floors or wings, single rooms, traditional dorms, apartments, or married student housing. Students have to pick one best suited for them. Choosing the right living arrangements can seem like shooting dice and hoping for a win.

Making new friends is not easy for many students causing some students to lean too heavily on the first few they meet even though they share few common interests or values. Students sometimes *put up with* friendships they would not ordinarily invest in when yearning for meaningful friendship.

Coed living can be a distraction for many who spend time trying to impress the opposite sex living in their dorms. Others feel overly self conscious in these new living arrangements. Studies show that students living in coed housing were more prone to binge drinking, and had more problem behaviors associated with drinking than students in other types of housing."[15]

Certainly, the relocation effect can cause insecure feelings to erupt. It is always easier to maneuver in familiar settings. Rooming with people you already know can be less stressful. In fact, local private colleges successfully compete with larger, less expensive, public universities because many students prefer to enroll in close-to-home, familiar settings than relocate to unfamiliar territory because it ensures knowing *someone* at school.[16] However, there are several good reasons why students should not room with old friends. Sharing a room with a close friend often serves as the death knell to that friendship. Even best of friends need space from each other; sharing a room often fails to provide needed space especially when one of the roommates is eager to make new friends. It is better to live in the same dormitory or complex that offers easy access to old *and* new friends.

High school seniors can begin to hunt for future friends when competing in sports events, drama, debate or music competitions, or church youth groups. Keeping contact information of interesting persons who plan on attending the same university can be a helpful start to finding college friends. Parents often ask co-workers where their students plan to go for college hoping to create another possible resource for you in the future.

While making new friends is not always easy, it is also not that hard either. Get involved in campus activities. University life offers a myriad of opportunities to meet and make friends. For example, new friends can be found where you work, in social, political, academic or athletic clubs or sororities and fraternities, at international organizations, at the fitness center and at Church, prayer groups or events sponsored by a Newman Center or another place of worship. Even volunteer organizations that help others are good places to make friends. The opportunities are immense. Research shows that it is easier to get involved in activities when students live on-campus; furthermore, graduation rates are better for students living on campus compared to those students who live off-campus.[17]

General collective living issues that tend to erupt when living nose to nose with other college students will be discussed in the last section of this chapter. The issues that can arise when living collectively with other people point to the need for communication, goal setting, and rules once more.

Who are your peers?

It is important to recognize and understand the world in which we live — its explanations, its longings, and its often dramatic characteristics.[18] This is just as important for college students, who can grow anxious when they don't *recognize* or understand their own peer group. All students worry about being paired up with someone they don't know. This explains why upper classmen orchestrate their living arrangements at the first opportunity. It is vital that you get to know many students in order to decide which ones complement your understanding of life, your longings, and your characteristics.

College students are a very diverse group of people. They demonstrate great differences in levels of intelligence, abilities and talents, ideas, morality, liberality of thought, word and actions, nationalities, religious affiliations, modern, relativist and atheistic influences, virtues and vice, understandings, personalities, securities and insecurities, longings, and characteristics. It is odd that any college student would be happy with group think in such a diverse setting. Find out about the persons you will be living, going to classes, and networking with. Eventually you will find out for yourself but here is a general heads up of who's who.

Most Millennials believe in God (76 percent)[19] yet only one-fourth of your age group regularly attends religious services (at least once a month). Compared to previous generations (23.6 percent in 1966)[20], more Millennials fail to claim (21 percent) a religious affiliation. The plurality of today's students regards themselves as more spiritual than religious. (This will be discussed more in chapter five.) Over 60 percent of Millennials would like to learn more about their religion.[21] A full 60 percent of Millennials believe the nation's moral compass is pointing in the wrong direction.

Yet, in general, the majority of your age group (82 percent) practice moral relativism – the belief that there is no definite right and wrong for everybody.[22] Moral relativism sets moral and immoral actions side by side for many college students and so they draw blurry lines between moral dilemmas. For example, the vast majority of your peers believe the following issues are clearly immoral: marital infidelity, plagiarism, greed, and increasing profits by decreasing the quality of a product or service. On the other hand, Millennials are more divided over the morality of other issues including abortion, whether it is OK for someone to practice more than one religion; whether religion should impact someone's professional life; whether people can have a different set of ethical standards for their business and personal lives; whether science should conduct medical testing on animals; whether environmental issues should take precedence over economic development, drug use, and euthanasia.[23] Finally, a great majority of Millennials *do not* believe that the following issues are necessarily wrong: divorce, pre-marital sexual relations, having a baby out of wedlock, human embryo stem cell research, and same sex marriage.

Your generation could be dubbed the Green Generation because you and your peers have been programmed to care a great deal about environmental causes (that may or may not be real) including decreasing polar bear populations, greenhouse effects, global warming, and/or shrinking acreage of the rain forests. Yet only 55 percent of your age group believes that economic development that causes environmental problems is always wrong.[24]

A full one third (37 percent) of your peers veer to the left on social and moral issues including abortion, same sex marriage, and the role of a government, legalization of marijuana, and taxes for the rich[25] even though the vast majority of students prefer the middle of the political and social road – neither left nor right.

It's fair to predict that the attitudes of Millennials will shift as they gain life experiences about commitments, marriage, personal responsibilities, the less fortunate, proper work ethics, having and raising children, and other general life questions.

The Marist Poll shows that your generation is the most different from your grandparents' generation, the Greatest or Silent Generation. Perhaps these contrasts have always been so. Differences between generations, within generations, and within cultures, can pose communication challenges for the different groups. It is likely that they will have difficulty relating to each other's *explanations*, *longings*, and *dramatic characteristics*.

Communication

We communicate because we are social beings who need social interactions, interpersonal connections and affiliation to be well. We communicate to bond, to bridge gaps with people who we are not as close to, and to maintain friendships. We communicate in a variety of ways — verbal and non-verbal.

Verbal language differentiates us from the animal kingdom even though we use words to convey thoughts, feelings, complex and simple messages, and ideas far less often than one would expect. Verbal communication requires that we hear, listen to, understand and interpret person's words and tone. The tone of our speech also conveys messages about moods, attitudes and opinions about 40 percent of the time. This is known as receptive language. The ease or difficulty of speech can be a function of intelligence, physical wellness, mental impairment, social wellness, and more. Being able to speak is a great gift! Therefore we should always mean what we say and say what we mean. What, how and why we communicate should reveal who we are, what we are really thinking, and what we believe. It should provide the means by which others can measure us accurately. Communication is normally a two-way street; we don't just talk while others are expected to listen. The proverb *two monologues do not make a dialogue* essentially hints at the fact that most of us prefer dialogues to monologues because we feel emotionally, personally, and socially connected through person-to-person conversation.

It is enjoyable to listen to great speakers who impart unique wisdom and knowledge; however, as stated earlier, most people do not relish having to listen to incessant lectures. We prefer dialogues to monologues.

Finally, all of us must learn to speak carefully and deliberately. Our words have the power to build up other people emotionally, personally and socially. Words can also destroy self esteem and social status. In fact, indirect aggression is most often carried out through gossip, slander, negative jokes, lies, exaggerations, or sarcasm. It is always important to recall the admonition: a spoken word can never be retrieved. Too many people and personal relationships have been damaged or destroyed via the quick tongue and the spoken word.

Perhaps some of you recall a recent story about cyber bullying that cost a young girl her life. As of this writing, police have not yet formally filed charges against the adult accused of cyber-bullying the young teen. The girls' parents maintain that the verbal bullying prompted their thirteen year old daughter to commit suicide because the bullying mortally wounded their daughter's mental and emotional wellness. The bullying occurred on the social networking site known as MySpace.[26] The old adage: "sticks and stones can break my bones but words can't ever hurt me" seems to have failed in this case.

Body Language

Humans also communicate with and through their bodies by non verbal communication, also known as body language. The science behind body language has been around for the past fifty years or so and is beginning to gain importance and acceptance as "science." Experts in body language have decoded ways to determine the meaning behind body movements, lack of movement, body positions, reflexive facial, hand or leg actions. Unconsciously, body language communicates mood, attitude, or opinion. Body language experts suggest that body language communicates non-verbal messages about 65 percent of the time. It is extraordinary to think that humans use non-verbal communication much more often than verbal communication, 65 percent to 35 percent, respectively. [27]

Body language is highly individualized and varies from person to person. What may indicate relaxation in one person may signal tension in another. Courses have even been designed to teach people how to read another person's body language. For example, courses are taught to help people discern whether someone's words are sincere or disingenuous by observing their body language as they speak. Professionals and self-interest attendees learn the language of the body for different reasons. Consider that one day, experts may be called on to testify about someone's body language in a court of law to determine his or her innocence or guilt. Human resource departments may use body language to assess when to hire or fire employees. Body language experts may become invaluable during marriage therapy sessions or other cases when people's sincerity or truthfulness is called into question; it could become useful indeed if proven to be an objective scientific tool.

How well do your peers communicate?

Your generation is the first to grow up completely familiar with various types of electronic communication technologies. Today, most college students have their own laptops, cell phones with text messaging capability and more. More than likely, all of you have already created your own web page on Facebook or MySpace. Your generation is adept at up linking, downloading, twittering, and texting unlike generations of older Americans. You are able to maintain a huge friend base extending back to junior high or grade school via these electronic technologies. It seems your generation has a lock on the proverb: *Make new friends but keep the old; one is silver and the other gold.*

However, experts worry that students of your generation may be less effective face-to-face communicators, especially with strangers or business colleagues — but even when with friends. Similarly, there is growing concern that today's students are unable to speak about important subjects thoughtfully, clearly, or deeply because of this same dependence on technology. Potential employers worry about communication deficiencies in today's Millennials. Communications professors worry that today's impersonal, gadget driven, plugged-in student has more difficulty communicating – verbally and written.

They worry that Millennials lack the conversational skills necessary to make personal, sincere, and deep interpersonal relationship connections. Texting and online chats deliver messages and conversation that are brief, to the point, and often largely superficial: "Hey whatcha doin?"... "Nothin- bout you?" ..."C U at 8."

Young people complain that their friends have trouble *really being present to them* even when in close physical proximity to each other. Friends spend too much time texting or placing other calls even when sharing space with another person. For example, one evening, when my husband and I dined out, I found myself distracted by a young couple who said nary a word to each other while they sat at a table for two. Both spent almost the entire time texting or calling others on their cell phones. As I observed their body language, it appeared their personal relationship was wanting.

Studies have shown that college students turn to alcohol to feel more comfortable in new social settings; essentially they drink so they can talk. In fact, feeling uncomfortable, inhibited, or reserved in new social settings is a primary reason given by students for drinking in college. Therefore, it is important to fine tune interpersonal communication skills so that new social settings are not so discomforting. Fine-tuning occurs through continued use and practice. Students need to frequently converse face to face with different people about different subjects in order to hone communication skills.

Politeness and misuse of the English language has eroded among college students as well. It is not uncommon to hear vulgar or crass language mixed in to regular conversation. In fact, impolite comments, rude remarks, and shallow conversations rule the day for many Americans – not just college students. Impoliteness does not support nor build up social capital.

How do you communicate?

Like other Americans, college students communicate using electronic technologies such as instant messaging, text messaging, social networking sites, and more.

Thirteen million Americans send daily instant messages to friends, family, co-workers, instructors, and others. In fact, nearly half of all adults who use the internet also use instant messaging (42 percent).[28] Instant messaging has several advantages over text messaging since it is a computer-aided technology that basically functions as email, chat room, paging system, telephone, voice mail, caller ID and bulletin board all rolled into one computer.[29] Most (86 percent) college students use instant messaging despite its disadvantages.[30]

Internet usage is much higher for all Americans (69.6 percent) compared to Europeans (38.6 percent) since we have many more personal computers.[34] Furthermore, most American high school and college students own their own computers and are therefore very proficient with the computer keyboard.

Social networking sites essentially allow members to create their own personal web pages that allow the owner to restrict access to the online personal information. Roughly 90 percent of college students participate in one or more social networking site, including Facebook and MySpace. Studies argue that electronic messaging does not replace face to face communication but supplements it.[35] That would be good news considering that about ten million Facebook members are of college age. But, the effects of this and other social networking tools on individuals' ability to communicate has yet to be fully measured.

College students spend a lot of time on the internet but experts *uneasily* conclude that the internet provides more positives than negatives. The internet serves as a valuable tool when used as a research arm, fact checker, news finder, mail box, music source, instant messenger, friend finder, and shopping cart.[36] Even though college students spend an average of 4.4 hours each day on the internet, they do not feel that it disaffects personal relationships.[37,38] Preliminary evidence suggests that internet time does not appear problematic for the majority of college students. But for some, the internet poses real temptations and addictions as will be discussed in a later chapter.

Did you know that text messaging got its start in Europe in 1993 after the commercialization of the cell phone?[31] Text messaging plans are fairly inexpensive but cell phones are needed and Europeans have cell phones! Europeans were first to heavily replace land line telephone systems with cell phones; however, their dependence on personal computers lags American usage. While only 69 percent of Americans have mobile phones that number approaches nearly 100 percent for college students.[32] The disadvantage of sending a text message lies in its intricate abbreviations and being able to type quickly and proficiently with just two thumbs. American college students use cell phones more for voice functioning than for texting, unlike Europeans.[33]

Is there hard and fast evidence that Millennials have significant communication problems? Preliminary evidence merely suggests that their face to face communication is simply not that rich. Students admit they don't talk much about religion, politics, or other deep subjects while online. This begs the question about whether these technological communication tools stymie in-depth communication. Personally, I have my doubts – modern communication technologies may simply fit the styles of communication that the users already have and prefer. Personally, I question how many adult Americans were refined communicators when they were emerging adults. Even among adults, aren't religion and politics considered taboo subjects for coffee table discussions?

Body image and self esteem

Body image and self esteem can be a barometer of a person's social, mental, and physical health. Students must work hard to protect or develop positive body images and self esteem. They must discover their own self worth (self esteem) by looking within themselves at their character, personality, abilities, beliefs, passions, convictions, sociability, and more. They must value the whole of their being including body, mind and soul in order to suppress the temptation to let society judge them based on personal beauty.

When society tries to standardize beauty measurements (height, weight, eye color, skin color, etc.) we all lose. The social standards calibrating beauty make it doubly hard – especially for females – to pursue healthy habits. Body image standards obfuscate the need to eat well and to eat enough. Having good nutrition has been positively linked to social, mental, and physical health. Good health helps all of us maintain positive body images and self esteem. On the other hand, poor nutrition is linked to poor social, mental, and physical health. There is a vital interconnectedness between nutrition, body image, health, mental health, and social health.

Being social by nature, people observe other people; these observations frequently turn into comparisons, assessments, and judgments. We compare ourselves to other people; we also compare other people to our own friends, family, acquaintances, and co-workers. Unfortunately these comparisons sometimes develop collective social norms, or standards, of beauty. It is quite natural to observe physical differences and form opinions about someone's personal characteristics but it is quite inhumane to let physical standards dictate who we like or dislike.

Studies cannot instill positive self images or positive self esteem in any of us. It is important to recognize that when we model ourselves after a successful movie star, chances are high that we will be unhappy. We diminish our own body image and self esteem when we strive to look like someone we are not. When we rely on men's or women's magazines, Hollywood or other media, to make our social comparisons, we will become less satisfied with our own bodies and low self esteem issues will develop, eating disorders rise, and we will experience a decreased sense of wellness of mind, body, and spirit. College women who associate low, supermodel-thin body weight and size to positive body images will take measures that compromise their own general wellness.[39] Eating disorders have been directly linked to poor body image or low self esteem. This will be discussed more in a later chapter.

Social supports from parents and family

College students need the support from their families as they navigate through the difficulties and joys of collective living. Students may look "all grown up" but studies confirm that co-eds continue to need parental and familial support, guidance, and help throughout their college years. Strong support systems drive up student success and graduation rates. Frequently first generation college students, especially minority students, are at a significant disadvantage simply because their parents lack personal college experience to help support their student.

First time students often don't receive the proper motivation necessary to keep them on campus.[40]

Parental involvement has been proven to be helpful, even life saving in some instances. Parents are often the first to realize the degree of their students' inability to adjust; they are often the first to see the depth of an ongoing personal, mental or social problem in their student. Parental interventions can be vital in securing proper medical or mental health diagnosis and treatments for their student. Parents can also provide helpful tips and support for students facing severe homesickness, anxiety, difficulty coping with personal relationships, and other personal matters because of their own college experiences and wisdom.

On the other hand, there are some parents who simply do not know when or how to let go. They have been dubbed "helicopter" parents due to their hovering nature.[41] These people become a thorn in everyone's side as they interfere in matters that are best handled by their emerging adult. Professor Pamela Matthews reports that some helicopter parents call her with the expectation of jacking up their students' grades even though the student don't deserve the grade. Helicopter parents even provide routine wakeup calls to their sleeping students so they won't miss an important test or class. Little do these parents realize that wake up calls do nothing to ensure that their student is on the way to his or her class. Helicopter parents over-indulge their students and bail them out unnecessarily. Helicopter parents have been known to willingly pay students' parking tickets; complain about the unavailability of classes long past registration deadlines; expect professors to make an exception for *their* student; complain about grades, the difficulty of college courses for their children, and make excuses for their student's behavior.[42]

General collective living issues

Dorm living will *always* be problematic for a host of reasons. Dense living will always suit some more than others; humans are social beings but they differ greatly from each other. Conflicts arise when roommates' schedules clash, habits annoy, or personalities become incompatible. There are a variety of things that roommates, suite mates, and dorm mates need to discuss in order to head off conflict or tension when sharing space.

Take heart. As a Millennial, you like to work with other people, you like to work hard, and you expect success! This translates into having the ability to resolve differences amicably.

Never lean on the goodwill of a roommate who seems to put up with your infractions or rude activities. Draw up a mutually agreed-upon Student Bill of Rights the first day you room together even if you have handpicked your roommate. A sample Bill of Rights can be found in Appendix Four. Personalize it for both roommates, discuss it, sign it, and then post it as a reminder that you both agreed to its tenets. Mutually agreed upon contracts will save both of you angst and difficulties in the months ahead.

Stand your ground if a roommate makes unreasonable or immoral demands. Both of you should treat each other as you would want to be treated. Your moral counsel may be needed from time to time but should be given only when asked for. If someone decides that you are just too impossible to live with because you don't give into unreasonable demands, then it should behoove him or her to find *more acceptable* living conditions. But chances are high, when paired with this type of roommate, you will be the one who ends up moving or finding more civil living conditions. If you are painted as selfish, make sure you aren't. If you find yourself worn out because your roommate continually disrespects you or fails to hold up to his end of the mutually agreed upon Student Bill of Rights, one of you will have to move. Don't consider this a failure unless you have been the one who has been demanding and difficult to get along with. Good roommates understand that different people come with unique habits, values, and standards. Obviously fewer tensions and problems arise when roommates share common sensibilities and standards, values and habits. However, problems emerge when one or both roommates are inconsiderate or demanding.

Demanding or difficult roommates can be a thorn in the side of any college student. Some people are simply spoiled, narcissistic, rude, used to getting their own way at home, mean spirited, have entitlement issues or are simply immature. But that too can change with time. Some students may have a very difficult time coping with life at first and that too can change. When communication channels are open, there is always hope that roommates can turn differences and/or difficulties into common ground.

It will be important to sit down together and discuss who you both are, including likes, dislikes, and values. After the discussion, draw up that Bill of Rights that you both pledge to honor while living together. The Bill of Rights should be tailored to meet roommates' likes and dislikes, needs and wants. Sometimes the best roommates are those with the biggest differences because they tend to give each other a lot more space.

Roommates have the right to amicably draw attention to infractions against the agreement. Both should try to resolve any problems as soon as they emerge.

Sleep

Getting enough sleep can be problematic especially when a roommate, suite mate or dorm mate is noisy late at night. A sufficient amount of sleep is important to everyone's general well being – even yours. It is important to get enough sleep and enough good sleep each night. Adequate sleep, in length and quality, provides much needed energy for the next day. It is important that you feel well rested after a full night's sleep.

Sleep habits and patterns vary from person to person. People have different tolerances for noise, movement, and light. Some people are very light sleepers while others could sleep through a fire alarm. These differences must be discussed with roommates so each person can learn to respectfully navigate around the other's sleep habits. Respect the sleep needs of your roommate even if it is unusual compared to your own. Listed here are a few points to consider for your Bill of Rights regarding sleep.

Guarantee each other's sleep time to be free of sudden loud noises, unnecessary commotion, talking, unnecessary sounds, physical interference, unnecessary disturbance, or interruption.

Do not interrupt another's sleep time with unnecessary noise, lights, movements, or talking on the phone. Silence cell phones when the other roommate is sleeping or trying to get to sleep.

Invest in good ear plugs if the roommate is a snorer. There is not much he/she can do to stop snoring.

If you are sensitive to light coming from a clock, laptop screen, or iPod screen, invest in a good quality, room darkening eye mask. Make sure eye masks are kept clean and sanitary.

Students who go to bed earlier than a roommate can invest in good ear plugs and eye masks in order to tune out lights and sounds.

The early to bed student will need to train him/her self to fall asleep while the other roommate is somewhat active in the room. Walks to the bathroom, coughs, turning pages, moves in the chair, etc., cannot be avoided.

Study

Like sleep, study habits and the need to study varies from person to person. Some students are very deliberate and meticulous with homework and study time, while others will go through courses without opening a book.

Different majors require different course loads, types of class work, and types of assignments. Many courses encourage group projects. Others tend to assign individual homework. These differences affect students' plans to study with others or alone.

Some students slough off assignments or study until it's time for the exams and then they cram or pull an all-nighter. While you may not agree with this type of study habit, remember they are not yours to change.

Some students like to stay up late to study while others prefer to get finished early so there is enough time left for relaxation before bed. These students may find it relaxing to watch TV, listen to music, hang out with friends, etc. However, if one roommate has just begun to study or is still studying, his or her roommate needs to leave their room to find relaxation.

Late night studiers or early to bed students both can make good use of a nearby lounge at different times out of respect for and consideration of their roommate's needs. Remember, it's not an issue of whose rights are trumping whose; rather both roommates have the right to be in their room while neither has the right to interrupt the other's sleep or study time.

Again, different habits can turn into confrontations unless attended to before they reach the annoyance stage. Roommates must arrive at a mutual agreement about blocks of study/quiet time in order to accommodate the other's habits. These differences can normally be worked out amicably.

Here are some more points to consider for your Bill of Rights.

Busy environments can be extremely distracting when studying. Avoid creating a busy, distracting environment when the other is studying. These distractions include:

- Doors that are constantly opening and closing.
- Loud noise.
- Flashing lights.
- TV noise.
- Music – some students study well with music; others find music to be distracting.
- Students who like to study with music should invest in ear phones so they can listen to their iPod or other devise without disturbing the roommate.
- The music lover always needs to keep the volume down for everyone's sake. Students who stay up late must realize the one in bed has a right to uninterrupted sleep. This means no loud music or welcoming friends into the room once the roommate is in bed.
- A roommate must not turn up the TV or music or welcome friends into the room while the other roommate is studying.
- Avoid sharing each other's equipment or personal belongings; this is the best policy for both.
- Roommates do not have to "share and share alike."
- If you have a serious need to use someone's things, be sure to ask first.
- Do not presume to receive permission to use something ever! (First time, second time, or more.)
- Some roommates have a hard time refusing a request even though they dislike lending something out. They may feel

guilty that you don't have something; on the other hand you may feel entitled and use other peoples' things when you shouldn't.

- Never use up or break something of your roommate's without replacing it.
- Never allow your friends to use your roommate's things.

Visitors

Many roommates simply share living space. They are not the best of friends but they learn to adjust to each other and get along. Many times, this arrangement works out the best for everyone; it can, however, also make living together difficult. Having mutual respect and understanding of each other's needs and wants helps to get a shared living arrangement off to a good start.

When you aren't best friends, your roommate will normally invite in their friends who you don't know and vice versa. Visiting hours must be discussed and agreed upon. Roommates should be free to welcome friends into their rooms but only in accord with previously agreed upon visiting hours and/or other conditions. Sometimes, friends barge into a room unannounced. This is rude! It is very important to inform all friends of the mutually agreed upon Student Bill of Rights. Posting the Bill of Rights, informing friends, and sticking to your original plan *is* the best plan to follow unless both roommates agree that it needs revising.

Here are more points to consider for your Bill of Rights:

- Visiting friends must never be allowed to take or use your roommate's things.
- Visiting friends must never be allowed to use your roommate's space without his or her permission, or as outlined in the Bill of Rights.
- Visiting hours including time, spatial elements, noise, etc.

Romantic guests

Roommates need to discuss and set mutually agreed upon visiting rules about boyfriends or girlfriends; make sure the rules are included in the Student Bill of Rights. It is unfair for any person to expect their roommate to leave their room simply because they desire private time and space with a boyfriend or girlfriend. Respectful roommates will not ask you to leave either unless that was agreed to and expressly written in the Bill of Rights.

It is important to realize that you do not have to give into a roommate's request that you leave your room. Roommates who expect to have sexual relations with a romantic partner need to find other space for their liaisons. Furthermore, it is never anyone's right to have any sexual activities or relations while a roommate is in the room – even if they think that a roommate is asleep. This behavior is lewd, disrespectful of everyone present, and outrageous. Most roommates will be awakened by such activity no matter how quiet the coupling duo tries to be. The couple would not appreciate the sleeping roommate (who is suddenly awakened by their activity) to suddenly blast a very loud air horn alerting everyone to the cause of his interrupted sleep! On the other hand this may be just what needs to happen in order for the offending couple to realize that the sleeping roommate was awakened by the hook up.

Again, roommates who respect each other would not violate the other's sensibilities or privacy in these matters. Furthermore, you do not have to "put up or shut up" with regards to any morally offensive activity including sexual immorality, drug or alcohol abuse, violence, etc. Nothing increases stress faster than feeling like you have to put up with someone else's offensive behavior in order to be considered a good roommate. Instead, good roommates confront prickly issues at the start of their room sharing, honor their pre-agreed rules for the duration of their time together, and resolve whatever differences emerge quickly and amicably.

Listed are a few more points to consider for your Bill of Rights:
- Clearly outline the rules of shared space with regard to boyfriends and girlfriends.
- Clearly outline the rules of shared space with regard to use of alcohol and other substances. Dense living populations tend to spawn increased use of illegal drugs. This abuse can increase the student's risk and incidence of mental disorders ranging

from mild depression to mental psychosis.[43]

- Clearly outline the rules of shared space with regard to room parties.
- Clearly outline the rules of shared space with regard to co-habitation.

Cleaning your room

As ridiculous and petty as this might seem at first glance, the lack of tidiness and cleanliness of a room or roommate can strain even decent roommate relationships. Listed are a few bullet points to consider for your Bill of Rights.

- Keep both sides of the room clean and clear out of respect for the other.
- Both roommates need to keep shared bathroom spaces clean.
- Set cleaning schedules for room and bathroom and any other shared spaces.
- Keep bathrooms and dorm rooms free from foul odors.
- Keep your room uncluttered and safe for walking around.
- Closet doors need to close.
- Fragrances or room deodorizers can be offensive to sensitive noses and allergy prone individuals. Always ask your roommate about strong fragrances before using them.
- Clean up the bathroom sink, shower, and toilet after using.
- Keep dirty laundry out of sight.

Personal hygiene

This discussion might also seem ridiculous and petty however these issues can also come between roommates. Listed are a few points to consider for yourself – you might not want to include these in your Bill of Rights but they might come in handy for your personal goals.

- Keep your physical body clean and free of body odor. Always use deodorant.
- Keep your clothes clean and laundered. Fold your clothes when done washing/drying.
- Shower daily.

- Comb your hair with your brush/comb, not your roommate's.
- Do not use someone else's toothbrush or toothpaste.
- Clean up toothpaste from sink. Do not spit all over sink unless you clean it up immediately.
- Clean up hair/beard shavings from sink.

Germs

Colleges are breeding grounds for infectious diseases. Germs are basically given open access to you, your roommates, classmates and friends. Close living quarters facilitate the rapid spread of common germs, infections and disease because you live in small, cramped quarters, you touch bacteria-laden surfaces, breathe the same air, use the same bathroom facilities, get sneezed and coughed on by each other, and shake hands and share hugs and kisses with infected people. Students also frequent parties or social functions where they share drinks, utensils, even food. These conditions allow easy transmission of viruses and bacteria.

College students also are more susceptible to contracting disease or illness because they often have depressed immune systems compromised by stress, inadequate or irregular sleep, poor diet, excessive or inadequate exercise, dressing inappropriately for cold weather, smoking, pre-existing disease, or infections (including STIs), and drug/alcohol use.[44]

The United States Centers of Disease Control (CDC) advises college students to get vaccinated against meningococcal meningitis, a type of bacterial meningitis, simply because of the increased risk of contracting this rare infection on college campuses. Studies show that nineteen- to twenty-two-year-old college students have higher risk for contracting bacterial meningitis. Annually, about a hundred cases of meningococcal meningitis infections occur on college campuses. Fifteen students die annually as a result of this infection.[45] Furthermore, the 2009 H1N1 outbreak on college campuses readily exposed how rapidly and severely infectious disease can spread when living in close quarters.

While getting vaccinations are prudent, it's critical to remember that these preventative measures can't eliminate the world's germs. In fact, many germs or bacteria can't be vaccinated away! It is important to pay close attention to your college's quarantine procedures and policies about illnesses, excused absences for illnesses, etc. Finally, it is always important to practice good, clean, common sense hygiene when sharing living spaces with other persons. Good hygiene measures include:

- Cover the nose and mouth with a tissue when coughing or sneezing.
- Throw tissues in the trash after use.
- Wash hands thoroughly and often with soap and water, especially after coughing or sneezing.
- Use alcohol-based hand cleaners.
- Avoid touching your eyes, nose and mouth, as germs can be spread this way.
- Try to avoid close contact with sick people.
- If you are sick with a flu-like illness, stay away from others for at least 24 hours until after your fever is gone, except to get medical care. Have roommates bring you food from the cafeteria. A fever is considered to be gone only if you do not have a fever and you have not had to use fever-reducing medicine.
- Keep away from sick people as much as possible.
- If sick and sharing a common living space with others, wear a facemask if available and tolerable.
- Do not drink from another person's cup or eat using their utensils.
- Drinking games put you at risk for disease.
- Have soap readily available in your dorm bathroom.
- Keep your bathroom clean.
- Make sure your bathroom counters are kept clean; use disposable cleaning wipes and have them readily available.
- Clean door knobs when roommates are sick.

Collective living has many advantages and disadvantages – it is simply part and parcel of the collegiate life for at least the first two years at most universities. Use it to your advantage as you attend college – you will be glad you did. Use it to your disadvantage and you will wish you hadn't.

Conclusion

This chapter summarized some of the social challenges and opportunities that come your way when living in a collective environment. Think about the various goals you want to have for your social wellness before moving on to the next chapter.

Reflection questions:

1. List your personal and social goals in the worksheet in Appendix Two.

2. How would you rate your self esteem and body image?

3. What/how do you feel about the social capital at your college? What do you contribute and how?

4. Are you a positive or negative game changer for friends? Explain.

5. How are your different or similar to your peers?

6. How well do you communicate? Explain.

7. Have you drawn up your Bill of Rights? How is that working out for you?

Chapter Four

Mental and Emotional Health

Emotional Wellness

Our mental and emotional states of health or wellness are interrelated. Each affects and is affected by our physical, spiritual, academic, and economic state or status. Each personal dimension of self depends on the other to maintain a more perfect balance of wellness; each are positively or negatively impacted by the health or illness of the other dimensions. For example, good mental health has been found to be a significant factor in maintaining good physical health and well being.[1] Conversely, poor mental health causes physical illness and lack of well being.

Our health, both mental and emotional, is affected by what we eat, how we sleep, whether we exercise and how much we exercise. It is also affected by our personal choices, behavior, and belief system. Poor nutrition, lack of sleep, lack of exercise, risky behavior, making poor choices, adopting negative attitudes, having poor self esteem and body image, can lead to development of mental or emotional illness. Chronic stress also can lead to the development of physical and mental health problems including "unexplained physical symptoms;

mental disorders; feelings of anger; depression; sleep disorders; mood disorders; cardiovascular diseases (hypertension, atherosclerosis); immune, endocrine, and metabolic functions; and other functional disorders."[2]

Mental health is much harder to define than physical health. In fact, Rosemary Anderson[3], author and doctor suggests that when professionals add the word "illness" after the word "mental" it implies that the mental health system has evolved into a medical model that can identify all disorders, diagnose all problems and fix brain disorders even though it cannot. Therefore, it is very difficult to determine what exactly constitutes mental health or mental illness.

Mental *health* may be harder to generalize or characterize but we all know it when we see it. Mental health experts suggest that mental health allows us to think clearly, feel good about ourselves and our accomplishments, adjust adequately to normal and everyday stressors, and cope with life in general. When we are mentally healthy, we make deliberate and good decisions, analyze possibilities and consequences and choose well accordingly. Choosing well means that persons take appropriate actions to meet the challenges while exhibiting generally good mood, rational and coherent thought in accord with their physical age and intellectual ability. Note that most of the words used are very subjective and qualitative measurements supporting the earlier assertion that mental health is much more difficult to define than physical health.

The opposite of mental health is mental illness (or disorder). Anderson suggests that most mental illness is not the result of brain disease but the result of people's everyday life choices, actions, or ineffective mental health strategies.[4] In fact, Anderson goes on to blame poor mental health on people's poor choices thereby creating self-inflicted stress and trouble. Therefore, many problems that fall under the heading of mental illness are actually social issues.[5] On the other hand, mental illness can also be the result of genetic vulnerability, brain damage, traumatic life experiences, abuse, and failure in life's affairs.[6]

Mental disorder[7] is the state by which a person develops abnormal thinking. The various categories of mental disorder determined by the

American Psychiatric Association include the following:[8]

Anxiety	Mood
Eating	Impulse Control
Personality Adjustment	Dissociative
Factitious	Sexual and Gender
Somatoform	Tic
Psychotic	

The various mental diseases defined within each category is quite extensive; this information can be found in the back of the book in the Appendix 7. The names of the various diseases and the categories have changed often over the course of the last century. New disorders have been added in recent years while others have been de-classified as a mental illness.

Mental Illness

Mental illness is the opposite of good mental health. Similar to physical illnesses, mental illness can negatively impact someone's everyday life. In fact, mental illness can be even more socially debilitating than physical disorders. While the body's immune response often *cures* certain physical illnesses or disease; mental illness just can't go away, according to mental health experts.

Treatments for mental illness are uniquely complex and difficult for several reasons. Diagnosing a mental disorder can be very difficult as oftentimes a patient presents inconsistent behavioral patterns, lacks obvious symptoms, or is in denial about having problems. The differing degrees or severity of mental health diseases can also make a diagnosis and the development of a treatment plan challenging. The most common protocol for treating a mental disorder combines psychological treatment or therapy with potent drugs. Psychiatric patients often complain about the bothersome, negative side-effects from the drugs. The side effects can range from minor to more serious to include: affecting memory, impairing sexual or physical function, affecting reasoning and clear thinking, and more. In other words, the side effects often make it difficult to stick to a treatment plan.

All college students – all people – will experience an occasional day when they feel oddly fatigued, moody, irritable, cranky, sad, anxious, or worried. But these feelings normally dissipate and we forget having a bad mood. Mental illness, however, does not go away on its own; chronic negative feelings, anxieties, phobias, distorted thinking and reasoning, erratic behaviors, voices, hallucinations, paranoia, or "moody blues," do not vanish suddenly when someone is afflicted by a mental illness. We can't expect a student with mental illness to "just get over it," "get a grip on it," or "get on with life." Mental disorders can linger and will begin to interfere with personal friendships, family relationships, roommate relationships, concentration, and academic success. Unless they receive proper treatment, people with mental illness often lose their zest for life. Dozens of mental disorders can disaffect people's lives. Most need to be treated immediately and appropriately with traditional or alternative medicine and therapies.

Experts report that adults between the ages of eighteen and twenty-five — the typical age of most college students — have the highest onset of major mental illness.[9] This risk coincides also with risky experimentation, including the abuse of drugs, alcohol, sexuality, and personal relationships. Furthermore, risky behavior can trigger the development of mental disorder. Approximately one in four Americans are diagnosed with a mental disability each year, and that number includes a disproportionate number of college-age students.

Family members, school faculty, roommates, or students who come in contact with a person with a mental disorder too often assume that the person is simply "having more difficulty following the rules or behaving in a socially acceptable way."[10] Therefore, it is important that family members, faculty, and students learn to recognize when someone has a mental illness or disorder and is not simply a person who has trouble following rules. The number of college students who *self report* a psychiatric disability is consistent with national statistics of self reporting."[11] Many people self report, but too many don't or can't seek treatment on their own. Many students who fail to self report don't seek help simply because they feel they would be stigmatized by other students or faculty if or when they sought the help they need.

Stress

Stress is not a mental illness but it has been proven to be one pathway that leads to the onset of a mental disorder. Stress should be viewed as a warning sign; it provides a signal to each of us that we are not coping well with some aspect of our lives, be it academic, physical, social, spiritual, or mental. Feeling stressed also provides the warning sign that we need to seek or receive help with the aspect of our life that is causing the added pressure in order to prevent it from escalating further. Without help, intervention, or relief the stress can cause our mental state to spiral downward until we acquire a mental or physical disorder.[12]

College students need to be aware that ongoing mental pressure is problematic. Rosemary Anderson teaches that a person under stress – whether it comes from performing either pleasant or unpleasant tasks – has the same physical response. First, stress causes the changes to our body chemistry which changes certain body functions. For example, stress increases our *fight or flight* reactions which in turn increase the body's output of stress hormones resulting in changes to the body's overall chemistry.[13] Persons affected by chronic, elevated levels of stress hormones have increased risk for developing immune or cardiovascular disorders. They can tend to feel angry or depressed; they may over- or under-eat to feed their sagging emotions. Stress can make us feel unusually worn-out thereby reducing any desire to get adequate exercise. Stress causes the buildup of visceral (gut) fat. Finally, high levels of stress hormones can slow our body's metabolism."[14] The fight or flight response - also known as the stress response - can also cause faster heartbeats; the sensation of anxiousness or fatigue; headaches; a feeling of "knots" or "butterflies" in the gut region; and other physical symptoms. Anderson reminds us that all of these feelings and emotions are normally fine as long as stress is temporary and "we have time to recover" from it. Furthermore, it is important that the effects of the response do not continue to increase. If the stress response continues without a break, it can eventually lead to disorders, both mental and physical."[15]

Stress leads to depression when the pathway (stress) remains unbroken. When the pathway is interrupted, a person can begin to experience relief and a reduction in mental pressure. Reducing mental pressure gives us the opportunity for recovery. Anderson essentially plots the pathway to depression this way: *Stress moves the person away from his/her normal, healthy emotional state to one in which he or she feels pressurized. Mental pressure causes symptoms including that of tearfulness or snappiness. Without relief, the pressure just continues to increase causing us to have significant issues with self doubt and/or poor self esteem. When this happens, we often begin to withdraw socially. We continue to feel stressed and this is exhibited by feelings of anxiety and anxiousness. With continued pressure a student can become highly stressed or excessively stressed – a state known as clinical depression.*[16]

College life is replete with inordinate amounts of stress, especially when students fail to set or stick to realistic personal goals each semester. Students can have any number of challenges coming their way on a daily basis including money troubles, poor grades, higher expectations than results, difficult tests or academics, worries about future job placement, or relationships gone bad. Stress also increases with physical ailments. For instance, students who face chronic illness, acute illness, pain or injury, and even allergies can experience increased emotional or mental stress. Also, skipping meals, having poor nutrition, and using combinations of different therapeutic/prescription drugs can contribute to physical and mental stress. Also, students who arrive at college with pre-existing mental health issues will be at a significant disadvantage if the college cannot provide adequate support, treatment, and continued diagnosis. These students must consider whether a campus has adequate mental health facilities when exploring college options.

College success is generally proportional to the collective success of each individual marker — academic, social, spiritual, and physical wellness. However, as stress levels mount there can be a downward, cascade of wellness factors including health, mental, spiritual, physical, economic, social wellness. It is important to understand that each person differs greatly from others who also must manage stressors and stress levels. Balancing one's life turns into a juggling act of many different, colorful balls. When we drop one of the balls, we directly disaffect the general state of our life. Adverse results can throw us into disarray making it easier to continue dropping balls. Overall we can become less adept at handling life's challenges.

Stress Management

Males and females tend to approach stress differently. Females seek out social connections when they feel stressed; unfortunately not all relationships are stress breakers or productive. Experts tell us that females can find effective relief against stress by becoming a positive care giver, by being nurturing.[17] On the other hand, males who are stressed out often turn to physical aggression, anger, or violence. Aggression and violence only serve to perpetuate stress. In fact, aggressive forms of relief actually introduce additional legal, social, mental, and physical stressors. Experts tell us that males get effective relief against stress by participating in strenuous sports including boxing, wrestling, weight lifting, and others.

Mental health issues stem from a variety of factors including those with genetic, biochemical, or social components. Regardless of the causes, stress needs to be dealt with. Our whole person reacts positively or negatively to what we think, do, say, and believe. We are one body with many different, complex components which must be kept in balance to maintain mental and physical health and wellness. Therefore it is important to maintain mental and emotional goals. Think about them as you continue reading the book. Make notes that are helpful.

Consider the following broad-scope suggestions for your mental health goals:

- Avoid overloading on personal and social activities that take time away from necessary study and contribute to the feeling of being academically overwhelmed. Set goals around the amount of time spent on social activities vs. academics.
- Avoid social interactions that increase personal stress, fear, or loss of self control and self determination.
- List the biggest stressors in your life.
- Maintain good, wholesome friendships at school and home.
- Seek counseling when you begin to feel overwhelmed or

stressed out; get tutoring help as needed

- Learn good time management skills – this goes a long way toward reducing stress.
- Evaluate your mental and emotional health routinely – do you find that you are feeling weepy, snappy, or aggressive? Find out why and take charge of trying to change the factors that contribute to these feelings.
- What are your mental and emotional health goals this semester? Long term?

Depression

As stated previously, the final stage of chronic stress is clinical depression. It is critical to realize that stress is not the disease but provides the pathway to depression. Stress is a state of feeling pressure or strain because of many different factors whereas clinical depression is classified as the disease. Clinical depression is a mental/mood disorder that negatively affects our lives. The classical definition for depression requires that a "person have five or more symptoms of depression for at least two weeks."[18]

The symptoms or emotions/feelings associated with clinical depression include sadness, hopelessness, worthlessness, or pessimism. Depressed people tend to become overly focused on guilt, inadequacy or illness. In addition, people with major depression often change eating and sleeping patterns, exhibit agitation, restlessness, anger, and irritability. They can also experience hallucinations or delusions. Clinical depression can make it difficult to concentrate or cause fatigue and lack of energy. Clinical depression increases the feelings of hopelessness or helplessness and can cause people to think about or attempt suicide. In fact clinical depression significantly increases a person's interest in committing self-harm.[19] Finally, clinical depression increases the incidence of risky behaviors causing many to become dependent on alcohol, drugs, and tobacco.

Some students enter college seemingly well adjusted but end up dropping out due to depression or the development of other mental disorders. Perhaps their college experience was a steady stream of personal setbacks. Anderson warns us that many mental disorders are the secondary consequence of making poor choices. Furthermore, students who begin a downward decline tend to make even more bad choices as they near the latter stages of feeling stressed out – clinical depression.

Suicide

Depression increases a person's risk to commit suicide. Suicide occurs when all glimmer of hope has been replaced by despair. Unfortunately, despair often can result when we pursue false decoys resulting in negative consequences that are personal, debilitating, isolating, and depressing. These effects cause some people to consider ending the misery by their own hand – never the real solution. Suicide just succeeds in passing one's pain onto an unsuspecting family member or friend. We are all hurt by someone's decision to attempt suicide. If only the depressed person could see the depth of pain they pass onto others through their desperation. This subject will be dealt with more in-depth in future chapters when we talk about the calamities that result when students follow harmful decoys

Reflection Questions:

1. Despair is the lack of which theological virtue? Explain.

2. What is mental health? How would you rate yours?

3. List your preliminary mental health goals here.

4. What are the signs of depression?

5. What are your responsibilities when living with a person who is depressed or suicidal?

Chapter Five

SPIRITUAL WELLNESS

Illness always opposes health and wellness regardless of the dimension affected. In other words, illness affects the body *and* mind and will incrementally and in proportion to the severity or degree of the disease. It naturally follows that *spiritual* illness or disease opposes spiritual *health* no matter our age or background. In this chapter we will examine spiritual illnesses and cures. Unlike physical and mental illnesses, spiritual sickness can always be cured! This chapter will draw heavily from the encyclicals, the Bible and the Catholic Catechism — all rich sources for today's spiritual dilemmas.

As observed previously, mental *health* is much harder to define than physical health due to the subjectivity of mental wellness and illness; yet mental and physical health are both recognizable and something to strive for. Spiritual health and opposing spiritual illnesses are also recognizable. Spiritual health is therefore something to strive for. Let's draw heavily from the definitions for mental and physical health to define spiritual health.[1] Spiritual wellness allows us to: think more clearly about our direction or purpose in life; to have a peaceful heart even when facing physical or social challenges; to make deliberate and morally sound decisions that are consistent with deeply held values and beliefs; to strive for a deeper understanding of God; to publicly express our faith in God; to seek a deeper appreciation and understanding of our faith and moral/religious principles; and to seek wisdom. When we are spiritually strong, we will recognize our dependence on the grace of God to transform us. This transformation allows for a closer synchronicity with the Divine Heart, Soul, and Will. Furthermore, the depth of our Faith, Hope, and Charity should grow in proportion to our spiritual health which is directly linked to physical, mental, emotional, intellectual, and social wellness.

Alternate definitions suggest that spiritual well being is a strength or wellness which promotes positive thinking, positive ideals, positive habits, positive attitudes, and positive efforts. All together spirituality advances our mental well being by "leading one to strive for a state of harmony with oneself and others while working to balance inner needs with the rest of the world."[2] Note how this definition is completely devoid of any mention of God. This is the first hint that spirituality is not necessarily related to religiousity.

Exposing the spiritual diseases should allow for healing, treatment, and/or eradication of spiritual illness; therefore, it is necessary to delve into the spiritual diseases, their consequences, and their cures!

Spirituality vs. religion

Religiousness has been proven time and again to motivate people to help others in need by giving of time, talent or treasure. We know that Americans are more generous givers than people from other developed countries. In fact, no other country even approaches America's charitable giving levels!"[3] But are we a religious nation? Let's find out.

The Marist/KofC 2010 Poll strongly suggests that a whole lot of Americans – young and old – consider themselves to be believers; a full 84 percent of Americans and 76 percent of Millennials agree with the statement that they believe in God.[4] These same groups of people are also generous givers of money to charities (70 percent) although the Millennials are less generous (56 percent) by way of comparison. Their charitable giving rate probably reflects a lower income status compared to the older generations. Many Americans perform volunteer work (67 percent) and/or make significant charitable donations (67 percent).[5] In 2006, Americans gave just under $300 billion to charity and that amount continues to increase.[6] "About a third of the individual gifts go toward religious entities and the remainder goes to more secular outreaches such as education, health, and social welfare activities.[7]

While it is laudable that most Americans believe in God, only a slim majority of those polled by the Marist/KofC Poll believe that religion plays an important role in their lives (51 percent). The Poll reveals that people's beliefs also do not automatically transfer into "faith in action" including going to Church; attending missions or retreats; attending adult religious instruction; volunteering for service projects; digging deeper to understand one's faith; praying regularly; or bringing their faith into the workplace.

The Marist Poll results offer "promise and challenges" for the Catholic Church (and all traditional religions) with its startling revelations. Some of the good news for the Catholic Church depicted by the survey includes:[8]

- 85 percent of Catholic Millennials (those 18-29) believe in God.
- The top priorities for Catholic Millennials are getting married and having a family (33 percent) and being spiritual or close to God (18 percent).
- 82 percent of Catholic Millennials believe commitment to marriage is under-valued. 63 percent say the same about concern for the less fortunate.
- 66 percent of Catholic Millennials say abortion is morally wrong, while 63 percent say the same of euthanasia.
- 80 percent of Catholic Millennials see religion as at least "somewhat important" in their lives. 98 percent of practicing Catholics agree.
- 55 percent of Catholic Millennials think that religious values should influence business decisions. 75 percent of practicing Catholics agree.

On the other hand, the Church faces the following challenges as it reaches out to young people:[9]

- The majority (67 percent) of Catholic Millennials do not view getting married or having a family as a top priority.

- Most Millennials (82 percent) do not set getting closer to God as a top priority.
- On the other hand a slim majority (55 percent) of practicing Catholics see themselves as more "religious."
- 61 percent of Catholic Millennials believe that it is all right for a Catholic to practice more than one religion. 57 percent of practicing Catholics disagree.
- 82 percent of Catholic Millennials see morals as "relative." The majority of practicing Catholics (54 percent) disagree.

"Despite whatever differences Catholic Millennials may have with the Church, nearly 2 in 3 (65 percent) are very or somewhat interested in learning more about their faith." The majorities of "all Americans – regardless of age – state that they have an interest in knowing more about their religion but fail to regularly attend church or sign up for ongoing religious education instruction. A large majority of these same Americans (63 percent)[10] agree with the statement that they consider themselves to be (wholeheartedly or somewhat) more spiritual than religious. A majority (61 percent) of Catholic Millennials vs. American Millennials (50 percent) believe that it is acceptable to practice more than one religion at the same time. Finally, a very large majority of all Americans practice moral relativism — the belief that there is no definite right and wrong for everyone. In fact, your peers are more likely moral relativists (64 percent) compared to the older generations."[11]

Another piece of good news offered by the Marist Poll results, show that roughly 81 percent of Americans think that people's ethical standards are different in business than personal lives even though *they do not believe this should be the case.* Sixty percent of Americans believe that religious beliefs and values *should* influence a business executive's decision making; however, bear in mind that means that a significant number of people — four out of ten — do not feel strongly that executives' decisions should be influenced by religious beliefs and values.[12]

The lack of understanding and appreciation for "religion," coupled with widespread acceptance of moral relativism proves the need for the Church to offer a New Evangelization. It's clear that it must begin right now. Also clear are the stiff challenges to the New Evangelization.

Donna Freitas, author of *Sex and the Soul: Juggling Sexuality, Spirituality, Romance and Religious on American's Campuses,* found that a large number of college students see little or no connection between sex and religion despite the fact that sexual immorality is considered a grave sin by Christian, Jewish, and Muslim faiths. Religion only seems to play a significant role (with regard to chastity) for students attending evangelical colleges — not for students attending Catholic or public universities.

Many college students have had very limited faith and religious formation and so they experience ethical and personal dilemmas disaffecting their public and private lives. It is curious that all generations of Americans (more than two-thirds of all Americans), including your age group, worry that the nation's moral values are headed down the wrong path. They also overwhelmingly believe that the nation comes up short in its commitment to social values. Yet these same groups are hard pressed to offer viable, concrete, and objective moral solutions for this slippery descent. Instead, they continue to embrace the *live and let live* principle – another term for moral relativism.

The Marist Poll also shows that a majority of Americans believe that virtues such as obligation to marriage, personal responsibility, respect for others, hard work, and honesty and integrity are not valued enough in this nation.[13] Therefore, college students (and indeed all Americans) need to take their faith and witness to the college classroom, the frat party, the football game, the dormitories, and the workplace; this is the call for discipleship. It may be the only time someone hears this witness to the truth. If all believers were committed to developing moral communities within their spheres of influence there would be less need to worry about declining moral or social values and commitments.

In sharp contrast, people who identify themselves as practicing Catholics regularly attend religious services. They also are twice as likely to attend religious retreats, mission teams, and volunteer projects as those who view themselves as spiritual but not necessarily religious. Like other practising religious groups, most practicing Catholics also want to learn more about their religion. Practicing believers are also more generous with their time and money. Arthur Brooks reported that "in the year 2000, religious people (the 33 percent of the population who attend their houses of worship at least once per week) were 25 percent more likely to give charitably than secularists (the 27 percent who attend less than a few times per year, or have no religion). They were also 23 percent more likely to volunteer. Religious people gave nearly four times more dollars per year, on average, than secularists ($2,210 versus $642). They also volunteered more than twice as often (12 times per year vs. 5.8 times)."[14] Brooks concludes with this commentary: "We can predict that the churchgoer will be 21 percent more likely to make a charitable gift of money during the year than the non-churchgoer, and will also be 26 percent more likely to volunteer."[15] These people tend to bring their faith and values into their workplace, community, and private lives.

The signs and symptoms of spiritual poverty or deficiency (illness)

A. Spirituality

Claiming to be *spiritual rather than religious* is both a contradiction and a sign of spiritual poverty. Today it is wildly more popular to label oneself spiritual rather than religious; it is not popular to readily advertise one's active membership in a traditional religious denomination. This also tells us that spirituality and religion are not synonyms. So, just what is *spirituality?* The internet serves up a treasure trove of definitions for spirituality. Let's read a basic description about spiritualism from one who is a "consumer of spiritualism": "It is, in the most basic sense, matters pertaining to the spirit and is based on the idea that there exists something, be it a state of mind, a being, or a place, that is outside the experience of our five limited senses. Spirituality is the personal relationship of the individual to this state of mind, being, or place and often emphasizes the notion of a path, that spirituality is a goal in achieving understanding, or an improved relationship with the sacred. Spirituality can be either a part of a particular religion or independent of religion; it is a self directed and personal inner path. As part of a larger religious journey, spirituality is usually descript and predictable, relating to one's personal relationship to god or the divine goal. For the unaffiliated seeker, spirituality may be adapted and modeled after the sacred practices of a number of different religions or none at all. In either case *spiritual matters are contrasted to the world of the senses and the needs of the human corporeal body and often involve an effort to reject, limit or transcend these senses and needs.*[16]

This spiritualist does not appear to be motivated to practice a traditional Christian religion that offers a fuller understanding about the Trinity; rather her spirituality motivates her practice of "ahimsa" — nonviolence toward all living beings. As a result, Cary eats only "cruelty-free vegan foods, refuses to purchase goods produced in sweatshops, and also refuses to drive gas-guzzling SUVs. She also likes to spend time reading (especially the *Bhagavad Gita* on mountaintops), blogging, munching vegan cookies, and browsing the blogosphere."[17]

Yoga is another activity of many *spiritualists*. Yoga teaches us to get in touch with our inner voice or spirit in order to live well. And this is perhaps why many spiritualists are not religious. Christian faiths call followers to look outward rather than inward in the quest for truth and God. Yoga urges us to look inward for strength and truth. This does not mean to infer that yoga is bad when used for relaxation or exercise; however, it becomes problematic when it replaces love for God with a love for self.

Pride is considered to be the deadliest of all sins because it is the root of all other sins. Fr. Robert Barron disputes that slightly by suggesting that sloth is the greatest sin of the 21st century because it prevents people from doing something about growing their faith![18] Sloth convinces believers to become like bumps on a log – unmoving – when it comes to learning more about their faith or putting their faith into action! Sloth makes people lazy about searching for God, moral answers, truth, or religious principles. Instead, slothful individuals think it is good enough to look inward and feel content about simply believing. Sloth fails to convict our consciences when we miss Mass on Sundays; neither does it place blame on our hearts when we stop learning about our faith. It convinces us that we can figure things out for ourselves. Sloth even stops us from worrying about being slothful. Sloth doesn't call us to pray or to seek answers about moral or religious questions we may have. Sloth produces a disinterest in discovering Truth. Sloth causes us to become completely lazy in matters pertaining to God. Sloth convinces us that any in-depth spirituality or religious efforts are just not worth it. Sloth is to blame for the decreasing popularity of religiosity. Sloth has made getting religion insidious. On the other hand, a true spirituality should cause us to examine our relationship to God. It should push us to want to find out more about Him, His Truth, His Wisdom and His Love. This journey should take us back to Church rather than the mirror or yoga class.

B. Moral Relativism

Spirituality is linked to the practice of moral relativism – the second symptom of spiritual poverty. Previously, it was noted that the majority of Americans believe in moral relativism — regardless of age — while worrying about the decline in American moral and social values![19] In fact, the 2010 Marist Poll states that "most Americans believe that the nation comes up short in its commitment to social values. These views are largely shared across the generations."[20]

It seems odd to worry about the direction of other people's morals while holding to the philosophy that there is no right or wrong moral standard for everyone! Herein is the contradiction for those who are moral relativists. Many have rightful fears or concerns about the downward trajectory of values in this country. Yes, Americans in general, "believe that virtues are not valued enough, including commitment to marriage, personal responsibility, respect for other people, respect for hard work, honesty, integrity, concern for the less fortunate, tolerance for diversity, respect for the law, respect for authority, work ethics, and more.[21] But fixing the problems necessitates affixing a collective set of moral standards and values, infusing moral virtue, and defining black and white – right and wrong actions and/or practices — to people's behaviors. Therein lies the weakness of moral relativism; it's a phony principle. There *are* moral absolutes.

Moral relativists can only hope that people will follow a generally appropriate path forward even as they worry that it isn't happening. People can only assume virtue when their moral compasses are hard-wired to the source of Virtue – God! We have previously discussed the fact that even civilized people do not necessarily continue along virtuous paths. People need to have fundamental beliefs in order to be motivated to practice a living faith. Pope Benedict XVI recognizes that cultural (moral) relativism is an illness; it requires the church to teach with a New Evangelization.

Clearly, the Church's influence on public debate should take place on many different levels. In the United States, as elsewhere, many laws are immoral (abortion, mandatory sexual sterilization and more). The Catholic community, needs to offer a clear and united witness on such matters. Even more important, though, there needs to be the gradual opening of the minds and hearts of the wider community to moral truth. Here much remains to be done.[22]

C. Abandonment of Religion

Moral relativism is a sign of spiritual poverty. All spiritual diseases/illnesses wear down our Faith and our commitment to Faith. The abandonment of traditional religions is more pervasive than in past centuries – especially among developed nations disaffecting the ability to discern Truth.

Many persons are achieving a more vivid sense of God. On the other hand, growing numbers of people are abandoning religion in practice. Unlike former days, the denial of God or religion or the abandonment of them are no longer unusual and individual occurrences. For today it is not rare for such things to be presented as requirements of scientific progress or of a certain new humanism. In numerous places these views are voiced not only in the teachings of philosophers but on very side they influence literature, the arts, the interpretation of the humanities and of history and civil laws themselves. As a consequence many people are shaken. [23]

D. Personal Sin

Personal sins – acts of omission and commission – hurt us because they draw us away from God's grace. Sin harms social capital and camaraderie. In fact, the Bible teaches that if one member suffers, all suffer. If one member is honored all rejoice together. You are the body of Christ, and individually, members of it.[24] We see the effects in our secular world as well. Recall how experts note that mental illness is largely the result of making bad choices. Mental and physical illnesses certainly disfigure and harm us. Many of these illnesses are the direct result of sin.

Sin disfigures and wounds us spiritually and physically — even mortally. The Church teaches that sinful persons remain in the image of God and in the image of the Son but are deprived of the glory of God – of His likeness.[25]

Grave (mortal) sin has a double consequence – it deprives the sinner of being in communion with God and prevents him or her from receiving His grace thus rendering us incapable of sharing eternal life with God. Venial sin, a less serious offense, causes us to develop unhealthy attachments to things of this world. Therefore, it is necessary to purify our bodies, minds, and souls in order to be cured from sin. This requires a continual conversion or turning away from sin.[26]

Socrates taught in ancient times that "an unexamined life is not worth living." Is it because an unexamined life turns lives into an accumulation of personal sin? Fr. Bede Jarrett writes: "The Pharisee is self satisfied, but the Publican is never content because he realizes the great gulf fixed between what he is and what he should be. All the saints must be forever discontented with their own sins while longing to restore all things in Christ."[27]

We must live like the saint who is never satisfied with personal sin and unlike those who, without examining their actions, remain oblivious to sinful habits, lifestyles and choices. Even when we fail to examine our lives, personal sin still accumulates and has consequences on our physical, mental, social personal, economic and emotional well being. A personal conversion requires a turning away from sin; we must seek forgiveness in order to be forgiven by God and others. Unforgiven sin induces spiritual weakness and disease and delivers us up to judgment – both now and at death — that render the unexamined (sinful) life not having been worth living. "Christ took upon himself the whole weight of evil and took away the sin of the world of *which illness is only a consequence.*"[28]

E. Scientific Advancements

Today, science is used to reveal and deny the existence of God. It is not unusual for astronauts to marvel about the extraordinary order of the created world. On the other hand, it is also not unusual for reproductive technologies to presume they are creating life or are masters of life itself. Scientific endeavors that cause other people to deny the existence or relevance of God only serve to increase social and spiritual chaos. When scientific endeavors fail to examine moral implications behind the discoveries, spiritual poverty is afoot.

Scientific advancements should try to address man's longings and questions even as it supports our understanding that God is Master Designer. Science must always acknowledge that God is infinitely greater than all His works (the sciences) and his greatness is unsearchable.[29] Too often science gets coupled with political agendas; at that point it has morphed from physical science.

Furthermore, when human beings think that science can genuinely and totally emancipate them from all trouble they effectively switch from hope and dependence on God to hope in self reliance, and man-made accomplishments.[30] *Gaudium et Spes*, an encyclical released in 1965 by the late Pope Paul XVI, contains wisdom and prophetic pronouncements pertinent today. It forewarned against science undertaking rapid developments that introduce contradictions or imbalances between our collective intellect and our theological understandings. These imbalances are generated when the latter lags the first. Over the past forty years, technologies have certainly introduced moral contradictions; simultaneously, catechesis of the faithful has been largely remiss with regard to moral contradiction. Consider how birth control measures, artificial reproduction, designer babies and many other "advances" fail to raise moral antennas.

Gaudium et Spes also admonished against sacrificing individual rights and stamping out moral objections in the name of gaining practical efficiencies. It also warned scientific advances not to generate moral confusions through wholesale devotion to practical efficiencies at all costs. Consider how legalized abortion, in-vitro fertilization, and abortifacient birth control methods (the Pill, The Shot and Implants, etc.) go against all the warnings. They sacrifice pre-born fetus' right to live; stamp out moral objections to abortion or contraception by promoting their practicalities, and thereby confuse our moral principles with regard to human life.

Much of today's moral confusion can be traced back to the general failure to question the good of scientific advancements. We allow the practical results to trump personal rights introducing moral confusion. This will continue because many are simply not interested in pursuing advanced theological understandings as they advance intellectual growth (i.e., college). Moral confusion will reign as long as we tolerate and promote the false worship of science, self-styled spirituality, moral relativism, and give free reign to research. Instead we allow research – especially in the life areas – to plunge ahead without limits or moral considerations. The Book of Sirach advises; "All our works are to be performed meekly … we are not to seek things that are too complex … we are not to examine things beyond our abilities … not be too curious in too many of His works for it is not necessary to see with our own eyes the things that are hidden. Uncertainty in these things has undermined many persons and had detained their minds in vanity."[31]

F. Moral Contradictions

Secular societies push God, Heaven and Hell included, into oblivion when they allow contradictory moral positions to create wedges between man and God, between practicality and human dignity. Human designs are capable of creating changes that actually "recoil upon us, our decisions and desires, as individuals or collective persons." The human technologies "recoil upon our collective (and individual) manner of thinking and acting with respect to things and to other people. Hence, cultural and social transformations can have repercussions on man's religious life as well."[32]

People pushed into moral confusion often turn to atheism, secular spirituality, or agnosticism rather than religiousness. Few people assert that there is no God but many suggest that there are no moral absolutes or absolute truths. In this way they push God into irrelevance which has the same effect as convincing people there is no God.

Readers, who are indifferent to God, sin, Heaven, or Hell, should read the book *Life After Death* by Dinesh D'Souza. He reminds us that what we believe about life after death does matter now and later! D'Souza writes that people with an indifferent attitude about life and death "couldn't be more wrong. It makes all the difference in the world. Therefore choose as if everything depends on your decision - because it does!"[33]

G. The Seven Deadly Sins

The seven deadly sins — pride, envy, avarice (greed), lust, gluttony, anger, and sloth — are considered "deadly" because they cause us to develop "serious sinful habits that cultivate a deeply sinful nature (lifestyle/habits) which harden our hearts against God and His Mercy.[34] By contrast we are taught by God and His Church to put on the virtues opposed to the seven deadly sins, including: humility, kindness, temperance, chastity, patience, generosity, and diligence. Each of these virtues is covered in depth in the Catholic Catechism.

H. Self Love

Self love is one more sign of spiritual illness. This does not mean that we should walk around hating ourselves! Self hate or loathing is very bad for our overall wellness for it translates into the adoption of risky behaviors, suicide, mental problems, and more. Rather, we are to live like we believe that we are adopted children of God! We need to know that we are made in His image and likeness. Righteous understandings of who we are, in relation to God, props up authentic love instead of selfish love.

We have free choice, which can take us on a journey toward God or away from God. When we move toward God, we develop a deeper, more profound, personal love for Him which consequently causes us to abandon self-love, selfish interests, and self-centered demands. On the other hand, when we move away from God, we begin to disregard Him, His Truth, His Wisdom, His Love and the Ten Commandments. This causes us to cling to self, to turn inward and to dial up the number of selfish demands we impose on others. Selfish love is a sure sign of spiritual illness.

If spiritual illness can cause mental and physical illness, it must follow that spiritual health promotes general health and well being.

How does religiosity promote health and well being?

A number of studies verify that religiosity promotes general health and wellness including physical, social, mental, and emotional wellbeing. Religious people tend to be healthier; have less stress or depression; are less likely to attempt suicide; live longer; are happier; have more fulfilling sex lives;[35] are more generous with their time, talent, and money; they more readily help others through works of charity or other types of volunteerism, are more open to marriage and having children; and display positive personal characteristics and traits. This generosity benefits all of society.

I recall hearing about a very public debate between a Christian and an atheist which clearly illustrated how different belief systems impact society needs. For example, an audience member asked the atheist how he/other atheists have helped the poor and disadvantaged as compared to the Catholic/Christian religious outreach services in the Philippines. The question stumped the atheist because he was unable to cite one instance in which an atheist organization funded a hospital, an orphanage, or other charitable services for needy people in their country. The same, starkly different levels of generosity have been noted around the world. Christian organizations are normally the first to step up to provide relief efforts for the poor and needy; they are also the most consistently generous. Faith moves people to commit acts of generosity whereas atheism merely seems interested in debating issues.

The Wellness and Behavior Inventory Study conducted in 2006 with college students, concluded: "If a student has a low spiritual health score, beliefs about good health are not a concern of theirs because their outlook and purpose in life are not priorities. In this case, intervention activities to improve spiritual health may need to be addressed before targeting direct, physical health behaviors."[36]

In just a few generations, society has moved hearts away from being concerned about spiritual fitness but this seems to have produced negative results. Major health trends across colleges show overall declining physical fitness and emotional health; increased stress, fear of failure and concerns related to relationships issues and sexual violence.[37] This coincides with lower student religious affiliation and church attendance.

The Cures:

A. Be open to the Grace of God

The major difference between spiritual illness and physical or mental illness is that all spiritual illnesses can be fully and completely *cured* no matter the sin; the cure for sin is the reception of God's grace. We receive God's grace when we exercise the "responsibilities of the Christian life" which include reception of the Sacraments including Holy Eucharist and Penance, doing works of mercy and charity, asking for forgiveness from God and those we offend; praying; collaborating with God in all parts of our life; obeying the Commandments; living out the Beatitudes; putting on virtue; avoiding vice; and freely choosing to live as disciples in our everyday life. St. Paul advises the Ephesians (and us) more about the cures for spiritual disease Take note of the highlighted portions in particular.

"**Be strong in the Lord**, and in the strength of His might. **Put on the full armor** of God that you may be able to stand firm against the schemes of the devil. For our struggle is not against flesh and blood but against the rulers; against the powers; against the world forces of this darkness; against the spiritual forces of wickedness. Therefore, **take up the full armor of God** that you may be able to resist the evil day and having done everything to stand firm. **Stand firm having girded your loins with truth and having put on the breastplate of righteousness,** and having **shod your feet with the preparation of the gospel of peace**, in addition to all, **taking up the shield of faith** with which you will be able to **extinguish all the flaming missiles of the evil one. And take the helmet of salvation and the sword of the Spirit which is the word** of God. With all **prayer and petition pray at all times in** the Spirit and with this in view **be on the alert with all perseverance and petition.**"[38]

B. Arm yourself with Virtue

And then there is virtue — "the habitual and firm resolve to do good."[39]

"Virtue gives truth to our intelligence, justice to our will, goodness to our heart and consequently the same mode of thought, will, and feeling as God himself who is by his essence truth, justice and goodness."[40] Virtue allows us to reflect the likeness of God; it allows us to more closely integrate our body, mind, will, and soul to God. We are called to reflect the likeness of God because we are made in His image. We are called to love ourselves and others authentically; this means we are called to love as God loves — with a sacrificial love!

There are various groupings of virtues: human virtues, moral virtues, and theological virtues (faith, hope, and love). The human virtues are normally grouped within the four Cardinal virtues: fortitude, justice, prudence and temperance. The moral virtues – acquired by human effort – increase through education, deliberate acts of charity and perseverance.[41] Furthermore, the practice of a moral life gives us spiritual freedom. We no longer stand before God as a slave but as a son or daughter.[42] The virtues enable us to perform Christian responsibilities, which include carrying out the Charitable and Spiritual Works of Mercy.

Charitable Works of Mercy

Feed the hungry – *donate to food shelves*
Give drink to the thirsty – *donate money*
Shelter the homeless – *help at homeless shelters*
Clothe the naked – *donate to clothing drives*
Visit the sick – *volunteer in hospitals*
Minister to the imprisoned– *prison ministry volunteer*
Bury the dead – *give the dead a proper burial*

Spiritual Works of Mercy

Instructing – *teaching catechism classes*
Advising – *volunteer in crisis pregnancy center*
Consoling – *in hospitals*
Comforting – *relief services*
Forgiving – *family, friends, and self*
Bearing wrongs patiently – *from friends, family members or others*

Examine your Life – know where you are headed

The faithful person examines his purpose in life; he or she also examines habits and lifestyles. Earlier you read that Socrates taught that the unexamined life is not worth living. By way of contrast, the examined life is indeed worth living because it draws us closer to perfection – God.

Examine your college culture – know where it is headed

The faithful person examines his surroundings. It is always important to examine the influences around you. When necessary, switch to a support system that enhances overall success. You will also be called to influence the culture in which you live. Pick a group of friends that help support this examination of life. Also, get involved in the campus Newman Center, Focus (Fellowship of Catholic University Students), Catholic Studies Groups or other volunteer activities. Help bring supportive and constructive faith curriculums to your campus. Live in community housing that is supportive of your spiritual goals. Seek out the same gender living communities. Work with your college to bring about measures that promote respect and dignity for all students. For example, strive to create alcohol-free living communities. Work on normalizing visiting hours to match wellness goals. Seek out professors who support your fledgling faith and philosophies about life. Take classes from professors who respect and uphold the teachings of the Magisterium of the Church.

Wisdom

Godly Wisdom is a means by which God cures spiritual poverty. The Bible teaches us that Wisdom is a pearl of inestimable worth. The search for Godly Wisdom will require "great effort on our part" but God reminds us that this time and effort will be well spent.

Wisdom is not the same thing as knowledge, nor is it gained through an accumulation of knowledge. If it were, all college graduates would be wise and there would be no need to search for godly wisdom. Thomas Aquinas taught that while we can "all work to attain intellectual virtue (grow in knowledge) by human effort, Wisdom descends from above." Wisdom allows us to "taste and see the goodness of the Lord because it is God – directed and portioned out." He is the source of Wisdom. We are gifted with Wisdom in proportion to our faith and humility. This gift rewards us with interior peace and a clearer understanding of God's plan for our lives. Wisdom allows us to realize that there is a greater purpose in life – it lets us see the living God active in the world around us. Wisdom calls us to make routine self examinations. Wisdom does not harden our hearts.

King Solomon, ruler of Israel for forty years during the 10th Century B.C., was the son of King David. He was credited with having a very keen intellect, understanding, and righteous (godly) judgment. In other words, King Solomon had Wisdom but he rightfully credited that gift to God. Like him, we ought to continually praise the Source and the Gift of Wisdom using his words:[43]

"Therefore I prayed, and understanding was given me; I called on God, and the spirit of wisdom came to me. *I preferred her to scepters and thrones, and I accounted wealth as nothing in comparison with her. Neither did I liken to her any priceless gem, because all gold is but a little sand in her sight, and silver will be accounted as clay before her. I loved her more than health and beauty, and I chose to have her rather than light, because her radiance never ceases. All good things came to me along with her, and in her hands uncounted wealth. I rejoiced in them all, because wisdom leads them; but I did not know that she was their mother. I learned without guile and I impart without grudging; I do not hide her wealth, for it is an unfailing treasure for mortals; those who get it obtain friendship with God, commended for the gifts that come from instruction.*"

The principle difference between faith and wisdom is that "while faith is simply the knowledge someone possesses about the articles of the Christian belief, wisdom goes on to a certain divine penetration of the truths themselves."[44]

The following example tries to explain Fr. Harden's comparison between faith and wisdom by using a secular example. Years ago, a Nobel Physicist named Richard A Feynman wrote a book titled *Surely You're Joking Mr. Feynman* in which he compared a genuine scientist with an average one. According to Mr. Feynman, most scientists are average at best. The average scientist learns to apply existing scientific theories and equations to solve problems. The genuine scientist generates the scientific theories, principles, and relationships. In other words, a real scientist watches an apple fall from a tree and understands why it drops, that it will be repeatable (including the how and why), and develops equations that allow others to calculate how fast it will drop and where it will land, etc. The average scientist is indebted to the genuine scientist for the deeper insight. There is a similar relationship between knowledge and wisdom. We should realize that knowledge is only average at best when compared to wisdom. Knowledge is the material we can all wrap our brains around whereas to have wisdom requires a "divine penetration of the Truths themselves". Knowledge is obviously important and necessary but Wisdom is its clear director. God is the ultimate scientist. Humans are merely average. We are indebted to God for Wisdom.

Wisdom remains elusive due to lack of faith, sloth, or pride. We can be easily tricked into thinking that knowledge and wisdom are synonymous and that they are attained through self-help efforts. It is essential to know that Wisdom is a gift from the Holy Spirit. Any Wisdom received will bring great blessings to us. It is indeed the valuable pearl that is worth searching and praying for over the course of a lifetime.

Faith and Truth

Faith and Truth get us to our final, hoped-for destination — Heaven. Atheist philosophies try to derail us from this reward. Nietzsche, Ernest Nagel, Bertrand Russell, and others cleverly call for the removal of all moral boundaries for specific reasons. They realize that moral boundaries help people maintain virtue, moral lives, and faith. On the other hand, removal of sexual restraints, for example, erodes religiosity and Faith, Hope and Charity. These philosophers recognized that "sexual liberation is one of the *benefits* of a decline in the belief of God and the afterlife."[45] In effect the fight for the removal of sexual boundaries is simply the ultimate fight against God.

Faith also beckons us to think about the path we follow as well as where life meets death – the final horizon. Everyone will eventually die – it is actually the great equalizer since death does not discriminate or hold any partiality for wealth, culture, philosophy of life, disposition or way of life. And so the subject of death should cause us to ponder it and discover where it leads. People who have had near death experiences provide us with clues to the afterlife, but the best evidence was given to us by Jesus Christ, who died and rose from the dead in order to reveal God's love to us.

We derive truth and meaning from both life and death since it is part and parcel of our "fallen" design. Searching for the Truth hinged to spiritual health and well being (faithfulness) allows us to acquire a reasoned understanding of the Creator *and* life and death.

Authentic Love

The Greek and Jewish cultures distinguished between the different modalities of love by having three or four words to describe love's various states. The different words distinguished between the love of parents for their children, romantic love, friendship, and love of God. Unfortunately, the English language only has one word for love and so the word is used to describe various types of commitments, feelings, emotions, devotions, and states. Thus, love has lost much meaning and depth.

God loves us freely, permanently, and unconditionally. He loves all of us even though He knows many freely choose to reject Him. God's love is always life-sustaining and invigorating. Tim Moser, coach and advisor for college students, describes God's love this way: It's free, full, faithful, fruitful and forever.

Jesus modeled God's love for us as He died for our sins. He taught us that love is patient, kind, trusting, modest, humble, and considerate. Love looks out for others, it is agreeable, forgiving, and permanent, and it rejoices in the right, bears all things, believes all things, hopes all things and endures all things. Love is not jealous or envious, it is not immodest, impatient, unkind, arrogant or rude, and it does not insist on its own way nor is it irritable or resentful. Love does not rejoice at wrong doings.[46] Love is a whole lot more than feelings; it is a choice we make.

Human sexuality gives us the unique opportunity to express

authentic love in and through our bodies with our beloved. We become the gift to our spouse. God has given us the free choice to reserve this gift only for true love, to withhold it selfishly, or to give it away foolishly and prematurely. We also decide how we want to treat other people. Either we will strive to treat others with dignity and respect (this is how we want to be treated) or we choose a more uncivil attitude which disrespects, maltreats or uses others. When we use others we hurt them *and* love. This manifestation of love can only be temporary, conditional, manipulative, hurtful, arrogant, insisting on its own way. Furthermore, it serves to decivilize society, disrupt family life, and wound men, women and children. Hurt people will turn around and hurt other people and so the cycle of use continues.

Discovery of the Purpose in Life

Fr. Maurice Zundel warns that: "few of us would have the courage to live if we didn't believe in the value of our own human life."[47] D'Souza argues this as well when he states: "most people want (and deserve) to be treated as persons rather than perishable bodies."

Sometimes college students have an odd way of looking at the value and purpose of life. Consider the following coed's statement: *"If people value their body as a temple (presumably she means of the Holy Spirit) then taking drugs is a risk because you're harming your body. If you see your body as just a vessel that you're in then it's not really risky; then it's just experimentation. How much can you do to this vessel before it collapses?"*[48]

Her logic seems to argue that students are morally bound — at least to themselves — to discover what type of *vessel* they are before indulging in risky social behaviors. She unintentionally seems to argue that students who take risks are mere vessels while student who don't take risks live with purpose and meaning; this implies there are two separate species of human beings. We know differently.

Human beings will always wonder why they were made. This questioning completely separates us from the rest of the animal kingdom. The gift of speech allows us to express our thoughts and desires. We freely, fully, faithfully, fruitfully and forever express our personhood with our bodies — unlike the animal creatures.

Searches for truth and/or purpose cannot just spur us to mirror our friends' searches. Quests must not start and stop with the study of social, political, scientific, or anthropological constructs. All of us have to take the search beyond intellectual or social spheres in order to get closer to the Truth, which is always constant and unchanging because so is God. The Bible teaches us that He is who He is (I am who Am). While some find this discomforting, it is mostly reassuring that God of today is the same God of tomorrow. What matters today matters tomorrow. Truth is the same – today or tomorrow.

Ongoing Catechesis

It is absurd to consider religious instruction complete after Confirmation. Most of you realize fully that ongoing instruction is vital for keeping sharp on the job, in the classroom, and in all secular areas of life. New studies show however, that few Catholic students bring a strong catechetical background with them to college. They are weak in theology and scripture due to poor grade school and high school catechesis.[49] Therefore, like other college students, young Catholics are ill equipped to deal with moral questions.

Did you know that boredom (lack of intellectual stimulation) can cause premature death among the elderly? Similarly, I pose this theory: Lack of spiritual stimulation can certainly cause premature spiritual death for all age groups.

It follows that if we continue growing toward God by studying theological matters, religious matters, and faith and morals, we will be better equipped to help advance civilization humanely and justly.

Most of us hate to admit that we have sinned. We frequently sidestep the issue by saying we made a bad choice. We also hate to admit a lack of spiritual formation even as we openly challenge those who are well formed. Recently, Rep. Patrick Kennedy (D.-R.I.) picked a very public fight with his bishop, Thomas J. Tobin, over the requirements for being Catholic. The debate turned into a classic dispute in which a theologically under-educated person (Rep. Kennedy) challenged the expert. Clearly, Kennedy did not really want to hear the Truth. The Bishop's response is important for all of us. (His letter can be found in the Appendix Nine). Clearly Kennedy, like many others, simply did not understand what it means to be a Catholic. Congressman Kennedy also doesn't appear willing to explore the Truth beyond his own understanding.[50]

The moral of the story is that we all need ongoing catechesis. Sometimes this ongoing education will be challenging to grasp; in fact it may provide answers we don't want to hear or direction we didn't expect to take. Consider the following true story of one woman's passionate, spiritual search. Her name is Mary.

Mary's journey took place over the course of a decade. Her search for truth meant joining and subsequently leaving quite a few different Protestant denominations. Mary described how each temporary stopping point deposited at least one nugget of truth in her. Nevertheless, Mary felt the need to search for "fullness and enduring originality." Unexpectedly, Mary found herself drawn into the Roman Catholic Church — the last place she expected to land. During her preparation for entry into the Church Mary was surprised to discover that each and every nugget of Truth (previously discovered) was perfectly preserved within the Catholic Church. For the very first time of her life, Mary felt at peace and at home. The discovery of the *Total Deposit of Faith* made her realize that all of the "nuggets" were contained within one Church because it was and is the original, apostolic beginning of Christianity. Mary understood that God never changes because He is the same Creator who was, who is and who is to come. Therefore, His Church is the same; it has unchanging moral and theological Truth. Protestant denominations had divided up and scattered various truths as they split from the Church and each other over the centuries. Mary admitted to receiving great blessings from each of the previous faith experiences she had, but she felt great peace and joy to have finally *come home*. Mary received spiritual healing and peace because of her genuine, humble quest for Truth.

The Gospel of St. Luke warns us not to build something without first acquiring enough resources because otherwise we will be mocked for our lack of foresight.[51] Similarly, we are to build a solid foundation of faith lest we be mocked for flailing along under the banner of faith and the banner of relativism. Christianity is incomplete at best when we fail to learn how to witness to the unbeliever, when we fail to be good public disciples, and when we fail to love authentically.

The Golden Rule

We all hope to be treated with respect and dignity; humans rightfully expect to have rights and liberties, freedoms, dignity, and honor. We seem to recognize that we deserve these rights because we have been created with inestimable worth. But this privilege means that we must also examine how well we treat others and their rights. Treating others as we would want to be treated is known as the Golden Rule.

The Golden Rule is actually a condensed summary of the last seven Commandments which instruct us how to love our neighbors. Recall, that the first three Commandments teach us how to know, love, and serve God. Together, the two subsets of commandments form the Ten Commandments – the basic laws for Jewish and Christian believers as well as those in the secular world. God sent his Son to clarify — not detract from — the Ten Commandments. Jesus' famous Sermon on the Mount provides the framework for the Golden Rule. He established the Law of the Gospel (Beatitudes) which perfectly fulfilled the Commandments of the Law.[52]

The Gospels record almost the exact wording of the Golden Rule as we know it. For instance St. Matthew recorded these words of Jesus: *"Whatever you wish that men would do to you, do so to them."*[53] St. John's Gospel shows that the Golden Rule is simply the way by which we are called to imitate Jesus' actions. This message is to: *"Love one another as I have loved you."*[54]

The Golden Rule "requires people to make decisive choices and then take decisive actions which support others and avoids harming our neighbor. It also puts into practice the words of the Lord in the New Testament."[55] Choosing to love God advances social capital, spiritual wellness, and civilization in supernatural ways and degrees because love for God moves us to love ourselves and His children authentically.

College students are keen on asserting and demanding rights and freedoms: academic freedoms, freedom of self-expression, civil rights, social freedoms, and more. Many rights debates turn into discussions about me, me, me, and my rights! Many times we fail to examine how our own demands and behaviors square with the Golden Rule, which calls us to show no partiality to self over others.

When people insist on exercising their rights, they often fail to uphold God's Truth. For instance, insisting on the right to have an abortion fails to uphold the fact that the unborn fetus is nevertheless a very young human being. This fact guided the passage of fetal protection laws in which a criminal is charged with two counts of murder if he or she causes the death of a pregnant mother and her unborn baby. Abortion is just one example whereby the dignity and freedom of all human beings is upended by individual rights.

Our culture tries to equate freedom and knowledge; yet it is godly wisdom that secures true freedom. College students need to see the link between personal sin and the demand for secular-based freedom, rights, and truth.

Unfortunately, many students define freedom as the right to do or say anything they please. Isn't freedom a *right* after all? However, God actually gives us the power to exercise or not exercise our rights in order to preserve *someone else's rights*. An exercise in real freedom demands that we first order our passions and desires around sound judgment, reasoning, and free will. In other words, we direct our thoughts, words, and deeds; they don't just spill out. True freedom requires that our decision to act (or not act) be deliberate and self-directed. It demands that we question the morality or ethical nature of decisions. True freedom arrives after we allow a spiritual maturation to settle within us!

There are three fundamental and universal truths that apply to all of us regardless of religion, sex, race, or nationality. Jeff Cavins, noted speaker and author, teaches that these are:[56]

1. **No person has any right to indulge in a pleasure or demand liberties and rights that could ruin another person.**

2. **What is safe for one person may not be safe for another, even if it is a right.**

3. **We must always judge from love not knowledge.** When we judge from love we are going to be willing to forego pursuit of a liberty if that liberty becomes a stumbling block for another

person. When we judge from knowledge we will not be willing to forgo the pursuit of our liberties but instead will demand our rights and liberties without regard for our fellow citizen.

False definitions of freedom only wind up enslaving us to someone, something, our own passions, weaknesses, or inabilities. Enslavements convince us to reject or temporarily set aside supernatural Truth, Faith, Hope, and Love. Enslavements make us spiritually weak.

Pope Benedict XVI warns against confusing freedom with absence of limits. He teaches that human freedom is only possible when we have the capacity "to respond to the needs/calls of the world with genuine creativity."[57] Furthermore, he teaches us to have "a sincere compassion" for others' needs and rights in order to "release love into the world." Humans can love others authentically only when they first love God and strive to live by the words of the Gospel.

Conclusion

Members of any social community must never allow their personal rights and freedoms to supersede others' rights and freedoms. When this happens, civilization and humanity suffer. Students who honor the accumulation of knowledge but reject the authentic search for Virtue and Wisdom will endanger their own happiness. When they fail to realize that even the most intelligent human reasoning is limited and subject to God, civilization fades. Failing to be open to supernatural Grace prevents us from looking fully at the world — this causes spiritual blindness.

There is a wide gulf between spiritual holiness and spiritual death. The first calls us to live selflessly whereas the latter calls us to live selfishly. It is true there are few rational reasons why we should live holy lives; however, it's pretty obvious what happens when we don't — civilization retreats.

It is completely within your rights to demand your liberties; it is also completely within your rights to forego them. Loving God necessitates sacrifices. But it will also allow us to learn to love each other more and more. Living by way of the Beatitudes is His radical call to create genuine social capital that is more powerful than man-made constitutions, laws, rights, guarantees or civil liberties.

Reflection Questions:

1. Define spirituality and religiosity. List similarities and differences.

2. Why is spirituality sometimes a symptom of spiritual poverty?

3. List signs of moral relativism around you. Describe why they are offensive and harmful.

4. How does personal sin affect wellness? Give personal examples.

5. List moral contradictions in the scientific community. Explain why the contradictions are harmful.

6. List the cures to spiritual illness or poverty.

7. List the causes for spiritual illness.

8. Go to Appendix Eight; use it to think about (or discuss) your Freedoms vs. Rights.

Chapter Six

Physical Wellness

Human beings are the only persons created with both corporeal (physical) and incorporeal (mind, will and soul) dimensions. Animals have bodies but since they cannot think, reason, and freely choose they are not persons. Angels are incorporeal persons since they have not been created with bodies. The Trinitarian persons – three persons in one God – do not have bodies. (True, Jesus took on a body when He came to earth as a baby.)

The fact that humans were created with bodies causes us to philosophize that physical bodies are therefore important to our humanity. Bodies are an essential part of our unique design and purpose. This discussion should cause you to wonder how your unique design relates to your purpose in life. Each of us are uniquely different than anyone else. This is mind boggling considering the masses of people now on earth (approximately 6,853,019,414 people inhabit planet Earth as of summer 2010). Then consider the number of people who preceded us and who will come after us.

This special blend of body, mind, soul and free will points out the inherent challenge for all human kind. This challenge is to establish, maintain, and preserve wellness by integrating healthy bodies with healthy minds. In this chapter we will discuss physical wellness – particularly with regards to your age group. You will be challenged to live green lives! How does one do that?

The 'Green' Life

The green ecological movement is primarily concerned about saving Mother Earth. Even though many worry about saving the planet few have lifestyles that maximize physical health and wellness. Oddly though it may seem, Pope John Paul II had a lot to teach us about greening up our bodies and of course our souls and minds. He taught that human persons who begin to learn and appreciate their original design and purpose can more fully and freely participate in the world, recognize and identify with God's glory, and experience the Order of Creation in and through our bodies. If we do these things, it follows that we will also learn to live in ways that maximizes the health of our bodies as well as our minds, souls, and wills. His philosophy is really a practical and authentic way to live green lives.

Previously, you learned that what you say, do, and avoid affects your emotional, spiritual, mental and emotional dimensions. Similarly these same things affect your physical wellness now and later.

Why should you want to live a green life? Principally, because you only have one life to live and it ought to be maximized, energetic, fully participatory, and focused and because you should have few lost opportunities due to illness or lack of wellness. When young people feel good they often presume to be master of their wellness. This presumption causes many to be less focused on today's actual physical fitness and wellness or lack thereof. This presumption can also cause some to disregard potential health risks. Furthermore, limited proof between today's risks and tomorrow's illnesses and diseases causes many college students to fail to look ahead or connect the dots between today's behaviors and tomorrow's lack of wellness. Unlike gum under our shoes, physical fitness and wellness don't just stick without paying attention to them.

Today, young adults face declining physical fitness, increasing levels of stress and fears of failure, more emotional and health issues compared to previous generations, increasing rates of sexual violence and relationship issues.[1] These issues point to an ever increasing inability of young people to understand and appreciate the original design and purpose of the human person and its integrated dimensions.

Physical Wellness

Physical wellness is not synonymous with physical fitness. Physical wellness is most commonly regarded as the state of life that is not manifested by disease or illness. Physical wellness allows us to feel good, look healthy, and able to do whatever we like. If you would like to run a 26 mile marathon, most of you presume that you could do so given the proper training since you consider yourselves to be physically well. We often link wellness to age even though that is not necessarily the case. Physical wellness is determined in part by the active choices we make in life that maintain or promote positive health. Wellness also is sometimes determined by factors beyond our control such as heredity, aging, accidents, injuries, or natural disasters. Like the other components of our lives, physical wellness is inextricably conjoined to all the others and together they determine whether or not we are well. Appendix Ten contains some helpful information about health and wellness.

The 'What If' Scenarios

The aspects of physical wellness that are within one's control can be directly affected by four basic "whats". Physical wellness is affected by: what we eat (balanced nutrition vs. unhealthy food choices); what we avoid (junk food, drugs/alcohol abuse, obesity, risky sexual practices, etc); what we wear (helmets, seat belts, sun screen/hats, etc.); and, what we do (exercise, fitness training, etc.) Physical fitness is one necessary component for achieving wellness; it will be discussed in more detail in the What We Do section.

The in-house health/physical fitness centers housed on campuses across the US offer classes to improve overall wellness among the students. This means the centers try to positively influence what students do (physical fitness), what they don't do, what they eat, even what they wear (seat belts, helmets, life jackets, etc.). Classes vary from facility to facility but can include those that teach stress management, nutrition, the prevention of eating disorders, and personal safety. We live in a society that places a very high value on attractiveness. It is important – given the self esteem problems common to many college students – that health promotion practices also support healthy attitudes toward one's own physique. Unfortunately, too many college-age men and women have distorted body images that are related to a desire to be thinner even when they are in a lean or desirable body fat range."[2]

What We Eat

Good nutrition is vital for feeling good, having enough energy, and maintaining and creating good physical health overall. In fact, studies continue to prove that good nutrition is a critical key to having a long and healthy life. But, not any food will do! The key is balance, nutrition, and variety. Every meal should include a combination of protein; carbohydrates including fruits, vegetables, and grains; and good fats. The average meal should provide a kaleidoscope of color on the plate indicating variety and balance. The average meal should also strive to avoid manufactured foods, chemically altered foods, and other wildly popular but unhealthy human concoctions.

College students tend to scrimp on time and money when it comes to food and eating during their college years. Many students simply feel they do not have the time to eat well – especially when living off campus. They lack the time to shop for fresh fruits, vegetables, meats, and carbohydrates. They also feel like they do not have time to cook balanced meals and then clean up too. Other students simply go off to college hoping to save money on food and housing! So these students often resort to eating cheaply by purchasing fast foods or consuming cheap carbohydrates and bad fats. Neither scenario provides ideal variety, balance or nutrition. Marilyn Shannon writes in her book, Fertility, Cycles and Nutrition, that eating a meal consisting of only carbohydrates increases the body's blood glucose levels. This temporarily provides a needed short burst of energy but it is not very helpful for setting long term goals that establish life long, healthy eating habits, proper appetite control mechanisms, or getting well-balanced and wide varieties of good foods. By the way, Ms. Shannon adds that simply adding proteins and fats to carbohydrates counterbalances and slows the digestive processes and the release of glucose into the blood stream helping to create "a long absorption state with steady blood sugar levels."[3]

Establishing and maintaining healthy eating habits are key factors to eating nutritiously, something that should be set quite early in life. Unfortunately, a lot of college students have grown up eating pizza and other fast foods. Consequently, they have come to relish the flavors, salts and bad fats in junk foods making them more preferable than homemade dishes. Your current eating habits probably reflect your parents' habits, patterns and influence. When a family regularly eats well, they establish healthy eating habits among their youngsters; on the other hand, when parents have poor eating habits, children tend to follow suit. College does not have to be the excuse for throwing out healthy eating habits nor does it have to be the excuse for continuing to eat poorly even if that is a family tradition. True, some emerging adults have not been eating well and for a long time but now can be the time to change.

A recent report found that high school students' access to vending machines, snack bars, and stores within schools contributes to diets high in fat and sugar and with little nutritional value.[4] Granted, the original study evaluated the weight and health status of students in grades K-12 and not college students; nevertheless, similar implications can be drawn for the college students with easy access to fast food kiosks, vending machines, etc.

Students will find it harder to establish or maintain healthy eating habits while away at college because of their erratic personal schedules. Fluctuating schedules introduces frequent "eating on the run" meals. These meals typically lack careful planning, good choices, and varieties of food that create colorful plates. Likewise, stress, lack of money, peer pressure, feeling insecure about eating in large dining facilities, fear of eating alone, frequent "pizza runs", following the others' bad eating habits, and other factors contribute to either over-indulgence or under-eating. Night time snacks are most often stored as fat since they are generally not burned off before going to sleep. Therefore, students interested in maintaining weight should avoid eating late night goodies. Also, a diet of fast foods, chips, soft drinks, and pizza is the tried and true way to achieve the Freshman Fifteen.

College cafeterias offer plenty of variety; sometimes the sheer number of food choices makes it difficult to choose well. This is especially problematic for the student who is tempted to try a little bit of everything every day – including the foods loaded up with calories and sugars. Skipping meals makes it more difficult to avoid comfort foods high in sugars, calories, and carbohydrates. Stress also causes students to either over-indulge or starve themselves; they either eat too much, not enough, or too much of the wrong foods. Studies show that college students rely too heavily on carbohydrates, fats, sodium, sugars and proteins; they tend not to get enough dietary fiber, vitamin C, calcium, iron, and zinc. They also frequently substitute junk and alcoholic calories for real food.[5] This is harmful to a person's long term health and wellness.

It is always important to eat a daily breakfast. The Mayo Clinic teaches that people who eat a healthy breakfast are more likely to take in more vitamins and minerals on a daily basis, consume less fat and cholesterol, and have lower levels of cholesterol; these factors reduce the risk for developing heart disease. Breakfast eaters show better concentration and productivity throughout the morning, have better control over their weight, and have better problem solving skills, alertness, and creativity.[6]

Heavy drinking is associated with reduced intake of good nutrition. Students who intentionally skip a meal or two if they plan to drink high-calorie alcoholic beverages later that day deliberately limit the intake of essential vitamins and minerals. These habits need to change in order to stay physically and mentally healthy.

Too many college students think they can beat the sugar effect (high blood glucose levels and calories) by drinking or eating foods and beverages laden with artificial sweeteners. Yet artificial sweeteners cause the body to release insulin in proportion to the amount of the sweetener consumed. Insulin production over-corrects "blood glucose levels" leaving many people feeling lethargic.

Caffeine and nicotine act as stimulants in the body; both increase heart and respiratory rates. Caffeine can also increase metabolism rates. Caffeine (over 600 mg/day) presents a significant health risk to users. The negative side effects include "increased nervousness, sweating, tension, upset stomach, anxiety, and insomnia. It can also prevent clear thinking and increase the side effects of certain medications."[7] Cigarette smoking is the "most preventable cause of illness and death".[8] Smoking increases the risk for developing many different types of cancers, wrinkles, bone fractures, and other problems. It is best to avoid consuming, drinking, or smoking these substances.

It is also important to consume good fats – by way of nuts, seeds, pressed salad oils, flax oils and fish oils. Normally, you will not have to worry about restricting your salt intake which can be a primary source of iodine unless you have been instructed by your physician to do so. College is also a good time to begin taking a good multi-vitamin loaded with vitamins B, C, D, and E, folic acid, magnesium, essential fatty acids, zinc and more. Studies show that the overall health trends of college students and emerging adults are sliding downward for many reasons including poor nutrition. The studies also show an average overall decrease in students' physical fitness along with increasing stress and emotional upsets.[9] Eating well, getting adequate exercise and sleep can turn this around.

Did you know that approximately 56 percent of college age students (from a multi-ethnic sampling) presented a "real age" that was older than their chronological age! Twenty six percent of these students had a "real age" more than 5 years older than their actual chronological age. This means they are aging faster than normal. Over 29 percent of the students had real ages between 0 -5 years older than their chronological age; this means that a full 55 percent of college students may be aging faster than their chronological age. Only 14 percent of the students had real ages more than five years younger than their chronological age. These students tended to be the nutrition majors![10] This study – though limited in nature – suggests that eating well is important to aging and overall wellness.

While many students gain weight in college, too many college students also become ultra-thin — especially female students. Most of the health and wellness attention has been focused on fighting obesity due to its link to a wide variety of diseases including diabetes and cardiovascular disease. Far too few hear about the very real dangers of being too thin, however. In fact it has been suggested that being too thin and having too little body fat is actually more dangerous to overall health and wellness than when a person is too heavy.[11]

The following list re-captures some of the dietary tips from above. This list represents the Important Dietary Recommendations for College Students:[12]

The Top Dietary Recommendations for College Students

1. Have a daily breakfast and don't skip meals.
2. Limit your consumption of empty calories, Trans fats, and sugars.
3. Eat a balanced diet; this is one that combines healthy amounts of food items from each of the food groups: carbohydrates; meats and beans; milk, yogurt and cheese group; and healthy fats. Planet Earth grows many different types of food for good reason! Each food type uniquely provide very specific micro or macro-nutrients that may not be found in others. Eating a variety of foods maximizes our intake of phyto-nutrients, vitamins, and minerals necessary for optimal health.
4. Try to eat fresh, homemade, unprocessed foods - they come out on top of the food hierarchy with respect to nutrition, taste and satisfaction.
5. Take a high quality, comprehensive multivitamin/multi-mineral supplement such as ProCycle or Optivite (for women) or Androvite (for men).[13] Also increase your calcium and vitamin D intake if it is below the recommended daily amounts.
6. Mix up the proteins that you eat by including fish, poultry, dairy, nuts, whole grains, legumes and red meat.
7. Increase your intake of non starchy garden vegetables such as spinach, lettuce, green beans, cucumbers, zucchini, brussels sprouts, asparagus, celery, peppers, cabbage, carrots, broccoli, beets, tomatoes, celery, onions, celery and cabbage. Vegetables

that contain fiber slow down the release of glucose from the intestines into the blood; this helps achieve steady blood sugar levels.[14] Steamed vegetables are better than boiled ones; frozen vegetables are better than canned fruits and vegetables. Fresh is always best.

8. Reduce alcohol intake. Do not substitute alcoholic calories for food calories.

9. Increase your intake of whole, fresh, ripe, and raw fruit like apples, pineapple, blueberries, grapes, oranges, strawberries, cherries, peaches and cantaloupes. Fruit juices or prepared fruits are not as good as whole fresh fruit. Furthermore, fruits canned in heavy syrup are not as nutritionally good as those canned in natural juices. Eat fruits in moderation and with protein or fatty foods to help prevent blood sugar swings.

10. Avoid foods containing Trans Fats. These types of fats are typically found in most processed foods including cakes, cookies, crackers, pies, bread, margarines, fried potatoes, salad dressings and snack foods.

11. Eat whole grain foods (oatmeal, whole wheat breads and crackers; cornmeal, popcorn, bulgur, rye, quinoa, sorghum, amaranth, millet and brown or wild rice) because they are superior to enriched or re-fortified grains which turn to sugar quickly during digestion. We obtain more vital macro and micro nutrients and fiber when we eat whole and hearty foods rather than their food supplements or even vitamins. Eating the whole food is important because normally plant food consists of a complex combination of compounds that work synergistically to give us maximum benefits; on the other hand eating food supplements provides only limited benefits.

12. Sharply decrease your sugar intake. Sugar is calorie rich and vitamin poor! Sugar is rapidly absorbed and therefore responsible for causing increased fatigue, irritability, depression, and headaches. Eating sugars cause you to crave more sugary foods. Women especially need to realize that excessive sugar intake generates high insulin levels which can adversely affect women's reproductive cycles. For instance,

excess sugar intake is linked to PCOS: polycystic ovarian syndrome and other menstrual cycling problems. Young women who are experiencing difficult or painful menses, irregular cycles, painful ovulations, or PMS symptoms should read Fertility, Cycles and Nutrition by Marilyn Shannon. This book connects the dots between nutrition, women's fertility cycles, and problems such as PCOS, cycle irregularity, endometriosis, and more.

13. Substitute water for soft drinks, caffeinated beverages, and coffee. Water is the most important nutrient in and for the body! It is necessary for every bodily function. Avoid all artificial sweeteners (NutraSweet, etc). Drinking one soft drink daily significantly increases your chances for obesity or developing insulin resistance and cardiovascular problems.[15]

14. Work toward improving your nutrition using the 80-20 rule.[16] Marilyn Shannon teaches that we should make sure that 80 percent of our diet is healthy, balanced, and varied and the other 20 percent allows us a bit of "wiggle room" for treats and special occasions.

15. Eat in traditional dining halls which offer buffet options; avoid the fast food courts when hungry.

16. Check out and visit all the "bars" in traditional dining halls. This is the only time I recommend visiting all the bars. Create your own kaleidoscope of color on your plates by visiting the salad bar, the main item bar, the fruit bar, the dairy bar, and more. Don't forget to visit the "make your own" bar, which offers freshly prepared dishes.

17. Don't wait until the last minute to get to the dining halls; many dining halls begin to remove entrees and salad choices about a half an hour before closing time.

18. Ask for foods that you would like to see on the menu; also provide positive and negative feedback to your dining hall. Comments/feedback can often be filled out online.

19. Limit yourself to one dessert per day – if even that. The ice cream, cookies, cake and pastries will be offered again in the future. Also, use prudence when scooping up the amount of ice

cream you plan to eat.

20. When you take too much food, don't eat it all.
21. Your dining hall probably has a website that provides detailed information about their menus, nutritional facts, calories, and advice.
22. Don't scrimp on food dollars necessary for healthy eating.
23. If living off campus, purchase an on campus meal plan to avoid the cooking and cleanup. This will not be a waste of money especially when you can't afford time or money to shop well, prepare balanced meals, and have the time to clean up afterwards.

Female students should take note of the fact that their current nutritional state creates a "maternal storehouse" that will be important to future pregnancies. High quality maternal storehouses help women have successful pregnancies, produce good quality breast milk after the baby is born, and helps to maintain her personal health. What women eat is important for their own future health outcomes as well as for the future health outcome of potential offspring. *The Art of Breastfeeding* points out that too often, young women fail to consider the direct and indirect role that nutrition plays in their health — today and tomorrow. They also disregard the direct and indirect role today's nutritional status will have on future pregnancies, their ability to produce milk, and maintain fertility. Male students need to take stock as well. Today and tomorrow's health and wellness is related to what we eat now along with the other three What Scenarios that follow shortly.

Visit the online food pyramid resources for information about eating healthily. These resources include the U.S. Department of Agriculture (My Pyramid)[17], the Harvard School for Public Health Food Pyramid[18] and the University of Michigan's food pyramid[19] People with ethnic food preferences can also find online information and food pyramids for the following tastes: Asian Diet Pyramid, the Latin American Diet Pyramid, or the Mediterranean Diet Pyramid. Even vegetarian food pyramids are available online. Each pyramid presents unique recommendations and guidelines most appropriate when following that food preference.

The 2020 Healthy Peoples' Initiative, launched by Federal Governmental Agencies on December 2, 2010, hopes to improve upon American's health and wellness and reduce chronic diseases by setting guidelines associated with diet, weight and other activities for everyone over the age of 2! This initiative warns that what we eat can seriously undermine health; they encourage the regular consumption of healthy diets in order to reduce incidence of obesity, malnutrition, iron-deficiency anemia, heart disease, high blood pressure, poor lipid files; Type 2 diabetes, osteoporosis, oral disease, constipation, diverticular disease, and some cancers. [20,21]

2020 Healthy Peoples Initiative Objectives With Regard to Nutrition[22]

Nutritional Objective (may/ may not include specific consumption goals.	Baseline (average current usage rates)	Goal (Target)
Reduce percent of iron deficiency.	10.4%	9.4%
Reduce percent of iron deficiency in pregnant women.	16.1%	14.5%
% office visits wherein physician provides nutritional counseling	12.2%	15.2%
% office visits wherein physician assesses patients' BMI	48.7%	53.6%
Vegetable consumption	0.8 Cups/1000 calories consumed	1.1 cups per 1000 calories consumed
Dark green/orange vegetables or legumes consumption	0.1 Cups/1000 calories consumed	0.3 Cups/1000 calories consumed
Whole grain consumption	0.3 cups whole grain/1000 cal.	0.6 cups whole grain /1000 calories consumed
Solid Fat consumption	18.9% calories consumed	16.7% calories consumed
Added sugars	15.7%	10.8%
Added solids and fats consumed	34.6%	29.8%
Saturated fats	11.3%	9.5%
Sodium	3641 mg.	2300 mg.
Calcium	1118 mg	1300 mg.
Vegetables – at least 5 servings of fruits and veg.	7.4% college students consumption rate [23]	25.5%

Nutrition for the College Athlete

Proper nutrition is critical for the college athlete. Increased levels of physical activity require increased intakes of water, protein, and carbohydrates in order to stay well hydrated and "well-fueled." The largest percent of an athlete's diet should normally come from carbohydrates – 50 percent — allowing the athlete to maintain energy and keep steady blood glucose levels; it also allows the body to restore muscle glycogen.[24]

Sports nutritionists urge student athletes to take in adequate protein for important reasons. Protein intakes helps to produce adequate amounts of hormones and enzymes, promotes nutrient transfer in the blood, and provides the necessary support and repair of the connective tissue. Athletes should eat 1.2-2.0 grams of protein for each kg of body weight. Excessive protein intake can increase an athlete's risk for dehydration and loss of calcium.

Athletes must consume proper amounts of wholesome fats in order to have adequate energy for the physical rigor of training and performing. Wholesome fats provide protection to the body's organs, provides insulation to the body, and helps facilitate the uptake of key vitamins and fatty acids. Athletes' diets should normally contain at least 20 percent fats in their total daily caloric intake.[25] When eating properly, athletes do not need protein supplements such as shakes, bars, or other types.

Athletes can time their meals to achieve peak athletic performance during competitive events. In fact, both performance and recovery from the physical activity is affected by a person's dietary intake before, during, and after the athletic event. Athletes should eat meals that are low in fats, fibers, and caffeine; moderate in proteins; and high in complex carbohydrates and fluids before the athletic events; these meals should be eaten at least 3-4 hours prior to competition. This helps to prevent or minimize gas, nausea, vomiting, cramps, and sluggishness during an event. Athletes performing in long endurance events should consume a minimum of 0.1-0.2 ounces of carbohydrates (30-60 grams) per hour by drinking sports drinks with 4 percent to 8 percent carbohydrate loads. Within several hours after any strenuous competition, it is important to consume adequate carbohydrates and proteins in order to replenish depleted glycogen stores and repair muscle damage and stress.[26]

It has already been mentioned that good hydration is important for achieving peak athletic performance. Conversely, dehydration increases one's risk for heat stroke, electrolyte imbalance, and serious cardiovascular problems. We sweat to help prevent any increases in the body's core temperature; however, sweating causes fluid loss which means the corresponding loss of sodium, iron, and calcium.[27] Experts remind athletes that they need to drink between ten to twelve cups (80-96 ounces) of fluids a day to maintain hydration! Furthermore, athletes should consume about 12- 20 ounces of fluids two to three hours prior to an athletic event and consume 6-12 ounces every 15-20 minutes during an event. Immediately after any competitive event, the athlete should drink 16-24 ounces of fluids for every pound lost.

What To Do: Stay Physically Fit

Physical fitness is not synonymous with physical wellness although it is one more measure of general wellness. When you are physically fit, you will have a higher degree of overall wellness than a person with a de-conditioned body. Today's colleges proudly showcase fitness or wellness centers built for students and faculty members for good reasons. Years ago, the non-athlete students had to time exercise around the schedules of the various athletic programs of the university. Scheduling conflicts often left little time – on a practical level – for the students not enrolled in athletic teams to regularly use the athletic facilities. Today that has changed with the introduction of these elaborate student fitness centers. These centers often feature state of the art weight lifting and strengthening equipment, gyms, running tracks, swimming pools, basketball and racquetball courts, classrooms for private and group training sessions, or wellness education. They offer many competitive opportunities for students to participate in. Students need to take advantage of these facilities for their own health.

One obvious purpose of these fitness centers is to counteract the mounting evidence which shows a gradual and continual decline of college students' physical fitness (and accompanying emotional health) compared to their earlier years. Appropriate exercise contributes to our overall energy and feelings of well being. Nutritionist Marilyn Shannon writes that the regular physical exercise – in the right amounts — is a powerful way of regulating blood sugar levels. This helps establish appropriate energy levels. Therefore all college students should be motivated and encouraged to use the student fitness facilities frequently. This is the only time when they will have free and unrestricted access to state-of-the-art facilities. Better yet, trainers are available.

Physical fitness measures help control the accumulation of harmful body fat; in this way it helps to control weight. Stress is reduced by physical activity therefore our ability to manage stress is well linked to our degree of physical fitness. When we are physically fit, we generally feel good about ourselves and our health, appearance, body strength, and energy levels. Exercise even makes us look healthier. Dr. Sherwin Nuland, author of The Art of Aging, says that "exercise makes us smarter while we're huffing and puffing in the interests of staving off the aging changes trying to overtake our hearts and blood vessels. It is a far better anti-aging treatment than all the elixirs, crèmes, lotions, potions and cosmetic surgeries in the world." Physical exercise and staying physically fit boosts our self esteem, self confidence, self assurance, and our ability to do things. This explains why physical exercise also promotes emotional and mental health. Adequate regular exercise is the key to providing these physical, social, and mental benefits. Remember that if you are not exercising regularly you are essentially giving up these related health benefits:

- Strengthens the muscles including the heart muscle
- Increases lean muscle mass and reduces fat weight
- Builds bone mass and increases bone rebuilding
- Helps maintain flexibility and balance
- Improves cardiovascular fitness
- Reduces blood pressure
- Increases the production of good cholesterol (HDL – High density lipids)
- Reduces risky blood clotting factors
- Improves bowel functioning
- Improves posture

- Increases blood flow in arteries
- Increases collagen
- Decreases fatigue, depression, and anxiety
- Decreases sleep disturbance (don't exercise before bed time however because exercise stimulates the Central Nervous System making us ready to keep going).

Young adults are advised to get a minimum of 30 minutes (the ideal target is 60 minutes per day) of heart pumping exercises every day. The type of exercise, intensity, and duration will vary according to individual preferences, endurance, abilities, physical fitness, physical strength and more. You can pick the exercise that best suits you from a wide variety of equipment, courts, and classes while in college.

Physical fitness is a measure of our cardiovascular health, muscular fitness and endurance, body composition, and flexibility. Standardized physical fitness tests determine a person's endurance; their cardiovascular fitness, core body strength or upper body strength (muscle fitness); flexibility; and motor skills. Standards vary according to age and gender. The cardiovascular tests measure one's ability to carry out strenuous work throughout a period of time without experiencing undue fatigue. Swimming, running, and walking tests are often used to measure cardiovascular fitness.

Flexibility is often overlooked when assessing our own physical fitness yet it largely determines the things that we can or cannot do safely. For example, we need to maintain flexibility in order to prevent damaging or injuring muscles or ligaments during exercise. We need limber muscles and supple ligaments in order to move well. The lack of flexibility, besides increasing our chance for acquiring a physical injury, makes it difficult to move without pain or discomfort. Exercises such as yoga promote flexibility and balance.

Muscular fitness is a subset of physical fitness; it measures a person's ability to sustain muscle contraction over a period of time without experiencing undue fatigue.[28] This type of fitness is measured by the number of push-ups, pull-ups, sit-ups, etc., that one is able to perform in a given time period. The U.S. Department of Health and Human Services and the U.S. Surgeon General's Office have determined that a college-age student ought to be able to achieve the following levels of fitness.[29] Take a peek to see just how fit you are compared to your peers.

Exercise Targets for Young Adults

	Level 1	Level 2	Level 3	Level 4	Your Score
Male - 1.5 mile run time (minutes)	12:52-15:12	10:17-12:51	8:14-10:16	≤ 8:13	
Female- 1.5 mile run	15:27-17:21	12:52-15:26	10:48-12:51	≤10:47	
Male sit-ups (2 minute)	46-57	58-86	87-97	≥ 98	
Female sit-ups (2 minute)	46-57	58-86	87-97	≥ 98	
Male push-ups(2 minute)	37-46	47-70	71-80	≥ 81	
Female push-ups(2 minute)	16-20	21-38	39-43	≥ 44	
Male swim 500 yds	11:31-13:00	8:46-11:30	7:31-8:45	≤ 7:30	
Female swim 500 yds	13:16-14:30	10:01-13:15	8:46-10:00	≤8:45	

The 2020 Healthy People Initiative[30] aims to support initiatives that significantly increase the number of adults (18 and over) who regularly exercise. The recommended standards for your age group include the following:

Exercise type	Intensity	Minimum number of hours per week
Cardiovascular	Moderate intensity	150 minutes
Cardiovascular	Vigorous intensity	75 minutes
Aerobic	Moderate intensity	300
Aerobic	Vigorous	150
Walking		Walk when destination is one mile or less.
Biking		Bike when destination is five miles or less.
Flexibility		No standard recommended due to lack of evidence.
Physical Activity [31]	Moderate intensity	30 minutes; 3 days per week
Physical Activity [32]	Vigorous Activity	20 minutes; 3 times per week

This amount of exercise is good for warding off bad moods, it increases energy, and helps maintain appropriate blood sugar levels. Physical exercise also can cause us to set personal challenges for ourselves that can be met and overcome. Meeting our personally set challenges builds additional confidence. Finally, physical challenges allow us to realize our limits — this is good.

If you routinely lack energy, you probably need some exercise. Fatigue leads to stress which decreases energy, which further increases stress. This vicious cycle of ongoing fatigue and stress can be broken by exercise. Conversely, the more physically fit one is, the better able he/she can normally manage stress.

Some of you may think that walking to class is enough exercise. Few students jog to classes or walk to class at a rate that gets their heart pumping fast. So, walking to class is not enough exercise for the average college student unless he/she is older than 65. But it does help to take stairs instead of riding up and down elevators and walking around campus rather than taking a bus or driving.

What to Do: Maintain a Healthy Weight

Weight maintenance is simple stoichiometry - or is it? Previously, experts preached that when a person's caloric intake is greater than his/her energy expended, weight will increase. They also taught that when a person's caloric intake is less than energy expended then a person will lose weight; likewise when caloric intake equals energy expended, weight is maintained. Thus, for decades people were taught to lose weight by simply eating less. Today, the experts think that effective weight loss isn't as simple as previously thought. "In fact, the calories in – calories out explanations about body weight are just too simplistic and don't account for many very real variables that have nothing to do with will or self restraint. Many people have always known this at gut level but it's good to see science bear that out. That said, people shouldn't assume that they're genetically precluded from ever being thin and healthy. All of us can learn new behaviors and adapt" says Dr. Caroline Cederquist who specializes in lifetime weight management.[33] Weight loss, weight maintenance, and weight gain are linked to other factors such as stress, amount of sleep disturbances, body types and even our genetic makeup. "Results from a study involving 133 overweight women showed that even strict adherence to a diet won't matter if people's diets are out of synch with their genetics."[34] But researchers have a pretty good idea about how much weight we should carry.

Earlier you learned that we measure a person's physical fitness by a number of cardiovascular tests, etc. Did you know that our body mass and shape is also a measure of our physical fitness? If we appear overweight, it is likely that we carry too much fat in proportion to our lean muscle mass. The health status of our body shape is measured several ways. Percentage of fat compared to lean muscle mass; using height to weight ratios to determine body mass indices; applying standards to hip/waist ratios and even skin fold tests help determine the health of a person.

The Body Mass Indices (BMI) are essentially height to weight ratios. This index, when used singularly, often fails to tell the whole story about whether a person is over or underweight or just right for his/her height. For instance, an athlete's weight may put him in the overweight category even though he may have a very healthy, low percent of body fat. Similarly, a thin college woman may have a low weight but high fat/lean muscle ratio. The body fat/lean muscle mass is an additional tool that can assess proper weight. Also, skin fold tests help to round out the full picture in determining a person's health status with regard to weight. It is not helpful to compare your body weight to a friend who may have a completely different frame than yourself. Students should maintain a healthy weight; increased exercise can help bring weight into the ideal range for your body type.

Results from a survey of college students revealed that nearly half of the male students surveyed were overweight or obese, while almost 30 percent of the female students were considered overweight or obese.[35] The 2010 data supports the previous survey results when it states that nearly 36 percent of college students are considered to be overweight or obese. The target goal is 16 percent.

The causes are attributed to poor diets, sedentary lifestyles, poor choice of foods, too much junk foods, and too much alcohol and too large of portion sizes. The experts are continuing to sort through data in order to establish the 2020 Healthy People Initiatives for weight and physical exercise. The 2010 Initiative showed that nearly half of college students do not receive adequate information about dietary behaviors and nutrition.

What to Do: Sleep

Sleep has already been discussed in a previous chapter; however, we will look at it a bit more in-depth as it relates to physical wellness and fitness. Sleep is critical to our overall health and well being. Sleep restores our mental and physical equilibrium; it is responsible for memory consolidation, stimulus processing, brain growth and repair of our immune systems."[36] As a person ages, his or her sleep needs decrease, but only subtly. Adolescents need at least nine hours of sleep per night whereas older adults normally operate well on six to seven hours of sleep. The emerging adult needs somewhere between six and nine hours of sleep every night.

On the other hand, the lack of sleep is bad for maintaining overall health and wellness. The lack of sleep compromises both our cognitive functioning and concentration/ memory functions. Sleep deprivation occurs when a person does not get enough sleep each night. A Canadian study found that about 85 percent of college students average six or more hours of sleep per night. This is good news! However, about 14 percent of students' average only about four to five hours of sleep. This amount isn't enough for anyone![37]

Sleep difficulties correlate with increased incidence of depression, anxiety, and somatic complaints.[38] One study found that with just two nights of sleep deprivation, students have increased incidence of making poor/risky decisions.[39] Sleep deprivation is blamed for causing depression, aggression, falling asleep in class, lack of energy, inattentiveness, risky decision-making, daytime fatigue, falling asleep at the wheel, and poor mental health. It also has been linked to obesity, high blood pressure, diabetes, and heart disease. Inadequate sleep leads to poor academic performance. In one study, participants who had been awake for seventeen to nineteen hours performed much worse than those with a blood alcohol concentration of 0.05 percent in a test of cognitive and motor performance.[40] Lack of sleep can become a vicious cycle; when we are stressed we need adequate sleep to restore our health and mental well being. However, when stressed out, many students develop sleep disturbances which prevent them from being able to sleep, thereby increasing feelings of being stressed out. Some college students stay up all night in order to "cram" for the semester exams. Little do they realize the extent of the harm they are causing themselves cognitively and psychologically.

On the other hand, adequate sleep has been shown to help us fight off infections, allows us to perform well, and work effectively and safely. Enough sleep also supports the proper metabolism of sugar preventing diabetes.

Students should plan on setting regular sleeping hours and wake up times that provide them with adequate, uninterrupted sleep. Oversleeping, frequently changing sleep patterns, irregular sleep patterns, or not getting enough sleep can leave a person feeling groggy or feeling like they have jet lag. Stress, alcohol, and smoking contribute to poor quality sleep or sleep disturbances. The key to knowing whether you are getting enough restful sleep is how you feel when you awake. If you feel awake, well rested, and ready to go you've gotten enough sleep. If you feel like you are in a perpetual jet lag, then you are probably not getting enough uninterrupted sleep and habits should be changed to correct this deficiency for your own good.

Sleep disturbances include: having difficulty falling asleep; waking early and not being able to return to sleep; having fitful or restless sleep; or not feeling refreshed or rested at waking. Failing to sleep well makes it impossible to get restorative sleep. Michael Jackson had numerous sleep problems compromising his mental and physical wellness. His repeated abuse of narcotics and anesthetics in hopes of getting a restful night's sleep eventually cost him his life.

You should learn to recognize when you or your college friends suffer from sleep deficiency. Get proper counsel for yourself or friends so that the problem does not worsen with time.

What to Do: Stress Management

Another vital "what to do" is to manage your stress during college. This is sometimes easier said than done but there are ways to learn these skills. Unmanaged stress can lead to depression and/or suicidal thoughts or attempts, and loss of control over mental and emotional health. Suicide is the third leading cause of death in young college age adults (ages 20 – 24).[41] The 2002 rate of suicide compared to other leading causes of death among college age students was reported to be 12.98 percent; this number involved the suicide of approximately 2497 students. We have already talked about the importance of stress management for maintaining wellness in previous sections so we don't need to elaborate any longer on this issue.

What to Wear

This may seem like an odd *What If* scenario for college students; however it isn't so oddly placed when things worn can help keep a student safe. The first worn safety device that probably comes to mind may be the automobile seat belts. Perhaps you thought of bicycle helmets. These are all devices designed to protect people of all ages. The unfortunate fact is that most moving vehicle deaths are caused by the failure to wear seat belts – even for college age students. And they tend to avoid wearing seat belts at the riskiest moments – when they drive drunk or allow someone else to drive drunk. Many students fail to buckle up when they intend to sleep in the back seat of a vehicle while their friend drives them home.

It has already been revealed in an earlier chapter that the leading cause of death among college age young adults is unintentional injury. In fact in 2002, over 8200 students were killed accidentally. Forty-three percent of all deaths are caused accidentally. The causes of death include being killed in motor vehicle accidents (29.7 percent), poisoning (6.2 percent), drowning (1.6 percent), falls (0.85 percent), other vehicle accidents (snowmobiles, jet skis, etc. - 0.6 percent), fire and burn accidents (0.57 percent), firearm accidental shootings (0.54 percent), pedestrian accidents (0.45 percent), personal attacks (0.24 percent), cycling accidents (0.05 percent)[42] and others.

While some accidents are unavoidable, others are mitigated when wearing seat belts, donning helmets while skiing, cycling, inline skating, snowmobiling, or participating in other fast moving sports.

Students who enjoy jogging outdoors are advised to wear reflective vests over exercise clothing during dark conditions in order that they can be seen by cyclists, motor vehicles and motorcycles. Other safety devices that students may wish to "wear" on their clothing include the MedFalsh (Medical Flash Drive) containing personal information such as medical history, prescription medications, X-rays, MRIs and more. This new safety device has been commercially available since 2008. Students should also consider having first aid kits and emergency blankets in their cars and/or dorm rooms. Small first aid kits can be carried in coat pockets also. Students should also think about wearing or carrying flashlights, and/or personal Mace spray devices and/or alarms that emit ear piercing decibels when activated.

What to Avoid

In the next chapter we will outline the various "pumpkins' or decoys that threaten student's wellbeing – socially, spiritually, mentally, emotionally, and physically. These include drug abuse, binge drinking, hooking up, casual sex, gambling, use of pornography, and others. They all represent the many "whats" to avoid while in college. Each disaffects the wellness in offending college age students whether they recognize it or not.

The 2010 Healthy Campus outlined the following goals for college students:[43]

- Reduce cancer in students by increasing use of sunscreen
- Reduce the transmission rate for STIs
- Reduce unintentional pregnancies
- Reduce relationship violence
- Reduce personal assaults
- Reduce smoking, cigar smoking and chewing tobacco
- Reduce sexual assaults
- Reduce average alcohol consumption
- Reduce substance abuse

Similarly, college students should strive to minimize personal accidents and injuries, especially those that are completely preventable. Students should also be aware that communal living presents fire safety hazards especially when people are careless or dismissive of potential problems. For example, the U.S. Fire Administration warns that drinking alcohol is almost always linked to college fire fatalities. Furthermore, they warn that cooking is the leading cause of fire injuries on college campuses, followed closely by careless smoking and arson.[44] The safety tips from the U.S. Fire Administration include:

- Students are to install and/or maintain smoke alarms in every dorm room and every level of their housing facilities.
- Students should keep their rooms clear of fire hazards.
- Student should also conduct quarterly fire drills and practice

escape routes or evacuation plans with fellow students.

- Students should not overload electrical outlets; furthermore extension cords must be used carefully.
- Candles must not be left unattended when burning.
- Cooking utensils must not be left on when unattended.
- Know how to call 9-1-1 for fire emergencies.

Conclusion

In the beginning, Adam and Eve fully appreciated the original glory and order of their own bodies including their sexuality. They appreciated their physical design as they noticed how complimentary they were to each other. That is until they gave into sin. This original sin caused our first parents to lose their full appreciation for, and understanding of, how and why they were made in the image and likeness of God. For the first time, Adam and Eve became embarrassed by their own bodies, its expressions (language of the body) and their sexual powers and so they hid from God.[45] John Paul II taught that Adam's first confession "of being afraid and so we hid confirms the collapse of the original acceptance of the body as a sign of the person in the visible world."[46]

Disorder entered the world through the original sin of Adam and Eve; as a result we suffer physically, emotionally, mentally, spiritually. We are still tempted to commit the same sins as our first parents. Misunderstanding the original purpose and meaning of human life leads to many abuses within our own lives. With that in mind we will now take an in-depth look at the decoys and temptations that will surely come your way while attending college.

Reflection Questions:

Think about the long- and short-term goals you plan to write up for your physical wellness. Go ahead, and jot down these thoughts here.

1. List goals for each of the "Whats" in your life:

A. What to Eat Goals

B. What to Do Goals

C. What to Wear Goals

D. What to Avoid Goals.

Chapter Seven

LIFE'S PUMPKINS

A Life Fable

Once upon a time, long ago, there lived a people who relished a certain species of duck. These ducks found the native's pumpkins very tasty. The people had difficulty hunting these clever ducks because they would readily take to flight after hearing the slightest whirring sounds emitted from flying arrows. Noting the duck's affinity for the pumpkins, the chief decided to float a few pumpkins down the river where the ducks loved to dive in and out of. To his surprise, the ducks began to swim beside the pumpkins to peck at the orange fruit.

Hoping to outfox the ducks, the chief hollowed out a pumpkin, fit it over his head, and went "hunting" while swimming in the river. The hollowed-out pumpkin proved to be a great decoy as a duck dove in to swim and peck at this delicacy. At the duck's arrival, the chief swiftly made a grab for its neck, broke it and tucked the dead duck into an underwater pouch for safe keeping. After gathering enough ducks, he swam back to shore. Using the pumpkins as decoys, the natives learned how to effectively and efficiently hunt this delicacy.

The Pumpkins

The moral of the story is to beware of "blindly" following decoys that beckon you with false promises to increase popularity, ego, fun or success. Personal egos and personalities can be compromised through insincere flattery, adulation or complaisance. Thus, even words can become a decoy when used to give insincere flattery, adulation, or complaisance.

Decoys are deceptive as they stoke entitlement attitudes, selfishness, egoism, self centeredness or even personal fears. Decoys provide unsustainable but often risky thrills. Many decoys are rightfully dubbed as Triple A Threats. This category is particularly dangerous because the decoys provide thrills that are highly anonymous, extremely affordable, and easily accessed. Illegal drugs, alcohol, online pornography, and online gambling pose this level of threat to college students and any others who chase after them.

Most decoys tempt in ways that are not that much different from those posed to Jesus and recorded in the Gospel of St. Matthew. This passage tells us that Jesus was hungry after fasting, so Satan began with the temptations targeting the human appetite. Next, Satan tempted Jesus to prove his worth. Finally, Satan promised power if only Jesus worshipped him![1] Like Jesus, you will also be tempted by "hunger." You may be taunted to prove you have the guts to do something which conflicts with your values. Or you may be tempted to direct your adoration away from God. We will be tempted to commit sin with our bodies, minds and wills. Each is the pathway to calamity. Each temptation comes with a price tag or consequence.

The decoys (pumpkins) attract us because they look good, taste good, and feel good – at least at the start. And then, like Edward in The Lion, the Witch, and the Wardrobe by CS Lewis, after getting a first taste of "Turkish toast," many continue to forsake reason, will, faith, or virtue to get more. Like pumpkins, Turkish toast can represent anything from drugs to sex to money or power. Like Edward, students who are unsure of themselves, their faith, or their personal values, are particularly open to the temptations posed by Turkish toast and pumpkins. Once you say yes to the temptation, the pathway to calamity gets wider and easier to follow as well. College students are naturally social and open to influence; however, seeking peer affirmation can result in blind chases after unsavory decoys.

So what constitutes a decoy? Wikipedia gives this definition of a decoy: usually a person, device or event meant as a distraction to conceal what an individual or a group might be looking for. Decoys lure, deceive, entrap, snare, trick, distract, and bait us into doing things we would not ordinarily do around church authorities, professors, public leaders or other respected adults. Decoys are red herrings. Decoys are people's actions, suggestions, or bullying that cause others to follow their lead or directives. Decoys are activities or things that conjure up curiosity about their effects. They are peer-popular activities that we want to be a part of. They are activities or things that seem to be the answer for fears, or raising hopes and dreams. Often it seems to be the norm. Finally, decoys never deliver their promises.

Why do we follow decoys? We don't chase after the decoys because we want to hurt ourselves; rather we are tempted to believe their promises of personal gain. Experts know that "sexual risk-taking, binge drinking, and substance abuse all peak during the early twenties."[2] This is the result of following social decoys that pretend to be the norm and therefore OK. In essence, these students ignore their Jiminy Crickets that warn against the decoys' causes and effects including overindulgence, capriciousness, irresponsibility, indiscretion, and more.

With this in mind, let's explore in detail the many decoys (fleshy pumpkins and Turkish toast) tempting college students as they float by.

Made in the Image and Likeness of Advertisers, Hollywood, and the Media

Advertising, Hollywood, and media of all types use men's and women's images to sell. [3] Regrettably these industries get to set the standards for beauty and attractiveness as they feature these images on billboards, in magazines, on runways and on television or in movies. These industries trade on beauty that is merely superficial and one-dimensional. Most images are highly sexualized — especially the females. Perhaps you already realize that the average runway model is an ultra thin creature. It is impossible to attain the super model figure when we consciously eat a healthy diet; however, it becomes possible when we starve ourselves. The average female in the United States stands 5 feet 4 inches tall and weighs 140 pounds. The average super model, by contrast, stands 5 feet 11 inches tall and weighs 117 pounds. These models weigh less than 98 percent of the American female population as a whole.[4]

The decoy exposed in this section is the desire to conform our image to others' standards. This decoy produces a secondary decoy which can turn deadly for many: eating disorders. These decoys affect both men and women – although women are more often disaffected. Parents know, practically speaking, that the more exposure their young girls have to media types, television, beauty magazines, Hollywood influences, and advertisers, the more their self esteems and self images tumble. In turn, negative body images cause eating disorders to surface.

Everyone forms their own body image; this is the image of yourself that you see in your mind. When this image differs from the image we see in the mirror it is distorted. Body images do not generally change once set nor do they allow others to convince us that we look differently from what we perceive; it is engraved in the brain and incapable of seeing a mirror image appropriately. This concept is important to understand especially when dealing with loved ones who may have an eating disorder and/or negative body image. People will not be able to convince the ultra thin person suffering from anorexia that he or she is starkly skinny because his or her body image will be negatively distorted. They see fat when everyone else sees malnourished bodies. Psychological counseling will be needed to get to the root problem.

People with poor body images often believe that most – if not all - people evaluate others on weight and outward appearance. Therefore, their desire to look thin for others becomes a critical factor in their choices.[5] Body images form consciously and unconsciously as we observe others, compare ourselves to others, and then form ideas of what or who we want to look like. The media also tells us what constitutes sex appeal, popularity, power, and likeability.[6] Those who constantly compare themselves to media-made standards for beauty will fit their square bodies into the idealized round pegs by adopting unhealthy eating practices, constant dieting, smoking, excessive exercise, or plastic surgery.

Self esteem and body image are complex constructs that are difficult to measure or change; nevertheless, having a low self esteem or poor body image disaffects a person's mental, social, and physical health. Even though self esteem seems only a relative measure of confidence, self worth, and self respect it "rules the mind" as it "dictates" self satisfaction, mental and physical health, and positive or negative social behavior. Depression, eating disorders, anxiety, suicidal thoughts, or other problems are risks for those with low self esteem.

All women – especially college and high school women – should learn about the important interplay between adequate body fat and fertility or reproduction. Why? Presently, reproduction is probably not going to be listed among your final goals and plans; however, it is important to realize that today's nutrition plan creates tomorrows' maternal storehouse that determines the state of health for women, future pregnancies, and their babies.

Twenty-two percent body fat is considered to be a healthy level for most women so they can maintain normal menstrual cycles. Maintaining a normal weight implies that we are eating well and for our health; achieving inordinate thinness implies that we are not eating well and are not healthy in body or mind. The fertility status of women who are too lean – i.e. having too little body fat – can be significantly compromised leading to infertility or difficulty in achieving pregnancy. When women are lean, they naturally begin to produce a less potent estrogen compared to women with a healthier percentage of body fat. Women who are too thin also produce high amounts of the sex hormone binding globulin which binds up estrogen making it less available for the important task of simulating the reproductive glands and bringing about normal reproductive cycles. Long cycles, scanty cervical mucus, amenorrhea, infertility, miscarriages, anovulatory cycles, short luteal phases or delayed ovulation result when a woman has inadequate body fat.[7]

Finally, male and female athletes may become too worried about meeting weight restrictions and/or body fat restrictions, thereby causing the onset of eating disorders. Female athletes with eating disorders are at risk for the Female Athlete Triad (FAT). This triad begins with the development of an eating disorder which causes amenorrhea (loss of fertility cycles and menstruation) which leads to the development of osteoporosis (unhealthy bone loss).[8] Any "situation that causes you to take in or to absorb fewer calories than you need will sooner or later result in low body fat causing long fertility cycles or no cycles at all. When a woman loses her cycles altogether, she is at risk for bone loss and eventual osteoporosis."[9] This is the FAT triad.

Your whole self benefits when you refuse to allow others to form you into someone else's image and likeness. Refusing to chase these false promises is an important first step toward acknowledging that you have been created according to the image and likeness of your Creator. This realization allows you to more fully appreciate and experience the order of God's creation in and through your body. What more could you want? Nothing, unless you have tasted Turkish toast.

The Internet

The Internet is a very congenial decoy. Parents, employers, teachers, and friends alike will encourage your acquaintance with and use of this technology; in fact they also use the internet – not as heavily as your generation however. Certainly, you have found that your college faculty highly encourages and even requires that you use the Internet because they "want you to make full use of the Internet's vast resources" and they also "want to see the college's major investment (wireless technologies, etc.) put to good use."[10] It appears that we love cyberspace technology for its obvious advantage. What are they?

First and foremost, the Internet allows us to reliably communicate with people around the globe in seconds. The cyberspace superhighway also gives all of us fingertip access to information that would not previously have been available. The Internet offers super convenient services including online banking and e-commerce. It serves as a job service finder. It also reports the news. Cyberspace allows us to keep in constant contact with friends and family. Most users feel that they can't live without the internet; this becomes apparent when internet providers knock users temporarily offline.

Not all use of the internet is healthy or beneficial. The internet has a shady side and that is why it is categorized as a decoy. The Internet allows students to have wide-open access to anything and everything; it's highly affordable (it's free), and students have complete privacy to the Internet access via their own computer every day of the week and every minute of the day. Internet access is free from any sort of parental monitoring or censorship; also students may be tempted to spend their largely unscheduled blocks of time inappropriately on the Internet. The Internet is problematic when students are distracted by instant messaging and chat rooms. The internet gets downright dangerous when predators anonymously and deceptively roam freely through its sites. Theft of personal identities and personal information is a very serious cyberspace problem. A significant portion of the internet use is for immoral activities including illegal sales of stolen materials, illegal acquisition of people's assets, solicitation for sex or prostitution, and more. The Internet becomes a nuisance when spam/junk mail clogs up inboxes. Verifying the accuracy or truthfulness of internet information is difficult for many reasons. Computer viruses interrupt many people's employment and personal activities. Many of us, at one time or another, have been prompted to wonder whether the internet is mostly good or mostly bad.

The Internet becomes a decoy when students sacrifice face-to-face interactions for impersonal ones. The Internet poses a problem for students who prefer the ideal life and experiences of living as an Avatar to real life with real people. The Internet is a very troublesome decoy when people think they can use it to expose details and photos of someone's private life world-wide with the click of a few keys. It is also a problem for students who fail to set personal limits on time or type of access. The internet evolves from a decoy into a calamity when users become addicted; this topic will be discussed in the following chapter.

The ability to use the Internet is very beneficial for most of us. We benefit personally when we refuse to allow the Internet to undermine our human dignity, to use other people's dignity, to waste our time or squander opportunities or to undermine our values. By controlling our use of the Internet – rather than allowing it to control us – we are free to more fully participate in the world.

Smoking

Today's college students are still tempted to smoke even though they know the risks – this makes it a decoy! In fact, today's college students smoke more than students from just a few years ago despite decades of data proving that smoking is the leading cause of lung cancer and preventable death in adults. Most students — in college and high school — know the facts; in fact 90 percent of people know the facts about smoking.[11]

The U.S. Centers for Disease Control (CDC) estimates that 24 percent of people between the ages of 18-24 smoke[12]; among this group, the "daily use rate" has recently risen from 9 percent to 14 percent.[13] These rates certainly mean that a whole lot of college students are smoking. These rates convince other students to try smoking. About a fourth of college students who smoke now began doing so in high school. Many other students smoke for the first time in college and do so at "fairly high levels."[14] Furthermore, smoking doesn't end when they graduate; approximately 75% of college students take their smoking into adulthood.[15]

Students smoke for a variety of social reasons including: wanting to fit in; it's the "party" thing to do; their friends smoke; weight management; cigarettes are more affordable in college; personal reservations against smoking diminish due to new influences; drinking and smoking frequently coincide; and smoking helps calm party jitters. Students smoke to be perceived as mysterious, manly, risk-taker, or cool. Also, students may not perceive smoking to be a very big risk.[16]

Not one of the reasons listed above support students' overall health and wellness. Instead, the decoy morphs into a habit that becomes very hard to kick. It also disaffects student's physical abilities and activities. For example, smoking is inversely associated with strenuous physical activity and strengthening activities. Conversely, non smokers are more likely to engage in strenuous and strengthening physical activity that contributes to their long term wellness.[17]

Nicotine, a mild stimulant, often precedes experimentation with illegal drugs, which is why it is sometimes called a "gateway" substance.

However, the use of alcohol, cigarettes, marijuana, and other drugs also have been found to occur in close proximity with each other rather than occurring in a sequential order wherein one abuse leads to another.[18] Others consider smoking to be a gateway for smoking pot or abusing inhalants.

Regardless of what abuse leads to another, most adults who smoke wish they had never started. This is particularly true when someone sees it as a direct consequence to a health problem or disease. Too many student smokers become tomorrow's regular smokers with similar regret. Students who don't smoke during high school or college are not likely to take up the habit later in life. Non-smokers have a higher likelihood of outliving friends who smoke.

Drug Abuse

Illegal drugs are a Triple-A Decoy: They are easily accessed and afforded and the purchases are made fairly anonymously. These substances become a temptation for students curious about their effects. Peers become persuasive decoys when they convince others to try it. Drug effects are often exaggerated by users when they sweep the negative effects under the rug. Drug abuse continues to be a worry for parents, health officials, college administrators, religious leaders, employers, and others — and for good reasons!

Nearly half of all college students have tried illegal or prescription drugs; of these students about half (22 percent) regularly use or are dependent on these substances.[19] Your peer group does not consider drug use to be wrong; a full 45 percent of Millennials (between ages 18-24) consider drug use to be morally acceptable or at least not a moral issue.[20] Joseph Califano, president of the National Center on Addiction and Substance Abuse (CASA) at Columbia University worries that drug abuse continues to increase due to easy access. He went on to say that "It's time to get the high out of higher education."[21]

The following table compares the drug abuse rates for full time college students between 1993 and 2005. The data provides a snapshot of the overall abuse rates in full time college students along with individual substance abuse rates. Note that several substances were not yet on the "radar" for health officials in 1993, including prescription drugs.

Substance	FT College Student use rate – 2005[22]	FT College student use rate – 1993[23]
Any Illegal Drug	37.5%	30.6%
Marijuana	33.3%	27.9%
Inhalants	2.9%	3.8%
Cocaine	5.7%	2.7%
Heroin	0.4%	0.1%
Hallucinogens	8.1%	6.0%
Crack Cocaine	0.4%	NA
Stimulants	4.5%	NA
Methamphetamines	0.8%	NA
Prescription drugs: Percocet, Oxycontin and Vicodin remain "highly sought after prescription drugs" by college students who abuse prescription drugs.	11.6% [24] - 12.1%[25] Students who abuse prescription drugs are more likely to also abuse alcohol, marijuana, ecstasy and cocaine and drive under the influence.	NA
Binge Drinking	63.4%	63.4%

Students use drugs primarily for social reasons. Experts tell us that students abuse drugs to relax; to reduce or escape stress, conflicts or personal problems; to decrease their social anxiety when in a crowd; or to heighten sexual encounters. Student participants of one study reported their primary reason for using drugs or alcohol was because they hoped it would heighten a sexual experience (40 percent); others used drugs in order to facilitate a sexual encounter (31 percent).[26] These college students buy into the myth that amphetamines, marijuana, GHB, MDMA (ecstasy), hallucinogens, and opiates increase sexual arousal and performance when – in reality — these substances can actually impair sexual function and sexual climax. For example, the drug called ecstasy causes erectile dysfunction. Students who get drunk or high are often left wondering whether they even had sexual relations. The sexual enhancement claims seem bogus at best when the few studies that report heightened sexual pleasure when using drugs compared to alcohol conclude with the disclaimer that the "acute administration of many substances disrupts learning and memory therefore study participants may not have been able to recall their experiences with sufficient detail."[27]

Illegal substances will always have side effects ranging from minor discomforts to more serious consequences including death due to overdose or organ failure. Many users simply do not understand the personal risks when abusing illegal substances. For example, did you know that marijuana is a possible carcinogen? "Using a highly sensitive new test, scientists in Europe report convincing evidence that marijuana smoke damages the genetic material DNA in ways that could increase the risk of cancer.[28]

Illegal substances produce side effects that can cause permanent or long term impairment of one's mental, physical, or emotional health.

Lately, drug cartels and "pushers" lace illegal drugs to make them go farther. Drug abusers cannot know whether the illegal substance they are using has been laced with other substances nor do they realize the side effects of the lacing products. In July 2009, the government reported that 70 percent of the cocaine that had been seized had been laced with Levamisole, a drug used by veterinarians to de-worm animals. Human consumption of this substance can cause serious side effects including death. Recently, the St. Paul *Pioneer Press* reported several deaths due to tainted cocaine.[29] It should be readily apparent that the drug cartels do not hold the best interests of abusers when lacing drugs with substances in order to stretch their inventory and make more money.

We know that abusing drugs and alcohol adversely affects decision-making, impairs memory, and increases personal risk taking. Substance abuse of any kind also increases a person's risk for developing mental health problems; attempting or committing suicide; getting hurt, injured or killed in a motor vehicle accident or other type of accident; being victimized or assaulted by someone committing a violent crime; or contracting disease or illness. Substance abuse is also linked to certain types of cancer and heart disease.[30] Finally illegal drug use only serves to finance drug cartels and drug pushers – dangerous people who use others for self gain.

Students who refuse to follow the siren call of drug use/abuse are free to experience the world with their full faculties intact. They can enjoy themselves knowing that they have not compromised their mental, physical, spiritual, emotional, or physical wellness. These students put their natural curiosities to work in all the right places. They also do not allow themselves to be used up by drugs or people with selfish motives. Good friends do not convince other friends to take risks to their health, minds, or souls. The students who rule their own lives – rather than letting passions, curiosities, and appetites rule – are better able to see God and his handiwork. In turn they are positioned to allow God to draw out their "true colors and musical notes" legitimately.

Alcohol

Excessive, illegal drinking is a big problem on most college campuses; therefore it is fair to rate it the number one decoy facing students. Many college students arrive on campus fully expecting to see and experience drinking – but many of you are not prepared for the excesses that you observe. Although heavy drinking is considered to be the most "urgent problem" facing health officials, not every college student drinks or drinks to excess. In fact, less than half of all students regularly engage in high risk drinking[31] and roughly one fifth of all college students abstain completely from drinking any amount of liquor.[32] But the students, who do drink, often do it at dangerous levels.

University officials recognize the problems associated with excessive alcohol consumption but don't know how to effectively deal with it – for many reasons. Alcohol awareness campaigns, for one, have not been very effective as observed by studies conducted between 1993 and 2001.[33] Yet, research suggests that personal social networks, perceptions about drinking, and effective communication of social norms with regard to drinking can positively or negatively influence risky drinking behaviors.[34] This means your social network can change perceptions; you can be the game changer for someone else when you hold onto the knowledge and conviction that binge drinking is too risky, it's not cool, and it is harmful. Advertisements for alcohol and alcohol-related products can be banned from college campuses. Student's families can also become game changers when they demand that universities change policies and/or practices that "unofficially" encourage underage drinking. College campuses must effectively communicate good social norms with regard to drinking! They must also be held responsible when they don't sponsor enough alcohol-free events. More importantly, you are your own game changer. The U.S. Healthy People 2010 Initiative Objectives set the goal to reduce binge drinking rates by nearly half – time will tell whether this goal will be met.

The overall drinking rate for college students is often reported to be 80 percent to 90 percent and so the conclusion drawn is that everybody is drinking. However, this data includes students who are of legal age, and those who have only an occasional drink. Inclusion of all drinkers – legal, moderate, underage, and excessive consumers — leads to the exaggerated perception that everybody is drinking and to excess! Recall that roughly 20 percent of all college students avoid alcohol altogether. Nevertheless, too many students are drinking and to excess and many students within this sub group are also under age!

This social decoy encourages college students to drink on and off campus in dorms, in social fraternity houses, in other student housing, in students' rental property or in bars. Many regard it as the social norm to drink at parties and celebrations or pre-game events. Students who join social organizations such as fraternities or sororities drink more than students who do not join these organizations; and they drink more excessively. One study showed that between 70 percent and 86 percent of fraternity men engaged in binge drinking; by way of contrast 45 percent of non-members engaged in binge drinking.[35] Eighty percent of sorority girls engaged in binge drinking compared to 35 percent of non- sorority members.[36]

Binge drinking (male) is defined as consuming at least five alcoholic drinks at one "sitting" and drinking this amount at least one time over the past two weeks. Female binge drinker is the consumption of at least four drinks successively in one sitting and drinking this amount at least one time over the past two weeks. More male students binge drink than do female students.

Students drink for multiple social and personal reasons. Social scientists tell us that the reasons to drink frequently align with students reasons to use drugs. Nobody drinks because they expect to get hurt or become an alcoholic! The following "reasons to drink list" is extensive:

Students drink as an icebreaker according to this ditty by Ogden Nash: *Candy is dandy but liquor is quicker.*[37] Students drink to relax. They like the feeling of being "tipsy" or high. They drink to seem cool. Students drink to fit in. In fact, they generally drink like others in their own social network. Students drink to experiment with alcohol effects. Students drink to elevate moods; they drink because they are bored, anxious, stressed out, lonely, or depressed. Drinking to cope with college life is the most concerning to mental health therapists simply because this sub-group of drinkers has been proven to have the highest risk for developing long-term alcohol related problems and abuse.[38] Students drink to meet a sexual partner or to enhance that sexual experience. Some students carry the perception that drinking is a rite of passage; others drink because they want to be perceived as a risk taker. Students drink to prove they can hold their liquor. Students feel drinking is fun. Students even drink so they have bragging rights to ridiculous behavior. Students drink to provide cover for ridiculous personal behavior. Students drink because they think it doesn't matter. Students drink to celebrate an upcoming school break, home football games, Halloween, and St. Patrick's Day. In fact, drinking to celebrate holidays has been dubbed *alcoholidays* in college circles.[39] Some students drink because they think they are supposed to! Some drink because they have been dared to drink. As already stated, students drink because they perceive it to be the social norm![40] All together, excessive and illegal drinking is an influential but deceitful decoy that hides potential calamities exceptionally well.

It will be hard to meet the 2020 Healthy People Initiative goals while university students honor the tradition of naming the Top Ten Party Schools in America. Sadly, students look for affirmation from organizations such as PubClub.com that provided the following unfortunate commentary: "What's all this fuss about national rankings in college football when we know the real action is not on the playing field but at the tailgate parties and in the bars."[41] The Pub Club's cheer: *Win or Lose, We Booze*, motivates students to act upon this praise. By the way, PubClub.com nominated the following schools as the Top Ten party schools for 2010: Texas, Florida, Wisconsin, Alabama, UCSB, Georgia,

Ohio State, Florida State, Arizona, and USC. Many universities actively support this cheer when they limit Friday and early Monday morning classes creating essentially a three day week. Faculty expectations have also plummeted in the past three decades as expectations for student drinking have increased. Thirsty Thursdays have come to signify the start of the weekends for students and college administrators alike.[42]

Students are under a lot of social pressure to drink but the personal price tag for giving up and surrendering to this peer pressure is high. Drinking naturally lowers inhibitions and impairs judgment; therefore drinkers often do or say things they ordinarily would not. Drinking and lowered inhibitions can produce a *beer goggle effect* – finding someone attractive because of the booze! Intoxication decreases brain activity causing drinkers to make poor or risky decisions/choices. Drinking is one of the primary causes for academic failure. Hangovers prevent students from getting to classes or preparing well for a final exam. Drinking can make students lose their commitment for why they are in school – academics.[43] Excessive drinking increases the risk for injury, trauma, or death due to fights, car accidents or falls; accidental drowning; pedestrian accidents, and more. Estimates blame excessive drinking for 1,400-1,700 student deaths annually. Driving while under the influence is still a serious problem despite the "effective" designated driving programs. A full 27 percent[44] of intoxicated students manage to convince others they can drive; therefore they get behind the steering wheel and cause more than 600,000 alcohol-related traumas, injuries, or deaths.[45]

Students who drink excessively increase their risks for developing depression, suicidal thoughts or actions, or other mental health problems. Excessive drinking increases the risk for developing certain cancers, heart disease, liver disease, or decreased fertility. Drinking is blamed for engaging in risky sexual behaviors that result in an unplanned pregnancy, unplanned sexual encounters, or the contracting of one or more sexually transmitted infections. Annually, 400,000 incidents of risky sex take place on college campuses. Another 70,000 reported incidents of sexual assault or date rape have been directly linked to alcohol use.[46] Each year, it is estimated that more than 100,000 students become "too intoxicated" to know whether they had sex or consented to have sex![47]

Students who drink to excess often think their friends will look out for them but too many intoxicated students are left behind. Unfortunately, many will not receive appropriate and necessary help to get back to their college dorm rooms safely. Some of these students are abducted, raped or murdered; others are killed mysteriously or simply found dead in houses, on streets, or in cars, still others are hit by cars as they try to get back home; others drown after falling down river banks, etc. The tragedies are very real.

Drinking can cause hangovers which include headaches, fatigue, vomiting, illness, loss of appetite, and sleep disturbance. Excessive drinking leads to death due to alcohol poisoning. Popular drinks on campus include beer, spirits, and caffeinated alcoholic beverages. Four drink manufacturers have recently come under FDA investigation because their malt beverages contain high concentrations of both caffeine and alcohol. They have been warned to stop adding the caffeine or stop selling the products. The warning came after the a yearlong investigation by the FDA into the all too numerous accounts from emergency rooms reporting severe physical illness and even death resulting from the consumption of caffeinated malt beverages.[48] The alcoholic energy drinks combine uppers (caffeine) with downers (alcohol) without knowing how powerful the effects of the combination are for average adults says Dr. Michael Romain of Austin Diagnostic Clinic.[49] He also said the drinks (caffeinated alcoholic drinks) concern him, not only because of the high levels of caffeine present but because of the potential effects when you mix two different drugs together. The body's natural sense to slow down with alcohol cannot happen because caffeine makes a person feel awake. This can lead to a false sense of sobriety even though judgment is already impaired by the alcohol. People think they are OK so they drive while impaired but awake![50] "Popular caffeinated alcoholic drinks contain on average 169 to 246 parts per million caffeine per drink. The FDA guidelines limit caffeine additives to 200 parts per million/drink. This is the equivalent of two Pepsi drinks.[51]

Finally, 10 percent to 35 percent of young drinkers will take their excessive drinking into adulthood. They will, essentially, drink their way to alcoholism from college to a later time in life. Regrettably, too many students fail to heed the warnings about excessive drinking because they don't think it pertains to them. Even more unfortunate is the fact that 100 percent of the tragic consequences that result from excessive alcohol consumption were preventable.

Students who refuse to allow their lives to be compromised by drinking to excess will graduate healthy, wiser, and focused than the peers who abuse alcohol. The abstinent drinker or the legal and moderate drinkers are more likely to accomplish their spiritual, mental, emotional, physical, and social goals for college. These students are well positioned to follow their personal and professional goals and dreams after graduation.

Bullying

So far, we have discussed several decoys for today's college students. Is bullying also a decoy? It has already been established that decoys are those activities or things that distract us or tempt us to do things we might not ordinarily do under the public's watchful eyes. Bullying fits this definition well. For example, the bully is often encouraged by friends to continue the aggression. Secondly, college provides a fairly anonymous atmosphere wherein bullies can get by with their aggression. Bullies may not even aim their aggression at specific targets but cast a wide net inflicting pain wherever or whenever it lands. After all, isn't college a place where students frequently poke fun at other students? Bullying consequences are often masked until tragedy strikes. Even the young adult who falls victim to a bully's aggression is often blamed for being unable to stand up for him/her self. Cyber - bullying is increasing in incidence among all ages of people. For these reasons, bullying is categorized as a decoy.

Bullies use aggression to gain the upper hand — either directly or indirectly. Direct aggression is physical harm carried out against another person. Indirect aggression is relational or social aggression; it intends to inflict indirect harm by resorting to slander, gossip, ignoring another person or even excluding them from the social group. Personal aggression is the act of deliberately harming oneself. Each type of aggression is either covert or overt. Young females use more indirect aggression compared to young males but this difference blurs as both groups mature. Overall, males commit more direct aggression than females in any age group. College men report relational aggression more often than college women.[52]

There is little concrete evidence to support the statement that once a bully always a bully because few large sociological studies have been conducted on the subject of campus bullying. However, it seems logical that bullies won't change behaviors until they improve their mental and emotional states. Consequently, there are still bullies in college and even in the professional work place.

A few studies that looked at campus bullying confirm that college bullying occurs. According to one study, approximately 20 percent of college women and 32 percent of college men complained of having been the target of a bully during the previous school year. Forty one percent of college males who were bullied were threatened with weapons. The others were pushed, grabbed, punched, or shoved.[53] Most of the incidents took place in local bars or at sporting events. One college student blogger wrote that "Bullying at college can be done to get an unpopular girl to quit a sorority. Instructors can also feel bullied by a student, or vice versa.[54] The existence and degree of bullying was explored at Union College; the consensus of opinions among students polled revealed that bullying existed (on campus). Furthermore, 82 percent of the respondents had witnessed bullying at higher rates than when they were in high school.[55] Jerif Vilardo, a former student at Daniel Webster College, says his school didn't do enough to protect him from a bully who forced him to drop out of college. Vilardo claimed that a certain student began "bullying, hazing, harassing, assaulting and abusing him in his dorm room, at the school cafeteria and elsewhere on campus," The bullying continued even though the perpetrator was ejected from the college. Vilardo blamed the school for doing nothing more.[56]

Bullying of any type – direct and indirect – inflicts emotional and/ or physical harm on victims. Bullying can cause targets to become anxious, lonely or isolated; it also can increase stress and risk of depression. Victims often begin to assume self-destructive behaviors such as suicide, especially if they experience wholesale rejection by peers who begin to blame them for being weak or social misfits. Blaming the victim rather than the perpetrator fuels ongoing aggression.

It is always inappropriate social behavior to bully someone else. Bullying is always inappropriate social behavior.

Think about whether you consider the following activities to be forms of bullying: Is it a form of bullying to pressure someone to drink or to have sexual relations? Is it a form of bullying when someone pretends to be hurt in order to make another person feel bad? What about these: publicly embarrassing someone; making abusive phones calls; sending threatening/hurtful notes or text messages; breaking confidence just to get an upper hand; criticizing the personal looks and appearance of someone; gossiping about someone; backbiting; ignoring someone; physically harming another person; threatening to bring physical harm on someone; date rape; road rage; stalking; flirting to deliberately hurt someone; giving dirty looks; slamming doors or breaking things; making negative practical jokes or pranks on someone; threatening to reveal damaging information about someone; insulting another person. Yes, these are all forms of bullying.

Sudents should not excuse aggressive acts because someone was drunk, "just joking" (inappropriately), or high or jealous or tired or whatever. Unnecessary aggression is never acceptable behavior; anyone making excuses for boyfriends, girlfriends, or friends should stop and ask themselves why. They are making excuses for a bully.

Unfortunately, bullies may personally benefit when acting aggressively. For example, the bully may attract a following from those who admire his or her aggressive behavior - that is until he or she gets too aggressive. There comes a point when even a bully is perceived as too aggressive; at that time the bully loses friends because he or she is perceived to be too aggressive, anti-social, or egocentric. A rejected bully then develops identity problems similar to those he or she instilled in the bullied victims.

Hazing is a form of "extreme bullying" that takes place on campus within limited windows of opportunity. Hazing rituals have become long standing traditions on most college campuses among social organizations such as fraternities, sororities, and athletic teams. It is a problematic decoy because of its tradition, popularity and acceptability! During hazing rituals, students blindly follow the lead of the oldest students. Newbie's can be subjected to dehumanizing rituals that often require the hazer to use another person in order to be accepted by a social organization or athletic team. For example, today's college fraternity hazing rituals often require a plebe to have at least one hook up experience with a sorority girl before being inducted into the social organization. Unfortunately, these hazing incidents often end up victimizing many people. Did you know that sorority women are at highest risk for being sexually victimized while attending college?[57]

Colleges know how to take disciplinary action against direct acts of aggression but have more difficulty assessing and/or controlling indirect aggression such as hazing, cyber bullying, and emotional or mental bullying.

Bullying and hazing fail to respect the dignity of all the persons involved. Bullying of any type should never take place; more importantly, bullying must never be socially accepted. Students who bully fail to love authentically. Bully behavior suggests that the person is not well mentally, psychologically, physical, or socially. They are the people to avoid on campus – not the people to copy. Students who refuse to become bullies or to allow friends to bully or even subject themselves to any sort of bullying are better off in every way – physically, mentally, socially, emotionally, and spiritually.

College Debt

Assuming large amounts of college debt is another tempting decoy for many students. College is the one arena wherein parents and students alike compare price tags but still tend to opt for the more "prestigious" or expensive institution. This decoy deceptively tricks students into putting off fiscal realities and responsibilities until later. College has come to be regarded as the place where different classes of students – rich and poor – can all afford the same opportunities and benefits of the prestigious institution they are attending. The hoped-for admission to a prestigious university often glamorizes educational goals.

The truth is that many students simply can't afford these types of colleges so accumulation of excessive student debt only serves to hamper long-term economic goals as well as other long-term personal goals. In order to defy this decoy, students and their parents need to objectively compare costs of different college options before falling in love with an institution. If you face financial limits, like most students, then it behooves you to choose a comparable but less expensive option. Most colleges are created equally when it comes to meeting overall educational goals and objectives, even though there is a high variability between price tags.

Furthermore, if your dream job has a very low probability of happening or pays a low starting wage, it is imperative that you compare academic costs. Each career path has its own debt ceiling related to the expected starting salary. The type of degree you plan to pursue should direct your debt load for college. Remember, there can be too much student debt just as there can be too much of any type of debt. High debt loads – no matter the future career – make it difficult to repay loans and still have enough money left over to buy a house or car, start a family, finish college, find the best job, make contributions to a personal retirement account, and more.

Financial strain increases student and post graduate stress levels. College can also be the time to waste a lot of money unless students live frugally according to their current state of life rather than the anticipated state of life. While the future appears rosy for every starting college student, it may not be rosy when you graduate. Many college graduates even complain about having to hold down jobs that don't require a college degree. Others can't find satisfactory employment after graduation. Alicia Dowd, Assistant Professor at UCLA's Rossier School of Education, teaches us that "no borrower can completely forecast what surprises life might throw at them that could make loan repayment onerous."[58]

College education becomes very expensive when students waste valuable time and resources unnecessarily. It should take, at most, four – possibly five (see endnote for explanation)[59] years to graduate with an undergraduate degree. Any additional time simply racks up student debt – possibly as much as tens of thousands of dollars.

Colleges are rated as high or low debt institutions depending on the total debt load the average student ends up carrying after four years. Low debt institutions generally provide significant financial aid packages, scholarships, grant money, or endowments that help cut down debt load for their students. The average debt load for students attending high-debt institutions ranges from $26,000 to $ 45,000, depending on whether the institution is private or public.[60] By contrast, students attending low debt schools carry below average amounts of, or no, student loans. Some of these institutions are "working colleges" whereby students work and pay as they go. The military academies are considered no-debt-load schools but they require a military commitment upon graduation. Naturally, it is always the most advantageous when a student does not have to borrow money to attend college.

Financial experts can still prove that it is worthwhile to go to college and graduate with a degree. College graduates consistently "do better than others when overall job creation is lagging," according to Christian Weller, a senior economist at the Center for American Progress. Our current economic recession has brought about high unemployment rates that also supports that premise. In September of 2009, the Bureau of Labor Statistics found that 4.9 percent of college educated women and 5.0 percent of college educated men were unemployed. By contrast, 8.6 percent of women with only high school degrees and 11.1 percent of men with only high school degrees were unemployed.[61] However, it is also true that the economic value of the university institution needs to be called into question as student debt increases faster than starting salaries. It is always important to calculate how much student loan is "too much" for your situation.

Just like the formula used for other adults, your total debt load after graduation – including any mortgages, car loans, credit card debt and education loans should not exceed 35 percent of your gross income. If your school loans will take up the full 10 percent of your starting salary, this means you only have 25 percent left to use for a car or housing and any other loans or credit card bills. Even a 10 percent college debt load becomes a significant monthly expense; it can severely hamper other long term purchases, goals, and plans and even your marriage-ability status.

Students shouldering low or little school or credit card debt have many more choices, opportunities, and options after graduation. These students will not have to feel like they are continuously paying back (for going to college) for 10 years or longer. They can take any job they like, and live any place they choose. They are also freer to marry and have a family compared to students burdened by excessive school debt. These students are less affected by pervasive or negative national or regional economic conditions. Indeed, debt free students are certainly freer to explore the world they have just launched into.

Credit Card Debt

Credit cards are alluring for many college students. Most college students have at least one credit card; some have three or more. Credit card debt can quickly consume or overtake incomes because of their high interest rates on unpaid balances. Students with credit cards are charged anywhere from 12.99 percent interest rates to 19.99 percent interest rates on unpaid balances. Did you know that the average non student generally pays lower interest rates on unpaid balances than students; these rates typically range between 14.72 percent - 17.43 percent.[62]

Today's average college student typically carries monthly credit card balances of $2,327 in addition to their student loans. Graduate students carry even more; 92 percent of graduate students carry average outstanding credit card balances of $8,612.[63]

A student's attitude toward credit is a significant predictor of the number of credit cards they possess. As positive attitudes toward debt increase, so does the amount of actual debt. Society as a whole has moved toward adopting a friendlier attitude toward consumer credit; correspondingly, as the attitude increases so does overall debt. In fact, as of December 2008, US consumers had amassed a staggering $988 billion in revolving debt up from $170 billion in January 1988.[64] Consumers tend to under-report their personal debt for obvious reasons: they hate to admit that spending exceeds purchasing ability.

The best advice that we can offer to college students with regard to credit cards and debt comes your way thanks to the input of several thrifty parents.

Their advice:

- Avoid revolving debt.
- Don't accumulate excessive debt.
- It's OK to have a credit card if you use it like ready cash. Pay off monthly credit card balances on time and in full.
- Buy cars only that you can afford today and commensurate with your driving needs and income.
- Live within your means for your state of life.
- Draw up a financial budget in college and stick to it.
- Work in college and use the earnings to reduce your debts rather than spending it on material items that vanish.
- Work during the summers to help offset college expenses.
- Forego frivolous or discretionary expenses.
- Live to appreciate your poverty; you will be more thankful when material blessings come your way after graduation.
- Avoid impulse shopping or spending that is often spurred on by using plastic instead of cash.

Credit cards are not inherently bad but they are a decoy because they entice us to spend more than we have. Credit cards are good to use if you already have the money in the bank but you prefer to buy with a plastic card that accumulates points. Pay the credit card bill when it arrives. Carrying balances from month to month strips away any good deals you thought you found. Compounding interest is the credit companies' American Dream — for them not you! Use credit cards only to buy things you need or can afford. Credit cards come in very handy while traveling. They also help to establish your credit history. Remember that having a bad credit history can negatively impact finding a job, or buying homes or cars; it will also make you pay more for large ticket items than someone with good credit. Credit cards "promote the feeling that you are not actually paying money for something you buy on a credit card" fueling over-spending and impulse buying. Another danger of having credit cards is that as you near the credit limit, the credit card company raises your credit limit making you feel like a "responsible" consumer. Credit card companies flatter you into higher credit limits. But the flattery disguises hidden dangers. Credit card companies do not care if you pay off the monthly balance.

They are simply interested in collecting the minimum payments which works to their advantage. As noted earlier, leaving unpaid balances will only cost you more in the long run.

Research shows that most college students rely on parental advice or example when using credit cards. Parents model these behaviors and attitudes — consciously and unconsciously — whenever they make purchases, negotiate prices, select items to buy, compare brands, overspend, carry unpaid balances, remain free of credit card debt, or get into trouble with credit card debt. Parents, in effect, set up their students to be a responsible consumer or an emotion-driven consumer. Secondarily, students follow the lead of their peers, schools, and mass media when it comes to using credit cards and making purchases, selecting brand names, comparing brands, etc.[65] Peers influence each other with regard to lifestyle purchases such as music, movies or clothing. This influence increases in college as the parent's influence wanes. Finally, it has been found that television influences our consumer behavior. The more television we watch, the more we want to buy!

Like the college graduate without school loans, graduating students who have no credit card debt will also have many more choices, opportunities, and freedoms available to them. These students have probably learned to live on less. This frugality – if maintained well – can positively impact their future marriage ability and even long term happiness. Frugal people are less impulse shoppers and are more conservative spenders and savers. These are all positive habits to develop in order to be able to more freely explore the world you have just launched into.

Gambling

Enter a gambling casino – even online gambling spaces – and you will immediately understand its lure. They are designed with bright colors and loud music; nobody is supposed to fall asleep in a casino! Going to a casino can feel like embarking on a fantasy getaway vacation complete with flashing lights, loud music, bright colors, food, alcohol, and celebrity guests. The atmosphere spells double jeopardy because drinks are free. These are a few of the reasons why gambling can be an enticing decoy for some college students – and many adults.

The lure of gambling can begin early in one's college career and colleges are becoming increasingly concerned about gambling among their students. Experts estimate that between "3 percent to 6 percent of college students meet the criteria for pathological gambling."[66] Student pathological gambling rates are two to five times greater than other adult samples. Like other addictions, pathological gambling confiscates the emerging adults' ability to have or maintain control over the habit. Pathological gambling disrupts study habits, test performance, relationships, and one's overall college success. It can even cause students to commit crimes. "When betting reaches a high-wager level and a player commits a crime to maintain that level of play, gambling is no longer about the money. It's about how the wagering itself makes the player feel. In the end, when people escape into gambling to avoid uncomfortable feelings, resolve pre-existing life problems, or get adrenaline rushes, it is the feeling that becomes addictive" says Dr. David Moore, a licensed psychologist and chemical dependency professional.[67]

College students face the same level of risk for becoming a pathological gambler as older adults although female students seem to have an even faster "progression to pathological gambling behaviors than male students.[68] The majorities of pathological gamblers were first substance abusers (alcohol, marijuana, and cocaine) or displayed impulsive/dysfunctional behaviors including suicide attempts, compulsive shopping, compulsive spending, and compulsive sexual behaviors.[69, 70]

While the gambling age varies from state to state, 21-year-old age restrictions often fail to keep underage college students away because they often have "easy access to fake IDs." College students are often attracted to gambling casinos because of the free liquor. Student gamblers also tend to be "sensation seekers" or risk takers, so the casino satisfies this desire. More than 40 percent of college students gamble at least once while in school; between 3 percent and 22 percent of college students gamble at least once a week or more.[71]

Finally, it may be important to recognize that men and women gamble differently. This shouldn't come as any surprise given the fact that men and women also spend and save differently. Typically, women prefer slot machines, lotteries, and bingo while men prefer active betting games including horse racing, card and dice games, and sports betting.[72]

The benefits of avoiding gambling should be obvious. First, you will have more money to put to better use. Furthermore, frequency is the untold secret trick behind any addictions including gambling. This means that if you never gamble you can never become an addict! By never gambling, you will not stoke any brain chemistry predispositions or personality tendencies that lead to addictions.

Sexual Decoys

Sexuality is a normal and significant part of who we are. The same center of the brain controls both our sexuality and hunger appetite. Nobody would ever recommend that students eat every time they thought about food or had an urge to eat. Yet, oddly enough, many fail to recommend any manner of restraint or self control in matters of sexual expression. And this is why so many college students are confused by the sexual decoys.

College students will find it important to divert sexual energy to the development and maintenance of virtue if they intend to practice sexual self control prior to marriage and even after marriage. This virtue is known as chastity and has become an "old fashioned" word and notion by many in secular society. Chastity is the virtue that helps us avoid temptations to commit sexual sins. Fortifying the virtue of chastity requires avoiding sexual temptation, keeping constructively busy, developing healthy study habits, setting personal goals, maintaining healthy personal relationships, and going to Church; receiving the Sacraments and praying daily. Unmarried persons need to harness their sexual feelings and behaviors for the good of themselves, their attitudes towards others, and for the good of their future spouse and marriage relationship. Adopting unhealthy sexual habits can cause a person to develop lifestyles that hurt and use others. Our personal sexual habits or behaviors either make it easier to love another person authentically or they make it more difficult to love someone authentically.

Committing to chastity is ongoing, daily in fact. Soon the habit of choosing chastity becomes a lifestyle and a commitment. Choosing pre-marital chastity is a deliberate choice made regardless of how much we love someone. Chastity always looks out for the best interests of the beloved person during any dating relationship. Chastity – a virtue – will always be protective and defensive of the other person's well being. Chastity allows love to grow naturally. These are the advantages that come from not falling for sexual decoys.

The following sections will involve a short discussion of each of the sexual decoys thrown out by modern culture – especially college culture.

Casual Sex

Civilization's primary purpose is to support families which create offspring that carry on the work of society. Today, casual sex along with many other risky sexual behaviors threatens both the primary purpose of civilization and the necessary support for families. Many students have been conditioned to believe that they "no longer have to enter marriage in order to have a regular sexual relationship." As a result, approximately 70 percent of young people support casual or pre-marital sex. Furthermore, about 80 percent of college students experience many types of casual sexual encounters. The average median number of lifetime sexual partners for many students will be four or more.[73]

Jeffrey Jensen Arnett, developmental psychologist and author of the "Emerging Adult" has a primary interest in your age group. He tells us that many people do not object to pre-marital sex either "as long as sex does not begin too early (whatever that is) or as long as the number of partners does not become "too many" (whatever that is). Americans may not be clear about what the precise rules ought to be for young people's sexual relationships, but there is widespread tolerance now for sexual relations between young people in their late teens and twenties in the context of a committed loving relationship."[74] Note how Arnett cleverly illuminates the moral relativism of such positions by inserting "whatever that is" at the various points in the sentence. However, the question– "whatever that is" – seems important enough to answer before engaging in any sexual relationship. Failure to answer the question at hand – whatever that is — introduces premature, casual, and demanding sex which introduces physical, emotional, social, spiritual, and mental calamities.

The word moral defines how individuals ought to behave. In contrast, immoral behaviors are those that people ought not to do because they harm others or self. Since sexual relations involve the behaviors of two individuals, questions about moral and immoral (right and wrong behaviors) naturally emerge. Arnett supports the notion that sexual behavior is connected with morality when he asked the question — whatever that is.

Nietzsche, Ernest Nagel, Bertrand Russell, and other atheist philosophers fought against sexual moral constraints because they knew that Christianity erodes when sexual moral restrictions are lifted. Furthermore, they recognized that sexual liberation leads to the general decline in the belief of God and the afterlife."[75] Unfortunately, sexual liberation has reached down into the main roots of Christianity as well. The 2010 Marist Poll found that only 34 percent of Americans, 40 percent of American Catholics and 38 percent of Catholic Millennials between the ages of 18 and 29 believed that sex between an unmarried man or woman was morally wrong or a moral issue. They also didn't believe that it was morally wrong to have a baby outside of marriage.[76]

As with junk food, "junk-sex" causes people's moral lives to decline precipitously. Junk food lovers deny eating badly, junk-sex lovers also deny behaving badly until lifestyles are exposed publicly. Consider the recent admission of celebrity sex addict Tiger Woods.

Even though moral relativism rules the day with regard to sexual morality, the hope remains that the "norms society imposes on itself in pursuit of its own self protection do not wholly disappear but rather mutate and move on. Farfetched as it seems at the moment, where mindless food is today's 'moral problems' requiring necessary strictures, mindless sex – in light of the growing empirical record of its own unleashing, may soon be seen as the new moral problem needing the imposition of necessary strictures once again, yet again, tomorrow."[77]

The state of marriage provides the only clear, consistent demarcation line that logically answers the question: "whatever that is." Marriage provides that state when sexual relations are authentic, appropriate, loving, safe, and healthy, and good. Any sexual relations outside of marriage render such behavior too casual, too soon, too often, and too wrong.

Many college students operate under the pretense that "love interests are supposed to be varied and transient even though their school and work experiences should be focused."[78] This type of attitude places more value on economics than human relationships. Little do these students realize that as often as they use another person for sexual self-gratification and other purposes, the more selfish, self-centered, and immoral they will become. In contrast, the more they love God and others, the less selfish and self focused they will be.

Hooking up

Hooking up is a very loosely defined form of sexual exploration involving an array of behaviors from kissing to more intimate activities. Hooking up is sometimes called *friends with benefits*. Many sociologists believe that hooking up has replaced former – more traditional forms of courtship and dating on college campuses. Let's hope they are off the mark.

While the sexual activities may be loosely defined, a full 78 percent of hooking up involves *unwanted* sexual activities. In fact, date rape has been upstaged by concerns over the riskiness of hooking up.[79] Consensual sex (oral and vaginal) occurs during approximately 20 percent of hookups. Limited evidence suggests that the average number of college hookups – for those who participated in the study and the practice — was ten partners per student; the range of the number of partners for all of the students participating in the study was one to seventy![80] A full 75 percent of college students have arranged or participated in a hook up.

Hooking up occurs in the expected places: dorms, fraternity houses, clubs, cars, and bars. Over half (58 percent) of all hook up participants used alcohol or drugs to facilitate the casual relationship. Furthermore, data shows that hooking up is even more prevalent among Catholic college students than students who attend secular or evangelical colleges![81] In fact, studies show that a female student attending a Catholic institution is four times more likely to hook up with a male partner compared to female students attending secular institutions.

Hooking up de-couples love from sex dismissing the original purpose and dignity of sexuality and personhood. Hooking up fails to integrate personal actions with real emotion. Hooking up deprives feelings and warmth from these actions. Students who participate in a hook up have set expectations for casualness, and the complete absence of having or fostering any emotional or romantic strings or entanglements.[82] Yet, students describe complex, interpersonal experiences during hook ups rendering the term "casual" as disingenuous as the act itself.

Research shows that this emotional detachment isn't working out quite as expected especially for many female partners. Only 20 percent of college females fully expected to or wanted to engage in oral or vaginal sex. The researchers noted that many of the women were looking for acceptance, some degree of communication, or other relational factors. The lack of communication left many of the female participants feeling empty, unfulfilled, regretful, confused or unsure. In sharp contrast, over 67 percent of college males participating in a hook up, "fully expected or wanted to engage in oral or vaginal sex." The male participants left with mixed feelings of pride, self-satisfaction and happiness, confusion and performance anxiety.[83] They also did not show any interest in starting up a personal relationship with the hook up partners. Research suggests that males instigate hook ups far more frequently than females.[84]

Both groups face increased risk for unintended pregnancy and getting infected with a sexually transmitted infection (STI).

Sexual relations always evoke emotion due to its original design and purpose! Every intimate act releases a "love hormone" called oxytocin! Oxytocin is on the loose even during hugging, eye gazing, holding hands, or any form of intimate touch. Oxytocin plays a key and central role in fortifying interpersonal bonds! It is meant to support and strengthen a sexual relationship. While it has been said that the eyes are the window to the soul...they certainly are the window to the emotional brain," says psychiatrist, Dr Kai MacDonald.[85] "We know that the eye-to-eye communication is affected by oxytocin, which evokes love, fear, trust, and anxiety. Oxytocin is called the love hormone because it is supposed to bond people – even those who unwittingly fall into its net.

This love hormone is designed by the Creator to establish appropriate psychological boundaries and maintain intimate relationships."[86]

Sexting

Sexting is a fairly new "worldwide phenomenon" primarily used by teens and young adults!" It's popularity morphs the practice into a social norm. Sexting is defined as "the act of sending sexually explicit messages or photos electronically, mostly between cell phones." Surveys hint that 33 percent of young adults between the ages of 20 and 26 have sent or received such videos or photos from another person.

The images sent constitute pornography – they are mostly nude or semi-nude pictures sent by one person (primarily females) to the other (primarily males). These images and sexual messages are sent without any guarantee of privacy. Even though a boyfriend may agree not to share it with other friends there is still no guarantee that others won't ever see it! About 17 percent of "sexts" are passed along, jeopardizing future employment opportunities, personal relationships, self esteem, while also introducing legal matters.

Several states have passed legislation that permits sexting between teens as young as fourteen years old in "committed relationships." It is outrageous that any legislative body would pass pretentious laws such as this! No adult can seriously believe that any fourteen year old in the United States has a committed relationship. Furthermore, it fails to protect lives – the sole purpose of laws. Authors of the law admit that it was passed to eliminate a backlog of legal cases involving charges of possession and distribution of pornography involving minors. Sexting remains illegal in many other states posing legal problems for college students who accept, receive, or send photos or videos of minors. In fact, college students face felony charges for possession of and/or distribution of pornographic photo images of minors in Florida, Ohio, Indiana, and Pennsylvania.[87]

Pornography

Regrettably, there are all kinds of porn: kiddie porn, heterosexual porn, and homosexual porn. This section will be confined to discussions regarding heterosexual male porn.

Pornography involves the use of any sexually explicit materials, erotica, and online sexual activity in order to cause sexual arousal. Pornography has crossed over into everyday lives and inserted itself into relationships that are marital, dating, cohabiting, and friendships. Pornography has even inserted itself into the business world jeopardizing jobs and careers. This insertion took a degree of stealth and cunning. Porn serves only two basic purposes: it is used for self gratification and it is used privately to satisfy sexual curiosities. Eighty three percent of men masturbate during or after viewing pornography.[88]

Approximately 40 million adults in the United States regularly visit Internet pornography sites. The pornography industry generates an estimated $100 billion of revenue annually; over $13 billion in revenue is generated within the United States. Furthermore, porn search engines fill about 70 million requests every day – this is one fourth of all search engine requests.[89] Porn use is highest among emerging adult males – between the ages of eighteen and twenty four; nearly 90 percent of these men dabble in or regularly use pornography.[90] Approximately one fifth of the college age porn users report daily use or at least three to five times weekly; half use porn on a weekly basis. Roughly half of the females from this same population group disapprove of pornography use and only 3.2 percent of women report a weekly (or longer) usage pattern.[91] The acceptance of porn use is limited by gender.

Porn is a Triple A decoy – it is easily afforded, readily accessed and anonymous. Internet porn sites provide all three features. The websites are open 24/7/365. Consequently, porn addictions are on the rise. Porn breaks down intimate, personal, and professional relationships and lives. There is limited evidence that pornography use also increases sexual and non-sexual violence and aggression.[92] Experts tell us that "even exposure to nonviolent pornography increases a male's likelihood to rape and hold rape acceptance attitudes". Rape acceptance attitudes are those that hold rape victims responsible for the sexual assault, or hold that there are "circumstances" when rape is acceptable. Frequently, convicted sex offenders claim that pornography made them rape someone! Porn users have five times more sexual partners over a lifetime and they are also more accepting of cohabitation and extramarital, premarital, and casual sex. Porn use is often linked to binge drinking.

Pornography often depicts sex using violence, subordination, bondage or even "rape" and the females are always shown enjoying these different levels of sexual aggression. Pornography re-defines and shapes male attitudes about authentic love, the purpose of sex, committed love, and marriage by depicting these violent and unrealistic portrayals. By way of example, researchers report that porn users often complain that their wives seemed needy, clingy, or overly demanding compared to online porn partners. In effect, porn users wanted to change their wives into "objectified partners" like their porn partners. Objectified women become things that dress and behave in ways that satisfy the desires and appetites of the male. Objectified women — those who allow themselves to become "things" likewise become course, detached, insensitive, insecure, overly-sensual or provocative, narcissistic, and self pampering. Self esteems tumble causing the adoption of self destructive behaviors.

Porn addictions are harder to kick than a crack cocaine addiction, according to some users and therapists. Sex addicts describe having feelings aroused by pornography similar to those described by drug abusers. David Mura writes in A Male Grief: Notes on Pornography and Addiction that, "In the pornographic perception, the addict experiences a type of vertigo, a fearful exhilaration, a moment when all the addicts' ties to the outside world do indeed seem to be cut off or numbered. The sense of endless falling; that feeling of a rush, is what the addict seeks." Addicts are powerless against this rush.

Exhibitionism

Everywhere we look, "Girls Gone Wild" conduct is very evident. It is obvious in Facebook shots, personal photos, sextings, dress, behaviors, attitude, language, and more. The media routinely covers incidents that show drunken females flashing their breasts publicly. So what do these public displays infer? Female flashing helps prove the point that moral sexual restraint is on the decline! The behavior itself can be blamed on the breaking down of traditional barriers between pornography and mainstream ideals of female sexuality.[93] Once again, the more we follow the sexual decoys, the less able are we to maintain traditional, moral, and religious ideals for sexual behavior or self restraint.

Porn portrays aggressive sexual behaviors for men and women as normal; essentially porn is very antagonistic toward traditional ideals of modesty and sexual limitations. Like porn, flashing behaviors are in-your-face and antagonistic of traditional behavior as well. True to the name, flashing behaviors prove that women can also be wild and shocking. The same goes for those who like to "moon" others.

Technically, experts argue the point that flashers and mooners are not typical exhibitionists since their behaviors do not normally represent exhibitionism, which is much more intimidating to observers. Mooners and college flashers are more than likely acting on a dare to perform publicly. On the other hand, exhibitionists come across as a "creeper" to those assaulted by their presence. As a result of the differences, Pamela Kulbarsh, RN writes: "A mooning at a high school football game does not, in itself, constitute exhibitionism, nor does flashing one's breasts at Mardi Gras. True exhibitionists take it farther."[94]

Cohabitation

Pro-cohabitation attitudes exist — not because people are necessarily down on marriage — but because so many unmarried adults cohabitate. Because so many couples are cohabitating, the collective behavior is forming a new social norm. Prior to 1960, cohabitation was rare; today it is widely practiced and accepted. Experts observe that within this new norm, cohabitation rates are highest among lower income couples, the less educated, and less religious. It is more common among couples wherein one or both spouses were previously divorced, or experienced parental divorce, grew up fatherless, or observed high marital discord in their parents.[95] Approximately, sixty percent of high school dropouts have cohabited compared to 37 percent of college graduates.[96] In fact, recently the Census Bureau added a question about cohabitation to its Current Population Survey in an attempt to help clarify the difference between single mothers living alone and those living with a partner. This question was inserted to make it "possible to measure how many new mothers are actually on their own."[97]

Cohabitations have increased twelvefold since 1960.[98] Today, most young people will live with someone before they marry.[99] Marriage experts tell us that many couple cohabit because they accept the myth that trial marriages deter bad marriages from forming and marriages that occur are now better because of cohabitation. Yet trends indicate from "representative samples of Americans that the percentages of men and women who rate their marriages as very happy has declined moderately over the past 35 years even as cohabitation rates have increased significantly."[100] In the year 2000, the United States had more than 4.1 million cohabiting couples representing nearly 8 percent of all couples living together. Cohabitation is also evident among Christian couples. The Catholic Diocese of Camden, New Jersey, conducted a small "marriage" study between February and May of 2009. The results revealed that of the 494 persons attending pre-marriage instruction, 72 percent indicated they were cohabiting; 26 percent were not cohabiting, and 2 percent gave no answer. Furthermore, 94 percent of the persons attending the conference admitted that they were sexually active. Only 24 percent of the attendees said that they regularly attended church; 41 percent attended sometimes; 29 percent rarely attended church and 5 percent said they never attended church. Yet 83 percent of the responders considered themselves to be Catholic, 11 percent Christian and 6 percent other.[101] Practicing Catholics differ significantly in their attitudes about cohabitation, divorce, and marriage from those who don't practice their faith.

Studies show that attitudes toward marriage also influence sexual behaviors in emerging adults. Increasing trends of cohabitation, casual sex, and planned pregnancy outside of marriage reflect a rising negativity toward marriage and the increasing acceptance of divorce.

Cohabitating couples do not necessarily ever proceed to the altar although most (75 percent)[102] expect to end up there. This expectation is invalidated by data that shows "considerable disagreement about the future of the relationship;" up to 74 percent of couples in the study disagreed about the likelihood of marriage or future together. Even securing a good job does not motivate many cohabiting couples to marry.[103] Cohabiting data reveals that only about half of all cohabiting couples marry within three to five years.[104] The Alternative to Marriage Project and the U.S. Census Bureau reported that roughly 10 percent of couples continue to live together as unmarried partners after five years or more."[105] Rather than being a stepping stone into marriage, cohabitation becomes a marriage alternative.

Sociology professor (Ohio State) Susan Sassler concludes: "Couples who use cohabitation as a trial period to test compatibility are far less likely to marry than couples who have definite marriage plans and a specific wedding date."[106] An Ohio State Study also showed that neither gender pushes marriage more or less often after starting to cohabitate.

A Canadian study concluded that cohabitation can negatively impact a future marriage because negative attitudes or behaviors acquired in a previous cohabitation are often carried forward into new relationships. Consider their findings: 63 percent of women whose first relationship involved cohabitation had separated several years later; by contrast, only 33 percent of women who had married first – prior to cohabitation — had separated within a similar timeframe. The authors of the study acknowledge the study had limitations.[107]

In general, many different sociologists agree that cohabitation is less likely to forge successful relationships because of different negative factors associated with cohabitation including increased uncertainty with regard to the intentions of either partner; financial and legal disputes; increased negative attitudes about having children or fidelity; decreased commitment levels; decreased levels of support for the other partner, decreased religiousness; less social support from other family members; decreased problem solving ability; and increased violent behaviors among those who cohabitate. Alex Roberts, author of "Marriage and the Great Recession" noted that "cohabiting couples are less likely to pool resources than married couples who feel obligated to sped wisely and save or invest in the future of the household".

Sociologists also warn that the "propensity to cohabitate soon after starting a romantic relationship leads to a pattern of instability. People who go through a series of de facto relationships are more likely to contract quick marriages, which are harder to remain faithful to."[108] Studies also show a positive correlation between religiosity and marital happiness and stability — the religiousness piece is generally missing in the majority of cohabitating relationships.

Many legal firms warn couples to first secure legal contracts and written agreements similar to pre-nuptial agreements prior to their cohabitating to ward off financial disasters in the event that their partner is unfaithful, dishonest, or both. Some live-in partners have successfully fought for "rights similar to those of married couples, in areas such as property, health insurance, pension plans, and child support[109] but neither the contract nor the living arrangements insure compatibility or happiness.

Furthermore, in sharp contrast to cohabitation, marriage adds to the economic welfare of couples and families. Studies show that men who marry typically earn more because marriage itself leads to increases in income; that is men who marry work harder, work smarter and earn more than their unmarried peers. Marriage brings along with it the expectation of accountability and fiscal responsibility that encourage the wise use of resources. Cohabiting couples in contrast are less likely to pool resources, or feel obligated to spend wisely and save or invest in the future of the household."[110]

Nearly 28 percent to 40 percent of all babies are born to unmarried, cohabitating mothers.[111] An "education gap" exists between mothers who have babies without benefit of marriage and those who give birth within marriage. More than 50 percent of new mothers without college degrees are having babies outside of marriage while only about 7 percent of college graduates are new mothers outside of marriage.[112]

Unfortunately, the majority of Americans of all ages believe that cohabitation has little to no negative effect on children.[113] This is a false promise of the decoy. It also helps explain the irony that "many people will not get married unless they can have a wedding and a savings account but are quite willing to have a child in a cohabiting relationship."[114] Data points out that cohabitation does have a negative impact on children even though more than 40 percent of cohabiting couple households are raising children.[115] In fact, children living with cohabiting adults have an increased risk for the following:[116]

- Emotional damage due to constantly changing adult parenting figures
- Physical abuse, injury, or death by mother's boyfriend
- Insecurity
- Other sociological problems

- Sexual abuse
- Lack of attention
- Poverty
- Behavioral issues in school
- Unstable family life
- Children living with single mothers or cohabiting mothers are less financially secure

It's time that Americans stop presuming that decisions made about life and love are inconsequential to self, future relationships, children's lives or all of society.

Moral Relativism

Moral relativism has been previously discussed, but never before with the proposition that it is a perilously popular decoy. Recall that a decoy has been defined quite broadly to include those beliefs, actions, or suggestions, which cause others to follow a lead without their full awareness of the decoy's hidden agendas or possible backlash. Thus, it can be argued that moral relativism is a decoy that welcomes others to support its philosophy lest they descend into judgmental criticism of others. And therein lies its pull. Few people relish the idea of being perceived as judgmental, a rigid ideologue, critical of others, or a person that just doesn't know how to get along with others. Furthermore, since moral relativism is so pervasive and convincing, it will be considered a decoy.

Moral relativism affects attitudes, beliefs and even moral positions. While many claim to practice moral relativism there are really few hard cord relativists. The majority turn into relative relativists, and in limited moral areas. For example, few people of any generation believe that it is OK to run a red light; most believe that red lights pertain to everybody! Similarly, most people would likely agree that it is not OK to dump toxic wastes into Lake Erie or Lake Superior. Most people would also agree that it is not OK to commit suicide. Yet many of these same people object to the imposition of moral standards for consenting people in select areas – especially moral sexuality. Dogmatic and principled stands are generally not welcome among many crowds including college students who "don't want to be lectured to". But we need to beware of moral relativism for many reasons.

It has been argued that there are seven fatal flaws of moral relativism.[118] They include the following:

1. Moral relativists, because of the very definition of its philosophy, are unable to accuse others of having committed a wrong. The underlying philosophy denies the existence of absolute truths that are universally true for everyone.

2. Moral relativists in theory are not able to complain about the problem of evil since they believe that neither objective good nor evil exist. Yet, many moral relativists do worry about the general downward direction this country is headed.

3. Moral relativists should not be in the business of praising or blaming since nothing in their definition of relativism is either better or worse than anything/anyone else.

4. Moral relativists are incapable of charging actions or people as being inequitable or unjust.

5. Moral relativists cannot understand the concept of improving moral beliefs and actions.

6. It is impossible to hold discussions about morals with a moral relativist.

7. Moral relativists often violate their own rule of tolerance by saying that the principled people are intolerant or judgmental.

Pope Benedict the 16th teaches us that "relativism has thus become the central problem for the faithful at the present time... In the relativist meaning (to dialogue) means to put one's own position, i.e. one's faith on the same level as the convictions of others without recognizing in principle more truth in it than that which is attributed to the opinion of the others.[119]

Therefore, this is the philosophy that produces muddled thinking about life and love in general and with regard to specific issues including cohabitation, abortion, divorce, marriage, casual sex, and more. Students falling into the trap of moral relativism will have a hard time arguing for anything founded on moral principles. Fundamental principles will be more cognizant of objective truth, good and evil, and the source of creation.

Cheating

Academic cheating is defined as laying claim to another's work, paying someone to do your work, representing another's work as your own. Cheating is also accomplished by having someone else take the exam on your behalf, bringing prohibited material into examinations, or purchasing "essays for hire." Academic honesty is needed to ensure that a student's work is his or her own.

Students most likely to cheat during college are the engineering and the business majors according to Cheating Fact Sheet Research Center. They also report that cheating does not end at graduation and resume fraud is one sign of that.[120]

Like the other decoys, cheating students copy other students' behaviors when it is to their advantage. Advantages to not cheating are obvious; students prove the degree by which they have learned new material. They also prove their reasoning and intellectual skills. These proofs positively influence social, academic, psychological and personal standing among peers and professors alike. Effort is indeed often its own reward.

Conclusion – One Last Story

Students are fooled by the decoys, not because they are stupid or ignorant, but because they are looking for affirmation in all the wrong places. We are all tempted by decoys for four primary reasons: we have various appetites that we try to satisfy; we aspire to be powerful or have influence (suggesting pride); we are afraid of loneliness or rejection; and we try to prove our worth by things we do. These powerful temptations can have very real effects on those who are not yet certain of who they are.

St. Augustine had wandered far and wide from the Church during his "emerging adult" years. In fact, Augustine roamed for many years before realizing that the path he traveled provided little by way of Truth, Joy, or Peace. After his conversion, Augustine spent time evaluating why he committed sin. One particular sin made him really think about why he had committed it! That incident involved him and other friends; together they picked most of the neighbor's harvest of pears. They didn't eat the pears, but used them to harass a nearby herd of pigs. Augustine was stumped as to why he committed this sin because he knew he didn't dislike pears or pigs or the neighbor. In fact, he had felt bad about wasting the neighbor's harvest. The pigs weren't the problem either. Finally, Augustine realized that he had committed this "stupid sin" in order to gain the "respect' and approval of a certain group of boys who had concocted the idea.

The moral of this story is to try and discover the underlying reasons for any temptations in order to prevent repeating the sin. Better yet, it is important to try and recognize the temptations for what they are in order to not commit the sin in the first place. All decoys cause us to stumble because they do not tell the truth of their sting; neither do they fortell the calamities we hear or read or see in real life. Some calamities are more private and won't evidence themselves until long after college graduation. It is important to identify the decoy long before it has its grips on you with regard to addictions, eating disorders, depression, sexual disorders, violence, despair, or failed relationships.

Reflection Questions:

1. Name the decoys present in your college culture.

2. Name some decoys that are particularly troublesome for you. Explain why you think they are so tempting. What "appetite" does it appeal to? How can you change that appetite?

3. Discuss how eating affects relationships.

4. Listed are the decoys discussed in this chapter. Which human appetite (body, mind or will) does each target for you/others?

Decoy

Advertising _____

The Internet _____

Smoking _____

Drug Abuse _____

Alcohol _____

Bullying _____

Debt _____

a. credit cart _____

b. gambling _____

Casual Sex _____

Hooking Up _____

Sexting _____

Pornography _____

Exhibitionism _____

Cohabitation _____

Moral Relativism _____

Cheating _____

Chapter Eight

PERSONALIZED
LANDMINES
AND CALAMITIES

In the previous chapter, you learned the decoys present to you and fellow peers. The sting of the various decoys will be discussed in this chapter. Of course all ages of people have their own temptations; however, your college years will reveal that you are more susceptible because your path forward is kind of a lonely one simply because you are alone. Most of you are like Adam, yearning for someone to share your life with. Discovery of this authentic love will help you forge ahead with spouse and children in tow. Meantime, your solitary and unfamiliar path for today and tomorrow will naturally be more anxious and edgy than when you travel with supportive and beloved companionship. It is true that two heads (or more) are better than one in most matters of life and love. Meanwhile you travel alone so make sure that path avoids all the possible landmines or personal calamities inserted there by different decoys. These landmines are most often responsible for causing you to miss cues that help identify your true vocation and your truly beloved.

The Personal Calamities

Personal consequences that emerge from following decoys can be ugly. Powerful addictions, sexual victimization, eating disorders, abortion, suicide, depression, violence, sexually transmitted infections, and accidental death are possible consequences that too many college students have tripped over when following the various decoys. These calamities are the direct result of failing to *civilize* appetites, desires, and fears. They are often permanent, and life altering. Most caring parents and other adults hope that their students would be spared from ever stepping on any of these landmines.

A. Abortion

Abortion is a major calamity befalling many female students. The decision to take the life of one's unborn baby comes after following *sexual* decoys. The subject has its own chapter (nine) because it has the capacity to change lives forever. Chapter nine will look at the various political and social arguments surrounding abortion, as well as its physical and emotional consequences.

B. Eating Disorders

Anorexia, bulimia and binge eating (Compulsive Overeating Disorder) are serious eating disorders that impair the abusers' physical, mental and emotional wellness. Early intervention is necessary to help prevent these disorders from completely ruining someone's life. All incidences of anorexia, bulimia and binge eating have increased significantly over the last several decades; in fact they have increased in proportion to societies' ever-growing preoccupation with thinness and self. Ironically, as personal preoccupation increases, self image and self esteem tumble and eating disorders increase!

In the United States, eating disorders have reached dangerously high levels according to some experts; the order of magnitude reached varies by source. Some sources suggest that up to 3 percent (diagnosed cases) of college women have anorexia nervosa or bulimia nervosa, unheard of generations ago. A total of ten million females and one million males have anorexia or bulimia.[1] Others suggest that 40 percent to 50 percent of female college students have varying types of eating disorders.[2] The following chart helps illustrate the rates of eating disorders in the United States.

Eating Disorder	All Males	All Females	College Males	College Females	Totals
Anorexia (diagnosed)	Slightly less than six tenths of one percent	Nearly 4 percent	Slightly less than six tenths of one percent	3 percent	10 million
Bulimia (diagnosed)	Slightly more than six tenths of one percent	Slightly more than four percent	Slightly more than six tenths of one percent	no data available	1 million
Binge Eating (diagnosed)		2x male rates[3]		2x male rates[4]	25 million
Other Eating Disorders	Bigorexia		Bigorexia: obsession with having a small, not muscular enough body.		
Over-exercising					

A significant number of college students have eating disorders; many of the eating disorders emerge around the age of 17 − 18 coinciding with the start of college. These disorders can be treated by attending to the various wellness factors. It is important that families eat regularly together in order to prevent the start of eating disorders in high school!

Women, too- often, feel they need to diet. One study (Kurth et al 1995) found that approximately 91 percent of college female students surveyed admitted to trying to control their weight through dieting even though this age group was not wholesale overweight. Of these students, 22 percent admitted to dieting often or always. This feeling of having to constantly diet is a first step toward the onset of eating disorders.[5]

Experts offer warning signs that may help detect or provide a signal for an emerging eating disorder. Students should be concerned when they observe friends develop a new or sudden preoccupation with food, weight, or calories; begin skipping meals while making odd excuses for this behavior; begin to steal food; irritability; making frequent trips to the bathroom, etc.[6] Unfortunately, eating disorders are very often associated with shame, covering up, dishonesty, and secrecy, making them hard to detect.

The various eating disorders limit the intake of nutrition, food, and calories differently but still pose dangers to the health and well being of the offender. Most eating disorders are not listed as the primary cause of death even though they are. Usually, the secondary health problems, generated by the eating disorder, cause death and therefore are noted on the death certificates as the primary contributor when in fact the eating disorder caused the secondary factor. As a result, the number of annual deaths due to eating disorders is under-reported.

Between 2004 and 2006, approximately 27,000 annual hospitalizations take place to treat the various types of eating disorders. The National Centers for Health Statistics (NCHS), a division of The Centers for Disease Control, informs us that eating disorders have the highest mortality rate of any mental illness; furthermore, the death rate for 15 to 24 year olds due to eating disorders is twelve times higher than the death rate of all causes of death for that same age group.

Without treatment, approximately 20 percent of people diagnosed with an eating disorder die prematurely from complications including suicide, development of heart problems, or other problems. With treatment, the mortality rates – due to eating disorders- reduces to 2 – 3 percent.[7] An estimated 5 percent to 10 percent of people afflicted with eating disorders die within ten years after initiating the disorder;

between 18 percent and 20 percent of people with twenty year long histories of eating disorders die. A full 30 percent to 40 percent of people with eating disorders never "fully recover" from the addiction. Unfortunately, the problem is masked by the fact that few deaths are attributed to eating disorders on death certificates. In fact, only 128 deaths due to eating disorders were reported in 2005.[8]

Anorexia is the eating disorder in which women (or men) severely limit their entire food intake, thereby starving themselves of calories and nutrition needed to maintain health and wellness. It is the refusal to maintain a normal weight for one's age and height. Anorexia is in play when a person maintains a weighs that is at least 15 percent below normal for a person's frame (BMI).[9] The person with anorexia takes comfort in seeing the weight scales fall; it becomes the one factor in their life that they have personal control over. Many people with anorexia are unhappy about their body shape and diet severely to try and alter natural contours. Anorexia can lead to severe malnutrition which contributes to amenorrhea, osteoporosis, and cardiac arrest. Anorexia is linked to dry skin, feeling cold, increased cholesterol levels, fatigue, hypertension, insomnia, hair loss, hollow facial features, gastrointestinal problems, shrunken breasts, and more. Anorexia can lead to death.

Bulimia (compulsive eating disorder) is the "recurrent inappropriate compensatory behavior taken in order to prevent weight gain. These behaviors purge food's effects from the body; behaviors include induced vomiting, use of laxatives or diuretics, self imposed strict eating restraints, and/or excessive exercise."[10] Purging provides bulimics with satisfaction and relief as they release pent up anxiety or stress. Food is always needed to purge and therefore a vicious cycle continues — eat-purge-eat-purge — in order for the bulimic to get and feel release from pent up stress or anxiety. The nature of the purging causes tooth decay; intestinal, heart, or kidney problems; acid reflux disease; gastrointestinal problems; muscle cramping; rupturing of the esophagus and/or stomach, and death. Anorexia and bulimia can disrupt friendships and family relationships; they can jeopardize a person's ability to attend to personal health and wellness — physical and mental — as well as other personal, social, and academic responsibilities.

Binge eating occurs when a person eats for comfort or security but is constantly worried about gaining weight. They may eat well but then go on starving sprees in order to lose weight or offset the caloric intake of a recent meal. The binge eating disorder does not involve purging. "A recent study of undergraduate college students found that higher levels of body dissatisfaction and eating disturbance among young people were associated with higher levels of interferences in their academic performance showing another path where eating problems lead."[11]

Compulsive exercising, compulsive over-eating, over-chewing and swallowing and "bigorexia" are also eating disorders that can generate negative outcomes and habits. The latter disorder can turn into an obsession to put on weight and muscle when a person regards his body to be too small and not muscular enough.

It has been impossible for psychologists to pinpoint why a person develops an eating disorder; they cite the following possible reasons including low self esteem, dissatisfaction with one's body image, imitation of others, social pressure, stress, anxiety, being a victim of a violent act, and depression. Did you know that date rape has also been linked with the initiation of an eating disorder – especially when the victim does not report the crime? The victim tries to "restore" personal control in order to cope with the assault and does so by initiating an eating disorder. While this measure is counterproductive, it happens all too often.

Some college students actively support and encourage types of eating disorders. They do this when they share laxatives, diet pills, or diuretics with friends or dorm mates. They also encourage eating disorders when attending Binge/Purge Parties whereby attendees come together to talk, laugh, and eat *forbidden foods* that are high in calories. Collectively, they purge the forbidden food — at the party — thereby mediating personal guilt since everybody is doing the same thing! These parties need to be boycotted.

C. Addictions: Sex, Drugs, Alcohol, the Internet, Gambling, etc.

All addictions cause people to lose control over important aspects of their lives. Addicting urges continue to beckon until they either take over someone's life or are dealt with head on and conquered. Addictions make it impossible for people to concentrate, or focus on responsibilities, interests and relationships. Addictions enslave people to the habits formed causing them to lose control over ordinary parts of their lives. Addicts suffer from the grave physical, social, psychological, emotional or spiritual consequences caused by the addiction.

Addictions are particularly troublesome when they begin by following decoys that are known as Triple A Engine Threats. These decoys offer affordability, accessibility, and anonymity. Addictions that are highly affordable, easily accessed and completely anonymous are much more "dangerous" to the addict compared to addictions that are expensive, hard to access and very visible. Addictions formed in college do not just suddenly stop at graduation! They continue until they disrupt the addict's work life or home life. Many employees have sacrificed jobs by going online at their workplace to access pornography (42 percent); or to participate in online chatting (13 percent) or gaming (12 percent); to place bets on or to watch sporting events (8 percent), to make or watch investment decisions (7 percent); or to shop from work (7 percent).[12] Vault.com estimates that Internet abuse by employees cost employers over $54 billion in lost productivity. Furthermore, addictions negatively disrupt marriages, family life, personal relationships, jobs, and/or school performance.[13]

Psychologists are beginning to argue that a "number of addictive behaviors may not even involve intoxicants such as drugs or alcohol." In fact, there is growing acceptance to label the following activities as addictions when they begin to disaffect people's personal, work, and social lives. These include: compulsive gambling, video game playing, overeating, exercise, pursuit of sex, the internet, and television viewing.[14] Workplace internet addictions have become so commonplace that employers are beginning to worry that recognizing *internet addictions* may in fact eventually protect their internet-surfing employees under the Americans with Disabilities Act.

Studies suggest that 6 percent of online users develop internet addictions; many of these habits are acquired in college. Kimberly Young reports that 43 percent of Alfred University students who had recently been dismissed from the college, failed school due to spending "extensive patterns of late night log-ins to the university computer system." Another study involving the University of Texas-Austin, found that 14 percent of students met the criteria for having an internet addiction. Internet addictions are the gateway to other addictions or abuses including online sexual affairs (cyber affairs) and pornography addictions.

Therapists have developed criteria to help assess whether or not someone is developing an *unhealthy* use of the internet. When a person's use meets certain criteria, they have likely developed an internet addiction.[15] The following set of questions assesses this possibility; the questions asked only pertain to a person's *non-essential* use of the computer or internet. This same set of questions can help assess unhealthy use of all *non-essential* online activities and electronic conversations including emails, chat rooms, Facebook dialogue, interactive games, instant messaging, other types of gaming, and more. Using the criteria, assess your own internet or online usage. If you answer more than five questions positively, you may have an emerging internet/online addiction. [16]

A.	Do you feel preoccupied with the internet? Do you think about previous online activity or anticipate the next online session? Yes or No. Circle one.
B.	Do you feel the need to use the internet with increasing amounts of time to achieve satisfaction? Yes or No. Please circle one.
C.	Have you repeatedly made unsuccessful effort to control, cut back, or stop internet use? Yes or No. Please circle one.
D.	Do you feel restless, moody, depressed, or irritable when attempting to cut down or stop Internet use? Yes or No. Please circle one.
E.	Do you stay online longer than originally intended? Yes or No. Please circle one.
F.	Have you jeopardized or risked the loss of a significant relationship, job, educational, or career opportunity because of the internet? Yes or No. Please circle one.

G.	Have you lied to family members, therapists, or others to conceal the extent of your involvement with the internet? Yes or No. Please circle one.
H.	Do you use the internet as a way of escaping from problems or of relieving a dysphoric mood (e.g. feelings of helplessness, guilt, anxiety, depression)? Yes or No. Please circle one.
I.	Have you experienced a change in sleeping habits as a result of your internet use? Yes or No. Please circle one.
J.	Have you experienced – or have others commented that you have experienced — a mood change, less enthusiasm, less energy, less responsive to friends, since using the internet? Yes or No. Please circle one.

D. Self Injury

About 17 percent of college students — 20 percent of women and 14 percent of men — report that they have cut, burned, carved or harmed themselves according to a new survey published by Cornell and Princeton University researchers. This is the largest study to date on self-injurious behavior (SIB) in the United States.[17] However, fewer than 7 percent of the students studied had ever sought medical help for self-inflicted physical injuries. Due to a severe lack of knowledge, experts are unable to ascertain exactly how many students are self injurers. The actual number is estimated to comprise less than 0.05 percent of the entire population. Experts also suggest that self injury is not very common but "is becoming at least a persistent uncommon behavior. Furthermore, it has symbolically migrated from being an activity of the fringe to an activity to those living on the edge but still unacceptable to the mainstream population." [18]

Self injury occurs in a variety of ways. Hospital records show that self injuries vary widely but include the following: self cutting, burning, branding, scratching, picking at skin, reopening wounds, biting, head banging, and hair pulling (trichotillomania), hitting oneself with hammers or other objects, and self breaking of small bones.

Lacking information about self injury, mental health experts and sociologists remain uncertain about whether to categorize self injury as a mental illness or a deviance. Classifying self injury as a "de-medicalized interpretation" groups it to other *deviances* including homosexuality, gambling, eating disorders, and drug use. Psychologists generally categorize self injury in this manner because they view it as a voluntary choice rather than an involuntary state.[19] Self injury is thought to be a symptom of other underlying impulse control disorders including post-traumatic stress disorder, anti social anxiety disorders, multiple personality disorders, and more. Some people inflict harm on themselves after learning about it through the media, the internet or books; to feel temporary relief from other tension or stress in life; as a ritual for hazing; or to be "hip." The latter suggests that self injurers may group themselves into a "subculture" that accepts self injury as a voluntary choice and lifestyle."[20]

Self injury has changed names over the last several years. Not long ago, it was called self harm or self mutilation; but today, most medical experts refer to the behavior as self injury. Note how the name change alone subtly changes how we regard the seriousness of the behavior or actions. The term self injury is the least *disapproving* of the three names. It could be easily argued that anorexia, bulimia, using excessive laxatives to lose weight, severe dieting, extreme tattooing or body piercing, even binge drinking and abusing drugs are forms of self injury. This argument has caused some therapists to conclude the new term is "misleading, overly generous, and too comprehensive."

Limited information on self injury is obtained from hospital records. These records show that all populations of people self injure themselves; the deviancy is not limited to adolescent or emerging adult populations. In fact, roughly two thirds of self injurers are reported to be older than 25 and nearly half were older than 35.[21] However, one large survey[22] involving 3,069 college students showed that "more than 41 percent of the self-injurers initiated the practice between the ages of 17 and 22; therefore nearly half began to self injure themselves in late high school and/or during college.

Self injurers tend to be female and bisexual (or those who question their sexual orientation). Asian-American populations are least likely to self injure themselves.[23] People who committed repeat incidents of self injury (SIB) exhibited the following characteristics:[24]

- Almost six times more likely to have considered or attempted suicide
- Three and a half times more likely to report a history of emotional abuse
- Three times more likely to report high levels of recent psychological distress
- Twice as likely to report characteristics of an eating disorder.

People who commit single incidents of self-injury had the following characteristics:[25]

- Nearly four times more likely to report high levels of recent psychological distress
- Two and a half times more likely to report a history of emotional abuse
- Nearly twice as likely to have considered or attempted suicide

E. College Dropout

College dropout rates have already been discussed thoroughly enough in the early chapters. It is important, however, to bring it up just once more to reinforce that current college dropout rates should be viewed as one more calamity for many college students. Too many students fail classes and coursework for all the wrong reasons. Many followed the decoys presented in chapter seven preventing them from earning a four-year degree. You have already learned that dropping out of college is costly economically, socially, personally, emotionally and psychologically. Consider this: the failure to graduate is associated with a 50 percent greater risk of suicide compared to graduating students."[26]

Unfortunately, the dropout rate seems to be increasing gradually over the decades. Consider the following. "The college dropout rates in the 1960s were one in five. In the 1990s, this increased to one in three. Now, according to U.S. Department of Education figures for 2000 through 2006, an astonishing 50 percent never graduate."[27] This dropout rate continues to climb even as cities and colleges within those cities boast of steadily increasing enrollment rates. For example, nearly two – thirds of the members of the high school graduating class of 2000 in Boston, who attended college, had not earned a college diploma within seven years.[28] This dropout rate statistic is discouraging news for many in the education business.

F. Suicide

Many college students struggle with mental health issues. You have already learned that mental problems often develop because college students (and others) take risks that deprive them of physical, social, mental, emotional, and spiritual wellness.

It is important that colleges, parents, faculty, roommates, and friends all work together to identify struggling students and then get them the necessary mental health services. Colleges continue to face "staggering" numbers of students who need counseling services for various mental health issues.[29]

Between the mid 1950s and the early 1980s, health officials began to take note of "rising suicide rates among college students. In that thirty-year span, data suggested that suicide rates had tripled among young men aged 15 to 24, and doubled for women in the same age group. These concerns sparked new research. More recently, the Lipschitz Study and the Big Ten Student Suicide Study, found that the college suicide rates (though different from each other) were consistently lower than earlier eras. The Lipschitz Study (Lipschitz et al) reported college student suicide rates ranging from 5 to 50 student suicides per 100,000 students[30], whereas the Big Ten Student Suicide Study reported suicide rates of 7 to 24 per 100,000 students.[31,32,33] Both studies show that college student suicide rates are significantly lower than suicide rates for the general population. However, suicide is the **second leading cause of death** for college students. (The leading cause of death for college students continues to be car accidents.) The Lipschitz and the Big Ten studies failed to account for the suicide rates of college dropouts; the suicide rate for college dropouts is significantly higher than the suicide rates for students currently enrolled in a university or college.

Experts acknowledge that it is critical to continue improving ways to identify students "whose impairment from depression, anxiety, substance or eating disorders puts them at high risk for suicide. These students must be enrolled in preventive treatment services."[34]

Lower student suicide rates have been attributed to the prohibition of use and presence of firearms on campuses and increased numbers of on-campus mental health facilities and services. Today, on campus mental health facilities are better equipped to treat depression or pre-existing conditions than they were before. However, concerns still exist as campus surveys reveal that on-campus facilities remain over-crowded or under staffed. Even more disconcerting to parents is that fact that 38 percent of colleges do not yet have mental health facilities even though they enroll students with preexisting mental health issues.[35] Students in these colleges will be unable to receive necessary mental health services and supports.

Parents, friends, and families, will always blame the college when their student dies on the university's watch especially when that institution failed to act on or recognize a student's cry for help. Today, many existing mental health facilities are now in place because parents put enough financial and legal pressure on universities after they failed to respond effectively to a mental health crisis.

Colleges and universities cannot be complacent with today's lower student suicide rates because their students still have plenty of mental health issues and problems. A full 39 percent of college women and another 20 percent of college men report feeling *overwhelmed* with college. A staggering number of students seek counseling services stressing out the campus mental health care facilities.[36] Furthermore, colleges report that their student populations have increasing rates of depression, eating disorders, history of major trauma, and personality problems that interfere with social and academic functioning.[37]

G. Depression

Many college students do not seek mental health help on their own because they worry about being stigmatized by peers or faculty; they lack the energy to go for help; they had tried to get help in the past but is wasn't there; they sought counseling that didn't help; they don't realize the problem; or they don't know where to go or from whom to seek help.

All students need to learn how to recognize mental health distress signals in order to get help for roommates, friends or classmates. Experts urge college students to remember that even though friends may get angry with them for trying to get mental help for the friend, an angry roommate is better than a dead one.[38] Nearly 15 percent of people diagnosed with major depressive disorder take their own life.[39] Appendix Six located in the back of the book provides a chart that outlines the warning signs of depression and suggested action items.[40] Additional information can be found also in Appendix Seven with regard to the contemporary classifications and types of mental disorders and their accompanying diseases.

H. Sexual Victimization

The majority of all rape and assault victims are college-age women; males (of any age) constitute a very small percentage of assault or rape victims.

A sexual assault or abuse occurs when someone forces sexual contact on a person without their voluntary consent. Sexual victimization can include forced kissing, fondling, rape or incest.[41] Any unwanted sexual aggression (even kissing or fondling) becomes an assault when the act is *unacceptable* to the "victim." Too many men and women receive unwelcome (without permission) fondling or kissing and in the oddest of circumstances. Any act of aggression is always wrong even if the act seems "harmless" to the perpetrator! Rape, assaults, and other types of sexual offenses violate the rights, dignity, and overall wellness of the victim. All sexual offenses are technically illegal and immoral actions.

Sexual assaults and abuse are painful, emotional experiences for the victims, who can suffer from ongoing fear, self blame, and other traumatizing emotional reactions to the initial attack. Victims sometimes begin self destructive behavior that further derails their mental and emotional health.

A National Crime Victimization Survey (NCVS) states that rape and sexual assaults are the most under-reported violent crimes taking place on college campuses (and elsewhere). Only 5 percent to 22 percent of all rapes and sexual assaults are reported to local, county, or campus police/security departments.[42] Small colleges report the lowest numbers of sexual assaults (2 percent to 4 percent) when compared to larger campuses.[43] But this doesn't necessarily mean they are safer. "Off the record" campus interviews reveal that women fail to report significantly high numbers of sexual assaults and victimizations; half of the female students interviewed in one study claimed that they had been sexually assaulted.[44] Assault victims were found to be much more comfortable telling friends about the incident; sexual assault victims are far less comfortable reporting the 'attack" to family members, authorities or police departments.[45] They are reticent to report the sexual assault to those who can do something about it for several reasons. So, sexual assaults go unreported and unprosecuted for reasons like failure to report, jurisdictional confusion, college cover-ups, and investigative mistakes. Why do so many victims fail to report the assaults?

First, male and female victims and their perpetrators often harbor "rape acceptance" attitudes. Secondly, many women are hesitant to report assaults committed by acquaintances or boyfriends because they don't want to get the perpetrator in trouble; victims may actually feel sympathy for socking it to the perpetrator. This is supported by statistics which show that 80 percent of sexual assaults are committed by someone the victim knew; yet most of these go unreported. Victims may also fear personal reprisals by the perpetrator or his/her friends. For example, the perpetrator may convince others to shun the victim. The victim also may be afraid of being accused or judged by friends, family, or others — especially the perpetrator and his friends or acquaintances. Thirdly, many victims carry around self guilt for the assault because they themselves had participated in activities with the perpetrator or other friends that involved the use of drugs, alcohol, or promiscuous/flirtatious behaviors. Victims who are depressed, have low self esteem or self confidence, are self critical, or suffer from disassociation after a previous sexual attack are also less likely to report the sexual crimes committed against them. These victims become their own enemy when they hold self blame or fear the scrutiny that comes with reporting sexual assault crimes. These women also have increased risk for becoming a "repeat" victim of rape and/or verbal coercion. [46]

Some sexual assault victims develop a degree of tolerance (rape acceptance attitudes) for sexual assaults before or after the attack. Victims or perpetrators develop rape supportive attitudes and tolerances for sexual assaults for different reasons. Many males begin to develop rape supportive attitudes after beginning to use pornography - especially porn that depicts violence as acceptable during sexual activities. When men view pornography as a normal way of life this deepens their rape supportive attitudes. Women also begin to have a degree of tolerance for being assaulted when they continually allow themselves to be used by men for sexual purposes.

Rape supportive attitudes show up when someone agrees with the possibility that there are acceptable situations in which a man might personally force someone into a sexual act! [47] This attitude allows men to hold negative opinions against the sexual victims (who report the crime). [48] These attitudes also reflect the growing acceptance of other immoral and/or illegal behaviors that may include substance abuse, alcohol abuse, deviant sexual arousal techniques and behaviors, hooking up, or the use of illegal drugs to facilitate sexual encounters. Unfortunately, the men and women who hold rape acceptance attitudes feel that some sexual victims have it "coming." Studies have found that rape supportive attitudes are more prevalent among dense groupings of men who are aggressive, who belong to social fraternities, college athletics or perceive of themselves as "macho." These men also tend to be sexually aggressive within their own personal/sexual relationships. They may coerce sexual partners (who begin to assume rape acceptance attitudes as well) by using verbal, chemical (date rape drugs or alcohol), psychological or physical measures; some admit that they participated in individual and/or gang rapes. One small study revealed that student athletes committed over 19 percent of all reported sexual assaults even though they represented less than 5 percent of the entire student body. [49]

Miscommunication, disregard for the intentions of the partner not wanting sex, and lack of consent (intoxication) are the three primary reasons why college women (and men) become victims of unwanted sexual assaults or victimizations. Males are more likely to believe that sex is the primary motivation for most rapes whereas women regard rape as a violent act of aggression because that is what it feels like to them.

Repeat sexual victimization is shockingly common. Statistics show that one fourth of all sexual victims are *repeat* victims of crimes. In other words, a disproportionately small percentage of victims experience a large proportion of the incidents. Slightly less than one fourth of the repeat rape victims experience nearly 40 percent of all rapes.[50]

Recently this scenario came very close to home. My daughter knows — told to her in confidence – about a friend's series of on-campus rapes. The rape victim felt remorse after the first attack for being intoxicated and unable to say *no* vehemently enough. She was raped by the same male student on at least three different occasions under almost identical circumstances (location, inebriation, post rape guilt, and failure to report). The victim refused to report any of the incidents primarily out of fear of reprisal and self guilt and she didn't want her parents to find out. Her friends began to lack empathy with her after the second incident. Little did the victims' friends realize that the victim may actually have begun to repress her emotions after the first sexual assault - including depression, post traumatic stress, anger, sadness, fear, anxiety, blame or shame. Repressed emotions cause some victims to respond uncharacteristically in future, but similar, circumstances. Repressed emotions can cause a person to have abrupt changes in personality, behaviors, and responses including avoidance, responding numbly, or placing blame on self rather than the perpetrator. If a victim is unable to favorably resolve the attack (via prosecution), he/ she may assume self-destructive behaviors including suicidal thoughts or attempts. These victims are also vulnerable to repeat assaults as was the case of the college woman described earlier.

Repeat victimizations often occur when the *situational contexts* are the same; for example, in the instance described previously, the assaults all took place in the same location, when the person was severely intoxicated and by the same perpetrator! Repeat victimization is more likely when the perpetrator knows that the victim has not or will not report the first sexual assault. Failing to report any sexual assaults only undermines the victims' abilities to appropriately resolve the first, or any, situation; it also serves to let the offender get away with the aggression. Sexual predators are able to identify attractive, vulnerable targets for their physical, sexual, or verbal abuse. Research suggests that women suffering from post traumatic stress or depression may be less able to recognize *risky situational cues* which normally direct her to take protective action, and so she falls prey to the predator's wiles.[51]

Exhibitionism, voyeurism, and pedophilia are reported to be the most common of all criminal sexual offenses.[52] Exhibitionism, or flashing "is often characterized by the achievement of sexual excitement through genital exposure, usually to an unsuspecting stranger."[53] Kulbarsh warns us that exhibitionists are not always older men in dirty trench coats. Most males who are actually arrested and charged with exhibitionism are emerging adults in their late teens and early twenties[54] (aka college students); many of them may be like the college football game streakers daring to running across the field during half time. There are many female exhibitionists also. Girls Gone Wild points that out all to graphically. An online search for articles about exhibitionism in college will lend information about college students' activities that none of us really need to know.

Typical exhibitionists yearn for attention from unwilling victims who express shock or surprise by the encounter with the perpetrator's lewd exposure. This reaction propels the perpetrator to offend again. It also brings them sexual excitement. Exhibitionists do not usually hide their identity! Statistics show that about 10 percent of all exhibitionists want to have personal sexual contact (touching, etc) with their victims. Exhibitionism generally involves: indecent exposure of sexual organs (63 percent), visible masturbation (51 percent), obscene language (15 percent), request for sexual favors (11 percent), and non-verbal request for sexual favors (21 percent).[55]

Pamela Kulbarsh, RN reveals that victims respond to exhibitionists in a variety of ways. Some laugh, others cry, scream, or express shock, fear or embarrassment. The exhibitionist normally thrives on all of the reactions with the exception of laughter or verbal ridicule/attack from the victim. The latter types of responses (laughter or verbal insults) actually increase the exhibitionists' feelings of inadequacy and insecurity; sometimes this causes the perpetrator to carry out additional and more aggressive/ violent crime against the victim. Exhibitionists are unpredictable because they act on uncontrollable impulses.

Dr. Joseph Carver states that "Exhibitionism is considered a sexual disorder in the field of psychiatry and psychology. In the community — it is considered a criminal act." Furthermore, he warns that exhibitionism can bring harm to the perpetrator when or if the victim's boyfriend, father, or public onlooker avenges the act. Carver warns that many exhibitionists themselves become victims of physical assault by bystanders before the police arrive or later by angry boyfriends or fathers.[56] He recommends that exhibitionists seek help from psychiatrists or psychologists who have experience treating sexual offenders. It is important to realize that there are suitable treatments and programs available for exhibitionists.

l. Date Rape

Date rape is all too prevalent on college campuses. It too often goes unreported for the same personal reasons listed in the previous section. Victims of date rape sexual assaults tell us that they thought they were raped for the following reasons: "I had impaired judgment due to drugs or alcohol; was intoxicated; I thought I wanted it but changed my mind; I found it easier to comply than to cause trouble; it happened before I knew it; I was pressured; I couldn't control myself; peer pressure; I was afraid to say no; and, I wanted a relationship."[57] This list helps to clarify why few women report date rape. Too often women seem more intent on placing self blame than placing the blame where it belongs.

We should all be shocked to read that some students admit this: "I get that sh-t (sex) for free. I just have to put a couple of drinks in them and then it's completely free."[58] He – like others — deliberately uses alcohol or drugs as "coercive tactics" in order to initiate sexual relations with a normally non-complaint partner.

Drug-facilitated sexual assaults are a fairly new and uncivilized social phenomenon. Certain types of drugs or alcohol work effectively to lower sexual inhibitions and these substances are very real threats for all young men and women in uncertain social settings.

Date rape substances erode victims' awareness, memory, and recall abilities even while increasing his or her sexual compliance. In essence, date rape drugs protect the predator from being charged with sexual assaults. This is one of the primary reasons the drugs are used. The most common types of substances used to facilitate date rape are illegal, including Rohypnol, GHB, and Ketamine. All of these drugs cause amnesia making it very unlikely that the victims will accurately recall any unwanted sexual attacks – thus the attacks go unreported! Date rape drugs have stronger effects than alcohol, even though both facilitate sexual compliance *among* the users. In one study, 7 percent of college females were purposefully drugged to facilitate sexual relations. Three percent of the male participants admitted to using drugs or alcohol to induce sexual intercourse even though they knew it to be against a woman's will. The researchers concluded that "rates of date rape drugging of women on campus may be higher than it first appears."[59] There are four principal date rape drugs.

1. Ketamine is an anesthetic commonly used in veterinary medicine; it is commonly referred to as Cat Valium, K, Special-K, or Vitamin K. This substance is odorless and tasteless so it can easily be slipped into victims' drinks. Ketamine causes victims to feel like they are in a dream; it can also cause hallucinations, amnesia, impaired attention, memory loss, delirium, high blood pressure, or fatal respiratory problems.

2. Rohypnol is a powerful sedative. It is not a legal drug in the United States. Rohypnol also does not have any taste or odor when the tablet is dissolved in drinks. Rohypnol lowers sexual inhibitions as it induces a drunk-like state; it also causes "users" to feel sleepy, relaxed, dizzy, and nauseous. It causes users to have difficulty walking and speaking. Rohypnol induces amnesia, blackouts, and loss of memory. Rohypnol's effects last for several (2-8) hours after ingestion. Rohypnol can cause physical and psychological dependency.

3. Gamma Hydroxyl Butyrate (GHB) is an illegal compound even though it is naturally produced in small amounts during normal metabolic processes. Street names for this drug include liquid ecstasy, soap, easy lay, and salty water. GHB is sold illegally in liquid or powder form. GHB causes users to feel intoxicated, happy, affectionate, playful, uninhibited, sociable, and relaxed. It also can cause users to lose physical coordination and muscle strength. Users sometimes take GHB willingly to enhance sexual experiences even though it has significant, negative side effects including nausea, headache, drowsiness, amnesia, loss of consciousness, inability to move, and difficult with concentration. GHB can cause death, especially when it is combined with alcohol or other drugs. GHB causes users to lose their natural gag reflex increasing choking risk.

4. Ecstasy (MDMA), a derivative from the sassafras tree, is illegally compounded into pills. MDMA is called the love drug because it makes users feel relaxed and happy; this drug, however, actually *inhibits* sexual performance. Ecstasy speeds up the central nervous system, increasing heart rate, blood pressure and breathing. MDMA can cause death.

Date rape substances have turned sexual assaults into gray legal disputes even though their use is clearly immoral and unconscionable. Only barbarians resort to using drugs to facilitate sex and to ensure they have a cover-up for any bad behaviors.

Males and females often have false perceptions about the other gender. Research suggests that a significant number of men expect sex if a woman sets up the date, comes to his apartment, has been drinking, is dressed provocatively, flirts with him, "gets things started", or only passively resists his advances. Studies show that men are less likely to correctly identify a woman's real sexual intentions if they themselves have previously had a number of casual sex partners, use pornography for self gratification, are narcissists, have difficulty attaching to the opposite sex, or have low levels of empathy for the other gender. In fact, research suggests there is a strong relationship between the frequency of one's misperception of sexual intent and actual sexual assault.[60]

Reasoning that it's OK to force sexual relations even if one has misread intentions, behaviors, or attitudes, never justifies the assaults. Young adult men must learn that youthful and fierce competition, risky behaviors, and enjoyment of dangerous pleasures have to give way to ordered civility and morality. Unfettered appetites only serve to instill selfishness and aggression, which cause men to consider women attractive prey. Similarly, women must help men order their passions and risky behaviors by never giving in or giving up.

J. Sexually Transmitted Infections

Satisfying sexual appetites via promiscuous sexual behaviors is the primary reason why sexually transmitted infections (STIs) are at pandemic proportions in the United States. It should be clear that there is no such thing as safe sex when having sex with someone who is infected with AIDs, has an STI, or is fertile. Furthermore, no one can guarantee 100 percent effectiveness when using condoms to try and safeguard against acquiring sexually transmitted infections or pregnancy, even though many assume this is the case. Many people – here and abroad – have been fooled into thinking that latex prophylactics won't break, leak, slip, melt, have manufactured defects, or tear. Such notions have led to the demise of large populations of people around the globe.

For years it was also thought that scientific advances would cure or wipe out all sexually transmitted infections. Westernized nations reasoned that if they could wipe out small pox, they could medically eliminate sexual diseases. These notions have not proven to be possible as evidenced by increasing numbers of new cases of sexually transmitted infections; many of these have no promise of cure. In fact, today more people suffer from STIs for their entire lifetime (65 million adults) compared to previous generations. Each year more than 15 million new cases of STIs are acquired; more than 60 percent (9 million) of these new cases are diagnosed among 15 - 24 year olds. College populations are considered to be a high risk population due to rampant promiscuity. A 2005 national survey, involving 17,000 sexually active college students, found college students, on average, have had four or more sexual partners per year without worrying about the associated risks.[61] When a person contracts a sexually transmitted infection, the immune system is compromised as it vigorously battles against the invading infection. Depressed immune systems and resulting symptoms increases a person's risk for contracting additional sexually transmitted infections. Any and all sexually transmitted infections exact huge psychological and physical consequences from the infected person's well being. The infections and subsequent treatments cost the medical health care system an estimated $14 billion annually.

Contracting a sexually transmitted infection hurts individuals psychologically, socially, and physically. Infected partners often become resentful or angry; others face depression, isolation, rejection or guilt when discovering that they are infected with a sexually transmitted infection. The physical consequences of the infections also detract from a person's psychological and social well being. Sometimes this damage is passed along to offspring as well.

Unfortunately, many infected individuals fail to disclose their sexually transmitted infection to their sexual partners. Their willingness to disclose the infection is often "dependent on the level of intimacy they felt that they shared with the sexual partner". In fact, the vast majority of people (up to 89 percent) may not feel compelled to disclose their STD with a current sexual partner.[62] The reasons for non-disclosure can be summarized with one word: self-interest. Reasons offered for failing to disclose included fear of discrimination; fear that the relationship would dissolve; fear of losing financial support; emotional (self) protection; self protection; and/or concealment of one's sexual habits.[63] Slightly more than half of the study participants believed that they *must always disclose* HPV infections whereas nearly one third were unsure about the importance of disclosing an HPV infection. Participants who understood the consequences of their STD did not show any greater obligation to inform their sexual partner about their own STD!

HIV/AIDS

One million Americans suffer from AIDS/HIV and more than another half million people have already died due to complications from the disease. "Of grave concern is the growing incidence of HIV infections in the United States among individuals aged 18 to 35, making this the population most likely to acquire HIV."[64] Many college students fail to realize that AIDS is contracted in a variety of ways including high risk heterosexual contact, male to male contact, injection drug use, mother to baby via breastfeeding, oral sex, and having contact with vaginal secretions including menses.

As of yet, there is no cure for the virus even though survival rates have improved due to new and expensive therapies and treatments. New AIDS/HIV cases continue to prove that people hold false senses of security about cures, invincibility, or sexual activities.

Human Papillomavirus (HPV)

HPV is the most common sexually transmitted infection in the United States; approximately 20 million Americans are currently infected with HPV. Another 6 million people are infected each year with this virus; furthermore, the 20 to 24 year old population has the highest new infection rates of any other population groups. Populations at high risk for contracting HPV are those that have multiple partners, practice early age sexual contact, smoke, use oral contraceptives, and have sex with uncircumcised partners.

Nearly 30 percent of all women are, or have been, infected with HPV infections – either high or low risk types.[65] HPV is difficult to contain because it is transmissible in the very early stages of the infection even when an infected person is unaware of having the virus. The CDC suggests that young people have a 50-50 chance of getting HPV when they have sexual contact with an infected person because it is easily transmitted through genital (anal, vaginal) contact with skin and mucous membranes. One of the first signs of infection is the appearance of genital warts. Normal skin cells turn into warts (abnormal skin cell development) under the influence of the virus.

More than forty types of HPV have been identified. The virus infects the genital areas of men and women, including the skin of the penis, vulva (area outside the vagina), and anus, and the linings of the vagina, cervix, and rectum. The virus is grouped into two general classifications including "low-risk" (wart-causing) or "high-risk" (cancer-causing) HPV infections. Most HPV infections (90 percent) are naturally cleared by healthy immune systems within two years,[66] however, fighting off additional new infections, or other types of infections can cause a person to develop long lasting infections which pose increased risk for developing cervical, anus, vulvae, or vaginal cancer. Men who have lingering infections are more susceptible to cancer of the penis. The following table shows the numbers of new cancer cases due to HPV. [67]

Estimated Number of New Cases Annually Due to HPV

Cancer	New Cases (women)	New Cases (men)
Cervical	3,700	
Vaginal	1,000	
Anal	2,700	1,700
Neck/Head	2,300 (not all related to HPV)	9,000(not all related to HPV)
Penis		1,000

Cervical cancer is normally *asymptomatic* until it is quite advanced; this makes it particularly dangerous. Pap smears are used to detect and screen for cervical cancers. Several vaccines, including Gardasil and Cervasil are available for young women and men between the ages of 9 to 15. These vaccines are supposed to be administered prior to beginning sexual activity.

The vaccinations target two specific high risk types of HPV – HPV 16 and HPV 18 — that cause most cases of cervical cancer. Preliminary studies show that the vaccines are highly successful in reducing the incidence of precancerous cervical lesions. Some worry that the vaccine will not prevent cervical cancer. Furthermore, the two vaccines tested showed promise in preventing only 70 percent of cervical cancers and 90 percent of genital warts. Vaccinations for the remaining strains of HPV (38 other strains) have not yet been developed or approved by the FDA. These other remaining strains cause 30 percent of the cervical cancers and 10 percent of the genital warts.[68] Dr. Charlotte Haug, Ph.D., cautions that we don't know whether the vaccine will prevent cervical cancer and death. This assessment needs more time. Dr. Haug also cautions against adopting wide scale HPV vaccination programs until there is more knowledge and facts regarding effective screening protocols, long range effectiveness studies, whether or when there is a need for booster shots, effect of vaccinations on natural immune systems, effect of the vaccine on the virulence of the cervical cancers, and more. She reminds us that "it is premature to assume these vaccines will be the cure-all; in fact "we won't know for generations whether or not these vaccines are useful for preventing cervical and other related cancers.

Unfortunately, published trials show increasing trends for precancerous cervical lesions caused by the less studied HPV serotypes.[69]

Herpes Simplex Virus (HSV)

HSV is another common sexually transmitted infection. The CDC suggests that about one in five college students will get, or already are infected with, HSV.[70] Similar to HPV, the spread of HSV happens easily because many infected persons don't realize they have the virus.

HSV is grouped into two types: HSV-1 and HSV-2. Both cause painful sores or ulcerations. HSV-1 is not considered to be a sexually transmitted infection when it shows up as the common cold sore in and around the mouth. However, approximately 15 percent to 25 percent of genital herpes (HSV-2) is caused by infecting the genital area with common mouth sores (HSV-1). HSV-2, acquired by sexual contact, causes genital sores and lesions on the thighs, buttocks, genitals, and rectum. Genital herpes is very painful when the lesions break causing open sores or ulcers. In general, infected women have more severe symptoms than infected men.

Genital herpes also cannot be cured although antiviral medications are used to boost the immune system, which helps heal open ulcers and sores. An infected person will have the virus and its accompanying flare-ups for the course of their lifetime; infected persons normally experience five flare ups during the first year following first infection. Subsequent flare ups which tend to be less frequent over time nevertheless produce painful blisters, fevers, itching, painful urination, swollen lymph nodes, pain in the legs, and tiredness. The open sores are troublesome because they make it easier to contract new and different infections (sexual and non-sexual). HSV has also been implicated as a cofactor in the development of cervical cancer. A mother can transmit the virus to her baby during childbirth; this infection can cause brain damage and other major problems in newborns. HSV increases the risk for miscarriage or premature labor.

Chlamydia

Chlamydia is a sexually transmitted infection caused by a *bacterium* known as Chlamydia trachomatis. Chlamydia is one of several possible bacterial sexually transmitted infections contracted through anal, vaginal, and oral sex. Thirty six percent[71] of all Chlamydia infections occur in the 20 – 24 year old age group; the incidence rate for this same age group is 401 infections per 100,000 people as of 2008.[72]

Chlamydia damages the female reproductive organs making it one of the leading causes of infertility. Chlamydia generally attacks silently and stealthily. Most infected women (up to 80 percent) and about half of all infected men have no symptoms. Young women have greater risk for infection due to the nature of the immature cervix.

The bacterium can silently infect and block fallopian tubes increasing women's risks for having an ectopic pregnancy, or developing pelvic inflammatory disease (PID) or infertility. Chronic pelvic pain, low back pain, fevers, nausea, pain during intercourse, abnormal vaginal bleeding are signs of infection. Nearly half of all cases of PID are due to Chlamydia. The bacterium can also infect the cervix, urethra, penis, rectal area and even the throat. Infections cause abnormal discharges, burning sensations when urinating, bleeding, swelling, and pain. These classic symptoms first begin to appear several weeks after first infection. Like HSV and HPV, Chlamydia also is linked to cervical cancer. Infected mothers can also transmit this infection to their newborn during childbirth which increases their risk for eye infections (conjunctivitis), pneumonia, and death.

Chlamydia is effectively treated and "cured" by the use of azithromycin or doxycycline antibiotics.

Gonorrhea

Gonorrhea, another bacterial STI, involves the *neisseria gonorrhoeae bacterium. This bacterium infects silently like the Chlamydia bacterium;* it also increases one's risk for becoming infected with HIV. Like Chlamydia, much of the damage is done before a person receives an accurate diagnosis and treatment. A *full 20 percent of infected men remain symptom free even though they will be able to spread the bacterium to all sexual partners.*

The gonorrhea bacterium prefers warm, moist areas of the body such as the cervix, vagina, uterus, fallopian tubes, urethra, mouth, eyes, throat, and anus. The infection damages the fallopian tubes, causing infertility, ectopic pregnancy, and/or chronic pelvic pain. Unusual vaginal discharges, urinary discomforts, and pelvic pain are early warning signs of having a gonorrhea infection. Gonorrhea also targets the male urethra and sperm ducts causing painful burning upon urination and sterility. Rectal areas of either gender can become infected during anal sex.

Gonorrhea increases an infected person's risk for arthritis, heart disease, eye infections, blindness, meningitis, and PID. Newborns infected with the bacterium are at increased risk for blindness. Infected pregnant women have increased risk for giving birth to low birth weight or pre-term babies.

Gonorrhea infects more of your peers than other age groups. Approximately one third of all gonorrhea cases involve 20 to 24 year olds;[73] the CDC reports that 112/100,000 young people are infected with Gonorrhea.[74]

Gonorrhea bacterium has become "drug resistant" over time making it more difficult to contain. Today the health care measures use the cephalosporin drug class to treat gonorrhea.

Syphilis

Syphilis is another sexually transmitted disease caused by a bacterium known as *treponema pallidum*. Syphilis is the great "imitator" because so many of its symptoms (sores on lips, external genitals) are indistinguishable from other infections. Syphilis transmission occurs when there is direct contact with a syphilis lesion. In the past, it was suggested that syphilis is spread through contact with toilet seats but this is not true. Pregnant women can pass syphilis to their unborn babies.

Today, the syphilis infection rates are considerably lower than 1940 rates, when the infection rates were highest. Until recently, health officials had held onto the hope that they would be able to successfully eradicate syphilis but thirteen thousand new cases of the "most contagious form" reported in 2008 have dashed these hopes. In fact, the CDC has observed a gradual increase in syphilis infections since 2001.

The 20 to 24 year old population group has the second highest syphilis infection rate (8.6/100,000 people); they are second to the 25 to 29 year old group (8.9/100,000).[75]

When undetected and left untreated, syphilis advances through three different stages. The first three weeks following an infection is known as stage one. During this time an infected person can develop painless lesions in the genital area which heals within several weeks. Six weeks later, more skin lesions appear along with flu-like symptoms: fever, aches, etc. The infection has progressed to stage two. The stage two symptoms generally subside within three weeks. Next, the syphilis infection enters the latent stage — stage three. Infected persons are generally pain free and comfortable at this stage of the disease progression. But it must be treated in order to avoid causing serious internal damage to organs including the brain, the central nervous system, eyes, heart, blood vessels, liver, bones or joints. Syphilis – left untreated — can cause paralysis, numbness, blindness, dementia, and even death.

Hepatitis

Hepatitis A (HAV), B (HBV) and C (HCV) are all viral infections affecting the liver. Hepatitis A is transmitted when someone ingests a feces (carrying HAV) contaminated object. This "fecal-oral" mode of transmission is not necessarily sexually transmitted, but it can be. Preventative vaccines have been developed which halt the spread of this infection.

Hepatitis B (HBV) is widely considered to be a sexually transmitted infection since it is most often transmitted when blood or other body fluids are shared or co-mingled through sexual intercourse. The Hepatitis B virus has been found in blood, semen, vaginal secretions, and saliva. This infection can be transmitted during birth to newborn babies. Persons considered to be most at risk for contracting HBV include people who have sexual relations (anal, oral, vaginal) with infected persons, have multiple partners, have pre-existing sexually transmitted infections, live with someone infected with HBV, are medical workers who are exposed to blood, hemodialysis patients, and students traveling to foreign countries with high rates of HBV. The HBV can survive for seven days outside of a human body; therefore it is easily transmitted when infected persons share needles, syringes, or other drug equipment.

Vaccines cannot cure the virus but are used to treat the symptoms of the infection which can include fever, fatigue, and loss of appetite, nausea, darkened urine, joint pain, jaundice, and more. The symptoms generally appear about three months after first exposure to the infection; many people remain symptom free for as long as six months after first infection. Infected persons recover after receiving early treatment but may have increased risk for developing chronic liver problems or liver cancer.

Hepatitis C (HCV) is transmitted person to person through the sharing of needles, receiving infected blood products, or using insufficiently sterilized instruments that pierce the skin including body piercing techniques, acupuncture, blood draws, tattooing, etc. HCV can be spread mother to unborn child via exchanges with mother's blood. Sexual intercourse is generally not considered to be the main mode of transmission of this viral infection although it is possible when blood is present (menstrual blood, break in skins, open sores, etc.). No vaccine is available to prevent the transmission of HCV.

Pelvic Inflammatory Disease (PID)

PID is often a cause of being infected with Chlamydia or Gonorrhea but it is also a stand-alone infection. Inflammation occurs when "bad" bacteria invade and infect a woman's vagina, cervix, uterus, or fallopian tubes. PID often goes undiagnosed because its symptoms can be elusive and confusing. The CDC estimates that PID goes unrecognized about two thirds of the time. The most common signs for PID include lower abdominal pain, fever, abnormal vaginal discharge, painful intercourse or urination, and irregular vaginal bleeding. When properly diagnosed, PID can be cured with antibiotics. The infection also causes infertility, which cannot be cured. Approximately 10 percent of women who have had at least one episode of "acute" PID experience infertility.

Women with a prior PID infection are at increased risk for having another infection. Each infection causes more damage to the reproductive organs. Sexually active women under the age of 25 are more at risk than older women. The nature of young reproductive organs and immature cervix tissue puts younger women more at risk for infection by harmful virus or bacteria.

Certain behaviors are known to increase women's risk of having a pelvic inflammatory infection. For instance, douching increases women's risk for infection because it eliminates or greatly reduces the amount of nature's good flora needed for a healthy vaginal tract. Douching also causes infectious bacteria to be forced up through the cervix and into the uterus. Failure to remove tampons on a timely basis can also cause pelvic infections. Furthermore, the Intrauterine Device (IUD), an abortifacient used to prevent implantation of a newly conceived life, increases women's risks for developing PID especially when she also has contracted a different sexually transmitted infection. IUDs were banned for sale in the United States in the late 1980s, but new, revised models attempt to reclaim the older IUDs' market share.

Trichomoniasis

Trichomoniasis, aka Trich or TV, is a sexually transmitted disease caused by a parasitic infestation. The parasite, *trichomonas vaginalis*, is a single-celled protozoan parasite that infests warm, moist places such as the vagina or urethra canals. The parasite can live outside of the body for several hours when it has found a moist environment including wet towels or sponges; therefore, it is possible to become infected by using "infested objects."

Trich affects both men and women although the symptoms are more obvious in women compared to men. Men experience a burning sensation after urination or ejaculation; they may also have a discharge or a feeling of irritation inside the penis. Women can see unusual vagina discharges described as frothy, yellow green, or smelly. Women also experience vaginal discomfort during intercourse, painful urination, irritation and severe itching in the genital area. These symptoms appear within five days to a month or longer after infection. Trich is curable with medication. The CDC estimates that 3 million new cases of Trich are diagnosed annually although not all cases are the result of sexual transmission.

Bacterial Vaginitis

Bacterial Vaginitis(BV) or *candidiasis* occurs when the vaginal tract has an upset of the natural balance of good and bad bacteria (yeast organisms). Candidiasis occurs when there is an over growth of the bad bacteria. BV causes abnormal vaginal discharges that are noticeably clumpy, gray, yellow, or foul smelling. Women with BV experience a lot of pain, itching, or burning sensations in the genital area or burning upon urination.

Candidiasis increases a woman's risk of contracting other sexually transmitted diseases and also facilitates the spread of this and other STIs to sexual partners. Gynecological procedures such as hysterectomies, tubal ligations, or abortions, increase a woman's risk for getting a candidiasis infection. Similarly, women who use the birth control pills, douche regularly, use feminine hygiene sprays, have multiple sex partners, ingest excess sugars or refined foods, regularly use antibiotics, are pregnant, have poor hygiene during bathroom visits (always wipe from front to back), or wear tight-fitting underwear or synthetic underwear or other tight fitting clothing, are more susceptible to getting candidiasis infections.

Limited studies show that there is an increased risk for acquiring BV when having multiple sexual partners. BV can be transmitted between sexual partners. Normally, candidiasis is more irritating and irksome than dangerous. BV can be difficult to eradicate because it is a stubborn infection. There are home and medical remedies for dealing with the infection. Men can also harbor BV in their penis and prostrate glands.

Pediculosis Pubis

This infection is caused by the parasite known as lice or "crabs." Up to three different varieties of lice can be found living off of humans — head lice, body lice, and pubic lice. All forms of lice are parasites that feed off of human blood causing itching and irritation of the area that they live in. Adult pubic lice are only about 1.2 mm in length. Of the various forms of lice infestations, only pubic lice are acquired by having direct sexual contact with the genitals and pubic hair of an infected person.

Pubic lice can also reside on "course hair" areas of the body including the head, underarms, and eyelashes. Pubic lice cause "pthiriasis" which causes intense itching of the infected area. Lice prick the skin to get at the human blood; these pricks cause severe itching, which in turn can inflame the skin tissue or cause the development of red, open sores. Pubic lice are more problematic during the winter months. Pubic lice are eradicated by using over the counter or prescription treatments.

Molloscum Contagiousum

Molloscum contagiousum is a viral infection that is triggered by the pox virus. This infection can be spread through sexual and non sexual touch. It has been regarded as a sexually transmitted disease since the late 1970s. The pox virus attacks only the outer layers of the skin. Normally this virus does not infect healthy people; it tends to occur in people whose immune systems are compromised by other viral infections including HIV/AIDS. This infection causes the eruption of small, white, pink, or flesh-colored lumps (benign tumors) or growths on the skin. These bumps tend to be round, smooth, and firm with a dimple or pit in their center. The growths can last anywhere from 6 to 12 months; they tend to go away on their own. If the lumps have grown too large or there are too many of them present on the face or body they can be removed by surgery or pharmaceutical products.

Scabies

Scabies are parasites that infest the skin causing pimple like outbreaks or rashes which tend to show up between the finger webbing or in skin folds. Scabies can be transmitted through direct and prolonged contact with the skin of an infected person. A hug or handshake does not provide sufficient skin to skin contact for transmission; however, infestation is facilitated through sexual contact, sharing bed clothes, and sharing unwashed under garments of an infected person. Scabies infestations cause inflammations which produce sensations of intense itching; the parasites can be eradicated by topical treatments.

Chancroid

Chancroid is a highly contagious yet curable sexually transmitted disease (STD) caused by the bacteria Haemophilus ducreyi. Cancroids cause ulcers in the genital area, swollen, painful lymph glands, or inguinal buboes in the groin area. Only 25 cases of Chancroid exist in the United States although this will increase as more infected persons migrate to the United States. It is very common in Africa. Left untreated, chancroid facilitates the transmission of HIV via the ulcers and open sores.

Other diseases can also be spread through sexual contact including the following: Cytomegalovirus (dangerous to newborns), Amebiasis (causes intestinal problems), and Giardiasins (Giardia is a common parasitic infection), Group B Beta Hemolytic Streptococcal Infection (also dangerous to newborns), Mycoplasma Infections (associated with infertility and spontaneous abortions), Shigella and Salmonella and other bacterial infections, and the Epstein Barr Virus (mono virus).

Infertility

Another calamity befalling too many college students, to their unawares, is the onset of reproductive infertility. This medicalized *condition* makes it difficult to get pregnant or sustain pregnancy. While infertility has been around since the early ages (even Abraham's wife, Sarah suffered from infertility until a visit from a "heavenly messenger" changed her condition), this status is increasing for a number of couples.

The reasons why infertility rates continue to increase can be directly attributed to excessive alcohol consumption, smoking, contraction of sexually transmitted infections, postponing pregnancy too long, abortion, contraception, career stressors, excess weight, eating disorders, and more.

Impaired fertility makes it difficult for approximately 11 percent of all married couples of childbearing years to achieve pregnancy within one year of trying. Infertility rates increase as women age. Studies show that females between the ages of 16 and 20 have a 4.5 percent infertility rate whereas women aged 35 to 40 experience an approximately 32 percent rate of infertility. Finally, women over the age of 40 have about a 70 percent infertility rate.[76] Infertility problems can also plague males. Approximately 40 percent of couple's infertility problems are male related, 40 percent female related, and 20 percent of the problems can be attributed to both spouses.

Infertility problems range from deficient sperm quality or quantity issues in males to endometriosis, tubal factors, ovulatory dysfunctions, cervical problems, and more in females. Unfortunately the rising infertility – of which many causes are self induced – prompt reproductive scientists to look to alternate reproductive techniques including in vitro fertilization, sperm donation, egg donation, surrogacy, embryo donation, and more, to resolve couples' infertility. The morality of these procedures has been long disregarded. We have arrived at the point where select men and women are recruited to sell their eggs and sperm (women can earn a whole lot more money than men) so that couples can have the perfect "blue ribbon" baby.

We will discuss this in more detail in chapter twelve.

Conclusion

All generations of citizens in the United States are beginning to conclude that our nation "comes up short in its commitment to social values."[77] Too often the obligation to marry, have a family, uphold personal responsibilities, respect others, work hard, and be honest and have integrity are no longer valued virtues or attitudes. As a result, social calamities will continue unless there is an awakening to truth, wisdom, faith, hope, and charity.

Until then, the Church must work to combat decoys which preach moral and cultural relativism. The efforts to combat this relativism are referred to as the Call for a New Evangelization and it began with earnest under John Paul II. Pope Benedict XVI continues that work; he instructs us not to fear even fear itself– we are to hope that we can and will resist the temptations and sins produced by modern culture.

Be the game changer!

Reflection Questions:

Once again, this chapter contains a lot of information to discuss. Look at each topic and list areas of disagreement and agreement. Discuss these in a large group discussion.

1. What information contained herein surprised you?

2. What is the difference between a decoy and a calamity?

3. Why are each of these topics presented in this chapter called a calamity.

4. Which are (if any) the bigger calamities? Or are there any differences?

5. Are there other calamities caused by college culture that are not mentioned in this chapter. List and explain.

ABORTION:
THE SOCIAL CALAMITY

Geneticists have long understood that a person's genetic code is determined when the male sperm fertilizes a female egg. The essence of who we are — including our gender, inherited characteristics, physical characteristics, and soul — is firmly in place long before we are implanted in our mother's womb. (Implantation occurs seven to nine days after conception.) Upon conception, the Creator *programs* new life with a "non-stop" mode. This *continual mode of operation* holds throughout life, from conception to natural death. It cannot be interrupted or put on hold unless another human being intervenes – in that instance life is at the mercy of the one altering the natural process.

Uninterrupted, all new life goes through a rapid progression of development involving cell division, cell multiplication, formation, and maturation. The first stage of life, called the pre-embryonic stage, takes place within the first twenty days after conception. The next stage – the embryonic stage – occurs from week three through week eight. Women at this stage of pregnancy begin to suspect pregnancy after having missed at least one menstrual period. (Natural Family Planning methods help women detect a pregnancy by twenty-one days after conception.)

By six weeks after conception, each new life has detectable brain waves. A stethoscope can pick up the heart beat of a new life just eight weeks after conception; by this time the new he or she responds to touch, movement, and sound, and begins to have alternate periods of sleep and wakefulness. He or she begins to be very active in the amniotic bubble.

The last stage – the fetal stage – is the longest and occurs from eight to thirty-nine weeks after conception. The word *fetus* comes from the Latin word for little one. By the "age" of ten to eleven weeks after conception, the baby's body is completely developed. Going forward, it just needs time, nutrition, and protection to develop into a full term baby that can survive birth.

Human bodies express our personhood. Even though a new life looks very different from older life, we remain the very same person throughout the process. Time and protection allows each life to achieve milestone after developmental milestone, both in the womb and outside of it.

How we look at life matters

While some argue that a pre-baby isn't yet a human person because of his or her dependence on a mother for sustenance, oxygen, and protection, consider the very same dependence the Chilean coal miners trapped underground in 2010 had on "another" in order to survive their ordeal. Trapped tightly in a mine they were tethered to the outside world via oxygen, food, and water lines – not unlike the preborn baby. These real world metaphors of life in the womb ought to jolt us to the realization that all human life is precious and needful of protection from those with selfish or misguided desires.

The real picture

Ultrasound technology reveals the story of what life is like inside the womb. The pictures and imagery show very young human persons sucking their thumbs; reacting to noise or light or discomfort, even

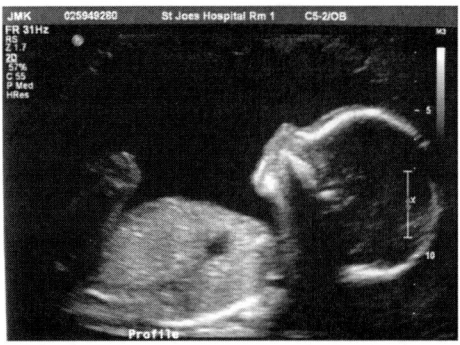

ultrasound frequencies; moving when uncomfortable; and listening to mother's voices. Unfortunately, some have been observed having to fight off abortionists' hands and tools. We have been told that abortion is pain free but ultrasounds show otherwise. *The Silent Scream*, a documentary about an abortion, clearly shows a baby silently screaming for help as her body is painfully torn apart. If she wasn't alive, she would sit like a rock in the forest, unmoving and rigid throughout the nine months of pregnancy and/or the process of the abortion.

In essence, the very tool used to help guide abortionists hands become instruments that show the horror of abortion. They also show the beauty and wonder of pre-born life. Ultrasounds prove that pre-born babies are just tiny human beings that should readily receive our love and compassion rather than revulsion.

Ultrasounds can change hearts. That is the principle reason abortion providers oppose legislation calling for mothers to see ultrasound images of their pre-born babies prior to making an "informed" abortion decision. Abby Johnson, facility director for Planned Parenthood's Clinic in southeast Texas, recently resigned from her position after witnessing an ultrasound guided first trimester abortion. First hand, Johnson saw a pre-born baby fighting for his life. This changed her pro-choice beliefs instantly bringing with it a complete conversion of the heart, mind, and will.[1] Johnson later revealed that Planned Parenthood constantly pressured her to "increase the number of abortions" and to "follow the money to determine the best direction for the clinic she managed, since abortions produce the "profits" for Planned Parenthood – not the pregnancy prevention educational programs! [2]

Dr. Bernard Nathanson, Joan Appleton, and others like them have also had changes of heart after performing many abortions. They discovered they could not go on killing any more tiny souls. Like Johnson, they found healing and forgiveness through a renewed faith in God.

The real question

When does life begin? It really is a no-brainer that life begins at conception. Yet pro-choice advocates have long tried to argue that life doesn't begin until a baby takes its first breath; it isn't a baby until it implants in the womb; it isn't a baby until it has reached the last trimester of pregnancy; it isn't a baby until it's at least three months old.... It's ironic how the definition of life seems to be a moving target even though science prides itself on being very exact. As you learned earlier, when science begins to advocate for something, it morphs from true science into political or social science.

While pro-choice advocates dodge the real question – the morality of abortion — it is crystal clear that abortion has essentially cheapened life within societies that allow it to continue and without wholesale objections. Let's talk about how abortion has cheapened life for everyone.

No physician would support or allow the cutting off of a human limb or organ just because someone no longer wants his or her limb or organ. Let's presume that the organ was not diseased, it was simply not wanted. Yet, we listen to judicial "intellectuals" argue that a pre-born baby is only a worthwhile life if the mother wants it. Abortion has also eroded our sense and appreciation for the uniqueness of each human person – born or unborn. What could have been accomplished by the exterminated lives will never be determined – but few ponder this lost talent and productivity.

Abortion has helped reduce life to accounting practices — unwanted babies are expenses and wanted babies are assets. It is no wonder that parents are not even ashamed to blurt out that their baby cost as much as their new home because he or she was "procured" by assisted reproductive procedures (ART) like In-Vitro Fertilization (IVF). Or to admit that they don't know what to do about the twenty or more frozen embryos waiting for release from icy wombs (cryogenic tubes).

Abortion gives parental desires extraordinary power that controls life and death. Ordinarily, it would be obvious to most members of any society that *desires alone* have never, and will never, be sufficiently protective of the rights of other autonomous individuals – especially those who cannot defend themselves. Someone's *desires* have never before trumped human rights – until now. Desires and self interests cannot be the backbone of civil societies. Yet abortion fosters such attitudes and vice in our society and we put up with it.

Abortion also changes the baseline by which adults regard children – especially babies. Previously children were thought of as gifts from God. Today, adults view children as a burden and an expense until they want one or until pregnancy fits in with their "planned parenthood" timeline. When this plan doesn't seem to be working according to schedule, adults spend inordinate amounts of time, energy, and resources eliminating the unplanned pregnancies, preventing pregnancy or designing, planning, and paying for genomes that will generate a "blue ribbon" baby.

Abortion permanently alters the futures of millions of unborn futures because of personal motives that fail to look out for the well being of our most vulnerable creations – the unborn. This mindset doesn't stop with babies, however. We are sure to find other people who are just as unwanted and unnecessary when we allow desires to dictate who has the right to live. It should seem rather obvious that when we begin to sacrifice the lives of our children because of self-centered obligations and desires, we have begun the descent into other uncivilized paths as well.

The abortion industry has carved itself into the economy as a legitimate business — the industry generates profits, employs large numbers of people, advertises its services, and heavily lobbies congressional offices. Planned Parenthood Federation, for example, receives approximately $350 million annually from federal, state, and county coffers. Early-term abortions cost approximately $350 per abortion while later term abortions cost approximately $2,300. Monthly *profits* at different facilities average more than $10,000 per month.[3] Planned Parenthood posts yearly profits from the abortion side of the operations[4] — so why do they receive tax dollars in that case?

Abortion has also changed the way adults view pregnancy, career, and family life. Contraception and abortion have technically leveled the playing field for women in the work world. Years ago, women wanted and expected equal work for equal pay. It appears they have accomplished that in part because of abortion and contraception. By the end of 2010, business predictions show that more women will be working than men; 40 percent of the working women will earn more than working men; more women go to college by a margin of 57 females to 43 males; female lawyers have increased tenfold and female physicians have increased three fold since 1970. Today, females govern as judges, Supreme Court justices, cabinet members, executives, governors and university presidents. Today's young women are close, very close, to equality. Women in fulltime year round jobs earned 77 percent of what men did in 2008; this is a 57 percent improvement since 1973. Many men do not earn any more than their fathers did nearly four decades ago. Over the past 50 years, men's median earning rose by just 33 percent — an average growth of just over 0.6 percent per year. Women's salaries increased much more significantly than men's. This increase occurred in part due to rising numbers of females in the workforce holding white collar positions.[5] Despite the leveling of the playing field, women still wonder if they are happy. A special *Time* magazine report concludes they are not happy.[6]

Where are we at today?

For more than three decades, Americans have debated and discussed whether or not abortion is a good thing, a bad thing, or neither. The debates haven't really been able to change the fact that this country persistently protects a woman's right to choose an abortion. Tax dollars are also used to financially support the abortion industry despite the fact that this use violates many citizens' religious and moral consciences.

Abortion continues to be one fight that the pro-life cause cannot compromise on because it directly involves the taking of an innocent human life. And so a great divide exists in this country. The only way out of this dilemma is prayer, sacrifice and a compassionate but truthful witness about the horrors of abortion. We have to take the debates out of the hands of the political and social gate-keepers and take the real facts, pictures, and stories to the younger crowd — college students, high school students, and young married couples.

Abortion advocates have failed to meet all of the many promises made since the late 1960s. In fact, abortion has not eradicated back street abortions or poverty. Nor has abortion become rare. It has not improved marriages or relationships. It has only created empty arms, empty hearts and empty classrooms. Yet, it continues to be a powerful decoy and calamity all rolled into one.

The pro-choice arguments tend to avoid moral questions so let's take a look at some of their arguments and disprove them one at a time.

What do the people think?

Poll numbers show that support for abortion is slipping slightly however it still has "powerful" political and popular allies that are vigorously fighting this trend. The 2010 Marist Poll, the 2009 Gallup Poll, the 2009 Pew research survey report less support for abortion among adults. The numbers of abortions performed are also lower than previous decades. The downward trend has been fairly steady since the 1990s. Abortion clinics are closing due to lack of abortionists to do the procedures, shrinking revenues, and fewer clients.

The following charts show a quick snapshot of the various trends mentioned earlier.

Marist Poll	Americans	American Catholics	American Millennials	Catholic Millennials
Is abortion morally wrong?	57% - wrong 19% -Morally acceptable 24% - not a moral issue	62% - Morally wrong 39% Morally acceptable or not a moral issue	58% - morally wrong 20% - Morally acceptable 22% not a moral issue	66% - morally wrong 34%- Morally acceptable or not a moral issue

The Gallup Poll results of 2010 (below) reported that "for the first time since they began asking the question more than 14 years ago (1995), a majority of U.S. adults identified themselves as pro-life." These new poll results "represent a significant shift from a year ago!" Up to now, the Gallup poll had not seen this high of a percentage of Americans who identified themselves as pro-life. The numbers suggest that almost the same number of Americans believe that abortion should be illegal in all circumstances as those who say it should be legal under any circumstances. "This is a sharp contrast from previous polls which had shown Americans leaning toward unrestricted abortion."[7]

Gallup Poll[8]	2009	2008	2002	2001	1995
Identifying themselves as pro-life	51%	44%	46%	42%	33%
Identifying themselves as pro-choice	42%	50%	49%	48%	56%
Abortion should be illegal in all circumstances	23%				
Abortion should be legal in all circumstances	22%				

A third national survey (results on opposite page) conducted by the Pew Research Center recorded an eight percentage-point decline (since August 2009) of those who support legal abortion in all or most cases. Support for the two broad positions is now about even, sharply different from most polling on this question since 1995, when the majority typically favored legality.[9]

Pew Research Center Poll[10]	2009	2008 (Aug.)	1995
Abortion should be legal under any circumstances	18%	17%	59%
Abortion should be legal in most circumstances	28%	37%	
Abortion should be legal in a few or no cases	28%	26%	40%
Abortion should be illegal in all circumstances	16%	15%	

Neither side wants to lose the battle for the hearts and minds of Americans so tempers flare at different junctures depending on who has the momentum. At the present time, the momentum seems to be turning against unrestricted abortion.

The 2010 Super Bowl featured an ad with Tim Tebow, NFL newcomer and his mother Pam. She told the viewers that her doctor had advised her to have an abortion "to save her own life" while pregnant with Tim. She chose to ignore the advice and gave birth to him; Tim responds with heartfelt gratitude that his mother was courageous and gave him life. The advocates for abortion came out swinging against the Tebows, the organization who sponsored the ad, and the network for running the *inflammatory anti-life message*. Choice only applies to one side of the aisle apparently.

Unfortunately, you have been mostly conditioned to think of abortion as a woman's right to choose. You have been told it is necessary because contraception doesn't work all of the time. You have been taught that abortion is a responsible way to prevent unplanned births. You have been told abortion is safe. You have been told that abortion is not a moral dilemma. These are all untruthful decoys that we will discuss next.

Have you heard the following adage? *"Fool me once, shame on you, fool me twice shame on me, fool me thrice, shame on both of us; and whoever deceives me once, God forgive him; if twice, God forgive him; but if thrice, God forgive us, because we could not beware."* God continues to forgive mothers who have been duped into having an abortion; it is necessary to have the humility to admit wrong doing and to ask for forgiveness. God's love is unconditional; but we have to accept it!

Are abortions safe for mothers?

Millions of women who have had abortions often discover that they face a new emotional dilemma that doesn't seem to go away. This dilemma is so commonplace that it has been given a name: Post-abortion Stress Syndrome. Post abortion emotional dilemmas can also affect the men involved with women who've had abortions. While pro-choice advocates try to dismiss the reality of the syndrome, too many women have reported the same symptoms time and again after having abortions. The word has gotten out friend to friend; as a result new organizations have been created that sponsor speakers and workshops, publish books, and counsel women who have had abortions. These avenues can't be censored by media that solely promote abortion. Studies also help prove that women have increased risk for depression, suicidal thoughts, and anxiety following an abortion. Symptoms of Post Abortion Stress Syndrome include the initiation of eating disorders, brief psychotic episodes, self-punishing behaviors, failure to bond with those who love them, and other emotional difficulties. Abortion can endanger a woman's emotional well being.

A Norwegian study reported that younger women who had abortions "clearly developed increased rates of depression" even though the authors could not explain the reasons for this increased risk after accounting for all confounding variables. Abortion is very widespread and "socially acceptable" in Norway; in fact by the time 1,000 Norwegian women reach the age of 50, they will have had a cumulative number of 470 abortions (47 percent of women have abortions). The Norwegian study conceded that "women who terminate pregnancies would *probably benefit* from post-abortion counseling."[11]

A New Zealand study also conceded that "abortion seemed to be a risk factor for inducing poor mental health including the likelihood of depression." However, the authors blamed the "degrading mental health of post-abortive women on the nation's overly-tight abortion restrictions. They stated that negative social stigma and negative sentiments about abortion were to blame." Researchers for both studies admitted surprise by the emotional effects after abortions.

A Finnish study reported that women who have abortions have increased risk of suicide compared to women who have given birth. Results from the study show that the risk of death from suicide within the year of an abortion was more than seven times higher than the risk of suicide within a year of childbirth. This finding was consistent with results showing that "undisturbed pregnancies actually reduced the risk of suicide."[12] The authors of the study concluded that "Abortion might mean a selection of women are at higher risk for suicide because of reasons like depression. Another explanation for the higher suicide rate after an abortion could be low social class, low social support, and previous life events or that abortion is chosen by women who are at higher risk for suicide because of other reasons. Increased risk for a suicide after an induced abortion can, besides indicating common risk factors for both, result from a negative effect of induced abortion on mental wellbeing. With our data, however, it was not possible to study the causality more carefully. *Our data clearly show, however, that women who have experienced an abortion have an increased risk of suicide, which should be taken into account in the prevention of such deaths.*"[13]

Dr. David Reardon (Elliott Institute) found evidence supporting his suspicions that "abortion is harmful rather than helpful to women" after conducting an examination of the medical records from more than 173,000 low-income California women who had abortions or gave birth in 1989. The results of the search found that women who had abortions were more likely (2.6 times) to commit suicide than those who had given birth. The average annual suicide rate per 100,000 women was 3.0 for delivering women, compared to 7.8 for aborting women; the national average suicide rate for women between the ages of 15 and 44 is 5.2 per 100,000 women. "This shows that abortive women have a higher suicide rate than women in general, and giving birth actually reduces women's suicide risk. The data clearly shows what we have long suspected: that abortion is harmful rather than helpful to women."[14]

Emerging data also suggests that post abortive fathers also have increased risk of suicide suggesting that many men are also extremely regretful of their partner's abortion.[15] Some fathers will never know that they were even a father-to-be. Others share complicity in the abortion decision as they prompted, coerced, or recommended that their partners have an abortion. Others share complicity when they fail to provide much needed emotional and physical support for their pregnant partner. Therefore it is understandable that men are also affected by abortion.

Chinese women have the highest suicide rates of women around the world; 56 percent of all female suicides around the world take place in China. The victims are mostly young rural women. China is the only country in the world where more women die from suicide than men. "Given the known link between abortion and suicide, can there be any doubt that maternally-oriented Chinese women coerced by their families and communities to participate in abortion are more likely to commit suicide?"[16]

Post Abortion Maternal Mortality Rates

Abortion advocates make the claim that abortions save women's lives; similarly they also claim that abortions are safer than pregnancies. Are these true?

During the late 1990s, the Kaiser Family Foundation claimed publicly that abortions are one of the safest surgical procedures in the United States. The Kaiser Foundation uses data from the Centers for Disease Control to make this claim. CDC data reports one maternal death due to abortion for every 100,000 abortions. This rate, 0.001 percent, would certainly be a near zero risk-free rate if true. The CDC data for maternal death seems suspect because even very safe surgical procedures normally report at least a one percent risk factor. CDC data also reports that the risk of maternal death due to pregnancy is ten times the risk of death due to abortions: 10 deaths per 100,000 women (100 deaths for every million pregnancies). We will contest that number shortly.

Other risk factors that the CDC fails to mention include the health risks — besides immediate death – of women who had abortions. The overall surgical complication rate attributed to abortion is estimated at 10 percent to 15 percent. Risks to women's health include perforated bowels, heavy bleeding, secondary infertility, and other problems. Abortion has also been linked to increased risks for breast cancer. In fact three states – Minnesota, Mississippi, and Texas — mandate pre-abortion counseling about the increased risk of breast cancer due to abortion prior to having the procedure. The risk for breast cancer is 30 percent higher for women who have had an abortion compared to women who have not had an abortion.

The CDC numbers used to compare death due to abortion and death due to pregnancy seem faulty at best and downright deceptive at worst. First, it is important to realize that the data used for abortion deaths do not separate data for early and late term abortions. The risks of death from late term abortions are statistically higher than the risks of death from early term abortions. However, since the numbers are combined, the heavier risk is diluted by the large number of early month abortions with lower risks.

Secondly, it is important to know that maternal deaths from abortions should be compared to maternal deaths after live births excluding troublesome factors such as tubal pregnancy, molar pregnancy, induced abortions, and natural abortions (miscarriages) because none of these pregnancies proceed to term or live birth. Excluding these conditions, Dr. and Mrs. J.C. Wilke , authors of *Why Can't We Love Them Both*, quite successfully argue that maternal mortality due to pregnancy and delivery drops below 4.7 deaths per 100,000 when these factors are taken into account.

Third, even though 4.7 deaths per 100,000 women are still higher than the 1/100,000 (death due to abortion) reported by Kaiser/CDC, it is important to know that the CDC lacks accurate data regarding abortions and maternal deaths. Their abortion statistics differ significantly from those given by the Guttmacher Institute (a division of Planned Parenthood Federation of America) for abortion by a factor of 20 percent. The statistics for both can be found in the Appendix Eleven. It's troublesome that the two agencies' numbers are so different. (Worldwide rates of abortion can be found in Appendix Twelve; the ranking is from highest numbers of abortion per population densities to lowest rates.)

Fourth, we know that real statistics about maternal death due to abortions is limited because abortion is rarely, if ever, cited as the cause of death on a death certificate for privacy and other reasons. Similar to eating disorders, the underlying cause often is unreported on death certificates. Instead, post abortive maternal deaths are attributed to the medical condition women present when arriving at the emergency room, such as septicemia (blood poisoning); pelvic abscess due to perforation of a woman's uterus or bowel; fever; hemorrhaging; blood clot; blood loss; failure to clot (disseminated intravascular coagulation); convulsions; cardiac arrest; urethra, bladder or intestinal damage; suicide attempts; pulmonary thrombo-embolism; or amniotic fluid embolism.

Several abstracts recently produced evidence of four post-abortion deaths linked to two rare bacteria known as Clostridium sordellii and Clostridium perfringens; the bacteria cause fatal toxic shock in the infected women.[17] The authors offer no clear explanation as to the bacteria's medical or epidemiological sources. The abstract reinforces the possibility that the cause of death cited on death certificates rarely finger abortion as the primary cause.

Data from other countries is often more relevant and factual because they actually run numbers on these types of risks as compared to the United States. Finland, a country with socialized health care, reports the following unadjusted morality rates for maternal death for 100,000 women.[18] Their data clearly disproves that abortions are safer than pregnancy, or safer than pregnancy with live births, or safer than pregnancy that ends in miscarriage or ectopic pregnancy. Yes, abortion is *safer* than all the anomalies of pregnancy added together but that comparison would be obviously flawed since most abortions occur during the early months of pregnancy.

Maternal death after live birth	27/100,000	
Death after miscarriage/ectopic pregnancy	48/100,000	
Death after abortion	**101/100,000**	**highest**
Death during pregnancy	75/100,000	

Finally, it is important to know that the Kaiser Foundation statistics fail to take into account the number of human babies killed during each abortion; for every abortion, one baby dies. Therefore, for every 100,000 abortions, 100,000 babies' lives are lost along with 1-100 maternal lives. Using these numbers, the death rate due to abortions is slightly more than 50 percent! Approximately 100,100 deaths occur for every 100,000 abortions. ($100,000/200,100 = 0.50$)

The Contradictions

Abortion advocates introduce many contradictions into their argumentation, still many people are beginning to see through the fog they have created. For example, advocates argue that abortion is safer than pregnancy yet we see ambulances parked out in front of abortion clinics. They argue that abortion is only for necessary circumstances but then we hear stories about women having three or more abortions. We also know of people who aborted a baby because it was the wrong sex, the wrong time for pregnancy, and the wrong partner.

The advocates claim that fetuses do not feel pain but then we see the horrible, bloody pictures of body parts and begin to wonder if that is true. Ultrasound imagery proves that pre-born babies do feel pain. Aborted baby bodies also evidence trauma having extended fingers and toes.

People hear stories about aborted babies born alive, inhumanely dumped in a bucket, and left to die. We also hear about the nurses who can't stand the fact that the baby is alone but alive in the bucket and picks him or her up and cradles the baby until death, which may take as long as thirty minutes or longer to come. Why do abortion advocates argue that we still must not intervene to save these "born-alive" babies' lives?

We hear advocates argue that abortion should be legal for all months of pregnancy, even up to the day of natural delivery. The technique used – partial birth abortion – completely reveals the lies underneath the statements that abortions are necessary to save the life of a mother. If she can undergo a surgical procedure such as a late term abortion, it is likely she could survive birth given our 21st Century advances in medical technologies. In fact new medical advances and technologies allow doctors to try and help both mother and baby when mothers are faced with real life threatening illnesses or disease. Mutually beneficial dates for delivery are drawn up so mother and baby both have a high probability for survival. The late Pope John Paul II saw how the power of abortion severs the connection with, and the recognition of, the other that defines us as persons. We need to wake up to this realization as well.

Advocates who argue that it's not a baby lose their point when women give premature birth to a 22-week-old fetus and the baby survives. And then we hear stories about young girls taken to abortion clinics by friends or authority figures without parental knowledge or approval, yet the same girls can't get their ears pierced or throat cultured without their parents' permission. In most states before a physician, nurse or other person can provide medical or surgical treatment to a minor, the parents must give consent. However, this consent evaporates for the exception clauses including treatments/procedures in areas of alcohol and drug treatment, sexually transmitted infections, abortions or contraception services.[19]

The many contradictions help reveal the lies and half truths of abortion. And then there is the most recent legislative contradiction of all — the same states that support a woman's right to choose pass legislation called the Prenatal Protection Act. This law allows states to convict someone for two homicides when his or her deliberate actions take the life of a pregnant mother resulting in her death and/or the death of her unborn baby. Texas passed a prenatal protection law in 2009 joining the ranks of twenty-eight other states that consider the killing of an unborn child and his or her mother by violent means to be two homicides. Fifteen of these states, including Texas, extend this protection for the entire term of prenatal development. In thirty eight states, parents can sue for the wrongful death of an unborn child."[20] How much more contradictory can we, as a society, get?

This gets us to the point where abortion assists social engineering. Let's examine that next.

Eugenics and Abortion

Eugenics is defined as measures that allow selective breeding for purposes of improving the human species by encouraging or permitting reproduction of only those people with genetic characteristics judged desirable. Eugenics fell out of favor after the Nazi period of terror – or did it?

The United States utilizes abortion as a tool for eugenics when used to create a disabilities-free society or a poverty-free society. Let's spend some time analyzing this statement.

Our youngest daughter, Kyra Therese, happens to have Down Syndrome. Since her birth we have awakened to a world that actually includes people with special needs. Prior to her birth we were oblivious to this reality. Since Kyra's birth, we have had the opportunity to meet many other parents whose children have a smorgasbord of disabilities and needs. We have also awakened to the fact that many other people are not sympathetic to children with special needs, nor do they regard special needs as very special. Each family we have talked to can relate stories of hostility shown to them or their children.

Kyra attends a large public school that has few children with Trisomy 21.[21] While there should be fifty or more children her age with this specific disability in the entire school district, given the incidence of the disorder, in fact there are less than ten. This isn't a case of being in the wrong school district; it is a case of parents given a prenatal determination of the genetic disorder who largely decide (or receive pressure) to terminate the pregnancy. "A systematic literature review shows that preborn babies diagnosed with Down Syndrome have very high termination rates, at least 92 percent! Termination rates vary by diagnosis and/or the disability."[22]

It is important to realize that there are actually well-respected people who actively push disability-free societies. Peter Singer, Decamp Professor of Bio-Ethics at Princeton University, is one of those people. He has made the following public statements: [23]

- Babies are not persons; "the life of a newborn is of less value than the life of a pig, a dog, or a chimpanzee."
- He would kill disabled babies if it were in the "best interests" of the family, because he sees no distinction in the child's life whether it is born or not.
- "Many people find my comments shocking, yet they support a woman's right to have an abortion." This statement by Peter

points out one more contradiction among abortion advocates.

- I would support killing a disabled baby.[24]
- "No newborn should be considered a person until 30 days after birth and that the attending physician should kill some disabled babies on the spot."
- "Human babies are not born self-aware, or capable of grasping that they exist over time."

The Groningen Protocol expresses similar sentiments. This protocol permits doctors to end the lives of babies born with disabilities or terminal conditions in the Netherlands. Up to 8% (80 – 90 per year) of all infants who die in the Netherlands (all were terminally ill or have very serious disabilities) die by the hand of the doctors.[25] Wesley Smith reminds us that the Groningen protocol seeks to "normalize infanticide by bringing the practice out of the shadows and into the light of day. Under this thinking, it isn't the killing that is wrong, but the secrecy." He gives further example of this lunacy by highlighting the case of a Dutch woman who killed four of her infants and was arrested for committing "infanticide." [26]

Today much of our society believes "that it is more responsible to terminate a pregnancy than to have a child whose health may be in question."[27] This constitutes eugenics! And we practice it on different populations of people as well.

Margaret Sanger intended to limit the African American population by administering birth control measures and recommending abortions. She fully supported the notion of eugenics when she formed the Planned Parenthood organization. Today, many social scientists and health officials believe that abortions are necessary in order to eradicate poverty. The same social scientists report that minority populations have excessive layers of poverty. Eugenics rears its head when officials link the two problems with one remedy — abortion.

Several years ago, a social worker/civil rights leader was shocked to discover more than 17,000 aborted babies in a dumpster outside a pathology laboratory in Los Angeles. Worse yet, she noted that approximately 80 percent of the fetus' were African American.[28] It should concern everyone that minority women are in the bull's-eye for targeted abortion marketing. Statistics support these statements. Minority women have a disproportionate number of abortions compared to majority white women. Thirty six percent of all abortions performed in the United States occur among minority women populations even though they represent only 13 percent of the child-bearing female population. African American women have five times more abortions than white women. Since 1973, over sixteen million African American babies have been aborted. This is a "tremendous loss for a minority group of people."[29] Furthermore, even though African American women have only one third of all U.S. abortions, more than 49 percent of the reported deaths due to abortion are among African American women.[30] Planned Parenthood should be very concerned about the lopsided nature of these statistics and work to ensure that poor or minority populations are not targeted for exploitation.

The Numbers

U.S. abortions have been on a gradual decline for at least the past decade; the highest numbers of abortions were performed in the late 1980s and early 1990s but the annual numbers of abortions performed have been sliding ever since. In total, since abortion was legalized in 1973, over 52 million U.S. babies — 52,008,665 to be more exact — have been killed by abortion through 2005.[31]

Planned Parenthood clinics have been forced to close due to lack of abortion providers or due to lack of clients. Operation Rescue reports that 2,200 abortion clinics were in full operation in 1991. This means that there were an average number of forty four clinics per state back then. Today Planned Parenthood operates with only 713 clinics, an average of 14 clinics per state. This represents a 67 percent decrease in sites. It is no wonder they are panicking and rancorous.

The U.S. abortion rate hovers around 22 percent; this means that more than one-fifth of all pregnancies end in abortion in the United States. Internationally, the U.S. abortion rate rests mid-range between Russia and Panama. Russia has a very high abortion rate (over 50 percent) while countries like Panama have a low abortion rate (less than 1 percent). The total numbers of abortions performed in the United

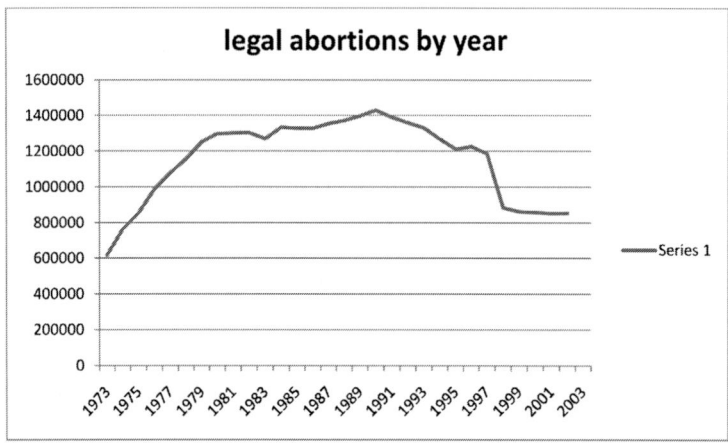

States, however, are significantly higher than in nations with very high abortion rates but low populations – such as Finland. The U.S. aborts – on average — 1.2 million lives annually (since 1973) however the annual numbers of abortions are dropping below 900,000 as shown in the chart above. Imagine if, in the blink of an eye, a city with approximately one million people just disappeared! That is basically happening every year in the United States.

Asia performs more than twenty-six million abortions annually in part because of its high population density. China alone aborts nine million lives annually. Forty six million abortions take place annually throughout the world; this translates to 123,000 daily abortions worldwide, or one abortion every second somewhere in the world. European countries face the dilemma where their numbers of annual abortions exceeds the numbers of their live births[32] and they have below replacement population growth.

Abortion Procedures: Chemical or Surgical

Before concluding this chapter, we must take a look at the abortion techniques. Eighty eight percent of all abortions occur in the first twelve weeks of pregnancy. This means that nearly 200,000 babies are aborted later in the pregnancy. In fact, the Guttmacher Institute provides the most comprehensive data with regard to abortion in the US; they show that more than 12,000 babies are terminated after viability (21 weeks)!

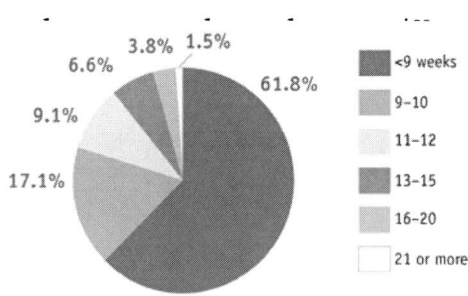

*In weeks from the last menstrual period.

Guttmacher Institute

Women have two options when choosing to have an abortion: a chemical/medical abortion or a surgical abortion. The chemical/medical options are limited by the gestational age of the fetus. Chemical/medical methods typically administer steroids — methotrexate and mifepristone — which blocks the hormone progesterone, which is necessary for the continuation of all pregnancies. Normally, the steroids effectively terminate pregnancies when the pregnancy has progressed for only a few (5-7) weeks. The fetus subsequently dies in the womb.

RU486

RU486 (Mifepristone or Methotrexate) is used to perform chemical (medical) abortions. It is different than emergency contraception in that it is more potent. **Early Option** or **Mifeprex** — brand names for the steroid methotrexate — is administered during chemical/medical abortions. The success rate of RU486 approaches 60 percent when used alone. This effectiveness rate is quite low and therefore RU486 is most often used in combination with another steroid, Misopristol. This additional steroid is generally administered within 48 hours after first administering the RU486. When both steroids are used within the first seven weeks of pregnancy, 92 percent of women had complete abortions; when used through the ninth week of pregnancy only 77 percent of women had a complete abortion."[34]

Side effects include nausea, vomiting, diarrhea, dizziness, fatigue, abdominal pain, uterine cramping, and vaginal bleeding or spotting. The bleeding generally last for an average of 9-16 days after starting the chemical dose, however, up to 8 percent of women experienced some type of bleeding for 30 days or more.[35] RU486 has already been linked to at least eight deaths in the US since gaining FDA approval, causing some physicians to withdraw their support for its continued use.[36] The death of Holly Richardson prompted her father to call for the banning of mifepristone usage in the United States; his unsuccessful efforts have been dubbed Holly's Law. *Banning* RU486 has limited support from physicians such as Dr. James McGregor, visiting professor of OB/GYN at USC who states: "because pill based abortions appear to be far riskier than surgical one, clinics should reduce or eliminate the use of RU486."[37]

Emergency Contraception (Morning After Pill)

Emergency contraception uses higher than normal doses of the birth control pill in order to prevent implantation or prevent pregnancy in women. It may also involve lower doses of RU-486. The emergency contraception – also known as the morning after pill – must be taken within five days after having sexual intercourse. Occasionally, physicians may implant an Intrauterine Device (IUD) instead of prescribing the higher dosage pills.

The emergency contraception drugs contain higher than normal doses of progestin (Plan B) or combination estrogen/progestin pills. The drugs prevent ovulation, impede the normal transport of the egg toward sperm, or cause the lining of the uterus to become inhospitable for implantation of a fertilized egg. The emergency contraception acts as an *abortifacient* when it prevents implantation of a fertilized egg or disrupts an implanted life.

The Copper T IUD is inserted into the uterus to kill sperm but also renders the uterine lining inhospitable for implantation of a fertilized egg. Like the emergency contraception drugs, this device has the capability of acting like a contraceptive when it kills all sperm thereby preventing pregnancy or as an abortifacient when it prevents implantation of a newly fertilized egg. The older IUD models were notoriously linked with causing pelvic inflammatory disease (PID) leading to female infertility.

Chemical Abortions

Saline abortions – or salt poisoning — are techniques first developed in the concentration camps of Nazi Germany. These types of abortions were widely used in the first decade after Roe V. Wade to terminate early pregnancies. During this type of an abortion, salt is injected into the amniotic sac of a pregnant woman poisoning the baby as he or she swallows. This type of an abortion causes convulsions, bleeding, edema, and ultimately death, within several hours of injection. Mothers normally deliver a dead fetus the following day. [38]

Surgical Abortions

Approximately 99 percent of all recorded abortions are performed by surgical means including suction aspiration, dilation and curettage (D&C), menstrual extraction, dilation and evacuation (D&E), and dilation and extraction.[39] All of these methods employ tools and equipment that break, suck, or slice away at the fetus' head and brain, legs, arms, spine, and chest. Each body part must be removed through a dilated cervix. The abortionists' tools comprise an arsenal of weapons, including vacuum or suction tools, curettes (looped steel knife), pliers, forceps, and scissor-like devices. The business is as grisly as the tools used.

What Can You Do?

There is plenty for you to do to help end this legal slaughter of innocent babies.

First, become convicted that all life – unborn, adolescent, toddlers, special needs, sick, homeless, the poor, the elderly, middle age, emerging adults – has meaning and purpose. Human life must not be expunged deliberately or reduced to meaninglessness by any means or devices or desires. It is always important to realize that legality of a matter does not guarantee its righteousness or morality.

Volunteer to help at crisis pregnancy centers; donate money to pro-life causes; write your legislators; give witness to friends and family members.

Also, seek out help for friends who face an unintended pregnancy. When you discover that a friend has had an abortion, be aware of the possibility that she may be suffering from post abortion stress syndrome. Several of the symptoms were described earlier but they include depression, feelings of guilt, anxiety, increased stress, the initiation of self destructive actions; or suicidal thoughts. Learn how to be an effective, compassionate friend from experienced pro-life counselors. Pray daily for the end to legal abortions and for spiritual healing of this nation. Pray also for the spiritual healing of all post abortive men and women. Finally, pray that our leadership turn to God for wisdom and understanding.

Reflection Questions:

1. What is your attitude toward abortion? Friends? How was that formed? What impacts your attitudes?

2. How would you convince someone not to have an abortion? What would you say?

3. What is an abortifacient? Did you realize that hormonal contraceptives are abortifacients? How does that affect you?

4. Do you believe that life begins at conception? Why/why not?

Chapter Ten

The Marriage Vocation

One of the most important choices we will make in life is choosing a vocation. In order to choose anything well we have to be mentally and emotionally fit. We also must be well prepared to transition into our chosen vocations. Choosing a spouse (if marriage is your future vocation) will be another critical decision for you to make– and it is a free choice! After all, when people marry they plan to spend the rest of their lives with that person, have children with them, and grow old together. In effect, choosing to marry someone should be consistent with the desire to wear ourselves out for the other in this lifetime. This choice should also be consistent with our hopes, dreams, goals, world view, and belief system. It is important that we know what we are doing and why we are doing it!

What is Vocation?

The term vocation has several classic definitions. A secular understanding of vocation is that it is a job, work, or profession – especially those *that require special types of commitment and education* such as physicians, lawyers, engineers, or, therapists. A second understanding of the word gets closer to the definition pertinent to this section of the book. Vocation is the special feeling or calling that allows a person to follow Christ more closely. It is a *specific type* of work that is designed (not chosen) for you. Vocations allow us to witness to the Christian life; they aim to order temporal things according to God. A carefully chosen vocation enables us to inform our world about the power of the Gospel, and to commit ourselves to the evangelical counsels appropriate for our particular state in life.[1] Thus, our vocation - either married life, religious life, or single life - predisposes us to be the best witness about God; life and love; and the Gospel.

Oftentimes, vocation is limited to mean the entering of a religious life, but that is too narrow of a definition. It is through marriage that most of us will *walk into* our vocation. This vocation entails becoming a holy spouse first, a parent (mother/father) secondly, and an employee after that.

What is Marriage?

Marriage is a vocation – this means that there has been a summons or a calling followed by our assent to this state of life. A spouse-to-be acknowledges that there is a higher purpose when he or she discerns and commits to the vocation of marriage. The Catholic Church teaches that marriage is an awesome blessing from God; that it is a natural institution established for the good of man, woman, family, and society; and that it is "intended to be the permanent, faithful, fruitful, and mutually-consented-to union between one man and one woman." But it's even more than that. Marriage has a purpose and that is twofold. Marriage is ordained for the mutual good of the spouses – this gives it its *unitive* purpose! Marriage is also ordained to conceive, raise and educate children, which gives it its *procreative* purpose.[2]

By contrast, the *legal* definition for marriage is merely contractual: "Marriage is a legally recognized state or relationship between two people who intend to live together as sexual and domestic partners."[3] This definition does not stipulate the type of people or genders required for the partnership thereby opening the door for non-traditional marriages.

The two views of marriage show completely different understandings. One views it as a no-strings-attached partnership whereas the other describes it as a higher calling. And while these two views clash with each other, it gives the Church opportunity to teach, clarify, and provide moral solutions to the challenges to marriage including: cohabitation, divorce, same sex unions, and contraception/ abortion. Many preparing for marriage simply do not appreciate the fullness of what marriage can and *should* be.

Let's talk about the terms *sexual or domestic partner.* These terms do not denote much depth of meaning in today's culture. In fact, using the word "partner" to refer to a spouse diminishes the spouse's unique value. Marital spouses are much more than a sexual or domestic partner. Everyone will have lots of types of partners in life. These partnerships can include tennis partners, business partners, dance partners, prayer partners, festival partners, bowling partners, and Bible Study partners. I have partnered with other mothers and fathers to carpool, babysit, organize mass mailings, and pray. I have even shared domestic partnerships with college suite mates, roommates, and dorm mates and our children! While these partnerships are affectionate and provided me with opportunities to grow, in no way do they compare to the depth and breadth of the relationship I have with my marital spouse. I have been blessed with only one very special spouse.

The state of marriage is further insulted when spouses are called *partners* by those who purport to be sensitive to the different types of families. Where has the special regard for marriage gone? Words reflect attitudes and these words suggest a dramatic shift in marital attitudes. Today, swapping the word partner for spouse suggests that marriages are no more special than domestic or sexual partnerships. These attitudes (and words) fail to relay the special dignity and sacramental nature that rightfully belongs to marriages and committed spouses. Presuming that a devoted spouse is not any more special than a domestic partner is an insult to God, His Church, married persons and their commitments. Furthermore, these attitudes remove any moral significance or distinction between sacramental marriage and civil unions or marriages. They also diminish marriage and peoples' regard for marriage. This is obvious when looking at marriage trends over the past fifty years. Since 1960, the US marriage rates have dropped from 76.5 to 37.4 marriages per 1,000 unmarried women.[4] The following table shows the marriage rates; the good news is that they appear to be in less of a free fall compared to the late 1970s and early 1980s but only time will tell.[5]

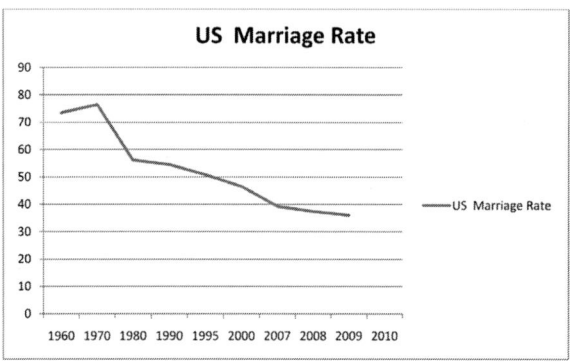

Partnerships do not provide the same level of commitment as marriages. Spousal commitments are emotional relationships as well as economic partnerships.[6] In other words spouses share and combine earning, spending, and saving; they share and build mutual assets; and together they hope for and beget children. All of these efforts do not apply equally to cohabitating couples. Furthermore, partnerships are not vocations. Few are wedded to their partner for life. Partners come and go as their partnerships are formed and dissolved. Dissolving partnerships are never annulled because nothing was ever promised to endure through good times or in bad. Cohabitating relationships simply melt away unless litigation is initiated.

Career and vocation are not interchangeable words and neither are spouse and partner. Studies find that men become better mates when they wed because they work harder and smarter for the family and they are more dedicated to the relationship emotionally and economically.[7] Therefore, marriage is much more than a private partnership between two people.

Marriage is a public declaration about the purpose and intent of two people. In fact, people need a marriage license for such a proclamation. Marriage is "good" for all of society because it provides the necessary foundation by which future children can be securely raised. Marriage fosters virtue, morality, values, and good citizenry when these public vows are honored and lived out. Marriage is the reason why a "man shall leave his father and his mother and shall cleave to his wife and they shall become one flesh."[8]

All too often college students indulge in casual sexual relationships which turn into quasi cohabiting relationships. At the end of one relationship, they start having another similarly premature sexual relationship with the next partner. Before long, they will have entered into and dissolved numerous sexual partnerships. This is not the solid preparation needed for entering into a vocation that demands emotional, physical, spiritual, mental, economic, and supernatural commitments from both spouses in order to last a lifetime. In fact, it's fair to wonder how multiple sexual partnerships differ from serial adultery.[9]

Faithful and permanent marriages are premier examples of God's love for the world. Love finds a special home in a marriage when both spouses are prepared well to live out this vocation; this state of life more naturally and excellently supports life and love.[10]

A. What is Love?

Today, love means many different things to different people. The ancient world recognized that love between spouses is vastly different from brotherly love, parental or even neighborly love. Consequently they used different "love" words for different types of love.

Contemporary society is constrained — figuratively and literally — by the word we use to describe various degrees and types of love. Society likes to portray love as simply an emotion or a feeling. But it is a lot more that. Love is the essence of the Gift (God). Audacious men and women act, talk, and presume to be a *gift to the opposite sex* – this is not what is meant when we say that "love is the Gift." The gift of love is real and permanent and it is freely given and freely accepted. John Paul II taught that "authentic human love must strive to imitate Divine Love which was modeled by Jesus. He willingly took on a human form for our sake. He also died so we could live." The fundamental characteristics of divine love are five-fold: His love is freely given; it is a genuine gift to mankind without strings attached. Love is freely received; God does not demand or require us to love Him back. It is given with full knowledge; God knows who we are but still loves us. Love is permanent; God's love isn't cyclic, temporary, conditional, or erratic. Finally, love is life giving; we need God's grace to complete the healing needed to recover from original sin.

Authentic marital love imitates God's love most completely compared to other types of love. Marital love allows the spouses to participate and experience *unitive* and *procreative* love unconditionally. In essence, it is given and shared when both spouses "wears themselves out for the other over the course of their lifetime." Together, unitive and procreative love is so much more than the sum of the two individuals' love.

Unitive love allows husbands and wives to freely become the gift of self to the other. It symbolizes the way that God gives Himself to us. There are multiple ways in which a couple expresses and shares unitive love. This love is given and received physically, emotionally, and spiritually. This love allows couples to express and share sexual unity. Unitive love is fostered when a couple intimately connects with the other spouse on an emotional level. It expands through the mutual sharing and fusing of individual spiritual and world views. It grows as the two spouses offer their mutual support and full commitment to the other. It is given when spouses serve each other. Unitive love is protective of the beloved and the relationship. It is harmonious and balanced. It shares tenderness, affection, and devotion.

Procreative love is a different aspect of the same authentic love and gift. Procreative love allows us to participate in God's love in a very special way through the co-creation of a new human being. This love unites a couple's mutual desire to have a child. It forges a mutual concurrence about staying open to God's plan for their family. It looks out for the welfare of every member – new and old – in the family. Procreative love encourages us to be open to the possibility of having one more child to share with the rest of creation. Fruitfulness mysteriously convinces couples living out procreative love that there will always be room for one more – and somehow there always is. Fruitfulness teaches couples how to better imitate God's super- abundant love. Fruitfulness generates exponential love between the spouses in part because of their shared love for the children. To stymie fruitfulness, is to stymie the couple's capacity to love; this only serves to foster independence and its related temptations of divorce, loneliness, or emptiness.

We can't engineer the love which arrives unexpectedly. Love is exhilarating because it is unconditional and freely given. We are not loved by our spouse because we deserve to be loved but because they have chosen to love us. It is indeed a blessing to be chosen by love and to be cherished by someone more than anyone else for a lifetime. What a blessing! What a love!

Authentic love allows us to see our beloved for who he (she) really is. When we love authentically, we choose to love a real person in spite of their human faults; authentic love does not foster "idealized" or unrealistic impressions of our beloved. It is necessary and OK to recognize our beloved's weaknesses and faults. Until we see them we don't really know our beloved. All human beings are less than perfect – in this life anyway! Lovers recognize these faults without drawing away from the beloved. "The attraction to a person based on feelings needs to mature into a *yes* to the value of the person independent of *feelings*. Only when the love has discovered and affirmed the person for what he or she is, can the lover say *yes forever*. Furthermore, when we finally learn to accept the beloved's dignity as someone other than ourselves, our existence is enriched by the new presence we thereby let into our inner world."[11] This *yes* moves us toward marriage.

On a practical level, authentic love precludes things like pre-marital agreements that presume eventual marital discord and divorce because of acts of fraud by a spouse, mistreatment, disillusionment, irreconcilable differences, abuse, or other reasons. Pre-arranged contracts hint that a future spouse is more worried about a future financial state than their marital responsibilities, vows of permanence or the state of the marriage. Lawyers, financial planners, and other professionals are primary beneficiaries of such pre-nuptial agreements. They convince modern couples to draw up the pre-nuptial agreements because it's smart financial planning that removes some of the *emotion* involved in the decision to get married.[12] It's important to know that the Catholic Church's Code of Canon Law objects to pre-nuptial agreements that presume an eventual divorce. This Code states that "A marriage subject to a condition about the future cannot be contracted validly." Father Vincent Serpa, a Catholic Answer's Apologist explains that "the Catholic Church teaches that marriage is the COMPLETE giving of the spouses to God through each other. Therefore, there can be NO strings attached. A prenuptial is a very big string!"[13] Resolution of estates in case of death of a spouse with children is better resolved through the use of Wills and Estate Planning Contracts; these make no statements about the future state of the marriage and only relate to matters of death.

B. Getting Ready for Authentic Love and Marriage

True love is a mutual gift shared between two people for their lifetime. Fortifying this love takes work but is well worth it! Unfortunately not everyone gets suitably ready for marriage or authentic love; neither do all work to maintain love or marriage.

Before committing to marriage, every young adult should have developed a positive attitude toward this vocation! They should also have arrived at the understanding that marriage is a vocation and not simply another possible next step after college. Young adults need to understand the meaning of marriage along with its twofold purposes as discussed previously. They must see *why* these two purposes of marriage are indivisible. Finally, they must believe that marriage is a commitment for a lifetime. They must see it as a unique state in life wherein spouses are called to holiness. Furthermore, they must realize the importance of living virtuously now in order to arrive at these fundamental understandings and attitudes before marriage. Today, many young people believe that marriage must be postponed because of social goals and standards which insist on college graduation and the securing of stable careers, large amounts of assets, and economic stability. These social standards are too high for many people to marry *responsibly* and so they wait! Unfortunately, these same social standards voice no opinions about postponing love, sex or having kids outside of marriage. As a result, cohabitation "is an increasingly popular alternative for couples skittish about marriage or not meeting preconceived preconditions."[14]

On the other hand, social standards urging couples to wait for marriage until after college bears some fruit. Marriage experts agree that "marriages of the college educated are better matched than ever before with regard to their educational and economic backgrounds. This produces marriages that are happier than those who are less well matched.[15]

When you become engaged, you will be asked to attend pre-marriage preparation programs. They are a small investment of time and money for something that will be life altering. All who plan to marry expect and desire joy filled marriages. Few couples would be happy to spend tens of thousands of dollars on a wedding if they didn't expect the marriage to last! So it is important to begin making worthy investments of time and money in programs that teach and help prepare you for marriage.

Believe it or not, in some ways you have already received a steady diet of marriage preparation since youth! This formation and preparation occurred as you lived with, were influenced by, and observed the state of the marriages of your parents, siblings, friends, and others. You absorbed attitudes and perceptions about marriage from real life thus far! You have also absorbed it from culture, the community you live in, and society. Unfortunately many cultural lessons focus on the negatives of marriage. For instance, one in three American children live with a divorced, separated, or never married parent.[16] You observe the social wrangling over marriage when people discuss and argue about same sex unions, having children, contraception, divorce, cohabitation, and more. You also absorb attitudes, beliefs, and perceptions from your Church provided you let it teach you.

How ready are you? One measure of your fitness for marriage is determined by the degree to which you have been drawn out of your original self by others, your beloved, and even yourself; it is the degree by which you allow yourself to be drawn out by love! Love that is true always beckons us to experience, learn and grow from the interests, feelings, world views, and relationships attributable to love's new connections.[17] Love that causes us to retreat into ourselves or become self absorbed is not true love nor does it make us fit for marriage.

Before marriage, we must *discriminately* search for our beloved's true face; we must readily realize that not anybody will do! The search for true love mandates that we grow personal virtue first so that we are better able to discriminately carry it out. Preparing for marriage will require many to have a conversion of heart, personal behavior, and attitude. Young people who have been pre-conditioned to believe that marriage is just not that special are those who have been hurt by personal relationships and experiences, divorce, abandonment, or lack spiritual formation. These young people can easily become dissuaded about the real purpose and meaning of marriage as they continue to hold onto false perceptions, hurts, and negative attitudes. Nearly 40 percent of Americans – mixed ages – say that marriage is becoming obsolete even though nearly seventy percent still feel upbeat about the future of marriage and family.[18] This mixed message will certainly continue to influence and/or confuse many young people. Personal behaviors tend to reflect one's "marriage attitude." For example, holding onto negative attitudes about marriage increases the likelihood that a college student will engage in binge drinking, hookups, or other risky sexual activity that jeopardize students' long- and short-term health risks. These negative attitudes decrease one's ability to develop healthy relationships further driving up negative perceptions about marriage.[19]

Marital attitudes develop from the positive or negative training you received in the past – also the present. Direct and indirect influences (positive or negative) have trained you heart as well as your brain. Is your heart afraid of commitment or ready for it; what is your general marital attitude? If you see marriage primarily as a private union with limited benefits, then it is more likely you will adopt habits, practices, and attitudes that promote self interests. If you have come to believe that the marriage relationship should primarily foster independence and individualism, it is likely you only have to give 50-50 in marriage. You might regard marriage as a partnership wherein you expect / anticipate having a limited but fair share of duties and responsibilities. In truth, spouses should look at marriage as a 100-100 proposition with each person giving their all for the other. If you fail to understand how marriage helps society, perhaps you see marriage as a state that should only satisfy your personal appetites.

Negative marital attitudes, materialism, and contradictory social perceptions cause people to postpone marriage for as long as possible.

When the purpose of marriage is thought to only serve me, me and me, then it is more natural to avoid it until selfishness has run its course or been changed by true love.

On the other hand, if you believe that marriage should be a loving vocation that requires commitment for a lifetime from both spouses you are more likely to uphold the nobility of marriage. Taken together, the personal behaviors and experiences of a person and the societal challenges to marriage lay the groundwork by which people approach marriage. Some take deliberate, purposeful steps while others stumble into marriage unwittingly. All young people need apposite training with regard to marriage and family life so they avoid the same paths by which too many blindly stumble into marriage.

C. Getting to Know Each Other

It is vital that people get to know each other during dating and courtship. Each person must be able to "measure" the virtuous nature and character of the other person; couples have to be able to see and know the mind and will of their beloved in order to love freely. Unfortunately, too many young couples worry solely about sexual compatibility rather than emotional, psychological, spiritual, social, and overall personal compatibilities. When the latter compatibilities are met, sexual compatibility is a given. However, when the latter compatibilities are not met, sexual compatibility is worthless.

Before you proceed down the aisle, both of you should have begun to arrive at a common world view. Also, each person should be fully supportive and understanding of the other's key attitudes, beliefs, and views especially with regard to spirituality, faith, and moral living. Communication is the key to discovering these thoughts, beliefs, expectations, dreams, and hopes. Couples need to merge world views smoothly and appreciatively. When the merger is too difficult or impossible, then it should become obvious that the relationship is not as ideal as it first appeared. The bitter pill of "breaking up" before marriage is much easier than that of divorce afterward.

Couple must learn to pray together and to share insights into their faith with each other. Couples must learn how to forgive and to ask for forgiveness. Humility is a necessary "marriage-ability" characteristic. Humor and laughter are also necessary ingredients for maintaining married love. Couples need to have positive support systems in place that respect and value their principles. All too often, dating couples are mocked or embarrassed into inappropriate behavior by friends or acquaintances; however, this won't happen if excellent and decent social supports are in place. Also, it will be necessary to build hedges around your relationship in order to better protect and defend your fledgling love; hedges keep good influences in and proscribe bad influences.

Nobody really falls heads over heels into *authentic love*; rather a person demonstrates an emerging authentic love when they freely choose to love someone. You will also choose to marry; it is never a good idea to slide into marriage because of social pressures, expectations, or family urgings. Take deliberate and thoughtful steps all the way to the altar.

So what characteristics do you hope to find in your beloved? Sociologists, Christine Whelan and Christie Boxer compared contemporary mate preferences with past preferences after interviewing 1,100 students enrolled in three different universities around the country. Whelan informs us that back in the 1930s, men hoped to find wives who would be dependable, kind, chaste and good cooks. Today's men aim to find love, brains, beauty and sizable salaries as well as dependability, etc. Today, women hope to find love, dependability and emotional stability in a future mate. You will find in the table on the opposite page a short list of today's preferences; they really are not completely dissimilar from generations past.

Table One: Male and Female Preferences of 2010[20]

What Today's Men Want	What Today's Women Want
Essential Characteristics: • Mutual love and attraction • Dependable character • Emotional stability	Essential Characteristics: • Mutual attraction and love • Dependable character • Emotional stability
Important Characteristics: • Education and intelligence • Good looks • Ambition	Important Characteristics: • Education and Intelligence • Desire for home and children • Ambition
Desirable Characteristics: • Good financial prospect • Good cook and housekeeper	Desireable Characteristics: • Good looks • Refinement
Un-Important Characteristics: • Similar political background • Chastity	Un-Important Characteristics: • Similar political background • Chastity

D. The Recipe for a Happy Marriage

The tried and true recipe for a happy marriage can be found in the Word of God. Saint Paul detailed for the Corinthians (and us) this perfect recipe. His description is basically a summary of many other passages that talk about love and marriage. He wrote:[21]

Love is Patient

Love is kind and is not jealous

Love does not brag and is not arrogant

Love does not act unbecomingly

Love does not seek its own

Love does not take into account a wrong suffered

Love does not rejoice in unrighteousness but rejoices with the truth

Love bears all things, believes all things, hopes all things,

and endures all things.

The following *secular* version, *The Recipe for Love Ingredients*, comes pretty close as well.

The Recipe for Love Ingredients

2 Hearts full of love	2 cups of joy	Stir daily with happiness, humor and patience
2 heaping cups of kindness	2 big hearts full of forgiveness	Serve with warmth and compassion, respect and loyalty
2 armfuls of gentleness	1 lifetime of togetherness	
2 cups of friendship	2 minds full of tenderness	

E. The Importance of Gender Differences in Marriage and Families

God created males and females, though it didn't have to be this way! God could have chosen a completely different design or He could have kept making us one by one. But He didn't and so this tells us that there is an original purpose and unique meaning behind the genders' design including their similarities and differences!

Neuro-science reveals to us even now something about both the purpose and meaning of the original design. It also reveals that God, not random evolution, created this original blueprint! The gendered differences and similarities permit a natural order and balance in sexual relationships as well as familial, educational, and professional relationships. The gender differences and similarities can also create calamities when we fail to understand the why and the how of the differences.

Each gender has a lot to teach the other. We need to listen to and study the "genius" of the two genders in order to neutralize misunderstandings and unnecessary gender conflicts! It is important that we don't neutralize gender differences in the process however! Dr. Leonard Sax remarked that "in order to feel at home everywhere we must be comfortable somewhere and that is being comfortable in our own skin!" It follows that little boys need to be allowed to be little boys and play with cars and trucks and make a lot of noise while little girls need to be allowed to nurture their baby dolls quietly and in singsong voices.

Dr. Sax tells us that genders really are hard-wired differently; furthermore brain studies prove this to be true from infancy onward.[22] Did you know that females have a seven-fold finer tuned hearing than boys? This carries through into adulthood. Men's hearing, on average, has been found to be significantly (by a factor of twenty) deficient compared to women's. This "fact" explains why women chronically complain that their husbands don't listen; the men are listening but they just can't absorb all the detail. The hard wiring differences of the gender brains affects even the connections between the eyes and ears and the brain.

The genders have major physiological differences as well. Men are normally bigger in size and weight; they generally carry more muscle mass but less body fat than women. Physically, top athletes manifest a 10 percent gap in performance and endurance between genders.[23] Men are "quantitative" thinkers, communicators, and evaluators whereas women are qualitative thinkers, communicators, and evaluators. Either gender has more difficulty communicating oppositely. In other words, women have more trouble thinking and communicating quantitatively whereas men have more trouble thinking and communicating qualitatively. Men internalize less – even after a competitive event. This means they do not dwell on the whys behind the successes or failures as do most women. This causes men to tell their wives and children to just get over it! On the other hand, women internalize more allowing them to get to the underlying reasons behind situations. This helps explain why women often tell their husbands – "you just don't care"! Both types of comments, under the right circumstances, can be valid. Both types of comments, under the wrong assertions, assessments, or circumstances, can be invalid!

When we don't understand the fundamental gender differences, we tend to create unfair gender stereotypes. For instance, Dr. Sax tells us that young boys tend to like to draw objects in blacks, grays, silvers and blues whereas girls like to draw people with a myriad of details and colors. Grade school teachers – mostly females – naturally prefer girls' art and this bias causes young boys to think that coloring is for girls. Similarly, too many girls sense the fact that adults prefer the aggressiveness and speed of young boys and therefore draw the conclusion that sports is for boys.

Too often, society stresses the problems generated by the gender differences. It has been a long time since it was first suggested that men are from Mars and women are from Venus, but this type of theorizing can cause some people to regard all gender differences negatively. Sociologists push the envelope even further when they name these differences negatively. Consider the college courses dedicated to the study of gender biases, gender differences, the sexual patterns of males, the socialization of women, the cultural construction of American masculinity, the theory of consensual sex, the dyadic contexts, or sexual liberation theories.[24]

All male and female conflict must be attributed to original sin. Any time the social sciences fail to acknowledge that bliss comes from God and disharmony comes from temptation and Satan, they will always be one study short of telling it like it is.

The gender differences help us all realize what it means to be a real man and a real woman. Mothers and fathers reinforce these characteristics in their children. Parents need to civilize both genders of their children in order to help form them into real men and real women! Mothers impart in their girls what it means to be a real woman and fathers instruct their sons what it means to be a real man. This formation occurs consciously and unconsciously. Finally, children need the influence of both male and female parent in order to sort out the "normal" differences and similarities of the two genders. Having the positive influence from the male and female parent enables children to positively develop their own *gender identity*; furthermore, having a positive identity allows them to be "comfortable in their own skin."

The role of father and husband has been marginalized by feminist theories; this role is also marginalized when men refuse to set aside juvenile-like tendencies. Some men don't even begin to take their social roles very seriously. When men are reduced to "indistinct androgynous images of large boys making money by themselves, and satisfying their own pleasures we are in trouble as a society."[25] These types of images only cause men to further retreat into themselves limiting their capacity to love authentically. The obvious consequences of this retreat include widespread child/family abandonment, divorce, sexual victimization, predatory behaviors, and more.

Men share commonality with a unique role model, Jesus Christ, who can teach them how to love authentically. Jesus faced the same temptations that all men face, without giving in once to selfish love.

Similarly, when women's roles are downgraded into ones that turn them into sexual servants, when women strive to be like men, or when women become androgynous moneymakers working for their own self, they retreat into themselves thereby limiting their capacity to love authentically. This is precisely why we see more and more vulgar or crude images of "Girls Gone Wild", Cardio strip teasers, porn queens, prostitution, hooking up, flashing, abortion, and female predators in the news.

Furthermore, when both genders assume self serving roles, this only paves the way for prolonged gender wars, incompatibility, divorce, and pain. These flawed characteristics make it more difficult to understand the purpose and meaning of marriage or gender.

"Noise prevents our hearts from hearing the *music of love*. This noise comes from three primary sources: concupiscence of the flesh, concupiscence of the eyes, and pride of life."[26] Furthermore, "unconstrained sexual urges threaten our real freedom, jeopardizing the very possibility of self-possession that enables us to be fully ourselves."[27] Self possession allows our gift of self to be real. The essence of self possession is to love willingly and readily. Failing to understand this can cause us to detach ourselves from the truth and to adopt negative attitudes towards life, love, and marriage.[28]

Finally, have you ever wondered why more men are convicted criminals, sexual perverts, or deviants than women?[29] John Paul II would likely explain it this way. Men commit more sexual deviances because they are not physically and intimately connected to new life; they are always at least one step removed from the personal and intimate connection between love and life. God's original design allows a mother to become one with her new baby. This unique vantage point naturally gives women the advantage of having more capacity to love (a new life) and thereby grow in virtue. Women are intimately in charge of a new life – both in the preborn stages and afterward when she cares for baby through breastfeeding, and giving baby good, general care. This vantage point makes it more inconceivable that mothers deliberately choose abortion. This intimate, personal connection with baby helps to explain why women suffer emotional and psychological consequences after choosing to have an abortion which ends the life of her own prematurely and violently.

Dr. James McKenna of Notre Dame University recently told an audience[30] about new research suggesting that fathers who hold, cuddle, and sleep with their new babies have temporarily reduced levels of testosterone. While this may sound disconcerting, it shouldn't be. Decreased testosterone levels facilitate attachment between a man and his wife and baby; the temporary decrease in testosterone allows a father to bond more closely with and be in touch with his wife and baby's needs. Essentially, it provides a civilizing and socializing effect so fathers stay close to family.

F. What About Money?

We have already discussed the importance of avoiding excessive credit card debt and accumulation of excessive school loans. Maybe you thought the debt caution only pertained to you personally. However, research shows that credit card debt "plays havoc with the lives of newly married couples whereas financial assets strengthen the marriage. Couples with no assets were 70 percent more likely to divorce than couples with at least $10K in assets. Furthermore, credit card debt was found to be associated with less time spent together, more fighting, and significantly lower levels of marital happiness among these couples."[31]

Money troubles cause couples to fight about many different matters including finances; as a result they feel less happy in their marriages. In fact, fights over money easily escalate into physical displays of anger. Men tend to react more negatively to their spouse's irresponsible use of money than women's reactions about their spouses' use of money. It is important to recognize your spending, borrowing, and saving philosophy now in order to compare it with that of a potential mate. Research suggests that when individuals feel their spouse does not handle money well, they report feeling less happy and more likely to divorce. Not liking how one's spouse spends money or handles money increases the likelihood of divorce by 45 percent. "Experts warn that only extramarital affairs and alcohol/drug abuse were stronger predictors of divorce."[32]

We have talked a bit about the dangers of materialism; when people base their self worth on material objects their general happiness and self esteem suffer. Materialism and materialistic spouses endanger marriages. Studies show that materialistic spouses increase both financial and marital strain into the relationship regardless of their social class.

We should not be surprised to learn that any type of vice causes marriage to falter or fail including vice associated with money matters.

G. The Role of the Family

In earlier sections, you have already learned that the two parent family is the cornerstone for society – it indeed takes healthy families to create strong villages. Families have the unique role (and duty) to form, educate, and love young children into adulthood wherein they have an increased capacity to love others authentically.

Deconstructing the importance (moral, spiritual, physical, emotional, psychological, and financial) of marriage and family diminishes the importance of motherhood, fatherhood, and children. It weakens society overall. Regardless of how experts spin the statistics with regard to divorce, poverty, the root causes of dysfunctional families, or lingering social problems, the fact remains that the basic building blocks for civilizations and positive social capital are stable, joyful human families consisting of one mother, one father, and their children. Two mothers simply are less able to teach boys about masculinity. Similarly, two fathers don't have a true feminine touch. Every single parent will have to admit that their children are raised with a shortfall when the opposite parent is missing, dead or derelict. These children lose the benefit of observing a masculine or feminine genius when that gender parent is missing or deceased or abusive. Unfortunately the following graph describes in reality what has happened since several decades ago with regard to two parent families.[33]

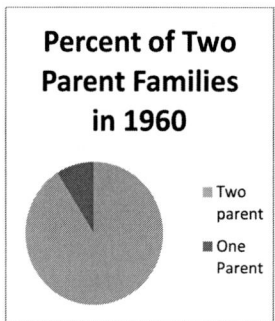

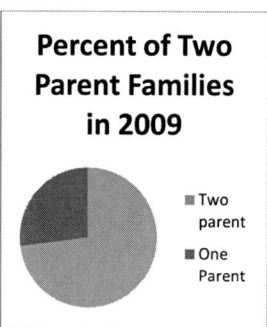

John Paul II tells us in *Familiaris Consortio* that the family is to become what it is. He writes: "Since in God's plan it has been established as an intimate community of life and love, the family has the mission to become more and more what it is, that is to say, a community of life and love. The essence and role of the family are in the final analysis specified by love. Hence the family has the mission to guard, reveal and communicate love and this is the living reflection of and a real sharing in God's love for humanity and the love of Christ the Lord of the Church his Bride."

H. Children

Spouses naturally expect their unions to be fruitful. In fact, the marriage can be fruitful in a variety of ways. However, the ultimate fruitfulness creates a new person made up of the two spouses. Nobody else in the whole world can create this same unique person. Humans yearn to be special, to have unique purpose, and to do something others cannot. Childbearing gives them this ability.

Parents do not normally have to be forced to love their children; adults are able to love their children well when they have *developed* an increased capacity to love others. This capacity grows when we willingly and joyfully accept children from God as a Gift and as Love. Unions that regard children as a burden rather than as supreme gifts of marriage, fail to appreciate the indivisibility of the twofold purposes of marriage which are two aspects of the same self giving."[34]

New life enriches parents because it provides the opportunity to love and come to know another new human person who has many talents, abilities, blessings to share with the world. New life provides freshness and newness within the family; this is priceless. New life energizes everyone unless it is viewed with a dim attitude; this attitude is generally the result of limiting one's ability to love more by resorting to contraception, abortion, serial adulterous relationships, and more.

Many people think that responsible parenthood is simply a balancing act between personal ambitions and parental/family guilt. In other words, people may eventually experience guilt over being childless or being absentee parents as they put the majority of their personal talents toward job-related functions so they can "get ahead" in life. This emphasis yields maximum material benefits and many personal rewards. However, many acknowledge that adults who seek only "material goods veer toward vice (selfishness and self centeredness), so eventually they have kids to mitigate any guilt for being "selfish" and "self centered." Meanwhile they continue to pursue personal ambitions. These families may be the model for some as it becomes the social norm, but little Truth supports this model explaining why divorce is often the next logical step.

As you might expect, more households had children living with them in the mid 1800s than in the mid 1900s; however, experts show that the number of households with children decreased even more significantly over the course of the next four decades due to contraception, increased divorce, fewer marriages, and other reasons. Fewer households with children mean that young children are less noticed by neighbors, shoppers, and other adults without children.[35] This explains in part why today's young families complain about the vexation displayed toward them and young children while going into restaurants, shopping malls, movie theaters, weddings, museums, and other places where adults prefer quiet and no children. This rate change in the percent of households with children living with parents from 1850 through 2000 can be observed in the following graph.

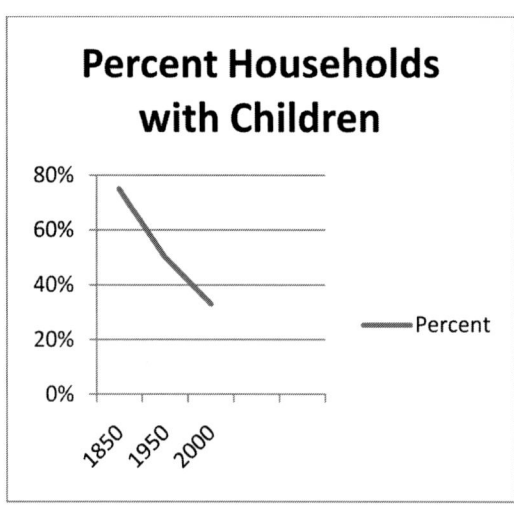

Furthermore, we ought to be concerned with the fact that education causes women to forsake having children. Did you know that college educated women in particular have far fewer children than women without a high school diploma! "In 2004, 24 percent of women aged 40 – 44 with a bachelors degree were childless while only 15 percent of those with a high school degree were childless. The National Marriage project has concluded that college educated women do not have enough children to replace themselves.[36]

The unique value of each child is diminished when society fails to appreciate any one of them. Children, like marital love, are created with their own individual dignity. We cannot buy a child or make them like widgets in a factory. Children have dignity because they are a gift to the couple from the Creator. Regardless of how hard biology tries to clone or artificially reproduce new life, it can never infuse the mind and the soul into the body! The very instant that new life is created, God is there to lovingly and spontaneously breathe in His life. This is the essence of our souls and our lives!

l. Sexual Intercourse

"Sexual intercourse lays bare the totality of our gift to the other." When we truly love another person we affirm this love by giving our self to the other freely and fully. Marital intercourse combined with authentic love allows us to give ourselves freely and fully and without shame, disgrace, embarrassment, humiliation, coercion, dishonor, vulnerability, anxiety, uncertainty, or fear of any type. Fears and negative emotions are simply not part and parcel of authentic love.

Continued intimacy is bolstered and watered with fidelity, faithfulness, and marital chastity. Intimacy increases when spouses serve one another by giving of themselves emotionally, psychologically, mentally, spiritually, and physically. Loving relationships do not seek sexual satisfaction; rather, they discover it naturally as they search for and fill up their spouse's emotional, spiritual, and psychological tanks. Intimacy increases our capacity to love. Marital chastity helps us honor our spouse's dignity and worth more fully.

J. Fertility

Fertility will be explained in much more detail in a subsequent chapter. For now, consider how new life impacts "old love" in remarkable ways. It serves to rejuvenate, revitalize, and surprise! New life lightens the heart. Natural fertility is the result of combining both sexual gifts of the male and the female.

Male fertility mimics God's love in that it is also continuous, steady, robust, potent, and passionate. Our combined male/female fertility and sexuality resembles the Trinity because it becomes the means by which new life is brought forth as a gift to the whole world. Essentially it takes two to make three just as it took the Father and the Son to love forth the Holy Spirit.

Finally, female fertility symbolizes the heart of mankind. The female fertility pattern cycles between fertility and natural infertility. The female fertility pattern is both hopeful and protective; the fertile phase offers hope for a new life whereas the infertile phases allow a woman to provide intimate protection for the newly conceived life. The infertile period of time concludes with a weeping - the menstruation – as if a welcomed guest failed to arrive. But hope is renewed by the next fertile cycle.

As a whole, society appears to be rejecting the value of fertility wholesale. Since 1960, fertility rates have dropped from 118 births per 1,000 women ages 15 – 44 to 69.5 in 2007. This impacts society, families, children, and our future significantly as we fail to be hopeful and rejuvenated by new lives.[37]

K. Challenges to Marriage

The US Catholic Bishops warn of four major challenges to marriage. These challenges include widespread use of contraception, growing acceptance of same sex unions, increased tolerance for divorce, and widespread cohabitation. Sexual permissiveness and moral relativism are a few of the underlying roots of these challenges. (Cohabitation has already been discussed in Chapter 7 so the subject will not be reopened in this chapter. Furthermore, contraception will be discussed in Chapter 12.)

These challenges convince people that traditional marriage between one man and one woman is old fashioned, transitory, and irrelevant. The challengers are modern day decoys that have quite successfully eroded understanding about the dignity, purpose, meaning, and importance of marriage.

You already realize that sexual permissiveness uses other persons; in turn, such use makes us forget what authentic love looks and feels like. When authentic love becomes foreign and unrecognizable it is seen as obstructive rather than constructive and the original bridge that was meant to connect two very different genders — men and women – becomes impassible.[38]

L. False Love

Relationships suffer when one or both of the mates behave poorly and fail to love authentically. Frequently, couples who abuse alcohol or drugs complain about feeling less satisfied with their relationship compared to those who do not use substances to enhance romantic relationships. "Risk taking, particularly heavy alcohol and substance use has been found to hinder healthy relationship formation and ultimately marriage."[39] Consider how this plays out in college where many students use drugs or alcohol to facilitate either sexual encounters or sexual climax. More than likely, these relationships will suffer in the long run!

Psychologist Cathy Mollner tells us that, "women use sex to get love whereas men use love to get sex." Men can more easily compartmentalize sex and love compared to women. One study revealed that over three fourths of sexually active men did not desire to be married in the near future even though their female partners did![40]

This study shows the chasm between sex and love or commitment. Men who use verbal sexual coercion (threatening the relationship, putting the woman down, swearing, expressing dissatisfaction with the sexual relationship) to "get sex" have a very limited capacity to love authentically. Women need to beware of forming sexual or romantic relationships with these types of men. Not surprisingly, women in verbally coercive types of relationships report more sexual depression, lowered self esteem, disappointment in the relationship and pervasive relational problems. Some men go so far as to suggest that rape is "less serious" for those who are married or in a sexual dating relationship.[41] Likewise, men need to beware of forming sexual or romantic relationships with women who use men.

"The sexual revolution has had negative effects on many people, chiefly the most vulnerable, and it has added financial burdens onto society at large. And this is true not only in the obvious ways like the spread of AIDS and other STDs but also in other ways affecting human well being."[42]

All along we have seen evidence that the best preparation for marriage is the commitment to chastity prior to marriage. We are once more reminded by secular studies of the importance for pre-marital chastity in order to have a loving marriage later on. The study found that "multiple premarital sexual partners increase the risk of having a later divorce and separation after marriage.[43]

M. Divorce

Divorce takes its toll on couples both economically and emotionally. Yet, the divorce rates continue to climb or at least remain elevated at twice the level that it was at during the 1960s. Divorce rates hit their highest levels in the early 1980s.[44]

Years ago, psychologists suggested that the number one cause for couples' divorce was due to lack of communication and/or the inability to effectively resolve conflict. Today, data suggests that couples divorce because they develop "unstable feelings toward their spouse." The unstable feelings are the result of having "interactive" differences, failing to respect each other, being antagonistic toward the other, becoming overly materialistic, and/or holding onto unrealistic, Hollywood-type expectations for marriage. These attitudes make it difficult for couples to "preserve the positive feelings they had at one time." In other words, these couples did not know each other before they got married; therefore they could not love each other authentically!

But there is good news; observable factors decrease a couple's likelihood to divorce. For example, couples are less likely to divorce when they have combined incomes over $50K, do not have a baby before marriage, marry when over 25 years of age, do not have divorced parents, have a religious affiliation, and have some college education.[45]

In early 2010, the U.S. Catholic Bishops produced a document which defined the four primary challenges to joyful, loving marriages. The document outlines the challenges to marriage as follows: contraception, divorce, cohabitation and same sex unions.

While every marriage has conflict, the new data suggests that spouses do not love each other enough to accept or overcome their differences. The data helps point out that certain factors will/can diminish one's respect for his/her spouse; increase antagonism toward a spouse; or decrease love and affection for a spouse. The U.S. Catholic Bishops believe these things are contraception, pornography, and society's attitudes toward marriage and divorce.

It is high time to shore up the foundations for marital relationships. And the way to do this is by looking for ways that support the resolve and stability necessary for happy marriages. Puppy love and affection is not the same thing as authentic love! Couples also need to understand the importance of respect and appreciation for their beloved within (and certainly before) marriage. There is further need for adult catechesis and evangelization to counteract the effects of moral relativism. It is time to restore systems and processes that support life-long marriages (natural family planning, pre-marriage prep classes that evangelize and provide catechesis about the faith).

It is the time to foster virtue – not vice – in college students before they plan to marry. It is also time to model authentic love in our own marriages for the sake of our children and grandchildren.

Today's divorce rates are nothing short of disastrous. In the US, first time marriages end in divorce more than 50 percent of the time and second time marriages end in divorce 67 percent of the time. Finally third or more marriages end in divorce more than 70 percent of the time.[46] Today, there are more than 2.1 million marriages per year in the United States; this represents a marriage rate of 7.1 per 1,000 persons. The divorce rate is half the marriage rate, or 3.5 per 1,000 persons.[47] This produces huge social consequences. By the way, it is important to note that religious couples with children have the lowest divorce rates!

Even though divorce is common and fast becoming a social norm, few experts tout divorce as beneficial for society, families, men, women, or children. Furthermore, the more that divorce becomes the social norm, the higher the divorce rates go. The short- and long-term consequences of most divorces are harsh. They attack both spouses' financial, social, psychological, health, spiritual, and emotional wellness. But it doesn't stop there. It also attacks the financial, social, psychological, health, and emotional well being of the children involved. Divorce also negatively impacts friends of the couple, families of both spouses, working partners of the spouses, and more. Finally, divorce has a profound effect on nearly everyone who knows the couple. It affects all of society but especially children.

Experts remind us that up to one third of children with divorced parents will suffer long term problems (emotional, behavioral, psychological, educational, and even physical consequence) after the divorce of their parents — even into their own adulthood. In fact, many children take these problems with them into their marital relationships reducing their own chances for success. Children from intact, happy homes do not face these same negative consequences. Furthermore, studies show that "children living with single parent families have negative life outcomes at two to three times the rate of children living in married, two parent families."[48] One of the negative life outcomes is that divorce and unmarried childbearing increases child poverty. Did you know that the majority of children who grow up outside of married families will have experienced at least one year of dire poverty?" Also, some have suggested that had the family structure not changed from 1960, today's black child poverty rates who be 28.4 percent rather than 45.6 percent and white child poverty rates would be 11.4 percent rather than 15.4 percent.[49] Furthermore, children who grow up without fathers are "far more likely to end up in prison than are those who grew up with both biological parents. Girls growing up without a biological father are far more likely to suffer physical or sexual abuse.[50]

Divorce is also costly to the public as well as to state, local and federal governments. "In 2002, the 1.4 million divorces cost taxpayers more than $30 billion due to increased need for food stamps and public housing, and lost revenues, etc."[51]

Blindly walking into a vocation has far more serious and moral consequences than blindly walking into a new job. Job swapping is as easy as 1, 2, 3. Swapping spouses is injurious and devastating to all involved because it renders the vocation – our calling – null and void and fruitless. While no one enters into marriage with the intention to divorce, this is often the end result because of all the factors discussed here.

Same Sex Unions

Complementary gender relationships were and are still the original plan for marriage as established by God. Man and woman, two different creatures, become one in marriage. God created male/female unions to be authentic and fruitful allowing natural love and life to flourish. For the most part, however, heterosexual marriages have been poor role models for authentic love, giving ammunition to those who would like to re-define marriage. It is much harder to defend traditional marriage when one's own ended in disaster. And so we have reached the doorstep of a time when it is argued with vehemence that to deny gays marital rights is to deny civil rights.

Marriage and same sex unions are different realities for many different reasons. Homosexuality is still classified as a mental deviance. Previously homosexuality had been classified as a mental illness but downgraded after gay activism worked actively to change the classification. Homosexuality is the state in which people experience an exclusive or predominant sexual attraction toward persons of the same sex. The genesis of the sexual orientation still cannot be explained despite decades of research and study. Some experts attribute the orientation to genetic factors while others attribute it to disease; environmental causes; family dysfunction; emotional/psychological harm; or choice.

Homosexuality is not common. Approximately 1 percent to 3 percent of the population has a homosexual orientation. The matter has been quite difficult to research due to fluctuations even within the various orientations. Research shows that sexual behavior can fluctuate over time for gay men and lesbian women. Public figures who have switched orientations as adults include Sinead O'Connor, Anne Heche, and Joanne Loulan. Sociologists acknowledge that there is a general lack of knowledge with regard to lifestyles, attitudes, values, and behaviors of gay men and lesbian women. Some sociologists contend that being gay, lesbian or bisexual is more of a political identity than actual sexual behavior. But this is opinion, not fact.

Same sex advocates argue that sexual differences and behaviors are irrelevant. It is understandable why they make this claim in light of the fact that homosexuality is not a complementary physical/sexual relationship. To discuss the points, it must be shown how same sex unions are different realities than heterosexual marriages. It must also be said that same sex unions do not meet the twofold purposes of marriage. Finally, we must defend the position that marriage is a public state that exists for the good of the two spouses, their children, and society as a whole.

It has already been stated that same sex unions are not complementary relationships. God designed man and woman to be physically compatible in order to live out the twofold purposes of marriage joyfully and faithfully. The twofold purposes are: procreative and unitive love. Gay sex does not have the capacity for procreative love nor does it have the capacity for a natural, complementary physical union. Gay sex has higher risk for disease for a number of reasons. Dr. John R. Diggs Jr., writes: "It is my duty to assess behaviors for their impact on health and well being. When something is beneficial it is my duty to recommend it. Likewise when something is harmful, (i.e. smoking, overeating, alcohol or drug abuse and homosexual sex), it is my duty to discourage it."[52] Diggs states that he believes we have the right to discuss aspects of this issue (homosexual sex) to cast light on how the teachings of the church intersect with the various social, moral and legal developments in sexual society.

Diggs says there are five basic differences between homosexual and heterosexual relationships; the differences highlight the fact that the two relationships are different realities. The differences involve the levels of promiscuity; physical health consequences; mental health consequences; general life span; and definitions of monogamy. Diggs says that the consequences of homosexual activity are distinct from the consequences of heterosexual activity. [53]

Gays do not hold to the premise that fidelity is primary to

relationships. In fact, gay liberation principles were founded on sexual promiscuity; if that (promiscuity) element is abandoned it would be tantamount to a communal betrayal of gargantuan proportions."[54] An older study revealed that 75 percent of white gay males had more than 100 sex partners. Within this same group, the average number of partners varied from 100 to more than 1,000 sexual partners in their lifetime.[55]

Dr. Diggs states that promiscuity is again on the upswing – especially among younger homosexual men. Gay couples have short lived relationships; the average gay relationship lasts generally less than three years.[56]

Gay men have higher risk for contracting sexually transmitted infections, the "gay bowel syndrome"; anal cancer; anorectal dysfunction; hemorrhoids; anal fissures, and colon blockage. The gay life expectancy is on average twenty years lower than the life expectancy of a heterosexual male. The majority of the physical or health problems teach us that the human body is not designed for anal/oral sex. Gay behaviors often veer toward sadism or masochism.

Same sex advocates have core principles concerns. They include:

- Provide a safe, supportive social structure for GLBT couples and persons.
- The removal of traditional concepts of marriage and family.
- Equalize the legal rights and status of GLBT persons/relationships with marital heterosexual relationships.
- Equalize right to parenthood via adoption.

Elimination of Sexual Social Mores.

The first concern is a basic right for all people and should not be disputed by either side. The last three concerns however are different. History shows readily that civilizations that remove the moral boundaries of sexual expression do not last.

Stripping the boundaries for marriage so that any or all sexual expressions are protected means condoning and accepting adult-child sexual relationships, incest, pedophilia, polygamy, and adultery. The Bible provides much needed counsel in this area; it teaches us that homosexual activities are grave (meaning serious) depravities; they are intrinsically disordered; are contrary to natural law, and are a sin that denies the sinner of his rightful inheritance of the Kingdom of God. The Bible reminds us of the consequences that befell Sodom and Gomorrah after they had given themselves over to homosexuality. Additional passages with regard to homosexuality can be found in Genesis 19; 1-29 Romans 1:24-27; 1 Cor 6:10; 1 Tim 1:10.

Finally, it is important to recognize that all children have the right to be raised by a loving and nurturing family which includes a father and a mother. Some people worry that denying same sex unions the right to marry is tantamount to committing a civil rights violations. U.S. Catholic Bishops teach that "these unions are not the equivalent of male/female unions. Therefore, it is not unjust discrimination to oppose legal recognition of same sex unions as the legal equivalent of marriage."[57]

Reflection Questions:

1. What is the purpose of marriage? Why can't same sex unions fulfill these same purposes?

2. What are the four primary challenges facing all marriages? Why would the U.S. Catholic Bishops lay claim that these areas disaffect all marriages – Catholic and non Catholic?

3. What is Love? Name the characteristics.

4. How are you getting ready for marriage?

5. Why did God create male and female complementary yet different?

6. What is the role of the family?

Chapter Eleven

RELIGIOUS VOCATIONS

Many of you who are reading this book will become our future priests, sisters, brothers, and permanent deacons. You will find your true purpose and meaning in the vocation of religious life. Not you? It is still important to pray for help in discerning all vocations – no matter what yours will someday be.

You have already read how "all of us can realize God's love more fully when we follow the vocation He designed for us. Furthermore, you will find the most happiness possible in this life when you follow God's designed path forward."[1]

Many men and women eschew the marriage vocation in order to answer God's call to become a religious order sister, monk or brother; ordained priest; or perpetual virgin. They find happiness and peace in following this call. Fr. Steven Rossetti indicates that today's priests are truly happy being priests. If they had to do it over again, the great majority would do so without question.[2]

How Do You View the Religious Life?

Oftentimes, the religious life is perceived to be reserved for someone who is already holy. Biographies of priests, sisters, or brothers prove this perception to be false, however. Those who answer the call to the religious life will be the first to tell you that they did not feel like they've led exemplary lives prior to the calling. Further, holy people are the first to realize that they are not nearly holy enough!

Some young people perceive the religious life to be too hard or limiting — no fun! This attitude develops because we live in a "culture that does not promote the benefits of serving others."[3] Further, it is well recognized that we have a "commitment crisis" in this country beginning with marriage and running all the way through family life, having children, and entering the religious life. This crisis is the result of discarding relationships, lifestyles, and vocations that matter – including a religious life. Catholic and Protestant denominations face vocation shortages precisely because of the country's failure to commit to the important matters of life. Even graduation numbers from major service industries like police[4], fire[5], military[6], and nursing[7] programs are significantly lower than hoped for or needed although other factors are also at play.

Some young people believe that they would have to sacrifice too many personal liberties and freedoms if they subscribed to a religious vocation. Let's not deny that making a lifelong commitment to the religious state (and married life) requires a person to forsake some types of personal liberties and civil and social freedoms in order to serve other people. These commitments restrict personal desires, liberties, and activities by necessity and for the greater good that comes from serving others selflessly.

The religious life can be demanding work. Priests, sisters, and brothers voluntarily give of their time, talents, and virtues to serve other people – and daily! They also must attend to the fine tuning of personal virtue in order to be an effective living witness of God's love. They can be tested by the monumental work and duties associated with providing the sacraments, counseling, instruction, spiritual help, prayers, masses, or other parish/order administrative work. This work demands personal sacrifices from our religious over and over. Committing to the religious life also requires personal devotion to prayer and the sacraments in order to renew their energy and faith. Religious servants spend up to four hours or longer in daily prayer because they are desirous of growing their personal relationship with God. They also mature in this relationship as they go about doing works of charity and making daily sacrifices so the rest of us have opportunities to grow in our faith, hope, and charity. The example set by the religious often spurs on the laity to perform works of charity and mercy - vital to helping keep their religious life intact and vice versa.

The religious accept personal/social restrictions in order to build up protective hedges from bad influences and temptations and making poor choices which lead to scandalous behavior(s) that hurt themselves and the whole Church. The hedges help keep in the good while preventing the discrediting of one's spiritual values, lives and authentic witness. Religious persons' public sins are particularly scandalous because we all expect more from someone who publicly declared his or her love and commitment to God and His Church.

Many non-believers regard priests, sisters, or brothers as anomalies or enigmas; John Paul II, for example, was admired by Catholics and non-Catholics alike. But public sins of any religious persons quickly discredit an entire religious institution by way of association. When even just one priest commits public scandal, nearly all of those in religious life are painted as phonies and flukes. Furthermore, the faith of the laity is shaken by religious scandals.

The Call

Many are called but few are chosen. Tens of thousands of people willingly accept the servitude of religious life in order to bring the Gospel to people around the globe. It is nothing short of miraculous that men and women continue to answer God's call even though society as a whole dismisses or discourages this life choice and commitment. The Lord himself invites young people to "become instruments of service, hence, an expression of the mission of the whole person who vouches for Him and brings Him to men and women. If human hands symbolically represent human faculties and, in general, skill as power to dispose of the world, then anointed hands must be a sign of the human capacity for giving, for creativity in shaping the world with love."[8]

Pope John Paul II, Mother Teresa, and Pope Benedict the XVI each have been instrumental in inspiring religious vocations among men and women during their lifetimes. These three have *walked the religious life* most excellently and passionately, leading by personal example, joyfulness, and commitment. The two Popes are regarded highly as *real men who dared to live a religious life* when many people in the secular world discriminate manliness from religiosity. They taught us that real men can become holy priests, brothers, deacons, bishops, and popes. Mother Teresa also set the ultimate example for 21st century women through her humble, inspirational service to the poor and outcasts of the world. Her example was nothing short of contagious! Just think, all three arrived at just the right time! Coincidental? Not when God calls!

It is difficult for young people to hear the call to any vocation – especially the vocation call to the religious life — when they are surrounded and bombarded by excessively negative noise and chatter from the culture with regards to these states of life. Nevertheless, you are each responsible for discerning the nature of your vocation – don't be afraid to investigate the possibilities before arriving at your decision. All *other possibilities* still help point you toward the path you are called to follow.

Many factors work against the call to religious life including materialism, moral relativism, sexual promiscuity, bountiful economic conditions, local cultural opposition, smaller family sizes, trying to satisfy parents' wishes, parental disapproval, political climates, and peer influences. It is important to know, however, that many factors also work *in favor* of fostering the call to a religious vocation including today's programs offered by dioceses, universities, parishes, local parochial grade and high schools, and seminaries that encourage and promote the exploration of religious life by the uncommitted teens and young adults. It helps when young people participate in or observe vocation promotional efforts including local *nun runs*, vocation "pizza" nights, and others. Institutions such as Ave Maria University in Florida and Focus – Fellowship of Catholic University Students[9] - promote vocational exploration among college age men and women. They also invite college students to examine the "meaning and purpose of their lives" through bible studies, peer ministries, and more. Vocations can be fostered within the group of Millennials who want to learn more about their faith or want to help their fellow man. Faithful and supportive parents and families are also great resources when they encourage their young adults to prayerfully and faithfully discern their vocation.

Big city parishes know that it is simply more difficult to identify and/or personally call potential candidates to the religious life. In former days, vocations were primarily fostered by mingling young people with religious sisters, priests, and brothers in schools, communities, and parishes. In the old days, the sheer numbers of religious personnel ensured that many young people knew someone (even from their own family) who was a priest or a sister. Young people were exposed to religious people regularly; they were their teachers, coaches, guidance counselors, principals, pastors, etc. Today, young people do not have this same opportunity or exposure to priests, brothers, and sisters because there are fewer of them around. Therefore, the Church has to attract candidates differently than it did in the past.[10] God works through all of the supports and distractions as He attracts and pursues those called to the religious life.

God might even use the mass media and internet to attract your attention. Many vocation's offices and religious orders have created attractive websites designed to answer questions about the religious life, track and keep databases of interested persons, and funnel pertinent inquiries and/or questions about the religious life to the right resource person. Check out the various websites online.[11]

There are other ways that parishes, dioceses, and religious orders try to attract young men and women to the religious life. The first way is to ask all parishes to pray for an increase in vocations. And, they do. Many parishes have inserted a *Diocesan Prayer for an Increase in Vocations* during the Mass. Parishes have seen positive results after implementing the *Called by Name* programs at the local parish level; this program personally invites students to consider a religious life by offering evenings of questions and answers, and presentations about the religious life.[12] A renewed interest in traditional spirituality and religious practices among emerging adults has generated a high level of interest in and curiosity about traditional vocations as well. Dioceses and parishes also have come to realize that many young immigrants are interested in and attracted to the religious life. First, however, the dioceses must successfully communicate and interact with the cultures of these young immigrants.

Lacking open access to seminary training used to be a barrier for enrollment in diocesan seminaries. Most dioceses have dropped the requirement that candidate students live in the diocese for at least five years before applying to the seminary. This has translated into more applications.

Vocation offices know that the personal witness of clergy and religious persons is always one of the most effective "recruiting" tools and they use it as much as possible to identify or get to know candidates and allow candidates to know the religious. As in all walks of life, it is very important to have effective and charismatic leadership at the top to help inspire young people to explore religious vocations.

Regardless of the recruiting tactics used, every individual must answer the call to become a religious priest, brother, or sister on his/ her own initiative. Each must come to believe that God is calling them by name. They must not choose the religious life for any other reason or expectation.

Today's young men have the opportunity to discern a religious vocation when attending minor seminaries. Approximately one third of the men who graduate from a college minor seminary undergraduate program enroll in a diocesan theological (major) seminary. [13] The remaining two thirds came to the conclusion that they did not have a vocation call. While some may think that this statistic is an indictment or failure of the discernment process in minor seminaries, it is not! Vocations directors are encouraged that so many young people take the time to discern God's call — whatever it will be — while in college!

In 2004, dioceses with the highest ratio of seminarians to Catholics include Lincoln, Nebraska; Yakima, Washington; Savannah, Georgia; Cheyenne, Wyoming; Rapid City, South Dakota; Wichita, Kansas; Tulsa, Oklahoma; Alexandria, Louisiana; Pensacola-Tallahassee, Florida; Steubenville, Ohio; Spokane, Washington; and Bismarck, North Dakota. [14] The recent upswing in seminary enrollments and new religious orders has been very encouraging especially since the Catholic Church in the United States had "suffered from a vocation collapse" even though vocations experienced a spectacular worldwide growth during the past several decades. Today's young men and women prefer orders and seminaries that are perceived as more vigorous, rigorous, traditional, and authentically Catholic. Several new religious orders for women come to mind, including the Sisters of Life, the Capuchin Sisters of Nazareth, the Missionaries of Charities, and the Poor Clare's. The first three were not around fifty years ago!

The Center for Applied Research in the Apostolate reports that the total number of American diocesan and religious seminarians decreased from 9,021 in 1978 to 4,790 in 2003 – a decline of nearly 47 percent.[15] In 1978, when John Paul II became Pope, there were approximately 64,000 diocesan and religious seminarians in training around the world. After twenty-four consecutive years of growth, the numbers of seminarians in training increased to 112,643 (worldwide). This growth represents a 76 percent increase.[16]

The Archdiocese of St. Paul and Minneapolis, under the direction of Archbishop Harry Flynn, ordained ninety priests in fourteen years.[17] Within this population of new priests only three have asked to be removed from their priestly duties and vocation. This dropout rate suggests that the seminary is thoroughly recruiting and preparing men for ordination and priestly function. It is highly unlikely that the divorce rate for new Catholic couples during this same time frame can come close to matching the 3.3 percent priestly dropout rate. It is apparent that the preparation for marriage must become more fine-tuned for Catholic couples asking to marry within the Church in order to have this same vocation satisfaction rate.

Types of Religious Vocations

All religious vocations have two permanent restrictions — celibacy and obedience. All religious vow to be obedient to God, the Church and/or a Mother Superior or Bishop/Pope of a diocese. Chastity is an important virtue for everyone including those called to live out the vow of celibacy. Chastity helps to build up those hedges necessary for faithful marriages and holy religious lives. Some religious orders also require their sisters, brothers or priests, take a vow of poverty. This vow essentially renounces ownership for any and all material possessions that are luxuries and desires rather than wants or needs. The Capuchin Sisters of Nazareth, for instance, go barefoot in the convent, sleep on the floor with sleeping bags and renounce all connection to material goods.

Religious vows are binding and permanent; so is the marriage vow for the laity.

There are three distinct types of religious vocations: contemplative, semi contemplative, and active orders; and two types of priests: diocesan and religious order priests.

Priesthood – Who and How?

Each year the Church ordains men from many different walks of life and types of families. The parishioners are especially curious about their new assistant pastor. You may be surprised by the diversity!

Men ordained to the priesthood have a myriad of life experiences and personality types. Some of our new young priests have been chefs, played guitar in a rock band, were martial arts experts, flew fighter jets, were practicing physicians, taught in medical schools, were "killers" on the football field, were successful lawyers, former atheists, carpenters, engaged to be married, lawyers, doctors, engineers, teachers, bicyclists (one rode a bike from St. Louis to Toronto with twenty other seminarians for World Youth Day), owned houses, drove BMWs, owned Rolex watches, are good looking, are great public speakers, are shy, are afraid of public speaking, get nervous in crowds, are humble, are funny, are friendly.[18]

These men are mainstream America with one twist: They all believe that God called them to serve fellow Catholics and Americans as priests, professors, and chaplains. The new priests come with different interests and some aren't even that young anymore. They are as varied as were the original Twelve Apostles who were fishermen, tax collectors, farmers, and more. Each of the men ordained to the priesthood come from a unique background and a personal story about the call to the religious life even though each "experienced the same Jesus Christ who asked them to leave everything to follow Him. And many of them will leave their old selves or "identities" behind to follow the Lord, for at ordination they will become an *Alter Christus*.[19]

The same diversity applies also to our religious men and women called to live as religious sisters and brothers. Recently, we have been privileged to know four young women who have joined religious orders. Each of them entered a different order. One young woman is in France, another in Spain, one chose an order located in Pennsylvania, and the last one is located in New York. All joined very traditional orders with restrictive lifestyles, yet each person is happy to be called as the Bride of Christ.

How Do You Know if You Are Called?

You should ask yourself if God has been calling you to the religious life. Some ask this question for all the wrong reasons including parental pressure, expectations of others, or because they have an overly scrupulous conscience. Others ask the question for all the right reasons.

What are some of these reasons? Vocation directors will tell you that there are some basic litmus tests for helping to discern whether you are being called to a religious vocation. They include:

The most important is **having a desire for the religious life**.[20]

God calls us through our natural inclinations. In other words, if someone has antipathy toward the religious life, it is less likely that they are called to the religious life – or at least at the time of the opposition. It is likely that young people may feel a bit afraid of the thought that they are called to the religious life but that is a lot different than being repulsed by the possibility. Students who love to be of service to others have a more natural inclination toward the religious life than those who dislike helping other people or find service work distasteful in every way. Students who love to help others are stronger candidates than those who don't like to do that. Those who prefer lots of friends are also better candidates than those who prefer close, personal, intimate relationships.

Certain personal qualities are best suited for the religious life including having a strong desire to grow in one's faith, natural generosity, enjoys being of service to others, prayerful, willingly shares their faith with others, and willingly and naturally imposes self sacrifices on themselves.[21]

Having the right motivation[22] is another important criterion for all religious candidates. Candidates must want to serve God first and foremost– this spiritual motive is the primary one needed in order to become a priest, sister, or brother. Personal motives — such as wanting to hide behind a collar due to social awkwardness, sexual identity issues or problems, having a prideful desire to lead, interest in power or recognition — are not good motives. These should become red flags for vocations directors to slow down a candidate's progress toward ordination or profession of the vows. The best candidates for the religious life are mostly interested in desiring to grow closer to God through their vocation path.

Having a natural fitness for the religious life[23] is another necessary criterion. For example, students who can live comfortably with less material things are naturally better suited for the religious life. Also students who are cheerful and feel invigorated or joyful when serving others are more likely candidates than someone who gets grumpy when dealing with difficult people. Young people who are obedient by nature are more likely called than those who bristle when having to obey superiors. When a young person can visualize themselves as a priest, sister or brother, they are more likely to be called than someone who can't picture this at all. Finally young people who can mesh personal dreams and interests with an active prayer life, the enjoyment of serving others, and the desire to witness to others about their faith are more likely to be good candidates for the religious life.

All people entering any type of religious life must go through a time of personal scrutiny and examination during which they ascertain whether they have the right motives, fitness, and desire, for the religious life. Simultaneously, the diocese or order also scrutinizes, investigates, and examines each young person to ascertain whether their response is to a *genuine* calling. The decision for ordination or entering the religious life is a joint decision made by the Church and the young person. Usually they both arrive at the same conclusion about the genuineness of the calling to the religious life. After the Church and the candidate determine that a person has a legitimate call to the religious life, then plans move toward ordination or the profession of vows.

Women entering a religious order normally enter the convent as a candidate, quickly become a postulant, then a novice, and finally make a profession of final vows. This process generally takes several years to complete. It is a similar process for men entering the religious order as a brother.

Can I Afford to go to Seminary?

Undergraduate students assume all educational expenses to attend minor seminaries. Most dioceses, however, pay for the graduate theological degree obtained during the seminary training. In most cases, the seminarians may not have to pay back the diocese even if they drop out before ordination. Other dioceses require seminary students to pay full tuitions. After ordination, the accrued expenses are revoked. The tuition for major seminaries cost students or dioceses approximately $50,000 per year or $150,000[24] for three years of seminary training. Only a few dioceses still require candidates to live in the diocese for five years before applying to the seminary. During priestly formation, seminarians are assigned to local parishes where they receive informal training in the life of a priest. A committee of lay persons is often formed to work with the seminarian assigned to their parish. They discuss topics of interest and pray together. This interaction exposes the seminarian to typical parishioners' questions, attitudes, concerns, and challenges.

Detachment for the Religious Ordination

Religious orders ask that candidates detach themselves from the world. This means that most religious orders will not accept a young woman (or man) into the community until she (or he) has paid off financial debts. This is an important consideration as you make college decisions about school loans. Nevertheless, there is help for overcoming financial impediments from organizations such as the The Laboure Society[25] and the Serra Club and others. These organizations are dedicated to helping young men and women find ways to pay off existing debt in order to enter the religious community. Contact your local diocesan vocations director or the above organizations if you have any questions about personal financial impediments.

What Do They Do?

The primary role of the priest is to accommodate the spiritual, religious, personal, and sacramental needs of the parish and the parishioners. In this role, they turn into counselors (pre-marriage, marital, and family), teachers, preachers, healers, and money managers. Religious sisters and brothers more directly connect with the people in their outreach. Normally, the religious communities choose one or more charism to follow. Consequently, some religious orders train sisters or brother or priests to be professors in college, or to serve as high school or elementary school teachers, doctors, nurses, retreat directors, or prayer warriors. Some orders work directly with the poor and underprivileged; others run and staff universities and colleges. Still others operate hospitals, schools, medical clinics, or nursing homes. Some religious communities provide care only for the elderly; others have an outreach to special needs children and adults. Still other religious communities serve populations disaffected by AIDS. The world is blessed to have a variety of religious brothers and sisters serving those who need their help. Both priests and religious can serve as missionaries at home or abroad.

Young people are advised to follow their hearts and their passions. They should join the religious community that matches their desire to grow closer to God with natural talents and passions. The religious sister or brother often feels like they are best suited to "be on someone's side when they are at someone's side."

What About Consecrated Virgins?

The Catholic Church retains a special rite for women called to profess vows as a consecrated virgin. This vow is not taken with the idea that it can be put aside if something or someone better comes along. The perpetual virgin professes to live out this vocation for her lifetime. It is distinctly different than religious life because the religious sister essentially binds herself to her community but the perpetual virgin binds herself directly to God without benefit of a specific religious community.

The consecrated virgin lives and works in the real world without a special uniform or garb. Her only outward sign is the wearing of a wedding band. For all the world knows, the consecrated virgin is a married woman until she describes her life.

"The Consecration of Virgins is one of the oldest *sacramental rituals* (a ritual that is used to show religious devotion) in the Church; it is the oldest form of consecrated life. The Rite for Virgins who live in and amongst the world was restored and promulgated on May 31, 1970."[26] Mary, the mother of Jesus, was the first consecrated virgin. She was later joined by Saints Agnes, Agatha, Lucy, and Cecelia.

The consecrated virgin promises several things to her bishop. She promises to remain unmarried; to live without violating the virtue of chastity; to dedicate herself to the service of the Church; to practice her faith; to accept the teachings of Scripture and the Church; to live a vibrant and grounded spiritual life; to grow personally; and to give herself totally to God and the Church.[27]

The consecrated virgin resolves to live a life of perpetual virginity for God. She professes her vows before the Bishop of the diocese where she resides. Her duties include:

- praying the Liturgy of the Hours daily
- receiving the sacraments regularly
- setting aside daily time to pray for the needs of the diocese, fellow Catholics, the Bishops, the Pope, and all of the clergy

Consecrated virgins have a "personal, spousal relationship with Christ." The consecrated virgin stands in the midst of today's culture as a living witness to the future life of all persons, a life in which there will be no giving or taking in marriage, but each person will live in intimacy with our Creator God."[28]

The Catholic Catechism teaches that: *The order of virgins is...a form of consecrated life. Through their pledge to follow Christ more closely, virgins are consecrated to God, mystically espoused to Christ and dedicated to the service of the Church, when the diocesan Bishop consecrates them according to the approved liturgical rite.*[29]

Pope John Paul II stated that "the consecrated virgin transforms any emotional pain endured by the decision to forsake marriage and natural motherhood for Christ's sake into joyful affirmation of the spousal meaning of the human body. The consecrated virgins teach us how we will live out authentic love in and through our human bodies after our own bodily resurrections take place at the end of the world."

We are all blessed by the example and deeds of all holy men and women, young and old, in the Church.

Reflection Questions:

1. Do you pray regularly for the discernment of your vocation?

2. Have you ever prayed about the religious life?

3. What do you expect your vocation to be? Explain why.

4. Do you know any religious men or women?

5. What is your opinion of these individuals? Do they live according to your expectations for this calling? Why/Why not?

6. Have you ever attended an ordination or final profession of vows? If so, what was it like? How did you feel?

Chapter Twelve

NATURAL
FERTILITY AWARENESS

You all got started quite naturally in your mother's fallopian tube with the mutual donation and union of your father's and mother's reproductive cells. Your father's sperm penetrated the wall of your mother's released egg cell and voila – here you are! Simultaneous to this physical reaction or synthesis, was another, even grander one. In the instant of fertilization, God breathed His life into the fertilized egg turning a natural synthesis into a supernatural one whereby you were endowed with body, mind, soul, and will. Granted, at that time, you were just a very tiny version of yourself. You have inestimable worth because of this breath; in fact, it molded you into an image and likeness of God! What you do with yourself and your life is up to you, but God loves you so much that He grants you the free will to choose whatever, all the while hoping (and knowing whether) you will choose to love Him.

This natural creation tells us a lot about what we can know and what we can't. This chapter will discuss what it is that we know about our biological beginnings. Appendix thirteen will be helpful if you are not aware of some of the technical terms used in this chapter. Also appendix fourteen contains an interesting timeline with regard to human sexuality issues compiled from a number of sources. Take a few moments now to look these two resources over before resuming reading this material.

Our Story

My husband and I learned about Natural Family Planning (NFP) at a pre-marriage retreat about a year before our wedding. Up to this point, we had not talked much about family planning matters although neither of us were very interested in the artificial birth control measures. Horror stories about blood clots due to the use of the Pill were enough to scare us off. So the topic of NFP intrigued us although the first question we had was: If it's so great, how come we haven't heard about this from others?

Pushing aside that concern, we decided to learn NFP from the Couple to Couple League for Natural Family Planning. The instruction seemed easy enough but we had yet to test the "user" effectiveness. About nine months later, we got married and the real test of NFP arrived. It turns out that it worked just fine for our early (and later) family planning intentions which were to postpone pregnancy. Three years later, we had our first son and twenty-one years later we gave birth to our last daughter.

Over the course of thirty-five years of marriage, we have used NFP to achieve pregnancy, postpone pregnancy, transition between natural infertility due to breastfeeding back into regular fertility, and also watched fertility wax and wane before menopause. We believe that NFP helped us live out our marriage vows better than would have been possible without this knowledge. NFP taught us to regard fertility as a gift to be treasured and not something to be spoiled or derided. And so we continue to teach NFP to young couples because we believe that it helped us think, talk, and act better toward each other, God, and our children.

Years ago, a woman wrote to Ann Landers complaining about the fact she had to pay for the cost of the birth control she and a boyfriend used and she felt this was unfair. However, she was uncomfortable bringing up the matter because she and the boy didn't know each other well enough to discuss money. She asked Ann what to do about this dilemma. We believe the use of NFP would end these types of dilemmas.

What is NFP?

Natural family planning is simply advanced instruction about human biology. It teaches couples to be aware of their combined natural fertility. It is very effective in helping couples realize when they are naturally fertile and when they are naturally infertile. It is the means by which couples read their fertility and infertility signs; studies prove that it is more 99 percent effective. Couples begin to understand more about themselves and the mystery of how they were created when they learn this system of awareness and knowledge.

Therefore, NFP entails the study of what makes fertility possible – the study of the **anatomy** of the adult human person. Furthermore, students who are learning NFP must discover how this fertility is made possible. They learn this by studying the **function** of the human reproductive cycles.

Male and Female Anatomy and Function

The male brain directs the anatomy and biochemistry of men just as female brains direct female systems. Ellen Grant writes in her book *Sexual Chemistry* that the different genders are just an extra carbon here, one more single hydrogen there, and voila we have two completely different genders with unique sexual characteristics and chemical operating hormones.

All sexual function begins in the hypothalamus and pituitary glands of the brain. You might not realize that the hypothalamus gland governs and regulates a number of metabolic processes including hunger, thirst, body temperature, and sexual chemistry. In females the interaction between these glands found in the brain and the sexual organs is known as the HPO axis (hypothalamus, pituitary, ovaries) whereas in males it is called the HPG axis (hypothalamus, pituitary, gonads). The hypothalamus sends out pulsating signals of gonadotropin releasing hormone (GnRH) to which the pituitary gland reacts by emitting intermittent secretions of luteinizing hormone (LH) and follicle stimulating hormone (FSH). These two hormones direct both the male and female reproductive systems; they are essential for both female and male fertility. (Enlarged diagrams available on page 381.)

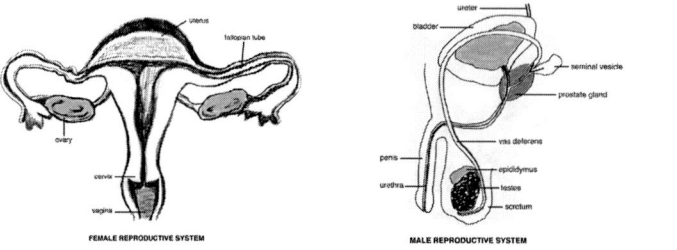

FEMALE REPRODUCTIVE SYSTEM   MALE REPRODUCTIVE SYSTEM

The above diagram shows the anatomy of the male and female reproductive systems. The male sexual chemistry is primarily designed to produce spermatozoa (sperm) capable of fertilizing a female reproductive cell (ovum). The primary target for testosterone is the testes which are located in the scrotum. Here, the male reproductive cells – the spermatozoa — are eventually manufactured and released. The testes are made up of two separate compartments called seminiferous tubules (adluminal compartment) and the Leydig cells (the basal compartment). The male luteinizing hormone is the key hormone responsible for stimulating the Leydig cells which produce testosterone. The first compartment produces the sperm and the second specializes in synthesizing male androgens such as testosterone.

Testosterone is an essential hormone that develops and maintains male genitalia and other sex glands, causes facial and body hair to grow, causes the male to develop a deep voice and large muscles and skeleton, and helps define the metabolic rate of the male body. When testosterone is adequately maintained it provides feedback to the hypothalamus and the pituitary gland; this is important for controlling the hormone production and balance.

Wet dreams or erections/ejaculations signal the maturation of a male's sexuality. These occurrences usually manifest themselves after boys have experienced other physical changes, including an increase in muscle mass; growth of pubic, leg and armpit hair; physical growth spurts; development of body odor and more.

Male fertility is the result of the male organs and glands responding to the brain's chemical signals in a uniquely male way. Conversely, female chemistry is the result of female organs and glands responding to the brain's chemical signals in a uniquely female way.

The female sexual chemistry is primarily designed to produce mature female reproductive cells (ova) that are capable of being fertilized by male sperm. Females produce four very important hormones that direct their reproductive systems, biology, skeleton, female characteristics and fertility. These hormones are follicle stimulating hormone, luteinizing hormone, estrogen and progesterone. The first two hormones are produced by the brain; the latter two are produced by the ovaries. (See previous diagram.) A girl's first vaginal bleeding episode, known as the menarche, is the final prominent sign that she has reached sexual maturity. Previously she will also have undergone other physical manifestations including the development of breast tissue and pubic, leg and armpit hair; physical growth spurts; development of body odor, changing moods, and other subtle changes.

Young girl needs to reach an average weight of about 100 pounds in order for menarche to occur. Menarche usually occurs around 12.8 years of age although the normal range for girls is reported as being 9.1 years to 17.7 years.[1] Research has yet to pinpoint what mechanism(s) activate puberty but menarche appears to result from combined factors including age, health, weight, and developmental growth. It is quite normal for girls who have reached sexual maturation to experience greater menstrual cycle irregularity over the course of the next several years while the hormones adjust. "Like menopause, puberty is a transitional period that culminates in a change in fertility. Puberty involves biological series of events that initiate fertility whereas menopause involves biological series of events that terminate fertility."[2] Ovulation of a female sex cell (egg) is a complex process initiated by the hypothalamus, a gland in the brain, which releases gonadatropin releasing hormone (GnRH). This hormone stimulates the pituitary gland to produce pulsating levels of follicle stimulating hormone (FSH) and luteinizing hormone (LH). FSH, in turn, stimulates the synthesis of estrogen and progesterone - also known as female sex steroids - within the ovaries of females to prepare an egg for ovulation. Each ovary is roughly the size of an almond and has a matching pair.

Within the ovary, various types of follicles exist; they differ by degree of development, division and maturation. They are known as granulosa cells, the oocytes, and theca and stroma cells; they work synergistically to cause one or more mature cells to ovulate.[3] In essence, the various follicles communicate and interact with the growing oocyte. Antral, also called primordial or resting follicles, are tiny (about 2-8 mm in diameter) but can be observed via ultrasound. Theca cells produce various ovarian androgens (including several types of estrogen). The granulosa cells produce estrogen (estradiol) and two important ovulatory limiting *factors* known as Inhibin A and B. Inhibin A is a product of the dominant follicle and rises with pre-ovulatory increases of estradiol. Inhibin B is a product of the pool of growing follicles and rises during the developing follicle phase of the cycle; it peaks mid cycle and then begins to fall. [4]

FSH levels rise at the end of the luteal phase (post ovulatory phase) and through the first week of the follicular development phase of the next cycle. Rising levels of FSH cause a dominant follicle to be selected for ovulation from the pool of *antral* follicles.[5] The hardiest and most mature oocyte is released at ovulation. Maximum levels of estrogen are achieved just prior to ovulation. The high levels of estrogen trigger pre-ovulatory surges of FSH and LH and together they cause the release of the egg from the pre-ovulatory follicle.

After ovulation, the corpus luteum (where the egg was released from) secretes progesterone using a more primitive pathway of synthesis than the estrogen producing cells.[6] This "yellow body" functions as a short lived gland and maintains production of the hormone progesterone for two weeks. The luteal phase or post ovulatory phase of the fertility cycle is detected by observing elevated basal body temperatures.

Meanwhile, the released egg begins its journey to the uterus after entering the fallopian tube. This trip takes about five to nine days. If the released egg is fertilized, the new life begins to produce Human Chorionic Gonadatropin (HCG) which helps maintain progesterone levels until the placenta takes over that function. If there is no pregnancy, the corpus luteum ceases to function after about fourteen to sixteen days and progesterone levels drop. The decreasing level of progesterone causes the basal body temperatures to drop, menstruation to begin, and the start of a new fertility cycle.

Females produce six different types of estrogens (E_1 through E_6). Estradiol (E_2) is the most powerful steroid of the bunch; it is produced within the ovaries, adipose (fat) tissue, the skin, bone osteoblast, smooth muscle cells, and the hypothalamus gland. Estrone (E_1) and estriol (E_3) are produced in the ovaries and other tissues as well but they exhibit *weaker* estrogen properties compared to estradiol. Women with higher percent body fat produce more estrone (E_1) than women with leaner bodies.[7] The less potent estrogens have to be re-synthesized into E_2 (estradiol) before producing significant steroidal effects.[8]

After menopause, the powerful estradiol (E_2) is no longer produced by the woman's ovaries in any significant amount, causing her estrogen levels to fall. This change produces a number of physical effects in females. Her pituitary gland continues to put out more LH and FSH in an attempt to orchestrate ovulation but the efforts are useless because there are no more viable eggs to develop. The brain doesn't know that the ovaries have been depleted of developing eggs consequently the FSH levels remain elevated in post menopausal women for the rest of their lives.

Male and Female Fertility

Male fertility is constant once sexual maturity has been achieved. On the other hand, women have cyclic fertility after reaching sexual maturity. Cyclic fertility means that the process of changing from being fertile to being infertile within each cycle is perfectly normal. It also means that the entire cycle will repeat the process in successive fertility cycles.

Disease, diets, environmental toxins, genetic abnormalities, sexually transmitted infections, alcohol or drug abuse, lack of exercise, illness, obesity and certain medications can disrupt or alter both male and female fertility, sexual hormone levels, sexual anatomy, or biofeedback signals.

Recent evidence suggests that a man's fertility appears to decline after the age of fifty until he is no longer fertile after the average age of 75. While controversial, some fertility experts suggest that even *if* the human male continues to be fertile after seventy five, his aging and lifestyle choices (if negative) may not be friendly to the process of spermatogenesis. Poor quality or damaged sperm increase with male aging adding increased risk for miscarriage, infertility, or other pregnancy problems.

Females have all the immature eggs (oogonia) they will ever have sixteen to twenty weeks after conception. (The more mature cell is called the oocyte.) In fact, pre-born females have more than seven million eggs at this time of her development! Yet, shortly after conception, the female reproductive cells begin to decline due to a process known as atresia. In fact, at birth, females are left with only about two million oocytes. By the time she reaches puberty, only 400,000 egg cells are still around. Yet this is normally plenty.

Women release between 150–400 total mature sex (egg) cells over the course of their natural fertility cycles depending on the number of pregnancies, length of lactational amenorrhea, and atresia. Over 99 percent of all oocytes/follicles that are in the ovaries simply degenerate and disappear at a steady rate. Research has discovered that when oocytes remain *naked* (i.e. without layers of granulose cells to protect them) they degenerate more readily.[9] Research has yet to determine all the causes that produce this lack of cover.

Fertility naturally declines as the numbers of viable oocytes dwindle. The fertility status of women older than forty years of age is considered to be less than half that of women who are thirty-five or younger.[10] Fertility plummets after the age of forty due in part to an increase in the rate of atresia.[11] Approximately 10 percent of women between the ages of forty and forty-four are able to become pregnant. Between the ages of forty-five and forty-nine, only 3 percent of the women are able to achieve pregnancy. It is extremely unlikely for anyone to achieve natural pregnancy after the age of fifty.[12] Menopause occurs when there are no more viable oocyte/follicles in the ovaries – this occurs for most women at the average age of fifty-one.

Some experts suggest that environmental toxins hasten atresia along with other factors. Environmental factors that disaffect reproduction are grouped into two categories: reproductive or developmental. Reproductive toxins prevent or impair reproduction by altering or interfering with the normal physiological processes including ovulation, hormone production, atresia and egg cell health. Developmental toxicants negatively affect, alter, or influence developing life. Exposure to toxicants during the first three months of pregnancy can cause birth defects or miscarriage. Exposure to toxicants during the latter months of pregnancy can slow the growth or alter the normal development of a fetus.

Infertility

Infertility is an adversity that affects up to one in seven couples of normal reproductive ages.[13] Infertility of any type can be emotionally painful for couples hoping for a baby.

Infertility can be traced to the male, the female, or both the male and the female in a relationship. Infertility is considered to be a medical problem. In many cases, the causes for a couple's shared infertility remain elusive. About one third of all infertility cases are either unidentifiable or traceable to combined conditions (synergy) of the couple. Another one third of the causes of infertility is attributable to each partner — male and female.

Factors that work against male and female sexual health include obesity, insufficient body fat, chronic alcohol abuse, chronic illness, systemic illness such as rheumatoid arthritis, and, cancer. All of these can negatively impact male testosterone levels and female estrogen/progesterone levels. Medications used to treat illness or disease can also decrease male and female fertility.

Infertility can also result from contracting sexually transmitted diseases, being exposed to environmental conditions or reproductive toxicants; having congenital or anatomical problems. It can develop after using contraceptives or having one or more surgical or chemical abortions. Infertility can even result from complications developed after giving birth – this subsequent infertility is known as secondary infertility.

Today, an infertile couple is often torn between accepting infertility or saying yes to the artificial reproductive techniques (ART) which promises them a baby. Turning one's back on this immoral decoy often means remaining childless.

Couples facing these moral dilemmas will have to lean on prayer and supernatural grace in order to be able to say: no and enough is enough. They also need to stand with conviction when presented with these options. The decoys will make it seem like only the results matter and the end point -a new human person – outweighs the illicit means used. These couples can look at the option of adoption, a moral means by which they are granted the same privilege of loving a child into adulthood. Infertile couples should consult with a wise spiritual advisor or pastor before undergoing infertility testing and procedures so they are not enticed by all that artificial reproduction has in store for them. Most medical centers do not operate with concern about Catholic medical and sexual ethics, morality or spirituality, nor do they have much respect for the moral or ethical beliefs of individual clients.

Male Infertility

Specialists often look to the sperm as the first possible culprit for a couple's infertility. The investigation will try to uncover any sperm deficiencies or abnormalities. They will also look for structural problems, medical conditions, or disease in the person. Male sexual health is determined in part by assessing and comparing the quality and quantity of his sperm to pre-established standards. Specialists evaluate the sperm's motility (movement and energy) and morphology (shape) factors, sheer numbers, and the volume of the male ejaculate. The sperm sample is graded. The possibilities are: too low, average, or high fertility.

Good quality sperm should move in straight, efficient lines. The heads of the sperm should be single, average sized, and oval-shaped. The tails ought to be long and fairly straight. These characteristics give the sperm a better chance of fertilizing the egg since they allow sperm to maintain strength and speed. Both strength and speed are necessary when striving to be the first to penetrate the hard outer coating of a female egg.

Female Infertility

Female sexual health is evaluated after conducting an investigation of possible underlying physical or structural problems, medical conditions, or disease including PCOS, endometriosis, anovulatory cycling, sexually transmitted infections, hormonal imbalances, eating disorders, poor nutrition, inadequate or excessive body fat; disease or illness; pharmacological side effects; age related factors; effects of chemotherapy; and more.

A general fertility assessment can look at the characteristics of the fertility cycle including luteal phase, mucus patterns and other ovulatory indicators. Different hormonal tests should also be carried out simultaneously. The uterus, ovaries and fallopian tubes will likely be evaluated as well to determine if there is any blockage, or presence of cysts, tumors, or other problems. An NFP chart can be a very useful tool to help look for infertility clues.

The entire evaluation process can become very complex, expensive, and frustrating for couples.

General Sexual Health

Men and women of all ages should be concerned about maintaining good general and sexual health because of the link between the two. As already discussed, environmental factors, genetic factors, sexual behaviors, nutrition, personal risk, and disease disaffect both.

The keys to maintaining health include the following:
- Eat a well balanced diet
    - Low in trans fat
    - High in fresh fruit and vegetables
    - High in good carbohydrates including nuts
    - Eat lean meats
    - Consume a variety of dairy products
- Maintain good blood pressures and cholesterol levels
- Exercise regularly
- Maintain proper weight
- Don't smoke or abuse drugs or alcohol
- Avoid exposure to radiation or chemical toxicants
- Men should avoid prolonged exposure of the groin to high humidity or heat sources, including hot tubs, jacuzzis, laptop computers. Avoid carrying cell phones in front pants pockets.

Post coital testing of sperm provides the best analysis of the female/male synergy. This test evaluates the quality and quantity of the sperm that is naturally deposited in the vaginal tract. The evaluation process may also require a sample of sperm that has not been deposited during intercourse. In this case, the couple may use a perforated, spermicide-free condom during intercourse in order to collect most of the sperm. The perforations allow the possibility of a natural pregnancy to still occur – albeit limited in nature.

Collection processes that ask the male to collect the sperm apart from natural coitus are an affront to his personal dignity. That process sends the man into a room where he is given pornographic literature and expected to masturbate in order to collect sperm. This is an illicit means that uses depersonalized efficiencies to satisfy scientific purposes. Measures such as this must be called into question by all persons of faith.

Infertility testing and medical evaluations can cause husband and/or wife to feel like they have been reduced to specimens or objects. It is time to stop infertility testing or procedures when a person begins to feel abused or violated or when infertility tests and procedures begin to damage the marital relationship or are illicit in nature.

Assisted Reproductive Technologies (ART)

Natural reproduction is fully protective; it does not manipulate, purchase, or control life. It allows newly conceived life to progress along a natural, uninterrupted continuum that begins at conception and ends with natural birth. All babies have the right to be conceived naturally within the marital embrace and to have the assurance of protection from their mother's body.

Assisted reproductive technologies are violators rather than protectors. They violate the Church's teaching about the sanctity and value of human life. They violate the dignity of male and female fertility; they violate the very personhoods of the people involved. They violate babies' rights to be conceived and protected within mothers' body. All babies conceived in test tubes are either manipulated, moved, discarded, frozen or used for experimentation. Only blue ribbon specimens are rewarded with a more natural home (womb). The violating technologies include in-vitro fertilization (IVF) procedures, sperm donation, artificial insemination, surrogate motherhood, and other variations thereof.

Procedures that replace the natural mother or father's reproductive cells or bodies, or artificially orchestrate the fertilization, are not moral methods. Artificial reproduction has come back to bite many people; this points to its unethical and immoral nature.

Despite the fact that there are many ethical issues surrounding assisted reproduction procedures, the assisted reproductive technologies don't stop doing what they do best: harvesting ova and sperm for profit while also generating millions of blue-ribbon embryos for sale.

We already realize that we cannot sell a body part, yet that is what happens with assisted reproduction. Women and men sell gametes. Some women even rent out their bodies like warehouses in the case of surrogacy. In the future, biological parents may have new reasons to conceive – perhaps their baby's organs will be used for financial or personal gain. Hold on. That has already happened. One couple conceived specifically so the new baby would be a perfect donor for their older daughter. And then there was the Octo-mom who had eight babies using IVF procedures. Finally, infertility isn't even made to seem like a barrier to pregnancy any longer. No, the barrier has become how much money and time couples are willing to spend to get a baby. Parents are not ashamed to state that their baby cost as much as their new car. People pay big bucks for that perfect, blue-ribbon baby. What happens when that blue-ribbon baby doesn't meet the expectations of the new parents? We will look at that shortly.

But first, consider how assisted reproduction technologies change the baseline for how we view fertility, infertility, and life in general. Modern society believes that nature is minimal but nurture is everything according to Toby L. Schonfeld. If that is true, however, then why are infertile couples paying hugely for gametes or embryos with the hopes of producing the smartest, brightest, tallest super-baby of all? To a large extent, they are paying for nature. Egg and sperm banks look for bright, intelligent, beautiful men and women; especially those enrolled in prestigious universities for their brains, athleticism and blond hair/ blue eyes. The national average egg donor is paid $4,200 for each cycle of harvested eggs. Sperm donors are paid anywhere from $50 to $100 per sample, and they are expected to contribute to the sperm bank for up to one year! [14]

But the unresolved ethical questions are coming back to bite. "The increased pressure to have one's own biological children, regardless of the cost, has led to problematic psychological effects for women undergoing these procedures."[15] Also there is emerging evidence that children produced by ART have adverse effects compared to children conceived within the protective confines of mother's body. Evidence suggests that these children have higher risk for cardiovascular problems, developmental delays, lower IQ[16], emotional difficulty, birth defects, and low birth weight and other prenatal complications related to multiple births.[17]

Egg donations are also physically invasive and risky. The American Society for Reproductive Medicine estimates that 1 percent to 2 percent of women undergoing the removal of her gametes will require hospitalization for secondary consequences including infection and other medical problems. A few women will require major surgery due to complications of the egg retrieval.[18] And then there are the examples of couples who unwittingly received another couple's frozen embryo(s); the embryos were switched – not at birth but in the laboratory. This unfortunate baby technically has three sets of parents: the genetic parents, the birth parents, and the laboratory technicians.

Couples have had custody battles over frozen embryos. Some divorcing couples perceive the frozen embryos to be financial assets during divorce settlements. If that isn't enough, ART often necessitates pregnancy reduction procedures when too many implanted embryos "took hold." But it doesn't stop there. ART allows couples to pick the gender of their baby. It also generates tens of thousands of excessive and *unwanted* embryos that are relegated to freezing, artificially induced limbos. ART promises to create a disabilities-free society if only we would all just get on board with those who promote gene pre-selection techniques including abortion and infanticide!

Egg banks offer couples the opportunity to choose from intelligence, eye color, height, or looks. Each characteristic costs additional money. What happens to the future offspring if he or she turns out not to be as intelligent, or tall, or good looking as the parents expected? Can the parents sue or return the merchandise? These unanswered ethical questions march us down the road into de-humanizing civilization.

Finally, Schonfeld warns that IVF and ART have contributed to an erosion of our sense of the uniqueness of what once was priceless. This erosion has been a long but gradual one. However, the erosion of what once was priceless was sped up after accepting the notion that life is only good when choice and desire are the trump card as happens with abortion and contraception.

Procedures that assist natural reproduction are generally considered moral methods.

Fertilization

The fertilization process creates a new person uniquely made up of the father and the mother. That means both parents contribute half to the genetic makeup of their new baby. The male sperm and female ovum are "miniaturized" designs that miraculously craft the human race; fertilization is more delicate and complex than many people realize. Both sperm and ovum need to be healthy in order to function properly. Do you know that it takes the average male over sixty-four days to produce mature sperm cells or spermatozoa? Just one high fever for several days can damage many of these sperm.

The sperm first become capable of fertilization after moving to the epididymus (see diagram on page 288). At this point the sperm become motile or capable of movement. Sperm undergo anaerobic respiration as they thrive and mature. The tail-like part of the epididymus provides the main propulsive force behind the male ejaculation. The ampulla serves as a storage reservoir for sperm until ejaculation; it produces fructose and other products required to keep the sperm healthy. The sperm remain viable in this region for forty to forty-five days.

The seminal vesicles are important because they provide a nutritious swimming medium (seminal fluid) for the sperm. Over half of the normal volume of male ejaculate (2-5 ml) is seminal fluid. The seminal fluid is alkaline in nature which helps to neutralize the naturally acidic vagina; neutralization is necessary to prolong sperm life. Sperm also need a watery field within the female tract to swim in search of an egg. Seminal fluid and female mucus secretions provide that swimming medium. The prostate gland contributes large amounts of the ascorbic (citric) acid to the seminal fluid which also help support sperm life. Bulbourethral glands secrete a mucoid (mucus like) substance giving semen a rather viscous consistency. The vas deferens joins with the urethra providing an exit pathway for both urine and semen.

Sperm are shaped like miniature tadpoles with a tail for swimming. Approximately 60 million sperm are released with each ejaculation however only about 10,000 sperm survive long enough to travel through the cervix and move upward into the uterus. Sperm viability is highly dependent on the presence or absence of female secretions. The optimal cervical secretions are stretchy and lubricative.

The sperm move slowly and randomly in search of the ovum. They swim roughly one millimeter every minute. Sperm take over two hours to reach the opening into the fallopian tubes after ejaculation! The journey of each sperm is nothing short of treacherous. After factoring in sperm size and distance between the cervix and the fallopian tubes, the journey has been likened to a person swimming a 100-mile race. Fertilization of the egg by the sperm must take place in the fallopian tube. Several thousand sperm eventually reach the oviduct (fallopian tube) but the journey is taxing. Only a few hundred finally reach the ovum which they surround and try to penetrate.

Sperm require travel time in the female reproductive tract for a reason. They fully mature during the journey. The final process of maturation is known as "capacitation," the process by which sperm gain energy and motility. This activation process alters the tail beat of the sperm so it is better equipped for quick penetration of the hard outer shell of the ovum. Prior to capacitation, the tail swept the sperm along with an effective wave like motion. Activation changes the tail motion into one that frenzily whips back and forth. This new movement gives sperm the best chance of being the first and only one capable of penetrating the outer crust of the ovum and fusing with it. Immediately after penetration, a chemical change takes place preventing other competitors from also penetrating the outer crust. Nearly eighteen to twenty-one hours later, the complete fusion of the pro-nuclei of the male and female cells is achieved; the process of fertilization is finished.

Estrogen, the predominant female hormone present in the first part of the fertility cycle is responsible for thickening the uterine lining and preparing it for possible implantation. The newly conceived life needs to implant in an endometrial lining that is rich in oxygen and nutrition. Progesterone, the predominant hormone in the second half of the fertility cycle, changes the lining of the uterus so that blood flow increases throughout the lining.[19] Progesterone helps maintain pregnancy for the nine months. Time and protection is all that is needed to allow this new tiny miracle of life to draw his or her first breath nine months later.

Natural Family Planning

"NFP is used to achieve and to postpone pregnancy. NFP makes use of periodic abstinence from sexual intercourse based upon the observation of the woman's natural signs of fertility in order to space births or to limit the number of children when there is a serious reason to do so. NFP requires that couples learn, accept, and live within the wonders of how God made them. This is essentially different from contraception."[20]

NFP has been proven to work as effectively as any of the hormonal contraceptives without having any of the serious side effects. There are various approaches to NFP around the world. They are categorized into three subgroups including the Sympto-thermal Method, the Ovulation Method, and the Temperature Method. My husband and I are familiar with the Sympto-Thermal Method as taught by the Couple to Couple League.

When couples use the Sympto-thermal Method of NFP they dutifully observe and record the observations of fertility and natural infertility. These physical manifestations are directly related to the dominant internal hormones that create the various phases of a woman's cycle. For instance, under the influence of estrogen, two changes can be noted by the observant woman. First, estrogen causes the cervix to begin producing mucus; this naturally clean discharge is necessary for sperm survival. Also the cervix undergoes changes (opens, softens, and rises) allowing sperm to migrate up and into the uterus. After ovulation, progesterone is secreted, which causes the cervix to lower, harden and close. Also progesterone maintains the lining of the uterus in hopes of welcoming a new guest – the fertilized life. Progesterone increases women's basal body temperatures and it also dries up the cervical mucus. Progesterone levels stay elevated approximately two weeks. If no pregnancy is detected, the levels drop and menstruation begins.

Fertility patterns vary greatly across the wide spectrum of women. Normally all women will see physical signs of the internal workings of fertility. If there is estrogen activity, women will see and sense cervical mucus and observe cervix changes. When there is an accompanying ovulation, women can note the "event" by observing a series of other changes that include surveying how the mucus changes from none to less fertile to more fertile and back to less fertile at the same time that the cervix changes from closed and firm to open and soft and then back again to closed and firm. These observations are also coincident with a thermal shift in basal body temperatures from a lower level to a higher level. She will notice whether these signs appear earlier or later than normal. Women also observe whether the mucus patches change in length and their overall pattern or progression from dry to less fertile to more fertile. They will also note changes in the length of the luteal phase which will stay quite consistent over the years unless transitioning between childbirth or into pre-menopause. The couple tracks overall cycle lengths, luteal phase lengths, first days of temperature rise, and lengths of normal mucus patches. Couples also chart secondary signs such as increased libido, breast tenderness, mood changes, and mid cycle lower abdominal discomfort known as the mittelschmerz (middle pain).

The NFP chart becomes the tool by which the couple records all stages of fertility. The chart can even serve as an invaluable tool for recording potential fertility issues. The NFP charts help couples determine which phase they are in each cycle. Normally each cycle has three phases. Phase one is the pre-ovulatory infertile phase; phase two is the fertile phase; and phase three is the post- ovulatory infertile phase. Couples apply the fertility awareness rules according to their intention to achieve or postpone pregnancy. They practice continence during the fertile time in order to postpone pregnancy or they enjoy unrestricted marital relations when hoping to achieve pregnancy. The NFP chart provides couples with the earliest record of conception and estimated date of delivery. Sometimes, miscarriages can be predicted through the observation of prematurely falling basal body temperatures after confirming pregnancy.

Pharmaceutical drugs (i.e. anti-depressants, allergy medications, etc), diet or weight loss; increased daily exercise; or other disturbances can affect hormones and fertility cycles. Always consult with a pharmacist before taking any medications about whether the drug will have an effect on mucus, temperatures, luteal phase, ovulation, or overall fertility.

NFP can be used by any woman, even those transitioning back into fertility after pregnancy or transitioning past fertility into menopause. This book is not meant to be a primary teaching text for learning NFP; for that turn to the *Art of Natural Family Planning, Student Edition.* Sign up for classes or home study courses offered by the Couple to Couple League or other NFP provider in your area when engaged.

Effectiveness of NFP

NFP is very effective and easy to learn but it involves more than just getting to class or having a chart. All couples using NFP must work hard to make it work. They should work at NFP as if it's effectiveness and virtues bestowed all depends on them while fully realizing that it really <u>all</u> depends on God.

We have used NFP through all stages of our marital life (breast-feeding, menopause, regular cycles, illnesses, etc.) without disappointment or surprise. NFP has been 100 percent effective for us as we planned our family. It is hard for some people to believe that it actually worked for us since we had seven children – but it did. All seven were planned and expected and hoped for. We will look at this in more detail later in the chapter.

The effectiveness rates of the NFP methods studied have been found to be as effective as the most commonly used contraception and abortifacients. The Pill, IUD, and NFP all have 99 percent method effectiveness rates. The user effectiveness rate for NFP is still highly effective when couples are motivated to postpone pregnancy. P. Frank-Hermann, et al 2007, found that the method effectiveness of the Sympto-thermal Method of NFP was 99.6 percent and the user effectiveness was 92.5 percent.[21]

NFP is unique from contraceptives for many reasons though one really stands out. NFP user effectiveness rate is 100 percent dependent on the combined cooperation, positive attitude, and sexual behavior of both husband and wife. Every other method or device puts the user rate effectiveness squarely on the shoulders of only one person in the relationship. I recall the frustration of a pregnant friend as she complained about having to bear the full responsibility for birth control. She grew tired of having this fall on her shoulders. Sadly the couple divorced about ten years later.

The Safety of NFP vs. Contraceptives

NFP is completely safe and natural. By contrast, all contraceptives have physical side effects ranging from minor discomforts to major concerns including breast cancers, blood clots, and even death. TV ads for the Birth Control Pill are quite interesting as they try to paint the Pill as the wonder drug but end the commercials with a lengthy list of possible side effects. Yaz was one of the wonder pills that quickly lost its appeal when the side effects came to light.

Vasectomies disrupt the healthy, major functioning reproductive system of the male body – that is to produce and release healthy sperm. Vasectomies cause males to absorb their own sperm which can then act as a foreign protein compromising their immune systems. This results in the formation of benign, sensitive lumps, decreases male sexual desire, increases risk of testicular pain, and other illness or disease.

Years ago, we were interviewed by the St. Paul *Pioneer Press* where we went on record explaining these side effects. One man called several years later to say that he had read the article, cut it out and planned to prove we were wrong since he had just undergone the vasectomy at the time the article was printed. Unfortunately, his health deteriorated just as forewarned in the article. His vasectomy cost him recurring leg clots, diminished health, and marital problems – he did get a divorce several years after having the procedure. He wanted to know if/ where he could get a reversal. He was referred to One More Soul, Inc., in Dayton, Ohio. They keep a list of physicians sympathetic to men and women like him.

Tubal ligations are also problematic since they damage a healthy major functioning part of the female reproductive system. Studies show that tubal ligations disrupt the blood supply to the tubes and related reproductive areas including the ovaries and uterus. This disruption causes the ovaries and uterus to malfunction increasing risks for serious premenstrual tension, bleeding irregularities, and hysterectomy.

The Intrauterine Device is linked to many side effects including ectopic pregnancy, increased menstrual bleeding, pelvic pain, PID, perforation of the uterus, and infertility. This device is considered to be an abortifacient since it does little to prevent conception although new devices are tipped with hormones that work to prevent ovulation and/or fertilization. The IUD alters the endometrial lining making it inhospitable for implantation.

Hormonal pills, patches and shots try to fool the pituitary gland into producing less FSH and LH. The pill acts as contraception when it suppresses ovulation which it does in 2 percent to 80 percent of female cycles. The pill is also designed to thicken mucus which slows down sperm motility. The designer pills also act in ways that deplete the endometrium of glycogen making it less hospitable to implantation of a newly conceived life. Lower dosage pills allow breakthrough ovulation (approximately 20 percent of the time) more often than higher, older dosage pills. If a given cycle is ovulatory the blastocyst (fertilized life) will have trouble planting in the inhospitable lining. Pills, shots, or patches can act as an abortifacient in any given woman's cycle.

Hormonal contraceptives have many negative side effects including the following:

- Hormonal contraceptives deplete women's vitamin levels
- Increase bad cholesterol levels
- Decrease good cholesterol levels
- Increases PMS symptoms
- Increases women's risk for developing yeast infections.
- Increases risk of breast cancer
- Increases risk for developing stroke or blood clots.

- Weight gain
- In 2005 the World Health Organization classified the contraceptive pill as a Group I carcinogen because of proven links with breast and some other cancers.[22]
- Compromises the female immune system.
- Recent findings wonder whether the Pill skews women's biological cues which help them choose compatible mates.
- German researchers have linked the Pill to female sexual dysfunction.
- Neurologists are concerned the progestin component may be affecting our ability to think.
- Gambles with women's well being.

Barrier Methods such as condoms, diaphragms, vaginal sponges and spermicides all present negative aesthetics for using couples. Most couples do not like having to insert, apply, or put on these types of things prior to intercourse. Women have increased risk for developing allergic reactions, toxic shock syndrome (vaginal sponges), vaginal dryness, and bladder infections (diaphragms) when using these methods.

The Intangible Risks of Contraception

Contraceptive use does not require men or women to develop virtues of chastity: sexual self control and self discipline. The lack of virtue can have a negative cascading effect in other personal areas also. The use of contraceptives is not 100 percent health-supporting nor does it promote the emotional and psychological well being of one's spouse – especially when that spouse begins to feel used or objectified by demands or expectations for sex. These concerns are several of the more frequent complaints heard from women who use contraceptives.

Contraceptive use occurs when one has conditional love — spouses do not love each other enough to be concerned about the possible health risks associated with contraceptive birth control. This type of conditional love is not concerned enough about the other person's spiritual, moral, emotional or mental health. Contraceptive love does not always try and make room for one more. In effect, contraceptive love changes the blueprint for procreative love. Contraceptive love does not rely on self control and self discipline to sustain the marriage but too often relies on sex to sustain the relationship. Therefore, contraceptive love also changes the blueprint for unitive love. Sex without limits is problematic for all couples. Recall that it is through our bodies that we express our attitudes and beliefs! What will your marital attitude about sex say about the depth of your love for your spouse?

A recent pro-life poster captures the essence of authentic love when it stated: "A true measure of love is when one loves without measure."

Environmentally Friendly – Going Green

It has already been said that NFP is 100 percent natural – for both women and men. It is also completely natural for society. NFP – of course – does not involve the use of contraceptives, which are manufactured, packaged and distributed using valuable natural resources and/or become pollutants in the waste water systems and landfills. Many people feel that going *green* is important but few realize that contraceptives do not contribute to this movement. Dr. Karen Kidd (University of New Brunswick) tells us that "for the first time since the formation of the earth, most U.S. waterways contain traceable forms of designed for human use estrogens that are not removed in wastewater treatment systems. Widespread use of hormonal contraceptives contributes to the water pollution."

Furthermore, Dr. Kidd tells us that the estrogen (from birth control pills) that is flooding into the water systems is not removable by our wastewater sewage systems and this is a problem since over 100 million women use the pill in some form annually.[23] Dr. Kidd says that we are drinking a toxic soup of chemicals. Dr. Susan Love, cancer surgeon, puts hormonal pollution on high alert because it is metabolized in our bodies as estrogen and it is the lifetime exposure to estrogens that has increased world cancer rates by 26 percent since 1980."(Carnevali & Mardonna, 2003; Davis et al. 1998)

Significant concentrations of the designer human estrogens have been found in highly urbanized areas. Biologists note that fish are affected by the higher concentrations of estrogen pollution. For example, fish populations are observed to have increased problems involving lesions, impaired reproduction, altered reproductive behavior, feminization of male fish, depressed male serum testosterone levels, decreased female egg and larva viability, decreased embryonic development, cellular damage, etc.[24] If you think these are only fish problems, they aren't. The fact remains that damaged fish "create a threat to the ecosystems because it eliminates important fish populations (specific) and allows for the eventual contamination of human beings via the food web dynamic.[25] Scientists worry that it is next to impossible to study the effects of estrogen contamination "since there is no place to find unexposed populations." Brittany Kimball from the University of Washington warns that "public notification of this accumulation has been limited due to a lack of comprehension of the implications by the scientific community." Isn't it also possible that public notification of this accumulation would necessitate first - the admission of hormonal pollution and secondly − a public repudiation of the use and/or production of hormonal contraceptives?

There is also increasing evidence that over-exposure to estrogen decreases male sperm contributing to the increase in male infertility rates and sexual dysfunctions.

NFP is Morally Defensible

The "responsible use' of contraceptives is to not use them at all since it increases human exposure to environmental pollutants; they also hinge personal responsibility to technology rather than to personal choices and actions. We have been conditioned to rely on pills or shots rather than self control or self discipline causing many to lose appreciation for the gift of fertility. Fertility is viewed as a condition to be held in check. The shifts in attitude toward fertility prevent us from seeing our own bodies (including fertility) as a gift. It also causes many people to disregard and dismiss the virtue of chastity.

Many couples use NFP. They build families with the hope of discovering God's plan for them as husband and father, wife and mother. It is a blessing to have a large family knowing that each was perfectly planned and wanted naturally. It is also a blessing to welcome surprise packages. The people who don't believe that couples want a large family are simply wrong. Pope John Paul II explains that couples using NFP often have large families because these "couples come to appreciate their importance of children to the marriage and they want to become generous with God."

Sexual abstinence naturally tests the credibility and reasonability of the couples' intentions to postpone or avoid pregnancy. Sexual abstinence is a form of self denial and therefore poses a slight "hardship" for all couples using NFP so their reasons to postpone pregnancy become real ones rather than frivolous, self centered ones. Monthly decisions about pregnancy are made.

NFP methods facilitate, allow, and support achieving and postponing pregnancy by consistently supporting and connecting life with love. It is the only method wherein sexual relations are left completely open to the possible transmission of new life. As you already recognize, everyone has the capacity to develop virtue. To simply give up on one's ability to develop virtue – as happens when couples practice contraceptive family planning — is to give up on ourselves.

Humane Vitae counsels us to know that "periodic continence develops self mastery, personalities, spiritual values, self sacrificing love which in turn opens hearts, driving out selfishness and enemies of true love." It also teaches us to dominate instincts and appetites by developing ascetical practices because they are required. Sexual abstinence – or continence – is an ascetical practice. Furthermore, self discipline bestows virtue on the family, which helps facilitate resolution of problems in other areas. It gives attention to the spouse, drives out selfishness, and deepens their sense of responsibility. By its means, parents acquire the capacity of having a deeper and more efficacious influence in the education of their offspring."[26] *Humane Vitae* has much more to say about the indefensibility of contraception.

The Church recognizes that couples must be the ones to determine the appropriate size of their family. But the Church calls couples to make these decisions based on a spirit of generosity. A wise deacon once remarked to me that the "decision must serve both love and life, and must be made with the realization that children are a stupendous blessing for their family.[27]

NFP in the full Catholic sense is so much more than about requiring abstinence! This is not the lynch pin of NFP; rather the central focus of NFP is the practice of authentic, responsible parenthood which is pro-child, pro-family, pro-marriage, pro-love! [28]

Many times we have been asked why we have so many kids if NFP works. This question always makes me feel a bit sad as we reflect on the implications of this question. Nevertheless, it is important to answer the question fully. Many young people just are not used to seeing families with seven children. Our response to the question is this: abstinence, time, prayer, and being changed by each pregnancy brought us to seven children. A miscarriage in the middle helped us more fully realize that fertility is a gift and not an absolute reality.

We have already discussed the many negative attitudes that society has imposed on us regarding marriage, children, relationships, etc. In essence, negative attitudes toward large families follow these attitudes. On the other hand, we personally believe in babies and children. Our children have made us better persons; they have indeed been a supreme gift to us and to our other children. They are also our gift back to God. Furthermore, when we believe the Church in matters of faith and morals, we have an easier time realizing that we are called to imitate God's generosity when it comes to planning our family. This made us realize that there is always room for one more.

All couples, young or old, must always consider the moral implication of their sexual actions when postponing or achieving pregnancy – throughout their married life. Simply put, we are what we do. Even within marriage, some sexual activities are illicit, including oral sex, anal sex, mutual masturbation, use of pornography, and other dehumanizing activities.

Providentialism

The further a society leans away from God, the greater the reactions against these shifts can occur. One of these counter-reactions is the philosophy that we must forsake any personal control for family size over to God's providential care. Providentialism is *letting go and letting God* accomplish His plans through us, including the generation of new life.

While this sounds virtuous, it has more commonalities with

contraception than virtuous family planning. Like the contraceptive philosophy, providentialists generally accept the notion that abstinence is bad for marriages. *Humane Vitae* and other encyclicals teach us otherwise. Further, NFP requires the active pursuit of chastity and other virtue whereas providentialism does not; this gives the impression that self control or self discipline is not highly valued. In fact, providentialists often have trouble with the mastery of self control and therefore feel the more acceptable antidote is learning to accept whatever comes rather than controlling (positively) what comes their way. NFP requires regular communication between spouses whereas providentialists develop a form of resignation to the unknown.

Authentic love is that love which chooses to fully cooperate with God. This is far different from burying one's head in the sand and hoping for "the best." It is better to actively choose life than to passively think that new life may happen. A prime example of this is given to us by the Virgin Mary. The Angel Gabriel gave her all the facts and then awaited her assent; he could also not have told her what was going to happen and expect the cooperation that she would have given. God loves and respects our free choice so much that He always awaits our full assent – even in matters of life. Knowing and choosing to say yes to life is far superior to ignoring but staying cooperative.

Final Notes

Attend NFP classes when preparing for your marriage. It is best to attend NFP classes as soon as you are engaged so you will have plenty of charting experience before your wedding day. It can be challenging to "stick to the plan" when couples lack experience in charting or have uncertainties about the method of NFP they choose.

NFP will change your attitudes and perceptions about marriage, pregnancy, babies, and life in general. At first couples may only regard NFP as another means of birth control – albeit a natural one. After years of use, they come to regard it as a way of life that they wouldn't set aside for any other type of birth control method or device. NFP helps couples put things into proper perspective. Selfish motives give way to selflessness and new found generosity is fostered.

We owe much to the Church who deemed NFP important enough to recommend it during our engagement. We are grateful to God for all of our physical and spiritual gifts that have accrued during our marriage. My hope is for you to realize these gifts as well.

Reflection Questions:

1. List the things you learned in this chapter.

2. What do you think about NFP now that you have read this chapter?

3. What do you think about fertility now that you have read this chapter?

4. What is ART? What do you think about ART after reading this chapter? Has it changed your opinions?

5. Discuss why ART is an unethical technology.

6. Discuss why Contraception is unethical and immoral.

THE CHALLENGES
OF BEING YOUNG

Young adulthood is increasingly complicated and challenging. You are constantly bombarded by decoys that look and sound appealing, but offer grave consequences when they grab hold of you.

You have a lot of juggling to do in order to maintain balance in your life. You will have to pay close attention to all facets of you including your physical, mental, emotional, social, financial, and spiritual dimensions. Failing to attend to each of these areas – your well being – means you will have trouble maintaining a balanced you! In fact, dropping just one or more of your "balls" will produce negative consequences to maturation and /or general health and well being. It is vital that you pay attention to all of your dimensions for the reasons outlined in the book. The thrill of the juggling should be interesting, challenging, and rewarding.

Goal Setting

Think about and plan for your short and long term goals. Ponder what your ideal life looks like compared to your real life. Maturation merges the ideal life with real life. Accomplishing your goals and sticking to the timelines actually helps you do that. Now it's time to put together this year's goals, action plans, and timelines. Use notes you made in past chapters to help you.

You will find a number of worksheets and other information in the appendices. Hopefully you took the time to answer the reflection/discussion questions at the end of each chapter.

Your Vocation

It is important to recognize and understand how it is that your body is like an artist's expressive medium - not shapeless raw material but a work of art in waiting. You are being drawn out of the marble by God's handiwork. You are an image and likeness that is designed after the Creator in order to co-create beauty that can be shared with the rest of the world.[1] Any denial of this will only serve to oppose maturation, and *much needed, advanced training* for your life ahead.

You have been created by God for a purpose; maybe you will find that purpose in married live, a religious life, or the single life. Your calling or *vocation* is the means by which you will allow yourself to be drawn out of the expressive medium that is you, a work in progress. Your vocation is unique for you and it is important that you discern it realistically, purposefully, and prayerfully. Until you discern this vocation, your search could feel slightly frustrating and subject to distracting temptations. Bear in mind that true vocations should not be stumbled upon accidentally. Nor should you follow friends into a vocation. It takes time to find this pearl for yourself. This should be your own journey.

It is always important to remember that if you are not moving closer to God, you are actually moving away from Him. Evil rejoices when we lose the guiding hand of God; after all it is God who provides the necessary grace so we can build up our spiritual and personal virtues and avoid temptations and sin.

Love You

You can't love what you don't know and that includes yourself! You also can't love others until you authentically love yourself which requires you to balance your life by paying attention to all of your dimensions! Finally, you can't authentically love yourself (or others) until you learn to know, love, and serve the Source of Love – God.

This is an exciting and challenging time for self-discovery and exploration of the bigger world around you. This bigger world may try to intimidate you – but take heart! All of your necessary supports are near you – look to your family, friends, Church, and those who love God.

This may be the first time that you realize just how insignificant you seem considering the world's population. After all you are just one among 6.8 billion people in the world and one of 310,737,330 people in the United States.[2] Nevertheless, you are special and endowed with purpose and mission. Find that mission and become the game changer God calls you to be.

The Decoys

A lot of the clamor that surrounds you will not be worth listening to. Today's young adults have had to live amidst a lot of untruths (that pose as truth), pumpkins (that are real decoys), appetites (that demand freedoms), and desires (that pretend to be rights). Older adults like me didn't have to battle against so many threats. We also didn't have to face as many imposters and fakes. There was a time, not so long ago, when most people believed that divorce was a calamity, premarital sex was wrong, using others only caused hurt, abortion was horrific, and same-sex unions were unimaginable. Complacency took over and now the morality of all of these is under contention by a drifting toward moral relativism and sloth.

This is the time of your life when you will have vibrant and sometimes perplexing and hurtful interactions with the opposite sex. It is time to search for your true love, which might be found in the vocation of a religious life or married life. Just don't let yourself be fooled into thinking that hooking up or casual sex is morally neutral in either the long or short run of life. Don't be confused by studies that suggest that casual sex is just that – no strings, no harm. Researchers are relieved to observe that suicide among women didn't climb in proportion to the number of incidents of "hooking up". However, their glee should be offset by disappointment over the behavior itself. Studies fail to look deeply into broken heart syndromes or diminished self esteem caused by being forced to drop out of college, contracting a sexually transmitted infection, have an abortion, or having an unplanned pregnancy. These consequences can affect people for their lifetime.

Truth

Regardless of opinion, there are moral certainties and you can know them by "clinging to your religion."

Polls show that your age group hopes to have a stronger spirituality yet few attend Church. This disconnect doesn't make logical sense. Unlike much of the greater culture, you must ensure that your life is not filled with inconsistencies and contradictions. That happens when you get to know yourself and integrate your body with your mind, soul, and will.

Unfortunately too many young adults have seen older adults say one thing but do another; these people create contradictions as well. Many of you have seen your parents split apart and therefore you have had to accept their divorce as a normal part of life. This prepares you less well for your own future marriage; your attitude about permanence in marriage will be slightly off-tilt. Divorce dims your appreciation for marriage. You have been taught that abortion is a woman's right, unfortunately this choice is not moral or ethical. You have watched adults make excuses for their immoral behavior so you kind of expect it from your peers. Responsible sex has been turned on its head. Too many of your peers think that making love involves a one night stand.

Attitudinal shifts and social constructs have opened the door to much pain. Few people need to be taught truth because it has been written on our hearts. Unfortunately, falsehoods and decoys have confused interior lives. The calls from the conscience have been hung up on – this makes it more difficult to know and understand wisdom and Godly truth.

Your age group is most often exposed to highly provocative ideas without having the benefit of infusion of truth or wisdom. Instead you hear mostly opinion even from those who are well-educated.

Longings

Every human person has interior longings and questions about the purpose and meaning of their life – this differentiates us from the animals. Because of these questions, it is always going to be important to "recognize and understand the world in which we live, its explanations and its longings and its often dramatic characteristics." Too often we believe that we can solve all of life's problems on our own. When we believe this, our "human intelligence and creative energies often recoil back upon ourselves."[3] Our reasoning and planning is not as superior as we think it is. These inventions recoil on us when we fail to take God's original design into account. They bite back when we fail to study God and His original blueprints. They bite when inventions and energies are built upon man-made philosophies. They especially bite when we believe that practical and efficient solutions are better than moral ones.

Your Choice

We live in a time when people worship choice, personal rights and liberties, and the freedom to do as they wish. We have set aside the worship of the One True God.

You have two basic choices in life. Either freely choose to love God more and more and thereby set aside your childish, selfish ways, or freely choose to love yourselves more and more and thereby disregard God, His truth and wisdom.

The Three Warnings

Remember the three things mentioned in the beginning of the book. Set realistic goals that minimize spent arrows, hurtful words, and lost opportunities.

The Living Word teaches us that peace comes from living as we were designed. You and I have been asked to forsake selfishness, love of money, arrogance, disobedience, ungratefulness, unrighteousness, hate, conceit, sinful pleasure, ungodliness, and a whole lot more. You have been told to hear your father's instructions and not to forsake your mother's teachings. You have also been told to observe the Commandments and to bind these commandments to your heart for they will guide you. The Commandments are like a lamp to show you the way.[+]

You have been encouraged in this book to do a lot of things and to avoid a lot of things. What is your response? It is time now to complete your final goals. Think about what you have previously recorded in Appendix Two after each chapter. It is now time to compile your thoughts, plans, and dreams into a cohesive working goal plan. Use the worksheet in Appendix Sixteen.

The Final Challenge

Challenges will come and go. Fortify yourself for these challenges by creating strong foundational supports that reinforce your spiritual, mental, emotional, physical, and financial well being. The Gospels advise us BE NOT AFRAID because fear is the underlying factor for all doubt and loss of faith. Fear also lurks under all calamities; fear itself is a decoy! You *are* only young once but don't let that be an excuse for foolishness, self centeredness, or vice. Live your life as though you really believe that life is…

    … an opportunity, benefit from it.

    … beauty, admire it.

    … bliss, taste it.

    … a dream, realize it.

    … a challenge, meet it.

    … a duty, complete it.

    … a game, play it.

    … a promise, fulfill it.

    … a sorrow, overcome it.

    … a song, sing it.

    … a struggle, accept it.

    … a tragedy, confront it.

    … an adventure, dare it.

    … luck, make it.

    … too precious, do not destroy it.

    … life, fight for it.

- Mother Teresa of Calcutta

Reflection Questions:

1. What arrows (actions) have you spent in college thus far? What changes will you make to avoid spending more lost arrows?

2. What words have you spoken that you can't ever take back? What changes will you make to avoid speaking lost words?

3. What opportunities have you lost in college? What changes will you make to avoid losing more opportunities?

4. Analyze Mother Teresa's poem with regard to you and your life. Insert your responses in the designated column.

Mother Teresa teaches us that …	**What is your…**	**Insert your response**
Life is an opportunity, benefit from it.	*Opportunity?*	_____
Life is beauty, admire it.	*Beauty?*	_____
Life is bliss, taste it.	*Bliss?*	_____
Life is a dream, realize it.	*Dream?*	_____
Life is a challenge, meet it.	*Challenge?*	_____
Life is a duty, complete it.	*Duty?*	_____
Life is a game, play it.	*Favorite game?*	_____
Life is a promise, fulfill it.	*Promise?*	_____
Life is a sorrow, overcome it.	*Sorrow?*	_____
How do you overcome a sorrow?	_____	_____
Life is a song, sing it.	*Favorite song?*	_____
Life is a struggle, accept	*Struggle?*	_____
Life is a tragedy, confront it.	*Tragedy?*	_____
How do you overcome tragedies?	_____	_____
Life is an adventure, dare it.	*Adventure?*	_____

APPENDIX ONE

Linda's Ten Top Tips for the Emerging Adult

1. Help create mutually supportive communal living environments where you attend college.

2. Help ensure that changes to the dorm living environments buoy up residents' well being, including their emotional, spiritual, mental, physical and social/career components.

3. Make friends with people who have similar purpose, goals, and interests in life.

4. Connect with people who build up your confidence, stability, happiness, and general well being. Associate with people who fully respect you.

5. Appreciate your college education. Make learning your highest priority; keeping your faith intact should be also your other highest priorities.

6. Don't lure or be lured down hurtful pathways.

7. Do not become your own adversary to the pursuit of general wellness and good health and interior balance.

8. Stop and consider the consequences of your behaviors. Everything has a consequence – good or bad.

9. Make a difference in people's lives. Take stock of your blessings and challenges; notice how merciful God is toward you. Imitate His mercy.

10. Stand up and be noticed.

APPENDIX TWO

My Short and Long Term Goals Based on Chapter's Input

Write down some quick-start ideas that will be helpful in setting your final goals and plans after finished reading *Surviving College*.

List goals here after reading each chapter	Chapter	Short Term Goal/Plan	Long Term Goal/Plan	Real or Ideal?	Date
Mental/Emotional:_____ Spiritual:_____ Physical:_____ Social:_____ Economic:_____	1				
Mental/Emotional:_____ Spiritual:_____ Physical:_____ Social:_____ Economic:_____	2				
Mental/Emotional:_____ Spiritual:_____ Physical:_____ Social:_____ Economic:_____	3				
Mental/Emotional:_____ Spiritual:_____ Physical:_____ Social:_____ Economic:_____	4				
Mental/Emotional:_____ Spiritual:_____ Physical:_____ Social:_____ Economic:_____	5				

List goals here after reading each chapter	Chapter	Short Term Goal/Plan	Long Term Goal/Plan	Real or Ideal?	Date
Mental/Emotional:_____ Spiritual:_____ Physical:_____ Social:_____ Economic:_____	6				
Mental/Emotional:_____ Spiritual:_____ Physical:_____ Social:_____ Economic:_____	7				
Mental/Emotional:_____ Spiritual:_____ Physical:_____ Social:_____ Economic:_____	8				
Mental/Emotional:_____ Spiritual:_____ Physical:_____ Social:_____ Economic:_____	9				
Mental/Emotional:_____ Spiritual:_____ Physical:_____ Social:_____ Economic:_____	10				
Mental/Emotional:_____ Spiritual:_____ Physical:_____ Social:_____ Economic:_____	11				
Mental/Emotional:_____ Spiritual:_____ Physical:_____ Social:_____ Economic:_____	12				

APPENDIX THREE

How I Spend My Time:

Daily Activities	Hours (%) of daily time	Areas that need more or less time per day?	How do you plan to change change your daily schedule?
Study/Homework			
Internet use			
Face-to-face communication			
Employment			
Sports/Fitness			
Computer/Video games			
TV/Video time			
Sleep			
Leisure			
Classroom hours			
Shopping			
Other (list)			

Appendix Four

OUR BILL OF RIGHTS

1. We acknowledge that we may have different values and ethics, principles, or standards, but we nonetheless will treat the other respectfully and with full dignity because we are both made in the image and likeness of God.

2. Each of us promises not to compromise, belittle, disrespect, or violate our roommate's values and ethics, religious and moral principles, political beliefs, religious practices, or standards.

3. We agree to resolve our differences respectfully, peacefully, and cooperatively.

4. We will not make demands on the other that cause them discomfort or anxiety.

5. There will be many occasions when each of us could "demand" a right but will agree to forgo making this demand out of respect for the roommate's sensibilities.

6. Both of us have the right to free, unlimited and full use of our room space and personal property without interference from the other. Neither of us will demand nor ask the other to leave the premises for any personal reasons.

7. We both recognize that unreasonable noise, distractions due to the presence of friends, or other interferences at improper times violates our mutually agreed upon free access/usage of our room space and personal property.

8. We will honor our roommate's right to sleep without unnecessary disturbances from noise, pranks, guests, or other personal behaviors.

9. We will honor our roommate's right to study in their room space without unnecessary disturbance from self or others.

10. We both agree to respect each other's personal belongings; therefore we will not ask to borrow anything that belongs to our roommate. If a personal belonging is voluntarily offered, we agree to immediately give back any items after using them. We agree to replace any items that we use up, lose, or break.

11. We will both keep our room and bathroom facilities clean and free of clutter. This is our weekly cleaning schedule of our shared living facilities: (Each roommate should circle one or more)

Bathroom:	M	T	W	Th	F	S	S
Room:	M	T	W	Th	F	S	S

12. Neither of us will gossip about our roommate's habits.

13. We have the right to invite guests into our room at the appropriate times designated on our Room Schedule.

14. Our guests shall respect the rights and property of my roommate, other residents of the floor or hall, and our mutually agreed upon Bill of Rights.

15. We both have the right to protest violations made against our Bill of Rights by our roommate or friends.

16. We agree to refrain from intimidation, coercion, name calling, and/or physical or emotional harassment or abuse.

17. We will equally share bathroom facilities and other common equipment or space.

18. We will pay our fair share of mutually agreed upon expenses.

19. We have the right to speak to an RA or other school administration about unresolved violations or problems.

20. We agree to practice good, clean, personal hygiene.

21. We agree to secure help for our roommate who is sick, in danger, or needs mental health help.

Signed,
this _____ day of _____ by

_____

_____

Post the Bill of Rights including this Room Hour Chart so both roommates have easy access to the mutually agreed upon information. This chart lists mutually agreed upon time slots for social time and entertainment and quiet time for study and sleep.

Room Hour Chart

	Mon.	Tues.	Wed.	Thurs.	Fri.	Sat.	Sun.
Study Hours: AM Afternoon Evening Nighttime							
Sleep Hours: AM Afternoon Evening Nighttime							
Social Time: AM Afternoon Evening Nighttime							
Entertainment: AM Afternoon Evening Nighttime							

APPENDIX FIVE

My College Budget[1]						
	Monthly Income		**Student Name**			
	Item	Amount				
	Estimated monthly net income		**Address**			
	Financial aid award(s)					
	Other income		**School/College**			
	Total					
	Monthly Expenses		**Semester Expenses**			
	Item	Amount	Item	Amount		
	Rent		Tuition			
	Utilities		Lab fees			
	Cell phone		Other fees			
	Groceries		Books			
	Auto expenses		Deposits			
	Student loans		Transportation			
	Other loans		Total			
	Credit cards					
	Insurance		**Discretionary Income**			
	Laundry		Item	Amount		
	Hair cuts		Monthly Income			
	Medical expenses		Monthly expenses			
	Entertainment		Semester expenses			
	Miscellaneous		Difference			
	Total					

[1]Used with permission from Tom Vetscher, CPA from Vetscher & Assoc.

APPENDIX SIX

Mental Health Warning Signs

Warning Signs:
- Depression.
- Sad mood.
- Reduced interest and enjoyment of life.
- Sense of hopelessness.
- Anxiousness.
- Hostility.
- Unusual calmness after a period of depression.
- Withdrawal from social interaction.
- A friend talks about suicide directly or indirectly.
- Friend gives away possessions.
- Observation of an abrupt change in personality and behavior.
- Use of alcohol or drugs changes.
- There is a sudden drop in school performance.
- Excessive dwelling on academic or relationship setbacks or other losses.

Facts to Know:
- All suicide victims had a treatable mental illness.
- Trust your instincts.
- You cannot put thoughts of suicide in someone's head.
- You will not be increasing their stress if you reach out to someone in need.
- Depression is linked to suicide.
- The best thing you can do is to reach out and offer support.
- Eight or ten mentions of suicide is often associated with intent to commit suicide.
- College students often do not voluntarily seek help for mental issues.
- Past suicide attempts or having been diagnosed with mood disorders increase risk of suicide.
- Alcohol, drug abuse and eating disorders are linked to suicidal behavior.
- Suicides are the consequence of not receiving treatment or lack of services.

What to Do:
- Reach out to the depressed student.
- Develop a relationship with the student.
- Be available to listen and talk – show them you care about them.
- Invite them to events.
- Find out what type of help is available on campus.
- Call their parents.
- Assess how easy it would be for that student to commit suicide by finding out how they think they would do it.
- Do not act shocked or scared by anything the student says.
- Find out when family is available to help.
- Find out what services are available on campus.
- Encourage student to seek professional help.
- Do not argue about morality of suicide with depressed student.
- Do not leave student alone if plan and means by which they will carry it out is obvious.
- Find out what professional help is available. You cannot be solely responsible for another's actions.
- Find out how to get help for your friend if school doesn't have mental health services.
- Maintain contact until help is secured.

What to Ask:
1. Are you thinking about hurting yourself or committing suicide?
2. When would you do it?
3. How would you do it?

Derived from several sources.

APPENDIX SEVEN

Mental Disorders and Disease

Anxiety Disorders
- Post Traumatic Stress Disorders (PTSD)
- Obsessive-compulsive Disorders (OCD)
- Panic Disorders
- Phobia Disorders

Mood Disorders
- Depression
- Mania
- Bipolar Disorders

Psychotic Disorders
- Schizophrenia
- Others with hallucinatory or delusional behavior

Eating Disorders
- Anorexia
- Bulimia
- Binge Eating

Impulse Control and Addictions
- Pyromania
- Kleptomania
- Compulsive Gambling
- Drug Addiction
- Alcohol Addiction
- Porn Addiction

Personality Disorders
- Antisocial Personality Disorder
- Obsessive Compulsive Personality Disorder
- Paranoid Personality Disorder

Adjustment Disorders
- Disorders due to stressful events such as natural disasters, major illness, interpersonal problems, loss of jobs, death of loved one, divorce.

Dissociative Disorders
- Multiple Personality Disorders
- Split Personality Disorders

Factitious Disorders
- Factitious Disorder with mostly Psychological factors
- Factitious Disorder with mostly Physical factors
- Factitious Disorder with both Psychological and Physical factors
- Factitious Disorder by Proxy
- i.e. Munchausen Disorder
- Sexual and Gender Disorders
- Sexual Dysfunction
- Gender Identity Disorder
- Paraphilia – Sadistic or Masochistic Disorders

Somatoform Disorders
- Psychosomatic Disorders

Tic Disorders
- Tourette Syndrome
- Disorders with quick uncontrollable body movements

Derived from Rosemary Anderson, "Stress and Mental Health", Journal of the Royal Society for the Promotion of Health(2004):112.2

Appendix Eight

Rights vs, Freedoms Worksheet

1.   List activities safe for you but not for someone else. Why are they safe for you but not the other?

2.   List instances in which you were willing to forgo a personal right out of consideration or love for someone else?

This section contains examples of actions taken by another out of concern for that person's well being rather than undue concern for toleration of rights. Are there any you disagree with and why?

1.   True, I am of legal age to drink, but tonight I will forego drinking because our group will consist of many underage students.

2.   True, my friend has the right to have an abortion, but I will talk to her about the studies which show that post abortive women have significantly increased risks for depression and suicide.

3.   True, sexual relations may "enhance" our dating relationship; however, there will always be the possibility of pregnancy even while using contraceptives. I refuse to do something that may result in a possible unintended pregnancy. We can learn about each other and have a great relationship without sexual relations.

4.   I will let my parents have access to my grades even though I don't have to. True, they may be disappointed but perhaps admitting my grades will help me set higher academic goals for myself. Besides, I need to realize that they have my best interest at heart.

5. My parents are setting a curfew for me when I come home from college. At first I was mad about that but then they told me how worried and anxious they get when I am driving around in the family car. After all, it isn't even my car. Also, I don't want them to worry about me. Besides that, late nights just make me that much more irritable the next day around my little brothers and sisters.

6. Nobody came into my room unless I allowed them in; but one day I realized it wasn't even my own room; after all, my parents own our home!

7. I used to wear low cut tops and tight fitting jeans until my boyfriend told me it really peaks his sexual mood. Neither of us wants to have sex right now because we want to wait until our wedding to unwrap our gift of self.

8. When I tell a lie, I just seem to wind up getting caught anyway. Besides, I hate having to lie. Maybe I need to look at what I am doing and why I am lying. I don't want someone to lie to me so why do I do it to others.

9. List other rights vs. freedom arguments here.

APPENDIX NINE

Dear Congressman Kennedy [By Bishop Thomas J. Tobin]:

Since our recent correspondence has been rather public, I hope you don't mind if I share a few reflections about your practice of the faith in this public forum. I usually wouldn't do that – that is speak about someone's faith in a public setting – but in our well-documented exchange of letters about health care and abortion, it has emerged as an issue. I also share these words publicly with the thought that they might be instructive to other Catholics, including those in prominent positions of leadership.

For the moment I'd like to set aside the discussion of health care reform, as important and relevant as it is, and focus on one statement contained in your letter of October 29, 2009, in which you write, "The fact that I disagree with the hierarchy on some issues does not make me any less of a Catholic." That sentence certainly caught my attention and deserves a public response, lest it go unchallenged and lead others to believe it's true. And it raises an important question: What does it mean to be a Catholic?

"The fact that I disagree with the hierarchy on some issues does not make me any less of a Catholic."

Well, in fact, Congressman, in a way it does. Although I wouldn't choose those particular words, when someone rejects the teachings of the Church, especially on a grave matter, a life-and-death issue like abortion, it certainly does diminish their ecclesial communion, their unity with the Church. This principle is based on the Sacred Scripture and Tradition of the Church and is made more explicit in recent documents.

For example, the "Code of Canon Law" says, "Lay persons are bound by an obligation and possess the right to acquire a knowledge of Christian doctrine adapted to their capacity and condition so that they can live in accord with that doctrine." (Canon 229, #1)

The "Catechism of the Catholic Church" says this: "Mindful of Christ's words to his apostles, 'He who hears you, hears me,' the faithful receive with docility the teaching and directives that their pastors give them in different forms." (#87)

Or consider this statement of the Church: "It would be a mistake to confuse the proper autonomy exercised by Catholics in political life with the claim of a principle that prescinds from the moral and social teaching of the Church." (Congregation for the Doctrine of the Faith, 2002)

There's lots of canonical and theological verbiage there, Congressman, but what it means is that if you don't accept the teachings of the Church your communion with the Church is flawed, or in your own words, makes you "less of a Catholic."

But let's get down to a more practical question; let's approach it this way: What does it mean, really, to be a Catholic? After all, being a Catholic has to mean something, right?

Well, in simple terms – and here I refer only to those more visible, structural elements of Church membership – being a Catholic means that you're part of a faith community that possesses a clearly defined authority and doctrine, obligations and expectations. It means that you believe and accept the teachings of the Church, especially on essential matters of faith and morals; that you belong to a local Catholic community, a parish; that you attend Mass on Sundays and receive the sacraments regularly; that you support the Church, personally, publicly, spiritually and financially.

Congressman, I'm not sure whether or not you fulfill the basic requirements of being a Catholic, so let me ask: Do you accept the teachings of the Church on essential matters of faith and morals, including our stance on abortion? Do you belong to a local Catholic community, a parish? Do you attend Mass on Sundays and receive the sacraments regularly? Do you support the Church, personally, publicly, spiritually and financially?

In your letter you say that you "embrace your faith." Terrific. But if you don't fulfill the basic requirements of membership, what is it exactly that makes you a Catholic? Your baptism as an infant? Your family ties? Your cultural heritage?

Your letter also says that your faith "acknowledges the existence of an imperfect humanity." Absolutely true. But in confronting your rejection of the Church's teaching, we're not dealing just with "an imperfect humanity" – as we do when we wrestle with sins such as anger, pride, greed, impurity or dishonesty. We all struggle with those things, and often fail.

Your rejection of the Church's teaching on abortion falls into a different category – it's a deliberate and obstinate act of the will; a conscious decision that you've re-affirmed on many occasions. Sorry, you can't chalk it up to an "imperfect humanity." Your position is unacceptable to the Church and scandalous to many of our members. It absolutely diminishes your communion with the Church.

Congressman Kennedy, I write these words not to embarrass you or to judge the state of your conscience or soul. That's ultimately between you and God. But your description of your relationship with the Church is now a matter of public record, and it needs to be challenged. I invite you, as your bishop and brother in Christ, to enter into a sincere process of discernment, conversion and repentance.

It's not too late for you to repair your relationship with the Church, redeem your public image, and emerge as an authentic "profile in courage," especially by defending the sanctity of human life for all people, including unborn children. And if I can ever be of assistance as you travel the road of faith, I would be honored and happy to do so.

Sincerely yours,
Thomas J. Tobin, Bishop of Providence
11/11/2009

APPENDIX TEN

A Hundred Health and Wellness Tips for College Students

Eating

1. Learn proper portion size.
2. Vary your meals. Each plate should be colorful and varied.
3. Eat breakfast.
4. Eat healthy snacks. Do not store unhealthy snacks close at hand.
5. Drink alcohol in moderation only. Do not drink to get drunk or to feel it.
6. When stressed, go work out. Do not eat to fight stress.
7. Drink plenty of water – at least 6-8 cups every day.
8. Limit sugar and caffeinated beverages. Avoid sugar free pops and juices – they contain aspartamine.
9. Eat plenty of fresh fruits and vegetables.
10. Limit junk food intake.
11. Stock your mini refrigerator with healthy foods only.
12. Do not skip meals.
13. Take a good daily muti-vitamin.

Exercise

1. Stretch before starting to exercise.
2. Walk to class.
3. Use the stairs instead of elevators.
4. Exercise daily.
5. Use helmets or safety glasses.
6. Take advantage of your campus fitness center programs.
7. Try different types of exercise: weight lifting, strength training, cardio and stretching, endurance.
8. Have fun – exercise with friends.

Sleep

1. Take a nap when you are feeling tired and worn out.
2. Take a break from homework a short while before trying to sleep.
3. Try to get to bed about the same time each night; wake up each day around the same time.

4. Get enough sleep- many people need at least 7-9 hours of sleep each night. Lack of sleep will make you feel cranky or less able to concentrate.
5. Work out night time schedules so that your sleep in not interrupted by roommates. Create a bedtime routine that works.
6. Avoid staying up all night.
7. Avoid drinking alcohol, eating meals or consuming caffeine before bed.
8. Keep your room dark and quiet.

Physical Health

1. Avoid risky sexual behaviors.
2. Get regular physical exams.
3. Do not abuse drugs or alcohol.
4. Take advantage of vaccination programs in college.
5. Avoid parties or circumstances that place you at risk for physical, sexual, or mental abuse.
6. Avoid binge drinking.
7. Get physical exams.
8. Get to the doctor when sick.

Illness

1. Wash your hands.
2. Do not share your cup, drinking bottle, or utensils with anyone.
3. Do not go to class when you have a fever.
4. Get to the doctor if your symptoms do not clear up within a few days.
5. Drink plenty of fluids when sick.
6. Get a flu shot.
7. Wear foot protection in showers.
8. Avoid going to rooms where a friend is sick.
9. Try to avoid touching mouth, eyes or nose with hands that are not clean.
10. Use hand and counter sanitizers.
11. Keep immunizations up to date.
12. Flu like symptoms can make your feel miserable; use over the counter medication when necessary.

Stress

1. Create a study routine that works.
2. Limit outside work and other activities that impinge on best study times.
3. Limit time spent on studying – avoid crash studying.
4. Give yourself study breaks.
5. Balance your social, academic time.
6. Get help before you feel overwhelmed.
7. Relax with daily hobbies and exercise.
8. Do not put off assignments. Put time between deadlines and completion dates.
9. Spend quality time with friends.
10. Do not over exercise, over study, over socialize.
11. Learn to manage your time productively.

Mental Health

1. Ask for help when you feel down.
2. Keep in touch with family support.
3. Build positive friendships.
4. Expect change in college.
5. It takes time to make good friends, don't rush the process.
6. Do not try to be a people pleaser.
7. Your friends will let you down, you will let them down.
8. Forgive and ask for forgiveness.
9. Know the signs of depression.
10. Build confidence by doing things well and doing things you do well often.
11. Volunteer.
12. Assemble a group of friends that share your values.
13. Get involved on campus.
14. Set goals.

If you study Abroad

1. Get immunized.
2. Avoid raw foods and water.
3. Bring a first aid kit.

4. Avoid contact with animals.

5. Swim only with friends and in safe places.

Spirituality

1. Get active in Church activities.

2. Go to Church regularly.

3. Attend Bible classes or other spiritual instruction.

4. Attend pre-marriage workshops prior to wedding.

5. Pray daily.

6. Sacrifice (make).

7. Be generous with time and talents.

8. Go on mission trips.

Financial

1. Use credit cards only when you have the money in the bank to pay your monthly bills.

2. Avoid spending unnecessary money.

3. Live frugally.

4. Do not take out large student loans that will be hard to re-pay.

5. Do not buy a car.

Other

1. Walk to class in appropriate attire in cold weather.

2. Avoid carrying heavy backpacks.

3. Do not smoke.

4. Set up emergency contacts with roommates.

5. Assert yourself.

6. Practice fire safety. Know where exits are in dorm rooms, houses, class rooms, etc. Practice fire drills.

APPENDIX ELEVEN

US Abortions Since 1973

Note the discrepancy in numbers of abortions reported by the U.S. Centers for Disease Control (CDC) vs. Alan Guttmacher Institute (AGI).

Year	Guttmacher Institute Report*	CDC+	Year	Guttmacher Institute Report	CDC
1973	744,600	615,831	1995	1,359,400	1,210,883
1974	898,600	763,476	1996	1,360,160	1,225,937
1975	1,034,200	854,853	1997	1,335,000	1,186,039
1976	1,179,300	988,267	1998	1,319,000	884,273
1977	1,316,700	1,079,430	1999	1,314,800	861,789
1978	1,409,600	1,157,776	2000	1,312,990	857,475
1979	1,497,700	1,251,921	2001	1,291,000	853,485
1980	1,553,900	1,297,606	2002	1,269,000	854,122
1981	1,577,300	1,300,760	2003	1,250,000	848,163
1982	1,573,900	1,303,980	2004	1,222,100	839,226
1983	1,575,000	1,268,987	2005	1,206,200	820.157
1984	1,577,200	1,333,521	Totals:	52,008,665	
1985	1,588,600	1,328,570	2006	Unreported	
1986	1,574,000	1,328,112	2007	Unreported	
1987	1,559,100	1,353,671	2008	Unreported	
1988	1,590,800	1,371,285	2009	Unreported	
1989	1,566,900	1,396,658	2010		
1990	**1,608,600**	**1,429,247**	2011		
1991	1,556,500	1,388,937	2012		
1992	1,528,900	1,359,146	2013		

* http://www.nrlc.org/abortion/facts/abortionstats.html
+ Lilo T. Strauss, Sonya B. Gamble, Wilda Y Parker, Douglas A. Cook, Suzanne B. Zane, Saeed Hamden, "CDC MMWR Surveillance Summaries"; Abortion Surveillance – United States 2003 by Division of Reproductive Health, National Center for Chronic Disease Prevention and Health Promotion)November 24,2006): 17.

APPENDIX TWELVE

Abortion Rates of Nations Ranked by Most to Least

Country	Year	%	Country	Year	%
Russia	2006	52.0	Montenegro	2006	18.8
Greenland	2005	50.3	Iceland	2005	16.8
Romania	2006	40.6	Spain	2005	16.1
Guadeloupe	2006	39.1	Finland	2006	15.3
Hungary	2006	38.9	Germany	2006	15.1
Estonia	2006	38.7	Channel Islands	2004	13.8
Belarus	2006	37.7	Dominican Republic	2005	13.7
Latvia	2006	34.7	Netherlands	2006	13.3
Cuba	2005	34.1	Turkmenistan	2006	13.3
Bulgaria	2006	33.5	Belgium	2005	13.2
Ukraine	2006	33.3	Greece	2003	13.1
Kazakhstan	2006	31.9	Andorra	1995	13.0
China (PRC)	2006	31.5	Taiwan (ROC)	1999	13.0
Martinique	2006	30.8	Switzerland	2005	12.9
Georgia	2006	30.7	Isle of Man	2007	12.8
Moldova	2006	29.5	Azerbaijan	2006	12.3
Cocos Islands	1978	28.6	Israel	2006	11.8
Belize	1996	28.0	Puerto Rico	2005	11.7
Czech Republic	2006	27.4	Bahrain	2002	11.4
Serbia	2006	26.6	Anguilla	2005	11.2
Slovakia	2006	26.1	Kyrgyzstan	2006	11.0
Korea, South (ROK)	1999	25.6	Barbados	1995	10.3
Sweden	2007	25.4	Costa Rica	2005	10.0
New Caledonia	1998	25.2	Bermuda	1984	9.9
Singapore	2006	23.9	South Africa	2005	9.2
Reunion	2006	23.8	Turks/Caicos Islands	2005	9.1
French Guiana	2006	23.4	Tajikistan	2006	8.6
Lithuania	2006	23.4	Tunisia	2001	8.4
New Zealand	2006	23.3	Uzbekistan	2006	7.5
Vietnam	2005	23.3	Ireland	2006	7.3
Seychelles	2006	23.2	Saint Helena	1990	7.1
Slovenia	2006	23.0	Faeroe Islands	2006	5.8
Armenia	2006	22.8	Kosovo	2006	4.6
United States	2005	22.6	Bosnia and Herzegovina	2001	3.2
Canada	2005	22.1	Austria	2000	3.0
Albania	2006	21.8	Suriname	1994	3.0
United Kingdom	2006	21.8	India	2000	2.7
Macedonia	2006	21.4	Gibraltar	2005	1.9
Australia	2006	21.3	Malta	2006	1.4
France	2005	21.0	Qatar	2005	1.3
Guyana	2003	20.9	Portugal	2005	0.8
Mongolia	2006	20.4	Venezuela	1968	0.8
Japan	2006	20.2	Poland	2006	0.09
Hong Kong	2005	19.9	Mexico	2005	0.07
Croatia	2006	19.7	Botswana	1984	0.04
Italy	2004	19.6	Chile	1991	0.02
Norway	2006	19.5	Luxembourg	1997	0.02
Denmark	2006	18.8	Panama	2000	0.02

Source: http://www.johnstonsarchive.net/policy/abortion/wrjp333pd.html

APPENDIX THIRTEEN

Definitions Of Terms Used In Chapter Twelve

Ampulla: serves as a storage reservoir for sperm until ejaculation

Azoospermia: zero sperm count in the ejaculate.

Bulbourethral glands: secrete mucus like substance giving semen a rather viscous consistency. This causes the semen to turn into a viscous, pearly substance after ejaculation.

Capacitation: is the process that takes place after ejaculation and in the female reproductive tract; it is a necessary process by which the sperm increase "energy" levels, enhance their motility and prepare for "activation".

CAVD: Congenital Absence of the Vas Deferens; occurs 1-2% of male infertility; often the diagnosis in men with azoospermia.

Corpus Luteum: Place where the egg was released from. It functions for about 2 weeks and then ceases to produce progesterone in the absence of pregnancy.

Dartos: the contractile tissue under the skin of the scrotum; also called tunica dartos.

DES (Diethylstilbestrol Sons): DES is a medication prescribed in the US to prevent miscarriage or premature delivery. Sons born to women who took DES while pregnant have a higher risk (slightly) of abnormalities of the scrotum and decreased sperm counts, epididymal cysts and autoimmune disorders, one testicle or both remain in the abdominal cavity.

DHT (Dihydroxytestosterone): twofold more potency than testosterone in epididymus, prostate, seminal vesicles, penis, kidneys, certain hypothalamus neurons and some skeletal muscles.

Diploid: division is necessary to reduce the diploid cell to a haploid cell prior to becoming spermatozoa.

Epididymus: sperm leave the semeniferous tubules and rete testis and enter the epididymus. This is where the sperm are concentrated by 100 fold. The epididymus adds fructose, glycoprotein, carnitine and other products so that sperm can become morphologically and biochemically mater.

Estrogen: a dominant female hormone that is important for reproduction and female sex characteristics.

Fallopian Tubes: the fallopian tube extends from each side of the upper end of the uterus. They transport released eggs from the ovary. The free end of the fallopian tube has loose, finger-like projections which easily pick up this released egg.

Fertilization: recombination of the male and female haploid gametes at fertilization; this means that each parent donates half the genetic material without increasing the number of chromosomes in the new life; this is how we all got our start.

Follicle: sac or container for immature eggs within the ovary.

FSH (Follicle stimulating hormone): released by the pituitary gland during Phase 1 of the woman's menstrual cycle. FSH stimulated immature eggs within the follicles in the ovaries to develop into mature eggs.

Germ Cells: immature reproductive cells, they progress through various stages until maturation to the spermatozoa.

GnRH: Gonadotropin Releasing Hormone

Gonads: testis

Granulosa cells: primordial follicles.

Haploid: a cell capable of supplying half the necessary genetic material needed for a new life.

HPT Axis: Hypothalamus-pituitary Axis

Hyposadias: a structural cause of infertility due to a birth defect of the urethra in the male that involves an abnormally placed urinary opening.

Hypothalamus: Located below the thalamus and posterior to the optic chiasma, this gland Controls Autonomic Functions, Emotions, Endocrine Functions, Homeostasis, Motor Functions, Regulates Food and Water Intake, Regulates Sleep Wake Cycle

Inhibin: ovulatory limiting factor

Inhibins: This Inhibin acts on the pituitary rather than on the hypothalamus.

Kallmann's syndrome: involving hypogonadism

Klinefelter syndrome: Affected individuals have at least two X chromosomes and at least one Y chromosome. The principal effects are development of small testicles and reduced fertility.

Leydig cells: sometimes called interstitial cells; produce testosterone.

LH (Luteinizing Hormone): this hormone signals the release of the mature egg.

Lumen: the cavity or channel within the seminiferous tubules.

Luteal Phase: post ovulatory phase of the cycle observable through elevated temperature patterns.

Meiosis: the second stage of spermatogenesis; it produces the haploid gamete (spermatids).

Menstruation: a woman's body weeping because a welcomed guest failed to arrive. It is the sloughing off of the outer layers of the uterus which had been prepared for reception of the new life.

Morphology: study and shape of the sperm cell.

Motility: biological term which refers to the ability of the spermatozoa to move spontaneously and independently.

Oligospermia: low sperm count.

Oocytes: further developed oogonia. Mature eggs.

Oogonia: immature sex cells.

Ovary: female reproductive organ which contains thousands of immature eggs or ova. Each woman normally has two ovaries on each side of the uterus.

Ovulation: when the egg is released from the ovary.

Pituitary: also called the hypophysis, is an endocrine gland about the size of a pea. It extends off the bottom of the hypothalamus at the base of the brain.

Progesterone: Another hormone which is necessary for the maintenance of the uterine lining. A woman experiences menstruation when her postovulatory progesterone levels decrease.

Prostate: compound tubuloalveolar exocrine gland of male.

Semen: contains two components; sperm and seminal plasma.

Seminal plasma/fluid: secretions of the accessory sex glands for purposes of transporting sperm.

Seminal vesicles: important source for the production of the seminal fluid.

Seminiferous tubules: structures inside the testis responsible for the manufacture of spermatozoa; also known as the adluminal compartment.

Sertoli cell only syndrome: a disorder that is the result of absent seminiferous tubules in the testes.

Sertoli cells: The Sertoli cells also produce and secrete Inhibin in amounts directly proportional to the successful spermiogenesis. Matured spermatozoa emerge from the Sertoli cells which are part of the semeniferous tubules. Increased activity in this cell due to the presence of testosterone allows spermatogenesis to go to completion.

Spermatids: formed by the division of the secondary spermatocytes completing meiosis

Spermatocytes: the resulting cells which are the result of the division of the Spermatogonia.

Spermatocytogenesis: the first phase of spermatogenesis; the proliferative phase.

Spermatogenesis: production of male gametes or spermatozoa through three stages; the final process that produces sperm containing half the number of haploid chromosomes; this allows a new person to have the same number of genes as both parents without doubling the genetic material. This process occurs in the seminiferous tubules.

Spermatogonia: the precursor cells (building blocks for sperm) which eventually develop into primary spermatozoa.

Spermatozoa: mature sperm; the male reproductive cell

Spermiation: process by which spermatozoa are shed into the lumen of the semeniferous tubule for transport out of the testis.

Spermiogenesis: the third stage of the spermatogenesis in which the spermatids now mature into spermatozoa; they morph from round spermatids into sex cells with a head and a tail; this stage ends with the release of the spermatozoa from the Sertoli cells.

Testis: the male gonads, testicles

Testosterone: influences the number of sperm produces but does not affect the rate at which spermatogenesis occurs; it is an important biological product of the Leydig cell; 4-10 mg. are secreted daily in men; 2% remains unbound in the bloodstream. (0.08-0.2 mg are normal levels).

Turgor: condition of being turgid; normal or other fullness.

Vas Deferens: The vas deferens is the tube that connects the epididymus, where the sperm are stored, to the urethra, the duct that can carry either urine or semen. Atresia: decline in the number of female eggs.

Stroma Cells: sex cells that are at different stages of development, division and maturation. These cells are further classified as being either granulosa cells, the oocytes, theca or stroma cells.

Theca Cells: sex cells that are at different stages of development, division and maturation. These various cells are known as granulosa cells, the oocytes, and theca and stroma.

Uterus: the human "bassinet" for the developing baby within the mother's body.

Appendix Fourteen

An Inclusive Timeline Regarding Human Sexuality Issues, Legislation, and Research

Attached is a timeline showing key dates and pronouncements with regard to sexuality. You will notice that the Church will always be called has to explain how and why "social advances" do or don't fit in with God's order of creation and plans.

Pre-modern era:

384 B.C.: Ancient peoples used natural chemicals such as cedar oil, lead ointment or frankincense oil as spermicides.

23 A.D.: Pliny, the Roman writer of Natural History advocates abstinence to avoid pregnancy.

Early history:

1758: "Ovist" (egg) understanding of embryology developed.

1766: von Haller classified thyroid, thymus and spleen as ductless glands; Bernard and Brown-Sequard advanced the concept of internal secretions.

1827: von Bain observed first mammalian female sexual reproductive egg. Prior to this discovery, fertility and sexuality was for the most part attributed to males- female bodies were only regarded as a host of the male "creation".

1831: Robert Brown identified nuclear core of the reproductive cell.

1832: Charles Knowlton concocted a birth control liquid from salt, vinegar, liquid chloride, zinc sulfate. It was popular for 40 years.

1838: German doctor, F. Wilde, offered his patients a small cervical cap – this model T of modern day diaphragms was not widely accepted or used.

1839: Charles Goodyear invents rubber and puts it to use manufacturing rubber condoms, intrauterine devices, douching   systems, and womb veils.

1843: Scientists discover that conception occurs when male sperm enters a female egg.

1869: Pope Pius 1X declared abortion to be murder.

1870: During the decade of the 1870's men and women were offered a wide assortment of birth control devises.

1873: Congress passed infamous Comstock law forbidding dispensation of contraceptives via postal service or interstate commerce. US first and only western nation enact laws criminalizing commerce involving birth control devices; passed by Protestant majorities.

1879: Scientist Fol observes union of sperm and ovum in animals.

1888: Waldeyer first uses term chromosome.

1890: Brown Sequard injected himself with testicular fluid; he claimed sexual rejuvenation at the age of 72; died 5 years later.

1890: Viennese gynecologist Knauer discovers existence of "chemicals" that control the body's metabolic processes.

1891: Henking discovers X chromosome.

1902: Landsteiner announces the discovery of four blood types: O, A, B, AB.

1905: Bayless and Stack discover existence/behavior of hormones. They also realized that genes are physical units of chromosomes. Hormones were so named after the Greek word meaning to stir up or incite.

1906: FDA created to protect consumer from fraudulent medical product or quackery.

1910: Thomas Morgan presents gene theory of inheritance.

1921: Margaret Sanger established American Birth Control League which was the antecedent of Planned Parenthood.

The same year Doctors Ogino (Japan) and Knaus (Austria) discover the key to ovulation. They discovered that ovulation was in relation to the next menstruation rather than the previous menstruation. The Rhythm Method of birth control was also developed.

1926: The first commercial estrogen preparation was made available. The discovery that pituitary gland functions as a remote control system in human reproduction leads directly to the invention of first pregnancy test.

1928: Scientist identifies the hormone progesterone.

1929: Zondek and Ascheim discover the hormone estrone.

1930s:

1930: Drug companies are eager to sell hormonal and barrier contraceptives but prohibited by commerce and interstate laws. , Drug companies used the term "feminine hygiene" to market a wide array of over the counter (OTC) birth control products. Drug companies marketed a Lysol douche that was found to be both dangerous and ineffective.

1930(Aug. 15): the Anglican church held its Lambeth Conference and voted in favor of birth control for hard ship cases only. This restriction later was found to be impossible to define opening the Pandora's Box to widespread acceptance and legitimization of contraception.

1930: (Dec 31) the encyclical named Casti Canubi was issued by Pope Pius XI. This encyclical was in response to the Anglican vote allowing birth control for hardship cases. In the encyclical, the Pope reinforced centuries/millenia of teachings against the use of artificial birth control drugs, devices, practices.

1934: Pincus achieved in-vitro fertilization of a rabbit.

1936: Courts legitimized birth control commerce among medical professionals; this caused the AMA to recognize birth control to be part of normal medical practices.

1940s:

Women primarily used douches for contraceptive purposes; these were very ineffective in avoiding pregnancy. I recall seeing a large, red bulbous device with a wooden handle during my childhood that was likely put to use for these purposes by my parents. My sisters and I would occasionally play with this and our mother would admonish us to put it back in the bathroom. We didn't realize its purpose back then.

1941: Marker discovers way to make synthetic progesterone from Mexican wild yams; this become the foundational work behind hormonal birth control.

1945: Albright writes an analysis that preventing ovulation prevents pregnancy and explores birth control by hormonal therapy.

1948: Anabolic steroid used for athletes participating in the Olympics and other world games; also used by the military soldiers.

Americans spent 200 million per year on contraceptives; "Rubbers" were the most popular method of birth control. Thirty states still prohibited or restricted the sale and advertisement of contraceptive devices.

1950s:

1951: Pope Pius XII announces that the Church will only sanction rhythm or abstinent behavior for limiting births.

1951: 200 Planned Parenthood clinics are operating.

1952: Pincus confirms that progesterone works as an "anti-ovulate" in rabbits and rats; his discovery was confirmed by Dr. Rock. Rock offered 3- 5 month "hormonal" therapies to infertility patients with goal of stimulating pregnancy.

1953: Watson and Crick prepared model for DNA.

Rock and Pincus performed the first human trials of the Pill with 50 women under the guise of conducting fertility testing. Searle provided the Pills for the "trial".

1955: Rock announces publicly that he and Pincus have found an effective birth control pill that inhibits ovulation.

1956: Searle's' birth control pill: Enovid is submitted for FDA approval. More tests are conducted but they are moved off the US shores into Puerto Rico; Haiti, and Mexico City.

1957: FDA approved use of Enovid for severe menstrual disorders; they required that the drug label carry the warning that it also prevents ovulation.

1959: Suddenly a large number of American women develop severe menstrual disorders and ask for Enovid. By late 1959 over half a million American women are taking Enovid for "off label" contraceptive purposes. Oct. 29 - Searle excited by potential market share-files for application to FDA to market pill for menstrual disorders and as a contraceptive. (Field tested 897 women).

1960s:

1960: The combination oral contraceptive marketed; $37 million in annual sales for "menstrual disorders".

The term: The "Pill" came from Adolph Huxley's New World Revisited. HRT introduced for menopausal women.

1960: Thirteen major drug companies were suddenly created or became involved in the development of new birth control methods. They were excited by the possibility of opening up even larger markets for contraceptive use.

1962: First word spread about the Pill's potential for causing serious side effects such as blood clots and heart attacks.

Searle denies any problems and claims they had no conclusive evidence demonstrating blood clots are direct result of   pill.

1963: By this date, 2.3 million American women use or used the Pill for birth control measures.

1964: Twenty five percent of all American couples use birth control pill for contraception.

1965: Pope Paul VI creates birth control commission to study the Pill.

1965: Courts strike down the Connecticut law prohibiting use of birth control as a violation of couples' right to privacy.

1966: FDA looks into issue of side effects of Pill and finds no "smoking gun" despite evidence of wide off label usage prior to approval for birth control. In fact, the FDA gives drug companies additional freedom to market hormonal   contraceptives   with less "red tape" concerns.

1967: Pincus dies from a rare disease of white blood cells due to exposure to lab chemicals.

1968: Sales of the Pill hits $150 million annually; there are now 7 varieties or brands.

1968 (July 25): Pope Paul VI issued the encyclical *Humanae Vitae*. A short excerpt from the beginning of the encyclical is enclosed here. "The transmission of human life is a most serious role in which married people collaborate freely and responsibly with God the Creator. It has always been a source of great joy to them, even though it sometimes entails many difficulties and hardships. The fulfillment of this duty has always posed problems to the conscience of married people, but the recent course of human society and the concomitant changes have provoked new questions. The Church cannot ignore these questions, for they concern matters intimately connected with the life and happiness of human beings. The changes that have taken place are of considerable importance and varied in nature. In the first place there is the rapid increase in population which has made many fear that world population is going to grow faster than available resources, with the consequence that many families and developing countries would be faced with greater hardships. This can easily induce public authorities to be tempted to take even harsher measures to avert this danger. There is also the fact that not only working and housing conditions but the greater demands made both in the economic and educational field pose a living situation in which it is frequently difficult these days to provide properly for a large family. Also noteworthy is a new understanding of the dignity of woman and her place in society, of the value of conjugal love in marriage and the relationship of conjugal acts to this love. But the most remarkable development of all is to be seen in man's stupendous progress in the domination and rational organization of the forces of nature to the point that he is endeavoring to extend this control over every aspect of his own life—over his body, over his mind and emotions, over his social life, and even over the laws that regulate the transmission of life."

1969: Journalist Seaman brings national attention to the dangers of the Pill.

1970s:

1970: Patient warning insert put in all packages of pill warning women by order of FDA. The Pill sales drop by 20% but remain the number one method of birth control choice.

1974: Government support for birth control clinics begins; first fertilization of human ovum outside body.

1979 (Sept. 5): Pope John Paul ll issues first address to the general audience with regard to Theology of the Body thesis.

1980s:

1981: Nov 22): Pope John Paul ll released Familiaris Consortio on the role of the family.

1984 (Nov. 28): Pope John Paul ll gave the last address to general audiences with regard to Theology of the Body thesis

1988: Drug companies at the urging of the FDA drop the high does oral contraceptives. Birth control dropped from the list of medical research 35 top priorities.

1990s:

1990: Viagra introduction, FSD and ED move to top of medical research priorities.

1991: The percent of teenage births to unwed mothers rose to 84 percent from 67 percent in 1980.

1993: (August 6): Pope John Paul ll released Veritatis Splendor with regard to the truth about human life.

1995: (Nov 21): The Pontifical Council for the Family released the Truth and Meaning of Human Sexuality document.

1995: (Mar 25): Pope John ll released the encyclical entitled Evangelium Vitae about the value and dignity of human life.

1998: (Mar 27): Viagra approved by the FDA in pill form to treat impotence.

2000s:

2000: Nearly $3 billion have been spent on federal Title X family planning services; yet teenage pregnancies and abortions rise.

Pope Benedict XVI cites moral relativism as the major problem for faith today.

2004; Society for Assisted Reproductive Technology (SART) formed.

2006: The CDC reported that 142,435 ART cycles were performed at 430 reporting clinics in the United States during 2006, resulting in 43,412 live births (deliveries of one or more living infants) and 57,569 infants.

2010: The use of ART has doubled over the past decade. Today, over 1% of all infants born in the United States every year are conceived using ART.

2010 (Feb.): USCCB name four primary challenges to Marriage: cohabitation, divorce, same sex unions, contraception. Approximately half of all couples cohabit prior to marriage.

APPENDIX FIFTEEN

Conditions/Drugs that Negatively Impact Testosterone Levels

Drug:	Side Effects:	Used For:
1. Spironolactone	Directly decreases testosterone levels.	Diuretic; eliminates excess water and urine from our bodies. Used to treat high blood pressure, edema or swelling from heart, kidney, or liver disease.
2. Chemotherapeutic Agents	Directly decreases testosterone levels.	Drugs used in the treatment of cancer.
3. Latoconazole	Directly decreases testosterone levels.	Used as an antifungal agent.
4. Flutamide	Directly decreases testosterone levels.	Used in combination with another medication used to treat prostate cancer.
5. Cimetedine	Directly decreases testosterone levels.	An antihistamine that blocks the release of stomach acid; used to treat stomach or intestinal ulcers and Heartburn from acid reflux.
6. Cyroproterone	Directly decreases testosterone levels.	Used to treat prostate cancer.
7. Progesterone	Inhibits GnRH secretions/ indirectly decreases testosterone levels.	Treatment for prostate cancer.
8. Estrogen	Inhibits GnRH secretions/ indirectly decreases testosterone levels.	Treatment for ED.
9. GnRH agonists	Inhibits GnRH secretions/ indirectly decreases testosterone levels.	Treatment for Prostate cancer, male breast cancer.
10. Glucocorticoids	Inhibits GnRH secretions/ indirectly decreases testosterone levels.	Prednisone & cortisols; used to treat arthritis, etc.
11. Antipsychotic	Elevates prolactin levels; affects testosterone.	Treats psychosis.
12. Tricyclic Anti-Depressants	Elevates prolactin levels disaffecting.	Used to treat depression; Zoloft, Prozac, Effexor.
13. Opioid analgesics	Same as above.	Provides pain relief; oxycontin.
14. Cocaine	Same as above.	An illegal drug substance
15. Reserpine	Same as above.	Anti-hypertensive; treats high blood pressure.
16. Verapamil	Same as above.	An L-type calcium channel blocker used to treat hypertension, angina pectoris, cardiac arrhythmia and cluster headaches. Brand names: Isoptin Verelan, Calan, Bosoptin, Covera-HS.

APPENDIX SIXTEEN

Analyzing Previously Set Goals

Analyze how well you accomplished your goals previously set here.

Today's Date: _____

Dimension	Accomplished Goals	Partially Accomplished Goals	Goals Not Accomplished	New Goals
Spiritual	1. 2. 3.	1. 2. 3.	1. 2. 3.	1. 2. 3.
Mental	1. 2. 3.	1. 2. 3.	1. 2. 3.	1. 2. 3.
Physical	1. 2. 3.	1. 2. 3.	1. 2. 3.	1. 2. 3.
Social	1. 2. 3.	1. 2. 3.	1. 2. 3.	1. 2. 3.
Emotional	1. 2. 3.	1. 2. 3.	1. 2. 3.	1. 2. 3.
Financial	1. 2. 3.	1. 2. 3.	1. 2. 3.	1. 2. 3.
Intellectual	1. 2. 3.	1. 2. 3.	1. 2. 3.	1. 2. 3.
Career	1. 2. 3.	1. 2. 3.	1. 2. 3.	1. 2. 3.

My notes:

APPENDIX SEVENTEEN

Final Short and Longer Term Goals

Use the previous appendix to compile your final three goals (short and longer term) for each dimension in this section. These should be updated at the end of this semester or year in college at the latest.

Today's Date: _____

Dimension	Short Term Goal - Ideal	Long Term Goal - Ideal	Short Term Goal - Real	Long Term Goal - Real
Spiritual	1. 2. 3.	1. 2. 3.	1. 2. 3.	1. 2. 3.
Mental	1. 2. 3.	1. 2. 3.	1. 2. 3.	1. 2. 3.
Physical	1. 2. 3.	1. 2. 3.	1. 2. 3.	1. 2. 3.
Social	1. 2. 3.	1. 2. 3.	1. 2. 3.	1. 2. 3.
Emotional	1. 2. 3.	1. 2. 3.	1. 2. 3.	1. 2. 3.
Financial	1. 2. 3.	1. 2. 3.	1. 2. 3.	1. 2. 3.
Intellectual	1. 2. 3.	1. 2. 3.	1. 2. 3.	1. 2. 3.
Career	1. 2. 3.	1. 2. 3.	1. 2. 3.	1. 2. 3.

CHAPTER NOTES

INTRODUCTION

1   William George Plunkett (1910 – 1975), printer and aphorist, said that "there are three things that never come back to us: the spent arrow, the spoken word; the lost opportunity". More information about Plunkett can be found online at the Australian Dictionary of Biography; Online Edition; http://adbonline.anu.edu.au/biogs/A160017b.htm.

2   Deepti Hajela, "Homeless Good Samaritan Left to Die - Man Was Stabbed After Intervening In a Fight To Help a Woman", Associated Press, http://www.msnbc.msn.com/id/36788569/ns/us_news-life/(January 4, 2010).

3   Cynthia J. Osborn, Dennis L. Thombs, R. Scott Olds, "Reconceptualizing Research on Undergraduate Alcohol Use: The Need for Student Engagement", *Evaluation and the Health Professions* (2007); 123.

4   Comparisons of Millenial's religious attitudes was demonstrated by the Marist Poll in collaboration with the Knights of Columbus, New Survey Comparing Religious Attitudes of Young Americans and Young Catholics, February 11, 2010.The Marist Institute for Public Opinion, founded in 1978, is a survey research center at Marist College in Poughkeepsie, New York that regularly measures public opinion at the local, state, and national level.

5   On April 25, 1799, Jedidiah Morse (1761-1826), American geographer and clergyman, warned listeners, during his election sermon given at Charleston Massachusetts, about the dangers of watering down core moral principles. His speech entitled Losing Freedom's Blessings can be found online at Christianity Today International's Christian History Timeline, Glimpse #99: The Amazing Morses: Sam and Jed: They Shrank and Expanded our World, (http://www.christianhistorytimeline.com/GLIMPSEF/Glimpses/glmps099.shtml).

6   Carl Anderson and Jose' Granados, *Called to Love* (New York: Doubleday, a Division of the Random House, Inc. 2009), 35.

7   David Van Biema, "Mother Teresa's Crises of Faith", (August 23, 2007),http://www.time.com/time/world/article/0,8599,1655415,00.html. 10 October, 2010.

8   Susan Pitman, Office for Vocations, Archdiocese of St Paul and Minneapolis, MN telephone interview with Linda Kracht, September, 2009.

9   *Catechism of the Catholic Church* (New York,: An Image Book by Doubleday, 1995), 928-929.

10 George Washington in a letter to Benjamin Lincoln dated June 29, 1788. The quote is recorded at Revolutionary War and Beyond, *Read a George Washington Quote*, (http://www.

revolutionary-war-and-beyond.com/george-washington-quote-1.html).

11   John Adams wrote a letter to his wife, Abigail Adams; the letter can be found in its entirely at Founding.com: a project of the Claremont Institute, *Letter to Abigail Adams July 3, 1776*, (http://www.founding.com/founders_library/pageID.2145/default.asp).

12   Jedediah Morse's Election Sermon given at Charleston, Mass. on April 25, 1799, taken from an original in the Evans collection compiled by the American Antiquarian Society. Verna M. Hall, *Christian History of the Constitution of the United States of America*, San Francisco: Foundation for America Christian Education (1975) 145.

CHAPTER ONE

1   James J. Heckman and Paul A. LaFontaine, "American High School Graduation Rates, Trends and Levels", IZA Discussion Paper No. 3216 (December 2007), 1 – 39.

2   A compilation of mission statements obtained online from William and Mary College, Harvard University, UCLA, MIT, U of MN, UND, and other university websites.

3   Stuart Kerachsky, Acting Commissioner for the National Center for Education Statistic Briefing on the Condition of Education; May 28, 2009.

4   Ibid.

5   MyGoals.com is a member- only Web site devoted to helping people identify and accomplish short and long term goals for any area of life. *Setting Goals*, http://www.mygoals.com/content/college-goals.html

6   Stephanie Armour, "Generation Y: They've Arrived at Work with a New Attitude", *USA Today*, 6 November, 2005, *http://*www.usatoday.com/money/workplace/2005-11-06-gen-y_x.htm.

7   Jeffrey Jensen Arnett, Ph.D, *Emerging Adulthood: The Winding Road from Late Teens through the Twenties* (New York: Oxford University Press, 2004), 12.

8   Jeffrey Jensen Arnett, Ph.D, *Emerging Adulthood: The Winding Road from Late Teens through the Twenties* (New York: Oxford University Press, 2004), 8.

9   Jeffrey Jensen Arnett, Ph.D, *Emerging Adulthood: The Winding Road from Late Teens through the Twenties* (New York: Oxford University Press, 2004), 12.

10   Marcia H. Magnus, PhD, "Which College Students are at Higher Health Risk", *American Journal of Men's Health Online First* (Volume XX, number X, November 25, 2008): 1

11   Jeffrey Jensen Arnett, Ph.D, *Emerging Adulthood: The Winding Road from Late Teens through the Twenties* (New York: Oxford University Press, 2004), 10.

12   Ibid.

13   Daniel, "Why College Freshman Dropout: the Undercurrent in Undergraduate Education", *CollegeScholarships.org*, September 5, 2007, http://www.collegescholarships.org/blog/2007/09/05/why-college-freshman-dropout.

14   Tamar Lewin , "Many Going to College Are Not Ready", *NY Times*, 17 August, 2005; www.nytimes.com/2005/08/17/education/17scores.html: 1.

15   Daniel, "Why College Freshman Dropout: the Undercurrent in Undergraduate Education", *CollegeScholarships.org*, September 5, 2007, http://www.collegescholarships.org/blog/2007/09/05/why-college-freshman-dropout.

CHAPTER TWO

1   WHO stands for World Health Organization; this agency has the directing and coordinating authority for health within the United Nations system. The definition for health was obtained from the document entitled "Defining Health and Wellness - The Health Of The United States, Birthrates And Fertility Rates, Infant Mortality, Life Expectancy" found at http://www.libraryindex.com/pages/2951/Defining-Health-Wellness.html#ixzz0egxmfjPV.

2   Dr. Halbert Dunn (1896-1975) coined the term wellness; he helped establish a national

vital statistics system in the United States. More information can be found at http://www. census.gov/history/www/census_then_now/notable_alumni/halbert_l_dunn.html.

3   William T. Hey, Kristine S. Calderon and Holly Carroll, "Use of Body-Mind-Spirit Dimensions for the Development of a Wellness Behavior and Characteristic Inventory for College Students", *Health Promotion Practice* (2006) 7: 125.

4   Jodi Dworkin, "Risk Taking as Developmentally Appropriate Experimentation for College Students", *Journal of Adolescent Research* (2005), 20:232.

5   Ibid. 231.

CHAPTER THREE

1   Kwame McKenzie, "Urbanization, Social Capital and Mental Health", Global Social Policy (2008, Vol. 8): 365.

2   Carl Anderson and Jose' Granados, Called to Love (New York: Doubleday Publishing Group, a division of Random House, 2009), 239.

3   Carl Anderson and Jose' Granados, Called to Love (New York: Doubleday Publishing Group, a division of Random House, 2009), 239.

4   Ibid.

5   Ann Sloan Devlin, Sarah Donovan, Adrianne Nicolov, Olivia Nold, and Gabrielle Sandan, "Residence Hall Architecture and Sense of Community: Everything Old is New Again", Environment and Behavior Journal (2008: 40): 488.

6   Brian J. Willoughby, Jason S. Carroll, William J. Marshall and Caitlin Clark, "Decline of In Loco Parentis", Journal of Adolescent Research (January, 2009: Vol. 24, No. 1): 23.

7   The great majority of US students – regardless of age or year in school - spend less than one hour daily on homework which is far less time than their counterparts in Europe and Asia. These results were reported by Brian P. Gill and Steven L. Schlossman, "A Nation at Rest: The American Way of Homework", Educational Evaluation and Policy Analysis (Fall 2003, Vol. 25, No. 3):320.

8   Sarath A. Nonis, Melodie J. Philhours, and Gail I Hudson, "Where Does the Time Go? A Diary Approach to Business and Marketing Students' Time Use", Journal of Marketing Education (August 2006: Vol. 28 No. 2), 121.

9   College students are advised to spend two to three hours studying per credit hour per week. This means that for twelve credit hours, a student should study at least 24 – 36 hours per week (3.4 hours - 7 hours/ class/week).

10   Ibid.

11   Kwame McKenzie, "Urbanization, Social Capital and Mental Health", Global Social Policy (2008: Vol. 8): 363.

12   Ibid.

13   Ann Sloan Devlin, Sarah Donovan, Adrianne Nicolov, Olivia Nold, and Gabrielle Sandan, "Residence Hall Architecture and Sense of Community: Everything Old is New Again", Environment and Behavior Journal (2008: 40): 488.

14   Ann Sloan Devlin, Sarah Donovan, Adrianne Nicolov, Olivia Nold, and Gabrielle Sandan, "Residence Hall Architecture and Sense of Community: Everything Old is New Again", Environment and Behavior Journal (2008: 40): 488.

15   Brian J. Willoughby, Jason S. Carroll, William J. Marshall and Caitlin Clark, "Decline of In Loco Parentis", Journal of Adolescent Research (January 2009: Vol. 24, No. 1): 24.

16   Ann Sloan Devlin, Sarah Donovan, Adrianne Nicolov, Olivia Nold, and Gabrielle Sandan, "Residence Hall Architecture and Sense of Community: Everything Old is New Again", Environment and Behavior Journal (2008: 40): 518.

17   Brian J. Willoughby, Jason S. Carroll, William J. Marshall and Caitlin Clark, "Decline of In Loco Parentis" , Journal of Adolescent Research(January 2009: Vol. 24, No. 1): 24.

18   Pope Paul VI, Pastoral Constitution of the Church in the Modern World (Gaudium et Spes), December 7, 1965, (http://www.vatican.va/archive/hist_councils/ii_vatican_council/documents/vat-ii_cons_19651207_gaudium-et-spes_en.html): 4

19   Marist/KofC Poll New Survey of Young Catholics Shows Promise and Challenges for

the Catholic Church, February, 2010, (http://www.kofc.org/un/eb/en/news/polls/index. html): 14.

20 John Lee, "Guess What College Freshman Think?" , Jan 27, 2009, (www.mindingthe campus.com/forum/2009/01/news_reports_on_uclas_latest.html): 1

21 Marist/KofC Poll New Survey of Young Catholics Shows Promise and Challenges for the Catholic Church, February, 2010, (http://www.kofc.org/un/eb/en/news/polls/index. html): 5.

22 Marist/KofC Poll New Survey of Young Catholics Shows Promise and Challenges for the Catholic Church, February, 2010, (http://www.kofc.org/un/eb/en/news/polls/index. html): 13.

23 Marist/KofC Poll New Survey of Young Catholics Shows Promise and Challenges for the Catholic Church, February, 2010, (http://www.kofc.org/un/eb/en/news/polls/index. html): 19.

24 Marist/KofC Poll New Survey of Young Catholics Shows Promise and Challenges for the Catholic Church, February, 2010, (http://www.kofc.org/un/eb/en/news/polls/index. html): Summary.

25 John Lee, "Guess What College Freshman Think?", Jan 27, 2009, (www.mindingthe campus.com/forum/2009/01/news_reports_on_uclas_latest.html): 1.

26 "Girl, 13, Commits Suicide After Being Cyber-bullied By Neighbor Posing As Teenage Boy", Mail online, 19 November, 2007, http://www.dailymail.co.uk/news/article-494809/ Girl-13-commits-suicide-cyber-bullied-neighbour-posing-teenage-boy.html.

27 Seema Marugan, "Non – Verbal Communication", (http://www.hss.iitb.ac.in/courses/n-v. pdf) October 10, 2010: 7/41.

28 Donghun Chung and Chang Soo Nam, "An Analysis of the Variables Predicting Instant Messenger Use", New Media Society (2007, Vol. 9): 213.

29 Ibid.

30 Donghun Chung and Chang Soo Nam, "An Analysis of the Variables Predicting Instant Messenger Use", New Media Society (2007, Vol. 9): 214.

31 Rich Ling and Naomi S. Baron, "Text Messaging and IM: Linguistic Comparison of American College Data", Journal of Language and Social Psychology (2007; Vol. 26): 292.

32 Textually.org reported that in 2000, over 33% US college students had cell phones on campus, according to a Student Monitor National Survey; by the fall of 2004 nearly 90% of college students owned a cell phone. This information can be found at Textually.org, (http://www.textually.org/textually/archives/2005/02/007109.htm), October 10, 2010.

33 Rich Ling and Naomi S. Baron, "Text Messaging and IM: Linguistic Comparison of American College Data", Journal of Language and Social Psychology (2007; Vol. 26): 292.

34 Ibid.

35 Nicole B. Ellison, "Introduction: Reshaping Campus Communication and Community Through Social Networking Sites", Students and Information Technology (2008: CCAR Research Study 8): 1.

36 Sally J. McMillan and Margaret Morrison, "Coming of Age with the Internet", New Media Society (2006, Vol. 8): 75.

37 Christine L. Ogan, Muzaffer Ozakca and Jacob Groshek, "Embedding the Internet in the Lives of College Students: Online and Offline Behavior", Social Science Computer Review (2008, Vol. 26): 172.

38 Kaveri Subrahmanyham, Stephanie M. Reich, Natalie Waechter and Guadalupe Espinoza, "Online and Offline Social Networks: Use of Social Networking Sites by Emerging Adults", Journal of Applied Developmental Psychology (2008, Vol. 29), 420–433.

39 Jung-Hwan Kim and Sharron J. Lennon, "Mass Media, and Self Esteem, Body Image and Eating Disorder Tendencies", Clothing and Textiles Research Journal (January 2007, Vol. 25, No. 1): 3–23.

40 Daniel, "Why College Freshman Dropout", (www.collegescholarships.org/blog/2007/09/05/ why-college-freshman-dropout/): 2

41 Pamela Matthews, "Beyond the Jokes on Helicopter Parents" (www.insidehighered.com/ layout/set/print/views/2009/09/09/matthews) September 9, 2009.

42 Pamela Matthews, "Beyond the Jokes on Helicopter Parents" (www.insidehighered.com/

layout/set/print/views/2009/09/09/matthews)September 9, 2009.

43   Kwame McKenzie, "Urbanization, Social Capital and Mental Health", Global Social Policy,(2008, Vol. 8): 362.

44   Thomas D Gore and Cheryl Campanella Bracken, "The Theoretical Design of a Health Risk Message: Reexamining the Major Tenets of the Extended Parallel Process Model", Health Education and Behavior (2005, Vol. 32):28.

45   Thomas D Gore and Cheryl Campanella Bracken, "The Theoretical Design of a Health Risk Message: Reexamining the Major Tenets of the Extended Parallel Process Model", Health Education and Behavior (2005, Vol. 32):28.

CHAPTER FOUR

1   Sean Joe, Emanique Joe, and Larry L. Rowley, "Consequences of Physical Health and Mental Illness Risks for Academic Achievement in Grades K12", Review of Research in Education (2009, Vol. 33): 297.

2   Dzung X. Vo and M. Jane Park, "Stress and Stress Management Among Youth and Young Men", American Journal of Men's Health (2008, Vo. 2): 354.

3   Rosemary Anderson holds a B.Sc and PhD in Biochemistry, BA in Psychology, and is a chartered psychologist. She is a member of the British Psychological Society, The European Academy of Occupational Health and a Fellow of the Royal Society for the Promotion of Health. She has lectured and written extensively on stress, health, and stress management. Rosemary is considered to be an expert in her field of studies.

4   Rosemary Anderson, "Stress and Mental Health", Journal of the Royal Society for the Promotion of Health, (2004, Vol. 124): 112.

5   Ibid.

6   Sean Joe, Emanique Joe, and Larry L. Rowley, "Consequences of Physical Health and Mental Illness Risks for Academic Achievement in Grades K12", Review of Research in Education (2009, Vol. 33): 298.

7   This is the most frequently used term by the WHO and the American Psychiatric Association(APA) to describe mental/psychiatric problems and illnesses.

8   "Psychiatric Disorders", Diagnostic and Statistical Manual of Mental Disorders, Fourth Edition (DSM Disorders- IV, (http://allpsych.com/disorders/dsm.html), October 10, 2010.

9   Sharlene A. Kiuhara, Sharlene A. and Dixie S Huefner, "Students with Psychiatric Disabilities in Higher Education Settings: The Americans with Disabilities Act and Beyond", Journal of Disability Policy Studies, (2008, Vol. 19): 104.

10   Sean Joe, Emanique Joe, and Larry L. Rowley, "Consequences of Physical Health and Mental Illness Risks for Academic Achievement in Grades K12", Review of Research in Education (2009, Vol. 33): 298.

11   Sharlene A. Kiuhara, Sharlene A. and Dixie S Huefner, "Students with Psychiatric Disabilities in Higher Education Settings: The Americans with Disabilities Act and Beyond", Journal of Disability Policy Studies, (2008, Vol. 19): 104.

12   Rosemary Anderson, "Stress and Mental Health", Journal of the Royal Society for the Promotion of Health, (2004, Vol. 124): 113.

13   Rosemary Anderson, "Stress and Mental Health", Journal of the Royal Society for the Promotion of Health, (2004, Vol. 124): 112.

14   Rosemary Anderson, "Stress and Mental Health", Journal of the Royal Society for the Promotion of Health, (2004, Vol. 124): 112.

15   Ibid., p. 112-113.

16   Ibid., p. 112.

17   Dzung X. Vo and M. Jane Park, "Stress and Stress Management Among Youth and Young Men", American Journal of Men's Health (2008, Vol. 2): 356.

18   "Major Depression", WebMD, https://health.google.com/health/ref/Major+depression. 10 October, 2010.

19   Ibid.

Chapter Five

1   A definition for wellness has been offered by many different social and governmental agencies and organizations. The National Wellness Association is one more that provides definitions of emotional, intellectual, occupational, physical, social, and spiritual wellness. This information can be found at: "Defining Health and Wellness - the Health of the US Birthrates and Fertility Rates, Infant Mortality, http://www.libraryindex.com/pages/2951/Defining-Health-Wellness.html, October 15, 2010.

2   University of California, Riverside. "Spiritual Wellness." Wellness, http://wellness.ucr.edu/spiritual_wellness.html, 10 October 2010.

3   Arthur C. Brooks." A Nation of Givers."The American; The Journal of the American Enterprise Institute. March/April 2008, http://www.american.com/archive/2008/march-april-magazine-contents/a-nation-of-givers, October 10, 2010.

4   Knights of Columbus. "New Survey of Young Catholics Shows Promise and Challenges for the Catholic Church" http://www.kofc.org/un/eb/en/news/polls/index.html. 10 October, 2010. Additional Poll Information: Who Believes in God? 88% Gen X (30-44 years of age); 83% Baby Boom (45-64 years of age); 90% Greatest Generation (older than 65) and 76% of Millenials/Gen Y (18 – 29 years of age) and 85% Catholic Millenials.

5   Knights of Columbus. "New Survey of Young Catholics Shows Promise and Challenges for the Catholic Church" http://www.kofc.org/un/eb/en/news/polls/index.html. 10 October, 2010: 7.

6   Arthur C. Brooks." A Nation of Givers."The American; The Journal of the American Enterprise Institute. March/April 2008, http://www.american.com/archive/2008/march-april-magazine-contents/a-nation-of-givers, October 10, 2010.

7   Arthur C. Brooks." A Nation of Givers."The American; The Journal of the American Enterprise Institute. March/April 2008, http://www.american.com/archive/2008/march-april-magazine-contents/a-nation-of-givers, October 10, 2010.

8   Knights of Columbus. "New Survey of Young Catholics Shows Promise and Challenges for the Catholic Church" http://www.kofc.org/un/eb/en/news/polls/index.html. 10 October, 2010.

9   Knights of Columbus. "New Survey of Young Catholics Shows Promise and Challenges for the Catholic Church" http://www.kofc.org/un/eb/en/news/polls/index.html. 10 October, 2010.

10   American Millennial: Generations Apart Religion, The Marist Poll, page 7; February 2010 with the K of C. page 27.

11   The Marist/ Kof C Poll 2010 revealed that the majority of all generations (>52%) believe in moral relativism.

12   By way of comparison, 88% of Catholic Millenials, 75% Americans, 66% Millenials think that people's ethical standards are different in business than personal lives.

13   Knights of Columbus. "New Survey of Young Catholics Shows Promise and Challenges for the Catholic Church: American Millennial: Generations Apart". http://www.kofc.org/un/eb/en/news/polls/index.html. (10 October, 2010): 3.

14   Arthur C. Brooks." A Nation of Givers."The American; The Journal of the American Enterprise Institute. March/April 2008, http://www.american.com/archive/2008/march-april-magazine-contents/a-nation-of-givers, October 10, 2010.

15   Ibid.

16   Jolinda Cary holds a dual degree in theology and anthropology and portrays herself as a consumer of spiritualism. Jolinda's blog analyzes many different topics from polygamy to paganism for military soldiers. Her message promotes equal co-existence. For more information go to: Jolinda Cary, "Jolinda Cary", Suite 101®.com. http://www.suite101.com/profile.cfm/jolinda. 10 October, 2010.

17   Jolinda Cary, "Jolinda Cary", Suite 101®.com. http://www.suite101.com/profile.cfm/jolinda. 10 October, 2010.

18   Father Robert Barron, "Seven Deadly Sins, Seven Lively Virtues (DVD)", (Skokie, Ill: Word On Fire Catholic Ministries, 2010): Lesson Four .This DVD and other materials can be found at http://www.wordonfire.org/WOF-Store/DVDs/Seven-Deadly-Sins-Seven-

Lively-Virtues.aspx. 10, October, 2010.

19   This includes the population of people who "believe" in the principle of moral relativism – the belief that there is no right and wrong for everybody.

20   Knights of Columbus. "New Survey of Young Catholics Shows Promise and Challenges for the Catholic Church" http://www.kofc.org/un/eb/en/news/polls/index.html. 10 October, 2010: 14

21   Ibid.

22   Michael Matt, The Remnant, Posting on May 5, 2008 with regard to the Pope Benedict XVl and his trip to the US. August 5, 2008.

23   Pope Paul Vl, "Pastoral Constitution on the Church in the Modern World (Gaudium et Spes), No. 7. December 7, 1965. http://www.vatican.va/archive/hist_councils/ii_vatican_council/documents/vat-ii-cons_19651207_gaudium-et-spes_en.html. 10 October 2010.

24   1 Corinthians 12: 26-27.

25   Catechism of the Catholic Church, (New York: An Image Book, Doubleday, 1995): 705.

26   Catechism of the Catholic Church, (New York: An Image Book, Doubleday, 1995): 1472.

27   Father Bede Jarrett, "Peace", The Magnificat (Tuesday, May 4, 2010): 63.

28   Catechism of the Catholic Church, (New York: An Image Book, Doubleday, 1995): 1505.

29   Catechism of the Catholic Church, (New York: An Image Book, Doubleday, 1995): 300.

30   Pope Paul Vl, "Pastoral Constitution on the Church in the Modern World (more commonly called Gaudium et Spes), No. 7. December 7, 1965. http://www.vatican.va/archive/hist_councils/ii_vatican_council/documents/vat-ii-cons_19651207_gaudium-et-spes_en.html. 10 October 2010. No. 9.

31   Sirach 3: 17; 22.

32   Pope Paul Vl, ""Pastoral Constitution on the Church in the Modern World (more commonly called Gaudium et Spes), No. 7. December 7, 1965. http://www.vatican.va/archive/hist_councils/ii_vatican_council/documents/vat-ii-cons_19651207_gaudium-et-spes_en.html. 10 October 2010. No 4.

33   Dinesh D'Souza, Life after Death: the Evidence (Chicago: Regnery Publishing, November 2009): 235.

34   Father Robert Barron, "Answer Key to Seven Deadly Sins, Seven Lively Virtues Workbook" (Skokie, Ill: Word On Fire Catholic Ministries, 2010): 1

35   Dinesh D'Souza, Life after Death: the Evidence (Chicago: Regnery Publishing, November 2009): 216.

36   William T. Hey, Kristine S. Calderon, Holly Carroll, "Use of Body-Mind-Spirit Dimensions for the Development of a Wellness Behavior and Characteristic Inventory for College Students", Health Promotion Practice (January 2006, Vol. 7, No 1): 130.

37   Marcia H. Magnus, PhD, "Which College Students are at Higher Health Risk", American Journal of Men's Health Online First (November 25, 2008, Volume XX, number X): 1.

38   Ephesians 6: 10 – 18.

39   Catechism of the Catholic Church, (New York: An Image Book, Doubleday, 1995): 1833.

40   Father Henri-Cominique Lacordaire, O.P , "Guarding against False Leaven", The Magnificat (Tuesday, February 16, 2010, Vol 11, No. 13): 242.

41   Catechism of the Catholic Church, (New York: An Image Book, Doubleday, 1995): 1839.

42   Catechism of the Catholic Church, (New York: An Image Book, Doubleday, 1995): 1828.

43   Wisdom of Solomon, 7:7-14

44   Father John A. Harden, S.J., The Catholic Catechism: A Contemporary Catechism of the Teachings of the Catholic Church (New York: Doubleday Publishing, 1975):201.

45   Dinesh D'Souza, Life after Death: the Evidence (Chicago: Regnery Publishing, November 2009): 208.

46   1Corinthians 13: 4-8

47   Fr. Maurice Zundel , "Human Life" ,The Magnificat (October, 2009, Vol. 11,No. 8): 192

48   Jodi Dworkin, " Risk Taking as Developmentally Appropriate Experimentation for College Students", Journal of Adolescent Research (2005, Vol. 20): 222.

49   Anne Henderschott and Nicholas Dunn, "Hooking Up: A Special Report", the Catholic World Report (June 2010): 28.

50   Bishop Thomas Tobin, Bishop of Providence, RI., "Without a Doubt: Dear Congressman

(Patrick) Kennedy", Rhode Island Catholic,11 November, 2009, http://www.thericatholic. com/opinion/detail.html?sub_id=263210 October, 2010.

51 Luke 14: 28

52 Catechism of the Catholic Church, (New York: An Image Book, Doubleday, 1995): 1968.

53 St. Matthew's Gospel 7:12; St. Luke's Gospel 6:31.

54 St. John's Gospel 15:12 and 13:34.

55 Catechism of the Catholic Church, (New York: An Image Book, Doubleday, 1995): 1970.

56 These truths can be found in 1 Corinthians, 8-9.

57 Carl Anderson and Jose' Granados, Called to Love (New York: Doubleday Publishing Group, a division of Random House, 2009):35.

CHAPTER SIX

1 Marcia H. Magnus, PhD, "Which College Students are at Higher Health Risk", American Journal of Men's Health Online First(November 25, 2008, Volume XX, number X): 1.

2 Lee N. Burkett, Cynthia Gayle Rena, Kathy Jones, William J. Stone and Diane A. Klein, "The Effects of Wellness Education on the Body Image of College Students", Health Promotion Practice (2002, Vol. 3): 77.

3 Marilyn Shannon, Fertility Cycles and Nutrition (Cincinnati: Couple to Couple League, 2009): 208.

4 Sean Joe, Emanique Joe and Larry L. Rowley, "Consequences of Physical Health and Mental Illness Risks for Academic Achievement in Grades K12", Review of Research in Education (2009): 289.

5 Marcia H. Magnus, PhD, "Which College Students are at Higher Health Risk", American Journal of Men's Health Online First(November 25, 2008, Volume XX, number X): 1.

6 Mayo Clinic Staff, "Healthy Breakfast: Quick, Flexible Options to Grab at Home", Healthy Breakfasts, http://www.mayoclinic.com/health/food-and-nutrition/NU00197/ UPDATEAPP=false&FLUSHCACHE=0, 14 October, 2010.

7 "Nutrition and Well Being A to Z: Caffeine", Faqs.Org. (http://www.faqs.org/nutrition/ Ca-De/Caffeine.html): 10 October, 2010.

8 "Cigarette Smoking and its Health Risks," Drugs.com (http://www.drugs.com/cg/ cigarette-smoking-and-its-health-risks.html), 10 October, 2010.

9 Marcia H. Magnus, PhD, "Which College Students are at Higher Health Risk", American Journal of Men's Health Online First(November 25, 2008, Volume XX, number X): 1.

10 Ibid., 6.

11 Lee N. Burkett, Cynthia Gayle Rena, Kathy Jones, William J. Stone and Diane A. Klein, "The Effects of Wellness Education on the Body Image of College Students", Health Promotion Practice (2002, Vol. 3): 80.

12 This list is a composite of several ideas and facts, obtained from two primary sources although others were influential as well. The two primary sources include: 1) Marcia H. Magnus, PhD, "Which College Students are at Higher Health Risk", American Journal of Men's Health Online First(November 25, 2008, Volume XX, number X): 1, and 2) Marilyn Shannon, Fertility Cycles and Nutrition (Cincinnati: Couple to Couple League, 2009): 208.

13 Marilyn Shannon, Fertility Cycles and Nutrition (Cincinnati: Couple to Couple League, 2009): 115.

14 Ibid., 4

15 Marilyn Shannon, Fertility Cycles and Nutrition (Cincinnati: Couple to Couple League, 2009): 115.

16 Marilyn Shannon, Fertility Cycles and Nutrition (Cincinnati: Couple to Couple League, 2009): 21.

17 USDA, "Steps to a Healthier You", My Pyramid.gov (http://www.mypyramid.gov/), 10 October, 2010.

18 Harvard School for Public Health, "The Nutrition Source: Knowledge for Healthy Eating", HSPH.edu (http://www.hsph.harvard,edu/nutrition source/). 10 October, 2010.

19 University of Michigan Health System, "Healthy Eating Overview", UMich.edu, (http://

health.med.umich.edu/healthcontent.cfm?xyzpdqabc=0&id=6&action=detail&AEProduc tID=HW_Knowledgebase&AEArticleID=nutri).10 October, 2010.

20   Health and Human Services, "Proposed 2020 Healthy People Objectives", www. Developing HealthyPeople.gov; http://www.healthypeople.gov/hp2020/Objectives/ TopicAreas.aspx ; 5 December, 2010.

21   This new initiative builds upon the information and results obtained from four preceding initiatives beginning with the 1979 Surgeon General's Report on Health followed up with the 1990, 2000, and 2010 Healthy People Initiatives. The primary US Agencies collaborating on the 2020 Initiative includes the USDA, Education, HHS, HUD, Justice Dept, and others.

22   Health and Human Services, "Proposed 2020 Healthy People Objectives", www. Developing HealthyPeople.gov; http://www.healthypeople.gov/hp2020/Objectives/ TopicAreas.aspx ; 5 December, 2010.

23   Obtained from the 2010 Healthy Campus Initiative – developed from the 2010 Healthy People Initiative.

24   Nancy Cotugna, Connie E. Vickery and Sheldon McBee, "Sports Nutrition for Young Athletes", The Journal of School Nursing (December 2005, Vol. 21, No. 6): 323-324.

25   Ibid., 324

26   Nancy Cotugna, Connie E. Vickery and Sheldon McBee, "Sports Nutrition for Young Athletes", The Journal of School Nursing (December 2005, Vol. 21, No. 6): 324.

27   Ibid.

28   Health and Human Services, "Annual Physical Fitness Test (APFT). (http://ccrf.hhs.gov/ ccrf/physical.htm:) 10 October, 2010.

29   Ibid.

30   2020 Healthy Peoples Initiative, "Topic Area: Physical Activity and Fitness", PAF 1-4; http://www.healthypeople.gov/hp2020/Objectives/files/Draft2009Objectives.pdf, December 5, 2010.

31   This goal is a specific 2010 Healthy People's Initiative Goal for College Students; obtained from Health Campus 2010.

32   The Healthy Campus 2010 set a specific physical activity goal for college age students. This task force set the goal of having at least 55% of college students engage in physical activity (moderate – vigorous) by 2010. The current level of participation hovered around 40% participation rate for college students at the start of the initiative. No data is currently available with regard to the average participation rate of college students as of 12/2010. The Healthy People's Initiative Goal for College Students was obtained from Healthy Campus 2010; an initiative of the American College Health Association Task force on National Health Objectives.

33   Caroline J. Cederquist, MD., "The Truth about Genetics and Weight Loss" , Newslbaze. com, December 7, 2005; http://newsblaze.com/story/20051207150658nnnn.nb/ tiopstorymhtml, December 5, 2010.

34   Ron Winslow, "Genes Point to Best Diets", The Wall Street Journal, March 4, 2010: 1. The article reported on the evidence provided by Interleukin Genetics, Inc. a Waltham Mass developer of genetic testing. They researchers admitted to the need for further confirmation from a larger study and additional research to determine the usefulness of determining whether a person's genotype is best suited for low carbohydrate or low fat weight loss programs. The diets used in the study included the Ornish Diet, Learn Diet, Zone Diet and the Atkins Diet.

35   "College Students, Hip, fly and fat", www.MSNBC, updated 5/14/2007, http://www. msnbc.msn.com/id/18659047/; 5 December, 2010.

36   Tamara Vallido, Debra Jackson and Louise O'Brien, "Mad, Sad and Hormonal: the Gendered Nature of Adolescent Sleep Disturbance", Journal of Child Health Care (2009, Vol. 13, No. 7): 8.

37   Kimberley A. Dawson, Margaret A. Schneider, Paula C Fletcher and Pamela J Bryden, " Examining Gender Differences in the Health Behaviors of Canadian University Students", The Journal of the Royal Society for the Promotion of Health (2007, Vol. 127, No. 38): 40.

38   Tamara Vallido, Debra Jackson and Louise O'Brien, "Mad, Sad and Hormonal: the

Gendered Nature of Adolescent Sleep Disturbance", Journal of Child Health Care (2009, Vol. 13, No. 7): 10.

39 Quishuang Jun and Qian Shi, "A Comparison of the Number of Hours of Sleep in High School Students Who Took Advanced Placement and/or College Courses and Those Who Did Not", Journal of School of Nursing (2008, Vol. 24, No. 417): 418.

40 Page 418; A Comparison of the Number of Hours of Sleep in High School Students Who Took Advanced Placement and/or College Courses and Those Who Did Not by Quishuang Jun and Qian Shi, Journal of School of Nursing 2008;24;417

41 "Statistics – Top 10 Causes: Leading Causes of Death – College Age", 2002, http://www. statisticstop10 .com/Causes_of_Death_college_Age-Adults.html, 5 December,2 010., page 1.

42 "Statistics – Top 10 Causes: Leading Causes of Death – College Age", 2002, http://www. statisticstop10 .com/Causes_of_Death_college_Age-Adults.html, 5 December,2 010., page 1.

43 The American College Health Association, "Healthy Campus 2010: making it happen" 2002, 1-15.

44 The US Fire Administration, "Fire Safety 101: a Fact Sheet for colleges and universities", March 2006,

45 Genesis 3:10.

46 Carl Anderson and Jose' Granados, Called to Love (New York: Doubleday Publishing Group, a division of the Random House, 2009): 109.

CHAPTER SEVEN

1   Gospel of St. Matthew, Chapter 4: 1- 11.

2   Brian Willoughby and Jodi Dworkin, "The Relationships between Emerging Adults' Expressed Desire to Marry and Frequency of Participation in Risk Taking Behaviors", Youth Society (2009, Vol. 40): 426.

3   Jung-Hwan Kim and Sharron J. Lennon, "Mass Media, and Self Esteem, Body Image and Eating Disorder Tendencies", Clothing and Textiles Research Journal (January, 2007, Vol. 25, No.1): 9.

4   Carroll College, "Eating Issues: Body Image", Carroll.edu. (http://www.carroll.edu/ students/wellness/counseling/eating.cc), 10 October, 2010.

5   Jung-Hwan Kim and Sharron J. Lennon, "Mass Media, and Self Esteem, Body Image and Eating Disorder Tendencies", Clothing and Textiles Research Journal (January, 2007, Vol. 25, No.1): 7.

6   Jung-Hwan Kim and Sharron J. Lennon, "Mass Media, and Self Esteem, Body Image and Eating Disorder Tendencies", Clothing and Textiles Research Journal (January, 2007, Vol. 25, No.1): 3.

7   Marilyn Shannon, Fertility, Cycles and Nutrition (Cincinnati: Couple to Couple League, 2009): 106.

8   Marcia H. Magnus, PhD, "Which College Students Are At Higher Health Risk", American Journal of Men's Health Online First (November 25, 2008): 2.

9   Marilyn Shannon, Fertility, Cycles and Nutrition (Cincinnati: Couple to Couple League, 2009): 107.

10 Kimberly S. Young, "Internet Addiction, a New Clinical Phenomenon and Its Consequences", American Behavioral Scientist (2004, Vol. 48): 409.

11 Mimi Nichter, Mark Nichter, Elizabeth E. Lloyd-Richardson, Brain Flaherty, Asli Carkoglu and Nicole Taylor; "Gendered Dimensions of Smoking among College Students", Journal of Adolescent Research (2—6, vol. 21): 216.

12 Ibid., 216.

13 Ibid., 216.

14 Mimi Nichter, Mark Nichter, Elizabeth E. Lloyd-Richardson, Brain Flaherty, Asli Carkoglu and Nicole Taylor; "Gendered Dimensions of Smoking among College Students", Journal of Adolescent Research (2—6, vol. 21): 216.

15   Nicole Vankim, Melissa Laska, Edward Ehlinger, Katherine Lust, and Mary Story, "Understanding young adult physical activity, alcohol and tobacco use in community colleges and four year post secondary institutions: A cross- sectional analysis of epidemiological surveillance data", BMC Public Health, 26 April, 2010: 1.

16   Mimi Nichter, Mark Nichter, Elizabeth E. Lloyd-Richardson, Brain Flaherty, Asli Carkoglu and Nicole Taylor; "Gendered Dimensions of Smoking among College Students", Journal of Adolescent Research (2—6, vol. 21): 216.

17   Nicole Vankim, Melissa Laska, Edward Ehlinger, Katherine Lust, and Mary Story, "Understanding young adult physical activity, alcohol and tobacco use in community colleges and four year post secondary institutions: A cross- sectional analysis of epidemiological surveillance data", BMC Public Health, 26 April, 2010: 3.

18   Fred C. Pampel and Jade Aguilar, "Changes in Youth Smoking, 1976 - 2002: A Time-Series Analysis", Youth Society (2008, Vol. 39): 459.

19   Donna Leinwand, "College Drug Use, Binge Drinking Rise", USA Today, 15 March, 2007. (http://www.usatoday.com/news/nation/2007-03-15-college-drug-use_N.htm), 10 October, 2010.

20   The Knights of Columbus in partnership with the Marist College Institute for Public Opinion conducted a survey that interviewed a cross-section of Americans from Dec. 23, 2009 – Jan 4, 2010. The results of this poll can be found in: The Marist Poll, "American Millenials: Generations Apart Religion"; February 2010. (http://www.kofc.org/un/cmf/resources/Communications/documents/poll_mil_religion.pdf), 10 October, 2010.

21   Donna Leinwand, "College Drug Use, Binge Drinking Rise", USA Today, 15 March, 2007. (http://www.usatoday.com/news/nation/2007-03-15-college-drug-use_N.htm), 10 October, 2010.

22   Donna Leinwand, "College Drug Use, Binge Drinking Rise", USA Today, 15 March, 2007.   (http://www.usatoday.com/news/nation/2007-03-15-college-drug-use_N.htm), 10 October, 2010. Her source for the statistics is derived from the National Center on Addiction and Substance Abuse at Columbia University.

23   Bureau of Justice Statistics, "Sourcebook of Criminal Justice Statistics; 1988 – 2003". (http://www.albany.edu/sourcebook/ind/DRUGS.Use.Among_students.College_students.3.html), 10 October, 2010.

24   "Study: Seven Percent of College Students Use Prescription Drugs as Stimulant for Non Medical Purposes", Science Daily, January 13, 2005 (http://www.sciencedaily.com/releases/2005/01/050111174901.htm), 10 October, 2010.

25   Donna Leinwand, "College Drug Use, Binge Drinking Rise", USA Today, 15 March, 2007. (http://www.usatoday.com/news/nation/2007-03-15-college-drug-use_N.htm), 10 October, 2010.

26   R. R Sumnall, C.M. Beynon; S.M. Conchie, S.C.E. Riley, J. C. Cole,"An Investigation of the Subjective Experiences of Sex After Alcohol or Drug Intoxication", Journal of Psychopharmacology (2007, Vl. 21, No. 5): 531 – 532.

27   R. R Sumnall, C.M. Beynon; S.M. Conchie, S.C.E. Riley, J. C. Cole, "An Investigation of the Subjective Experiences of Sex After Alcohol or Drug Intoxication", Journal of Psychopharmacology (2007, Vol. 21, No. 5): 531.

28   "Marijuana Damages DNA And May Cause Cancer, New Test Reveals", Science Daily.com , 15 June, 2009, (http://www.sciencedaily.com/releases/2009/06/090615095940.htm), 10 October, 2010.

29   Jeremy Olson, "Tainted Cocaine Kills Two People", St. Paul Pioneer Press, 8 June, 2010, sec 8: 8.

30   "Medical Consequences o f Drug Abuse", National Institute of Drug Abuse. Com. http://www.nida.nih.gov/consequences/), 10 October, 2010.

31   Students who regularly binge drink (43%) is a lower average than ever binge drinking rates (64%). This number will also differ significantly from those that report overall college drinking rates. These studies include students of legal age, and those who have only an occasional drink; their reported numbers inflate problem drinking rates when they cite numbers as high as 80- 90% .This information can be found at the following resource: Kent E. Glindemann, Douglas M. Wiegand, and E. Scott Geller, "Celebratory Drinking

and Intoxication: a Contextual Influence on Alcohol Consumption", Environment and Behavior (2007, Vol. 39): 353. In another study, North Dakota State University (NDSU) located in Fargo, ND, was found to have the highest binge drinking and alcohol poisoning rates across all age groups for nay university. Students at NDSU consume on average two more drinks per sitting than the national average. Over half (53.5%) of NDSU students engage in binge drinking which is a full 10% higher rate than the about national averages. This evidence was obtained from the following resource: "Program: Alcohol Poisoning: Mobilizing College Students Using Action Research Sponsors: Office of Orientation & Student Success, North Dakota State University Practice Notes", Health, Education and Behavior (2008 vol. 35): 438.

32   Kent E. Glindemann, Douglas M. Wiegand, and E. Scott Geller, "Celebratory Drinking and Intoxication: a Contextual Influence on Alcohol Consumption", Environment and Behavior (2007, Vol. 39): 353.

33   Soyeon Shim, and Jennifer L. Maggs, " A Psychographic Analysis of College Student's Alcohol Consumption; Implications for Prevention and Consumer education", Family and Consumer Sciences Research Journal (2005, Vol. 33), 255.

34   Alan Reifman, Wendy K. Watson and Andrea McCourt, "Social Networks and College Drinking: Probing Processes of Social Influence and Selection", Personality and Social Psychology Bulletin (2006, Vol. 32): 830.

35   Lonn Lanza-Kaduce, Michael Capece, and Helena Alden, "Liquor is Quicker; Gender and Social Learning among College Students", Criminal Justice Policy Review (2006, Vol. 17): 140.

36   Ibid.

37   Ogden Nash, "Reflections on Ice Breaking", (http://www.westegg.com/nash/ice-breaking.html). 10 October, 2010.

38   Cynthia D. Mohr, Debi Brannan, Josh Mohr, Stephen Armeli Farleigh, Howard Tennen, "Evidence for Positive Mood Buffering among College Student Drinkers", Personality and Social Psychology Bulletin (2008, Vol. 34): 1249.

39   Kent E. Glindemann, Douglas M. Wiegand, and E. Scott Geller, "Celebratory Drinking and Intoxication: a Contextual Influence on Alcohol Consumption", Environment and Behavior (2007, Vol. 39): 354.

40   This composite of reasons was obtained from the various resources cited with regard to alcohol.

41   "Where the World Goes to Party: PubClub.com's Top 10 College Party Schools: Win or Lose, We Booze!", PubClub.com. (http://www.pubclub.com/collegefootball/index.htm). 10 October, 2010.

42   Cynthia J. Osborn, Dennis L. Thombs, and R. Scott Olds. "Reconceptualizing Research on Undergraduate Alcohol Use: The Need for Student Engagement", Evaluation and the Health Professions (2007, Vol. 30): 125.

43   Lonn Lanza-Kaduce, Michael Capece, and Helena Alden, "Liquor is Quicker; Gender and Social Learning among College Students", Criminal Justice Policy Review (2006, Vol. 17): 131.

44   Laurel Sharmer, "Evaluation of Alcohol Education Programs on Attitude, Knowledge, and Self Reported Behavior of College Students", Evaluation and the Health Professions (2001, Vol. 24):339.

45   John D. Clapp. Megan R. Holmes. Mark B. Reed, Audrey M Shillington, Bridget Freisthler and James E. Lange, "Measuring College Student's Alcohol Consumption in Natural Drinking Environments: Field Methodologies for Bars and Parties", Evaluation Review (2007, Vol. 31): 470.

46   Cynthia J. Osborn, Dennis L. Thombs, and R. Scott Olds, "Reconceptualizing Research on Undergraduate Alcohol Use: The Need for Student Engagement", Evaluation and the Health Professions (2007, Vol. 30): 121.

47   Joan Burggraf Riley, Patrick T. Durbin and Mary D'Ariano, "Under the Influence; Taking Alcohol Issues into the College Classroom", Health Promotion Practice (2005, Vol. 6): 202.

48   Abby Goodnough, "FDA Warns Firms Making Alcoholic Energy Drinks", St. Paul Pioneer Press, 18 November, 2010, sec A, 7.

49   The most popular caffeinated alcoholic drinks are manufactured primarily by four companies including Phusion Projects (manufactures Four Loko), Charge Beverages Corp. New Century Brewing Co. and United Brands Co. Most of the drinks are carbonated malt beverages flavored with fruit juices. They have high levels of alcohol (up to 12%) and caffeine.

50   KXAN, "Popular Drink Among Students Mixes Caffeine, Alcohol", Updated: Thursday, 09 Oct 2008, 7:00 AM CDT,Published : Friday, 25 Apr 2008, 12:11 AM CDT, http://www.kxan.com/dpp/search/Popular_drink_among_students_mixes_caffeine_alcohol_28263918 November, 2010.

51   Ibid.

52   John Archer and Sarah M. Coyne, "An integrated Review of Indirect, Relational and Social Aggression" Personality and Social Psychology Review (2005, Vol. 9, No 3): 223.

53   Kenneth E. Leonard, Brian M. Quigley, and R. Lorraine Collins, "Physical Aggression in the Lives of Young Adults: Prevalence, Location and Severity among College and Community Samples", Journal of Interpersonal Violence (2002, Vol. 17): 545.

54   Blog by Melissa "Bullying At the College Level", http://www.stateuniversity.com/blog/permalink/bullying-it-happens-in-college-too.html , 23, April 2010.

55   Charles O. Cara, "The role of college bullying – does it exist?"; http://dspace.nitle.org/handle/10090/7029 August 1, 2009: 1. The study distributed short questionnaires to 82 students and conducted in-depth interviews with 10 students at Union College.

56   Newesday.com, "former Student Sues College Over Bullying", October 18, 2007; http://www.universitybusiness.com/newssummary.aspx?news=yes&postid=14515; 8 December, 2010.

57   William F. Flack Jr.; Marcia L. Caron, Sarah J. Leinen, Katherine G. Breitenbach, Ann M. Barber, Elaine N. Brown, Caitlin T. Gilbert, Taylor F. Harchak, Melissa M. Hendricks, Catherine E. Rector, Heather T. Schatten, and Heather C. Stein, ""The Red Zone; Temporal Risk for Unwanted Sex among College Students", Journal of Interpersonal Violence(2008, Vol. 23): 1190.

58   Alicia C. Dowd, "Dynamic Interactions and Inter Subjectivity: Challenges to Causal Modeling inSstudies of College Debt", Review of Educational Research (2008, Vol. 78): 236.

59   Co-operative educational experiences normally add another year to the four year plan for most degree programs. Co-op students alternate professional work experiences with on campus instruction. Beginning the students sophomore year, students alternate between living a semester on campus with a semester off campus to gain work experience in their field of study. Co-op students feel their work experiences are crucial to helping them sort out the fit of their major and the type of work they prefer within their field upon graduation. This job experience is beneficial for students and potential employers.

60   "Quick Facts about Student Debt", ProjectonStudentdebt.org, Updated January 2010, http://projectonstudentdebt.org/files/File/Debt_Facts_and_Sources.pdf, 10 October, 2010. This resource states that 62% of graduates from public university had student loans averaging $20.200. Seventy Two percent of graduates from private nonprofit universities had student loans on average of $27,650. Ninety six percent of graduates from private for profit universities had student loans on average of $33,050. These numbers are all at least 20% higher than in 2004.

61   W. Bradford Wilcox, "The Great Recession's Silver Lining?", The State of our Unions, December, 2009: 20.

62   Index Credit Cards.com , "Credit Card Monitor: Current Rates", November 30, 2010. http://www.indexcreditcards.com/credit-card-rates-monitor/, 8 December, 2010.

63   "Student Loan Debt Statistics", American Student Assistance Fact Sheet, (www.amsa.com/policy/resources/stats.cfm): 2, June, 2010.

64   Jeffrey Dew, "Bank On It: Thrifty Couples are the Happiest", The State of our Unions, December, 2009: 24.

65   Mary Beth Pinto, Diane H. Parente, Phyllis M. Mansfield, "Information Learned from

Socialization Agents: its Relationship to Credit Card Use", Family and Consumer Sciences Research Journal (2005, Vol. 33): 358.

66   Jeremiah Weinstock, James P. Whelan, Andrew W. Meyers and Claudia McCausland, "The Performance of Two Pathological Gambling Screens in College Students" , Assessment, (Dec. 2007, Vol. 14, No 4): 400.

67   "Growing casino culture and online betting mean gambling addicts must face constant temptation", NY Daily News ,Thursday, November 12th 2009, http://www.nydailynews.com/lifestyle/health/2009/11/12/2009-11-12_celebrity_gambling_addicts_are_only_half_of_the_story_as_gambling_addiction_grow.html, 8 December 2010.

68   Tavares, Zilberman, Beites, & Gentil, "Men, Women, and Gambling Progression" The Wager 2001. (http://www.basisonline.org/2001/08/the-wager-vol-3.html), 10 October, 2010. Also reported in: Lynn Blinn-Pike and Sheri Lokken Worthy, "Under Graduate Women Who Have Gambled in Casinos: Are They at Risk?", Family and Consumer Sciences Research Journal (2008, Vol.37): 72.

69   Lynn Blinn-Pike and Sheri Lokken Worthy, "Under Graduate Women Who Have Gambled in Casinos: Are They at Risk?", Family and Consumer Sciences Research Journal (2008, Vol.37): 79.

70   Jeremiah Weinstock, James P. Whelan, Andrew W. Meyers and Claudia McCausland, "The Performance of Two Pathological Gambling Screens in College Students" , Assessment, (Dec. 2007, Vol. 14, No 4): 400.

71   Lynn Blinn-Pike and Sheri Lokken Worthy, "Under Graduate Women Who Have Gambled in Casinos: Are They at Risk?", Family and Consumer Sciences Research Journal (2008, Vol.37): 73.

72   Ibid., 79.

73   Brian J. Willoughby and Jodi Dworkin, "The Relationships Between Emerging Adults' Expressed Desire to Marry and Frequency of Participation in Risk Taking Behaviors", Youth and Society (2009, Vol. 40), 430.

74   Jeffrey Jensen Arnett, Ph.D., Emerging Adulthood: The Winding Road from Late Teens through the Twenties, (New York: Oxford University Press, 2004):5.

75   Dinesh D'Souza, Life After Death: the Evidence (Washington DC: Regnery Publishing, Inc., 2009): 208.

76   Marist Poll: American Millenials: Generations Apart Religion; The K of C in partnership with The Marist College Institute for Public Opinion; February 2010;survey interviewed a cross-section of Americans from Dec. 23, 2009 – Jan 4, 2010. (http://www.kofc.org/un/cmf/resources/Communications/documents/poll_mil_religion.pdf) 10 October, 2010.

77   Mary Eberstadt, "Is Food the New Sex? A Curious Reversal in Moralizing", Policy Review (February and March 2009): 7.

78   Jeffrey Jensen Arnett, Ph.D., Emerging Adulthood: The Winding Road from Late Teens through the Twenties, (New York: Oxford University Press, 2004):9.

79   William F. Flack, Jr.; Kimberly A Daubman, Marcia L. Caron, Jenica A. Asadorian, Nicole R. D'Aureli, Shannon N. Gigliotti, Anna T. Hall, Sarah Kiser, and Erin R. Stine, "Risk Factors and Consequences of Unwanted Sex Among University Students: Hooking Up, Alcohol, and Stress Response", Journal of Interpersonal Violence (2007, Vol. 22): Page 150.

80   Elizabeth L. Paul and Kristen A Hayes, "The Casualties of Casual Sex: a Qualitative Exploration of the Phenomenology of College Students Hookups", Journal of Social and Personal Relationships (2002, Vol. 19): 644.

81   Anne Henderschott and Nicholas Dunn, "Hooking up: A Special Report", Catholic World Report, June 2010, page 26.

82   Suzanne D'Amato, "Modern Romance: From Kissing to "Sexting," Today's Hook-Up Culture is Changing How Teens Think about Relationships", TeenVogue.com (http://www.teenvogue.com/beauty/2009/05/teens-talk-about-sex-and-hooking-up) 10, October, 2010.

83   Elizabeth L. Paul and Kristen A Hayes, "The Casualties of Casual Sex: a Qualitative Exploration of the Phenomenology of College Students Hookups", Journal of Social and Personal Relationships (2002, Vol. 19): 645.

84   Ibid.

85   Dr. McDonald was voted San Diego's Top Doc for 2009 and 2010.

86   Laurie Pawlik-Kienlen, " How Love Hormones Work: Oxytocin Increases Intimacy & Bonding, Eases Psychological Disorders, Suite101.com. Feb 15, 2008 (http://psychology. suite101.com/article.cfm/how_love_hormones_work)10 October, 2010.

87   "Sexting? More Common Than You Think", St Paul Pioneer Press , 04 December, 2009, section A: 9.

88   Jason S. Carroll, Laura M. Padilla-Walker, Larry J. Nelson, Chad D. Olson, Carolyn McNamara Barry and Stephanie D. Madsen, "Generation XXX: Pornography Acceptance and Use Among Emerging Adults", Journal of Adolescent Research (2008, Vol. 23): 10.

89   Ibid., 7.

90   Jason S. Carroll, Laura M. Padilla-Walker, Larry J. Nelson, Chad D. Olson, Carolyn McNamara Barry and Stephanie D. Madsen, "Generation XXX: Pornography Acceptance and Use Among Emerging Adults", Journal of Adolescent Research (2008, Vol. 23): 16.

91   Ibid., 16-17

92   Lynn M. Pazzani, "The Factors Affecting Sexual assaults Committed by Strangers and Acquaintances", Violence against Women, (2007): 724.

93   Annette Lynch, "Expanding the Definition of Provocative Dress; An Examination of Female Flashing Behavior on a College Campus", Clothing and Textiles Research Journal (2007, Vol. 25): 184.

94   Pamela Kulbarsh, "Indecent Exposure: Exhibitionism, Flashers and Weenie Wagers", Law Officer (17 April, 2008) (http://www.lawofficer.com/news-and-articles/columns/ Kulbarsh/Flashers_and_Weenie_Waggers.html) 10 October, 2010.

95   Ronald T. Wilcox, "The Smart Money, She Saves, He Spends", The Sate of Our Unions, December 2009,: 61.

96   Social Indicators of Marital Health and Well Being: Trends of the past Four Decades", State of Our Unions, 2009, University of Virginia, Charlottesville, Virginia, December 2009: 84.

97   Tamar Lew," The New Transition: Single Moms With Live-in Partners, St. Paul Pioneer Press, 7 November, 2011, sec A, 4A.

98   "Social Indicators of Marital Health and Wellbeing", The State of Our Unions, University of Virginia, Charlottesville, Virginia, December 2009: 84.

99   Larry Bumpass and Hsien-Hen Lu, "America's Families and Living Arrangements: 2000: Trends in Cohabitation and Implications for Children's Family Contexts in the United States - Population Studies", U.S. Census Bureau. (2000): 29-41.

100   "Social Indicators of Marital Health and Well Being: Trends of the past Four Decades", State of Our Unions, 2009, University of Virginia, Charlottesville, Virginia, December 2009: 84.

101   Cecilia Le Chevalier, NFP Coordinator - Diocese of Camden NJ, personal email, 5 November 2009.

102   Living Together/Cohabitation (http://www.unmarried.org/living-together/cohabita-tion.html) 10 October, 2010

103   Susan Sassler, "Cohabiting Couples Not Likely to Marry - Study Finds", 2 February, 2004, http://www.eurekalert.org/pub_releases/2004-02/osu-ccn020204.php 10 October, 2010.

104   "Cohabitation, Marriage, Divorce, and Remarriage in the United States", CDC.gov, July 2002, (http://www.cdc.gov/nchs/data/series/sr_23/sr23_022.pdf): 49, 5 June, 2009.

105   Smock, Pamela, "Cohabitation in the United States", Annual Review of Sociology (2000): 1 -24.

106   Susan Sassler, "Cohabiting Couples Not Likely to Marry - Study Finds", 2 February, 2004, (http://www.eurekalert.org/pub_releases/2004-02/osu-ccn020204.php) 10 October, 2010.

107   "Cohabitation: a Recipe for Marital Ruin - Shown to Put Partners and Kids at Risk" Zenit News, 1 Oct 2005, (http://ewtn.com/library/ISSUES/zcohabit.HTM) 10 October, 2010.

108   Ibid.

109   "Cohabitation: a Recipe for Marital Ruin - Shown to Put Partners and Kids at Risk", Zenit News, 1 Oct 2005, (http://ewtn.com/library/ISSUES/zcohabit.HTM) 10 October, 2010.

110   Alex Roberts, "Marriage and the Great Recession" , The State of Our Unions, December

2009: 47-48.

111 Jane Dye, "Fertility of American Women: 2008", Current Population Reports , August 2008:6 Earlier reports had suggested higher rates accounting for the 40% number reported above. Demographer Andrew Cherlin, John Hopkins University and Pamela Smock said "they were surprised that the number of mothers living with a partner was not higher since previous estimated had put it at around half of unmarried mothers."

112 Social Indicators of Marital Health and Well Being: Trends of the past Four Decades", State of Our Unions, 2009, December, 2009: 72.

113 Lydia Saad, "By Age 24, Marriage Wins Out", Gallup.com, August 11, 2008, (http://www.gallup.com/poll/109402/Age-24-Marriage-Wins.aspx) 10 October, 2010.

114 Tamar Lew," The New Transition: Single Moms With Live-in Partners, St. Paul Pioneer Press, 7 November, 2011, sec A, 4A.

115 Social Indicators of Marital Health and Wellbeing", The State of Our Unions, University of Virginia, Charlottesville, Virginia,December 2009: 84.

116 Kathryn A. London, Ph. D, "Cohabitation, Marriage, Marital Dissolution, and Remarriage: United States 1988: Data from the National Survey of Family Growth, Division of Vital Statistics National Center for Health Statistics.(http://www.cdc.gov/nchs/data/series/sr_16/sr16_020.pdf2007).

117 "Cohabitation: a Recipe for Marital Ruin - Shown to Put Partners and Kids at Risk", Zenit News, 1 Oct 2005, (http://ewtn.com/library/ISSUES/zcohabit.HTM) 10 October, 2010.

118 "Seven Fatal Flaws of Moral Relativism", July 13, 2010, http://www.theologyonline.com/forums/showthread.php?t=67930, 10 December, 2010.

119 Cardinal Joseph Ratzinger, "Relativism: The Central Problem for Faith Today": May 1996 http://www.ewtn.com/library/curia/ratzrela.htm; 8 December 2010.

120 "Cheating is a Personal Foul" http://www.glass-castle.com/clients/www-nocheating-org/adcouncil/research/cheatingfactsheet.html; 8 December, 2010.

CHAPTER EIGHT

1   Some sources suggest that the incidence rate of eating disorders is significantly less. For example the South Carolina Department of Mental Health (http://www.state.sc.us/dmh/anorexia/statistics.htm) reports that (an estimated) 8 million Americans have an eating disorder – seven million women and one million men. Higher incidences are reported by MEDA (Multi-service Eating Disorder Association); they suggest that over eleven million people suffer from some type of eating disorder in the US. (http://medainc.org/help/about_disorders.asp.) Furthermore, nearly half of all Americans personally know someone with an eating disorder (Note: One in five Americans suffers from mental illnesses.)

2   "Eating Disorders among College Students", WaldenBehavioralCare.com. (http://www.waldenbehavioralcare.com/eating_disorders_among_college_students.asp.): 18 October, 2010.

3   Sean Joe, Emanique Joe, and Larry L. Rowley, "Consequences of Physical Health and Mental Illness Risks for Academic Achievement in Grades K12", Review of Research in Education (March, 2009, Vol. 33): 299.

4   Ibid.

5   Although the following information came from an older study, I believe it is still pertinent today. Kurth, et al. 1995 reported the results of a 1993 national survey of 11,467 high-school students and 60,861 adults; results revealed significant differences between genders with regard to eating and dieting. This information is available online at: "Perfect Illusions, Eating Disorders and the Family: the Facts", PBS.org. (http://www.pbs.org/perfectillusions/eatingdisorders/preventing_facts.html) 18 October, 2010.

6   In the previous chapter, it was stated that the average American woman is 5'4" tall and weighs 140 pounds while the average model stands 5'11" and weights only 117 pounds. This information was reported by the following resource. It is important that college men and women realist that attempts to transform the average college female or male body into

a super model body will only lead to the development of dangerous practices and habits. Some of these are listed in this section of the chapter. More information about eating disorders can be found at "Eating Issues", Carroll College.edu. (http://www.carroll.edu/students/wellness/counseling/eating.cc) 18 October, 2010.

7   "Eating Disorders", Focus Adolescent Services. com   (http://www.focusas.com/EatingDisorders.html.)18 October, 2010.

8   "Information Sheet 2008- NCHH Data on Eating Behaviors, Centers for Disease Control. gov.   (http://www.cdc.gov/nchs/data/infosheets/infosheet_eatingbehaviors.htm)   18 October, 2009. More information was obtained from "Body Image: Loving your Body Inside and Out: Eating disorders", Women's Health.gov. (http://www.womenshealth.gov/bodyimage/eatingdisorders/). 18 October, 2010.

9   "Eating Disorders", Focus Adolescent Services. com   (http://www.focusas.com/EatingDisorders.html.)18 October, 2010.

10   Jung-Hwan Kim and Sharron J. Lennon, "Mass Media, and Self Esteem, Body Image and Eating Disorder Tendencies", Clothing and Textiles Research Journal (January, 2001, Vol. 25, no. 1): 6.

11   Sean Joe, Emanique Joe, and Larry L. Rowley, "Consequences of Physical Health and Mental Illness Risks for Academic Achievement in Grades K12", Review of Research in Education (March, 2009, Vol. 33): 299.

12   Kimberly S. Young, "Internet Addiction: a New Clinical Phenomenon and Its Consequences", American Behavioral Scientist (2004, Vol. 48): 411.

13   Kimberly S. Young, "Internet Addiction: a New Clinical Phenomenon and Its Consequences", American Behavioral Scientist (2004, Vol. 48): 402.

14   Ibid., 404.

15   Ibid., 404.

16   This series of questions was developed by Kimberly S. Young, "Internet Addiction: a New Clinical Phenomenon and Its Consequences", American Behavioral Scientist (2004, Vol. 48): 404.

17   Susan Lang, "Self-Injury is Prevalent among College Students, But Few Seek Medical Help", The Chronicle Online, 5 June 2006, Cornell.edu (http://www.news.cornell.edu/stories/June06/self-injury.ssl.html), 10 October, 2009. Susan Lang reported the results of a Princeton/Cornell Study.

18   Patricia A. Adler and Peter Adler, "The De-Medicalization of Self Injury: From Psychopathology to Sociological Deviance", Journal of Contemporary Ethnography (2007, Vol. 36): 561.

19   Ibid., 560.

20   Ibid., 560.

21   Ibid., 547.

22   John Eckenrode and Daniel Silverman, M.D, conducted the Self Injury Survey with 3,069 Students attending Princeton and Cornell. Eckenrode is professor of Human Development and Director of the FLDC at Cornell; Silverman is Princeton's chief Medical Officer and Executive Director of University Health Services.

23   "Self-Injury Is Prevalent among College Students, Survey Shows" ScienceDaily.com, June 5, 2006, (http://www.sciencedaily.com/releases/2006/06/060605155351.html) 18 October, 2010.

24   Ibid.

25   Ibid.

26   Ann Pollinger Haas, Herbert Hendin, and J. John Mann, "Suicide in College Students", American Behavioral Scientist (2003, Vol. 46): 1227.

27   "College Dropout Rate Climbs as Students Face Challenges: Life Coach Offers College Tips to Success: Tools to Life Beta", NewsBlaze.com. September 12, 2007 (http://newsblaze.com/story/2007091202000800001.mwir/topstory.html) 18 October, 2010.

28   Thomas, "College Graduation Rates – Statistics Tell a Sad Tale", OpenEducation.net. (http://www.openeducation.net/2008/11/20/college-graduation-rates-statistics-tell-a-sad-tale) 18 October, 2010.

29   Ann Pollinger Haas, Herbert Hendin, and J. John Mann, "Suicide in College Students",

American Behavioral Scientist (2003, Vol. 46): 1228.

30 Ibid., 1225.

31 Ibid., 1226.

32 Ibid., 1225.

33 Ibid., 1226.

34 Ann Pollinger Haas, Herbert Hendin, and J. John Mann, "Suicide in College", American Behavioral Scientist (2003, Vol. 46): 1237.

35 Ibid., 1228.

36 Ibid.

37 Ibid.

38 "Preventing Suicide Among College Students", Medical News Today, March 22, 2008 (http://www.medicalnewstoday.com/printerfriendlynews.php?newsid=101326) 18 October, 2010.

39 "Major Depression", GoogleHealth.com. (https://health.google.com/health/ref/Major+depression) 18 October, 2010.

40 "Preventing Suicide Among College Students", Medical News Today, March 22, 2008 (http://www.medicalnewstoday.com/printerfriendlynews.php?newsid=101326) 18 October, 2010.

41 Rob McKinney, "Information Center for Sex Offenses: Rape, sexual Assault, Date Rape, Statutory Rape", McKinneyLawFirm.com (http://www.mckinneylawfirm.com/CM/FSDP/PracticeCenter/Criminal-Law/Sex-Offenses.asp?focus=topic&id=1) 18 October, 2010.

42 Bonnie S. Fisher, Leah E. Daigle, Francis T. Cullen and Michael G. Turner, "Reporting Sexual Victimization to the Police and Others: Results From a National Level Study of College Women", Criminal Justice and Behavior (2003, Vol. 30): 7. These authors also included data and information from several previous studies including Koss et al 1987, Fisher et al, 2003.

43 Bonnie S. Fisher, Leah E. Daigle, Francis T. Cullen and Michael G. Turner, "Reporting Sexual Victimization to the Police and Others: Results from a National Level Study of College Women", Criminal Justice and Behavior (2003, Vol. 30): 24.

44 Terri L. Messman-Moore, Aubrey A. Coates, Kathryn J. Gaffey and Carrie F. Johnson, "Sexuality, Substance Use, and Susceptibility to Victimization; Risk for Rape and Sexual Coercion in a Prospective Study of College Women", Journal of Interpersonal Violence, (2008, Vol. 23): 1730.

45 Bonnie S. Fisher, Leah E. Daigle, Francis T. Cullen and Michael G. Turner, "Reporting Sexual Victimization to the Police and Others: Results from a National Level Study of College Women", Criminal Justice and Behavior (2003, Vol. 30): 24.

46 Terri L. Messman-Moore, Aubrey A. Coates, Kathryn J. Gaffey and Carrie F. Johnson, "Sexuality, Substance Use, and Susceptibility to Victimization; Risk for Rape and Sexual Coercion in a Prospective Study of College Women", Journal of Interpersonal Violence, (2008, Vol. 23): 1743.

47 Joohee Lee, Elizabeth C. Pomeroy, Seo-Koo Yoo and Kurt T. Rheinboldt, "Attitudes toward Rape", Violence Against Women (2005, Vol. 11, No. 2): 180-181.

48 Joohee Lee, Elizabeth C. Pomeroy, Seo-Koo Yoo and Kurt T. Rheinboldt, "Attitudes toward Rape" Violence Against Women (2005, Vol. 11, No. 2): 189 – 190.

49 Leah E. Adams-Curtis and Gordon B. Forbes, "College Women's Experiences of Sexual Coercion: A Review of Cultural, Perpetrator, Victim, and Situational Variables", Trauma Violence Abuse (2004, Vol. 5): 106.

50 Leah E. Daigle, Bonnie S. Fisher, and Francis T. Cullen, "The Violent and Sexual Victimization of College Women: Is Repeat Victimization a Problem?", Journal of Interpersonal Violence (2008, Vol. 23): 1296.

51 Ibid., 1303, 1308-1309.

52 Pamela Kulbarsh, "Indecent Exposure: Exhibitionism Flashers and Weenie Wagers", LawOfficer.com , April 17, 2008 (http://www.lawofficer.com/news-and-articles/columns/Kulbarsh/Flashers_and_Weenie_Waggers.html), 18 October, 2010.

53 Ibid.

54 Pamela Kulbarsh, "Indecent Exposure: Exhibitionism Flashers and Weenie Wagers", LawOfficer.com , April 17, 2008 (http://www.lawofficer.com/news-and-articles/columns/Kulbarsh/Flashers_and_Weenie_Waggers.html), 18 October, 2010.

55 Ibid.

56 Dr. Joseph Carver, "Problems with Exhibitionism", Counseling Resource, http://counsellingresource.com/ask-the-psychologist/2007/10/10/problems-with-exhibitionism/, 9 December 2010.

57 William F. Flack, Jr., Kimberly A. Daubman, Marcia L. Caron, Jenica A. Asadorian, Nicole R. D'Aureli, Shannon N. Gigliotti, Anna T. Hall, Sarah Kiser, and Erin R. Stine, "Risk Factors and Consequences of Unwanted Sex Among University Students: Hooking Up, Alcohol, and Stress Response", Journal of Interpersonal Violence (2007, Vol. 22): 148-149.

58 My daughter Kelly reported this incident to me. The two college girls had taken the transit to Old-Town Philadelphia; a fellow LaSalle University male student was also on the train. During the train ride, the male college student had been approached by an elderly Chinese man asking him to prostitute the two college girls next to him. He declined the offer by suggesting the earlier statement to the pimp. The two girls – while shocked by the attempted assault – were very dismayed by the male student's response.

59 Meika Loe, "The New View in Action: College Students Discuss 21st Century Sexuality", Feminism Psychology (2008, Vol. 18): 495.

60 Angela J Jacques-Tiura, Antonia Abbey, Michele R. Parkhill and Tina Zawacki, "Why Do Some Men Misperceive Women's Sexual Intentions More Frequently than Others Do? An Application of the Confluence Model", Personality and Social Psychology Bulletin (2007, Vol. 33); 1468.

61 Georgia N. L. Johnston Polacek, Jennifer A. Hicks, and Sara B. Oswalt, "Twenty Years Later and Still At Risk: College Students' Knowledge, Attitudes and Behaviors about HIV/AIDS", Journal of Hispanic Higher Education (2007): 74.

62 Mary Keller; Victoria von Sadowsky, Barbara Pankratz, Joan Hermsen, Richard Sowell and Alice Demi, "Self Disclosure of HPV Infection to Sexual Partners", Western Journal of Nursing Research (2000): 287.

63 Mary Keller; Victoria von Sadowsky, Barbara Pankratz, Joan Hermsen, Richard Sowell and Alice Demi, "Self Disclosure of HPV Infection to Sexual Partners", Western Journal of Nursing Research (2000): 287.

64 Victoria von Sadovszky, Doris C. Vahey, Kristan McKinney and Mary L. Keller ,"Emotions Involved in College Students' Sexual Encounters", Western Journal of Nursing Research(2006, Vol. 28): 865.

65 "Study Estimates Overall HPV Prevalence in US Women", National Cancer Institute.gov. (http://www.cancer.gov/cancertopics/hpv-prevalence0307), 18 October, 2010.

66 Adapted from the NCI Cancer Bulletin Mar 6, 2007, Vol. 4, No. 10.

67 "Genital HPV Infection Fact Sheet", CDC.gov. (http://www.cdc.gov/std/HPV/STDFact-HPV.htm#Whatis), 18 October, 2010.

68 "Genital HPV Infection Fact Sheet, CDC.gov. (http://www.cdc.gov/std/HPV/STDFact-HPV.htm#common), 18 October, 2010.

69 Charlotte J. Haug, M.D., PhD, "Human Papillomavirus Vaccination- Reason for Caution", The New England Journal of Medicine (August 21, 2008, Vol.359, No. 8): 862.

70 Ibid.

71 "QuickStats: Percentage of Adults Aged 20--29 Years with Genital Herpes* Infection, by Race/Ethnicity+ --- National Health and Nutrition Examination Survey, United States, 1988--1994, 1999--2002, and 2003—2006", MMWR (Morbidity and Mortality Weekly Report (Feb. 27, 2009, vol. 58, No. 07). (http://www.cdc.gov/mmwr/preview/mmwrhtml/mm5807a6.htm?s_cid=mm5807a6_e) 18 October, 2010.

72 "Sexually Transmitted Diseases: Chlamydia CDC Fact Sheet", CDC.gov. (http://www.cdc.gov/std/Chlamydia/STDFact-Chlamydia.htm#WhatIs) 18 October, 2010.

73 2008 Sexually Transmitted Diseases Surveillance, Table 1. Cases of sexually transmitted diseases reported by state health departments and rates per 100,000 population: United States, 1941-2008, "http://www.cdc.gov/std/stats08/tables/1.htm) 18 October, 2010.

74 2007Sexually Transmitted Diseases Surveillance, Table 32. Primary and secondary syphilis — Reported cases and rates per 100,000 populations by age group and sex: United States, 2003-2007, CDC.gov, (http://www.cdc.gov/std/stats07/tables/32.htm) 18 October, 2010.

75 2008 Sexually Transmitted Diseases Surveillance, Table 1. Cases of sexually transmitted diseases reported by state health departments and rates per 100,000 populations by age group and sex: United States, 1941-2008, CDC.gov. (http://www.cdc.gov/std/stats08/tables/1.htm) 18 October, 2010.

76 2007 Sexually Transmitted Diseases Surveillance, Table 32. Primary and secondary syphilis — Reported cases and rates per 100,000 populations by age group and sex: United States, 2003-2007, CDC.gov (http://www.cdc.gov/std/stats07/tables/32.htm) 18 October, 2010.

77 "Infertility", Penn State's Milton S. Hershey Medical Center College of Medicine; (www.hmc.psu.edu/helathinfo/infertility.htm) 5 June, 2009.

78 We have referred to this Marist Poll several times throughout this book. The Survey was undertaken in partnership with the K of C and the Marist Institute for Public Opinion at the Marist College in Poughkeepsie, NY. This survey interviewed 2,243 Americans including 1006 Millennials. Data was collected from 12/23/2009 through Jan 4, 2010 posted Feb. 2010. A New Survey of Young Catholics Shows Promise and Challenges for the Catholic Church was released Feb 11, 2010; PR Newswire, United Business Media.

CHAPTER NINE

1   Joseph Abrams, "Planned Parenthood Director Quits After Watching Abortion on Ultrasound", FOXNews.com, published November 02, 2009, (http://www.myfoxhouston.com/ddp/news/national/Planned_Parenthood_Director_Quits_) 18 October, 2010.

2   Ibid.

3   Page 1; Planned Parenthood Director Quits After Watching Abortion on Ultrasound; article posted on MY FOX Houston.com; 11/4/09

4   The statement also includes data from 2002 abortion data provided by Blunt County Right to Life, "A Voice for the Unborn" BluntCountyRighttoLife.com, (http://voiceforunborn.com/) and (http://voiceforunborn.com/causeofdeath.html) 18 October, 2010. Abortions net $400 per procedure times 850,000 abortions per year, yields $340 million per year. This income turns the abortion industry into a very large business.

5   Edward Lotterman, "Stagnant Incomes, Restless Voters", St. Paul Pioneer Press, Sept. 3, 2010, Business Section, 5D.

6   Nancy Gibbs, "What Women Want Now: A Time Special Report", Time Magazine, October 26, 2009, Vol. 174, No 16: 25.

7   Lydia Saad, "More Americans "Pro-Life" Than "Pro-Choice" for First Time. Also, Fewer Think Abortion Should Be Legal "Under Any Circumstances", May 15, 2009, Gallup.com (http://www.gallup.com/poll/118399/More-Americans-Pro-Life-Than-Pro-Choice-First-Time.aspx) 18 October, 2010.

8   Steven Ertelt, "Gallup Poll: Majority of Americans Pro-Life on Abortion, Highest Levels in 15 Years", May 15, 2009, LifeNews.com (http://www.lifenews.com/nat5053.html) 18 October, 2010.

9   "Population Matters Policy Brief: Do Public Attitudes Toward Abortion Influence Attitudes Toward Family Planning?" Rand.org, (http://www.rand.org/pubs/research_briefs/RB5042/index1.html), 18 October, 2010.

10 Lydia Saad, "More Americans "Pro-Life" Than "Pro-Choice" for First Time: Also, Fewer Think Abortion Should Be Legal "Under Any Circumstances", May 15, 2009, Gallup.com (http://www.gallup.com/poll/118399/More-Americans-Pro-Life-Than-Pro-Choice-First-Time.aspx) 18 October, 2010.

11 Willy Pedersen, "Abortion and Depression: a Population-Based Longitudinal Study of Young Women, Scandinavian Journal of Public Health (2008, Vol. 36): 424 – 427.

12 Mika Gissler, Elina Hemminki, and Jouko Lonnqvist, "Suicides After Pregnancy in

Finland, 1987–94: register linkage study", British Medical Journal, December 7, 1996 (http://www.bmj.com/content/313/7070/1431.full), 18 October, 2010. S.J. Dower and E. S. Nash, "Therapeutic Abortion on Psychiatric Grounds", South African Medical Journal (1978): 604-608. Bengt Jansson, "Mental Disorders After Abortion" Acta Psychiatrica Scandinavia, (March, 1965): 21978.

13   Mika Gissler, Elina Hemminki, and Jouko Lonnqvist, "Suicides After Pregnancy in Finland, 1987–94: register linkage study", British Medical Journal, December 7, 1996 (http://www.bmj.com/content/313/7070/1431.full, 18 October, 2010): 1431.

14   David Reardon, "Suicide Rate Higher After Abortion, Study Shows: Elliot Institute Presents New Findings at International Women's Health Conference", the Post-Abortion Review (April-June 2001, Vol. 9, No. 2): 3.

15   David C. Reardon, PhD, "Abortion is Four Times Deadlier than Childbirth: New Studies Unmask High Maternal Death Rates from Abortion", the Post Abortion Review (April-June 2000): 3. The psychopathological effects of voluntary termination of pregnancy on post abortive fathers were gathered from fathers called up for military service. The data was reported in the following source. J.C. DuBouis-Bonneford and J.R. Galle-Tessonneau, "Psychopathological Effects of Voluntary Termination of Pregnancy on the Father, Called Up For Military Service", Psychologie Medicale (June 1982, Vol. 14, No. 8): 1187-1189.

16   Ibid.

17   AL Cohen, J Bhatnagar, S Reagan, SB Zane, MA D'Angeli, M Fischer, G Killgore, TS Kwan-Gett, DB Blossom, WJ Shieh, J Guarner, J Jernigan, JS Duchin, SR Zaki, and LC McDonald, "Toxic Shock Associated with Clostridium Sordellii and Clostridium Perfringens After Medical and Spontaneous Abortion", Obstetrics and Gynecology. 2007 Nov, Vol. 110, No. 5)1027-33.
Marc Fisher also presented this information to the CDC; his power point presentation entitled "Clostridium sordellii toxic shock syndrome following medical abortion" can be found at FDA.gov (http://www.fda.gov/downloads/AboutFDA/CentersOffices/CDER/ UCM183774.pdf): 11, 18 October, 2010.

18   Mika Gissler, and Elina Hemminki, and Jouko Lonnqvist, "Suicides After Pregnancy in Finland, 1987–94: register linkage study", British Medical Journal, December 7, 1996 (http://www.bmj.com/content/313/7070/1431.full, 18 October, 2010): 1431.

19   Guttmacher Institute, " An Overview of Minors' Consent Law" , October 1, 2010. Guttmacher.org. (http://www.guttmacher.org/statecenter/spibs/spib_OMCL.pdf) 18 October, 2010.
Too often, those who advocate for life are accused of spreading suburban myths with regard to minors' consent in for procuring counseling and services for securing an abortion, contraception, treatment of sexually transmitted diseases, pregnancy, drug and alcohol counseling. The following information proves the point that minors cannot get their ears pierced without parental permission whereas they (depending on the state they live in) can obtain an abortion without parental consent.
"The legal ability of minors to consent to a range of sensitive health care services— including sexual and reproductive health care, mental health services and alcohol and drug abuse treatment—has expanded dramatically over the past 30 years. This trend reflects the recognition that, while parental involvement in minors' health care decisions is desirable, many minors will not avail themselves of important services if they are forced to involve their parents. With regard to sexual and reproductive health care, many states explicitly permit all or some minors to obtain contraceptive, prenatal and STI services without parental involvement. Moreover, nearly every state permits minor parents to make important decisions on their own regarding their children. In sharp contrast, the majority of states require parental involvement in a minor's abortion.
In most cases, state consent laws apply to all minors age 12 and older. In some cases, however, states allow only certain groups of minors—such as those who are married, pregnant or already parents—to consent. Several states have no relevant policy or case law; in these states, physicians commonly provide medical care without parental consent to minors they deem mature, particularly if the state allows minors to consent to related services. The following chart contains seven categories of state law that affect a minor's

right to consent.
Contraceptive Services: 26 states and the District of Columbia allow all minors (12 and older) to consent to contraceptive services. 21 states allow only certain categories of minors to consent to contraceptive services. 4 states have no relevant policy or case law. STI Services: All states and the District of Columbia allow all minors to consent to STI services. 18 of these states allow, but do not require, a physician to inform a minor's parents that he or she is seeking or receiving STI services when the doctor deems it in the minor's best interests.
Abortion: 3 states (Maine, Connecticut, Maryland) and the District of Columbia explicitly allow their minors to consent to abortion services. 22 states require that at least one parent consent to a minor's abortion, while 11 states require prior notification of at least one parent. 4 states require both notification of and consent from a parent prior to a minor's abortion. 7 additional states have parental involvement laws that are temporarily or permanently enjoined. 6 states have no relevant policy or case law. Alaska, California, Montana, Nevada, and New Mexico current statutes with regard to minor consent have been permanently or temporarily enjoined by a court order and therefore their policies are not in effect. "

20   Paul Nowak, "Texas Pregnant Woman's Death Could Bring Unborn Victims Law Into Play", LifeNews.com
      October 14, 2003 (http://www.lifenews.com/state187.html) 18 October, 2010.

21   Trisomy 21 is the medical term for a condition commonly referred to as Down Syndrome.

22   Razib Khan "Down Syndrome and Abortion", Scienceblogs.com, September 8, 2008 Posting (5:16 PM) (http://scienceblogs.com/gnxp/2008/09/down_syndrome_and_abortion_rat.php)

23   Scott Klusendorf , "Peter Singer's Bold Defense of Infanticide", Christian Research Institute, (http://www.equip.org/articles/peter-singer-s-bold-defense-of-infanticide) 18 October, 2010.

24   World Net Daily: Matters of Life and Death, "'Bioethicist': OK to Kill Babies After They're Born 'Animal-rights' Promoter Asserts Actual Birth Makes No Difference", WorldNetDaily.com, Sept 14, 2006 (http://www.wnd.com/news/article.asp?ARTICLE_ID=51963) 18 October, 2010.

25   Wesley Smith, "Is the Dutch Groningen Protocol Akin to the Nazi Doctors?", Firstthings.com, March 22, 2005, http://www.firstthings.com/blogs/secondhandsmoke/2010/09/08/is-the-dutch-gronningen-infanticide-protocol-akin-to-the-nazi-doctors/) 18 October, 2010. Wesley J. Smith is a senior fellow at the Discovery Institute, an attorney for the International Task Force on Euthanasia and Assisted Suicide, and a special consultant to the Center for Bioethics and Culture.

26   Wesley Smith, "Dutch Woman Arrested for Infanticide; But Dutch Doctors Do It Without Consequence", Firstthings.com, August 8, 2010 (http://www.firstthings.com/blogs/secondhandsmoke/2010/08/08/dutch-woman-arrested-for-infanticide-but-dutch-doctors-do-it-without-consequence/) 18 October, 2010.

27   Rachel K. Jones, Lori F. Frohwirth and Ann M. Moore, "I Would Want to Give My Child Like Everything in the World; How Issues of Motherhood Influence Women Who Have Abortions", Journal of Family Issues (2008, Vol. 29, No. 79): 94.

28   "Abortion and the Black Community", blackgenocide.org (http://blackgenocide.org/black.html) 18 October, 2010.

29   Ibid.

30   Ibid.

31   Lilo T. Strauss, Sonya B. Gamble, Wilda Y. Parker, Douglas A. Cook, Suzanne B. Zane, and Saeed Hamden, "CDC MMWR Surveillance Summaries: November 24, 2006: Abortion Surveillance – United States 2003", Division of Reproductive Health, National Center for Chronic Disease Prevention and Health Promotion (2006): 16-18.

32   G. Sedgh, S. Henshaw, S. Singh, E. Åhman, IH Shah, "Induced Abortion: Rates and Trends Worldwide", Lancet (2007, Vol. 370): 1338–45.

33   Guttmacher Institute, "Facts on Induced Abortion in the United States: Incidence of Abortion", May 2001 "Facts on Induced Abortion in the United States: May 2010, Gutt-

macher.org (http://www.guttmacher.org/pubs/fb_induced_abortion.html) 18 October, 2010.

34   IM Spitz, S. Christin- Maitre, and P. Brouchard, "Early Pregnancy Termination With Mifepristone and Misoprostol in the United States," New England Journal of Medicine (1998, Vol. 338): 1241-47.

35   Mifepristone", Wikipedia, (http://tripatlas.com/Mifepristone), 18 October, 2010.

36   Ibid.

37   Gardinar Harris, "Seventh Death in Medical Abortion", New York Times, May 12, 2006 (www.nytimes.com/2006/05/12/health/12abort.html?_r=1&pagewanted=print)   18 October, 2010.

38   During induction abortions – aka later term abortions –the amniotic sacs of pregnant women are injected with salt for the purpose of poisoning the new life. When used in combination with prostaglandins and pitocin, the salt solution causes uterine contractions hastening the delivery of a poisoned, dead fetus.

39   Dilation and extraction is also known as partial birth abortion.

Chapter Ten

1   The Catechism of the Catholic Church (New York: Image Book published by Doubleday, 1995), 244, Numbers 928-929.

2   USCCB Committee on Laity, Marriage, Family Life, and Youth, Marriage, Love and Life in the Divine Plan: A Pastoral Letter - abridged version, (Washington, DC, Feb. 2010, Publication No. 7-113), 2.

3   "Definition of Marriage", Encarta Dictionary (http://encarta.msn.com/dictionary_/marriage.html_) 25 October, 2010.

4   Charles Martel, "The End of Marriage", American Family Association Journal(January 8, 2010): 1

5   "Social Indicators of Marital Health and Wellbeing" , The State of Our Unions: Marriage in America 2009 , The National Marriage Project (University of Virginia, February 2010): 65. The 2009 estimate is merely an estimate based on US Census figures for total populations extrapolated from 2008 figures. The marriage rate for 2010 has not been reported; however, preliminary reports suggest that marriage rates continued to slide downward due to the economic recession and the other reasons previously discussed (increased cohabitation rates, divorce rates, etc.).

6   W. Bradford Wilcox, "The Great Recessions' Silver Lining", The State of Our Unions: Marriage in America 2009 , The National Marriage Project (University of Virginia, February 2010): 16.

7   Alex Roberts, "Marriage and the Great Recession", The State of Our Unions: Marriage in America 2009 , The National Marriage Project (University of Virginia, February 2010): 47.

8   The Book of Genesis 2: 24.

9   This definition for illicit sexual relationships was coined by Fr. Jason Lefor, University of ND, Grand Forks; Newman Center.

10   USCCB Committee on Laity, Marriage, Family Life, and Youth, Marriage, Love and Life in the Divine Plan: A Pastoral Letter - abridged version, (Washington, DC, Feb. 2010, Publication No. 7-113), 8.

11   Carl Anderson and Jose' Granados, Called to Love (New York: Doubleday, an imprint of the Doubleday Publishing Group, a Division of the Random House, Inc., 2009), 54.

12   Bankrate.com, "Everything You Need to Know About Prenuptial Agreements", http://www.bankrate.com/brm/prenup.asp, 10 December,2 010.

13   Father Vincent Serpa, Catholic Q&A, http://forums.catholic.com/showthread.php?t=203402&highlight=pre-nuptial+agreement, 10 December , 2010.

14   Alex Roberts, "Marriage and the Great Recession", The State of Our Unions: Marriage in America 2009 , The National Marriage Project (University of Virginia, February 2010): 47.

15 National Marriage Project, "Social Indicators of Heath and Well being" The State of Our Unions: Marriage in America 2009 , The National Marriage Project (University of Virginia, February 2010): 72.

16 Hope Yen, "Four in Ten Polled Say Marriage is Becoming Obsolete", St. Paul Pioneer Press, 18 November, 2010, sec 8A, M.

17 These thoughts are an expansion of the original idea presented by Carl Anderson and Jose' Granados, Called to Love (New York: Doubleday, an imprint of the Doubleday Publishing Group, a Division of the Random House, Inc., 2009), 54.

18 Hope Yen, "Four in Ten Polled Say Marriage is Becoming Obsolete", St. Paul Pioneer Press, 18 November, 2010, sec 8A, M. Ms. Yen writes for the Associated Press . The data used by Ms. Yen was based on a Pew study which interviewed more than 2500 adults during the first three weeks of October, 2010. The survey claims a margin of error of +/- 2.6%.

19 Brian J. Willoughby and Jodi Dworkin, "The Relationships Between Emerging Adults' Expressed Desire to Marry and Frequency of Participation in Risk Taking Behaviors", Youth and Society (2009, No. 40): 430.

20 University of Iowa, "Study finds education and money attract a mate; chastity sinks in importance", University of Iowa News Release, Feb. 5, 2009, http://news-releases.uiowa. edu/2009/february/020509study_mate.html, 12 December, 2010.

21 The New Testament, 1 Corinthians 13: 4-8.

22 Dr. Leonard Sax, "Gender Differences in the Sequence of Brain Development", (http:// www.education.com/reference/article/Ref_Boys_Girls/), 25 October, 2010.

23 Stephen Seiler, "Gender Differences in Endurance, Performance and Training", Southington-Cheshire Community YMCAs, (http://homepage.mac.com/giarnellamd/ genderdifference.html), 25 October, 2010.

24 These were some of the course titles listed by various Sociology Departments for different institutions of higher learning.

25 Benjamin Wiker, "The Abolition of Man (and Woman)", National Catholic Register, November 1, 2009, Section: Indepth: 7.

26 Carl Anderson and Jose' Granados, Called to Love (New York: Doubleday, an imprint of the Doubleday Publishing Group, a Division of the Random House, Inc., 2009), 104.

27 Ibid., 112.

28 Carl Anderson and Jose' Granados, Called to Love (New York: Doubleday, an imprint of the Doubleday Publishing Group, a Division of the Random House, Inc., 2009), 113-114.

29 The 2007 incarceration rates for men range from 0.7% (for white men) to 4% (for black men) vs. 0.4% (for black women) to 0.09% for white women. "Of the 2.3 million inmates in custody, 2.1 million were men and 208,300 were women. Black males represented the largest percentage (35.4%) of inmates held in custody, followed by white males (32.9%) and Hispanic males (17.9%).

30 These statistics were reported by the following source: William Sabol and Heather Couture, Bureau of Justice Statistics, "Prison Inmates at Midyear 2007", (Washington, DC: US Department of Justice, June2008),NCJ221944, (http://www.ojp.usdoj.gov/bjs/ pub/pdf/pim07.pdf), 7.

31 The statement was made at the Couple to Couple League National Convention held in 2010 at Green Lake, Wisconsin.

32 W. Bradford Wilcox, "The Great Recessions' Silver Lining", The State of Our Unions: Marriage in America 2009 , The National Marriage Project (University of Virginia, February 2010): 18.

33 IBID; 26.

34 National Marriage Project, "Social Indicators of Heath and Well being" The State of Our Unions: Marriage in America 2009 , The National Marriage Project (University of Virginia, February 2010): 97.

35 USCCB Committee on Laity, Marriage, Family Life, and Youth, Marriage, Love and Life in the Divine Plan: A Pastoral Letter - abridged version, (Washington, DC, Feb. 2010, Publication No. 7-113), 8.

36 National Marriage Project, "Social Indicators of Heath and Well being" The State of

Our Unions: Marriage in America 2009 , The National Marriage Project (University of Virginia, February 2010): 94.

37   National Marriage Project, "Social Indicators of Heath and Well being" The State of Our Unions: Marriage in America 2009 , The National Marriage Project (University of Virginia, February 2010): 72.

38   National Marriage Project, "Social Indicators of Heath and Well being" The State of Our Unions: Marriage in America 2009 , The National Marriage Project (University of Virginia, February 2010): 91.

39   This sentence borrows on the idea originally suggested by Carl Anderson in Called to Love.

40   Brian J. Willoughby and Jodi Dworkin, "The Relationships Between Emerging Sdults' Expressed Desire to Marry and Frequency of Participation in Risk Taking Behaviors", Youth and Society (2009, No. 40), 429.

41   Brian J. Willoughby and Jodi Dworkin, "The Relationships Between Emerging Sdults' Expressed Desire to Marry and Frequency of Participation in Risk Taking Behaviors", Youth and Society (2009, No. 40), 434.

42   Jennifer Katz and Laura Myhr, "Perceived Conflict Patterns and Relationship Quality Associated with Verbal Sexual Coercion by Male Dating Partners", Journal of Interpersonal Violence (2008, Vol. 798), 799.

43   Mary Eberstadt, "Is Food the New Sex; a Curious Reversal in Moralizing", Hoover Institution Policy Review(February & March 2009), 6.

44   Russell D. Ravert, "You're Only Young Once: Things College Students Report Doing Now Before It Is Too Late", Journal of Adolescent Research (2009, Vol. 24), 389.

45   National Marriage Project, "Social Indicators of Heath and Well being" The State of Our Unions: Marriage in America 2009 , The National Marriage Project (University of Virginia, February 2010): 77.

46   National Marriage Project, "Social Indicators of Heath and Well being" The State of Our Unions: Marriage in America 2009 , The National Marriage Project (University of Virginia, February 2010): 80.

47   David Fagan, "Uncontested Divorce Information", ArticlesFactory.com (http://www.articlesfactory.com/articles/law/uncontested-divorce-information.html), 25 October, 2010. Fagan cited data from Jennifer Baker of the Forest Institute of Professional Psychology in Springfield, Missouri.

48   Centers for Disease Control and Prevention, "Marriage and Divorce", CDC.gov. (http://www.cdc.gov/nchs/fastats/divorce.htm), 25 October, 2010.

49   Ibid., 101.

50   National Marriage Project, "Social Indicators of Heath and Well being" The State of Our Unions: Marriage in America 2009 , The National Marriage Project (University of Virginia, February 2010): 88.

51   Mary Eberstadt, "Is Food the New Sex; a Curious Reversal in Moralizing", Hoover Institution Policy Review(February & March 2009), 6.

52   John R. Diggs, Jr. MD, "The Health Risks of Gay Sex", CatholicEducation.org (http://wwwlcatholiceducation.org/articles/homosexuality/ho0075.html, page 1), 25 July, 2010.

53   John R. Diggs, Jr. MD, "The Health Risks of Gay Sex", CatholicEducation.org (http://wwwlcatholiceducation.org/articles/homosexuality/ho0075.html, page 3), 25 July, 2010.

54   Gabriel Rotello, Sexual Ecology; AIDS and the Design of Gay Men (New York: Penguin Group, 1998), 112. (quoting gay writer Michael Lynch)

55   Alan P. Bell and Martin S Weinberg, Homosexualities: a Study of Diversity Among Men and Women (New York: Simon and Schuster, 1979), 308 Table 7.

56   John R. Diggs, Jr. MD, "The Health Risks of Gay Sex", CatholicEducation.org (http://wwwlcatholiceducation.org/articles/homosexuality/ho0075.html, page 14), 25 July, 2010.

57   USCCB Committee on Laity, Marriage, Family Life, and Youth, Marriage, Love and Life in the Divine Plan: A Pastoral Letter - abridged version, (Washington, DC, Feb. 2010, Publication No. 7-113), 23-24.

Chapter Eleven

1   Susan Pitman, Archdiocese of St Paul-MPLS Vocations Office, telephone conversation, Summer, 2009 (651-962-6890).

2   Fr. Stephen J Rossetti, "The Joy of Priesthood", God Spy, http://oldarchive.godspy.com/faith/The-Joy-of-Priesthood-by-Fr-Stephen-J-Rossetti.cfm.html, 2 November, 2010.

3   The USCCB Committee on Clergy, Consecrated Life, and Vocations, "Priestly Vocations, Cultural Challenges and Foundations of Hope", United States Conference of Catholic Bishops, www.nccbuscc.org/vocations/articles/challenges.shtml , 3 November, 2010.

4   John Pomfret, "Police Finding It Hard to Fill Jobs: Forces Use Perks And Alter Standards," *Washington Post*, Monday, March 27, 2006, sec. Nation.

5   "At least two-thirds of the nation's fire departments are understaffed, according to the National Fire Protection Association (NFPA), which sets firefighting codes and standards. The shortage is worst in rural volunteer departments that have trouble recruiting new members." Mimi Hall, "Police, fire departments see shortages across USA", USA Today, 28 November, 2004, http://www.usatoday.com/news/nation/2004-11-28-police-shortages-cover_x.htm, 3 November, 2010.

6   In 2004, the military faced a shortage of military recruits due to many factors including deployments, military operations, the impact of military life on families, and other factors according to Mark Mazzetti, "Army to Lower Bar for Recruits", Los Angeles Times, October 4, 2005. http://articles.latimes.com/2005/oct/04/nation/na-recruit4. More recently the military recruitment rates have improved due to the raising of enlistment ages, financial bonuses for signing up, the current tough economic times, and other factors. Recruiting for the military is always considered to be a challenge.

7   Officials state that "to meet the projected growth in demand for RN services, the U.S. must graduate approximately 90 percent more nurses from US nursing programs. Much of the shortage is blamed on a shortage of nursing school faculty rather than proof of an existing commitment crisis. American Academy of College Nursing, "Fact Sheet: Nursing Shortage", AACN, Updated September 2010, http://www.aacn.nche.edu/Media/FactSheets/NursingShortage.htm, 3 November, 2010.

8   The USCCB Committee on Clergy, Consecrated Life, and Vocations, "Priestly Vocations, Cultural Challenges and Foundations of Hope", United States Conference of Catholic Bishops, www.nccbuscc.org/vocations/articles/challenges.shtml , 3 November, 2010. This article included this prayer said by His Holiness Benedict XVI at the Chrism Mass Homily in St. Peter's Basilica on April 13, 2006.

9   Focus – Fellowship of Catholic University Students – has a ministry presence on fifty university campuses (some private but mostly public universities) in 27 different states and the District of Columbia. More information about the locations and mission and vision of this ministry for Catholic students can be found at "Fast Facts" , Focus, http://www.focusonline.org/site/PageServer?pagename=about_facts (November 2, 2010.

10   Even political atmospheres affect religious vocations; the USCCB reported that states which tend to vote Republican – aka the Red States – produce more vocations than states that historically drift toward Democrats – aka the Blue States.

11   The website for the Archdiocese of St. Paul- Minneapolis is: www.10000Vocations.org. There are many diocesan-specific websites available for your information throughout the country. Check out your diocesan website for more information. You might also be interested in visiting "Vocation Basics" www.vocations.com (3 November, 2010) and http://romancatholicvocations.blogspot.com/2009/04/young-nun-to-be-must-wipe-out-debt.html for a list of excellent sites that contain information about discerning vocations.

12   Called By Name is a program wherein parishioners nominate young people who they think would make good priests. These young people are then invited to an evening of fellowship and discussion about vocations in their parish.

13   These vocation rates are specific for St. John Vianney Seminary, University of St. Thomas, St. Paul, MN. Vocation rates vary by institutions. This number was obtained during my discussion with Susan Pittman, Archdiocese of St. Paul, Minneapolis.

14 Jeff Ziegler, "Priestly Vocations in America: A Look At the Numbers", Catholic World Report, 2005 http://www.ignatiusinsight.com/features2005/print2005/ziegler_seminarians_aug05.html (3 November, 2010).

15 Ibid.

16 Ibid.

17 Fr. Father Michael Creagan, Pastor of St. Joseph's Catholic Church, West St. Paul, Minn., conversation, Fall, 2010.

18 The USCCB Committee on Clergy, Consecrated Life, and Vocations, "Priestly Vocations, Cultural Challenges and Foundations of Hope", United States Conference of Catholic Bishops, www.nccbuscc.org/vocations/articles/challenges.shtml , 3 November, 2010.

19 Ibid.

20 Fidelis Tracy, C.D.P , "Vocations: How Is God Calling Me?", American Catholic.org, http://www.americancatholic.org/Newsletters/CU/ac0801.asp. 3 November, 2010.

21 Ibid.

22 Martin Pable, OFM Cap, "How to Know You Have a Vocation To The Religious Life", http://pathsoflove.com/articles/discernment-MartinPable.html

23 Ibid.

24 2009 tuition rates.

25 "Founded in 2003 (based in Eagan, MN), the Labouré Society has assisted over 200 individuals into priestly and religious formation through the resolution of financial impediments; substantially, in the form of school loans. They currently have over 70 men and women in their current portfolio. They invite others to partner with them in prayer and financial support! More information about the society can be found by visiting http://labouresociety.org/ (4 November, 2010) There are other organizations, groups of people and ways that young men and women can eliminate college debt including benefits, fundraisers, appealing to friends and family members, etc.

26 "Consecrated Virgins" Vocations.ca; http://www.vocations.ca/Questions/How_do_i_become/Consecrated_lay_person/virgins.php, 3 November,2 010.

27 Ibid.

28 Judith Stegman, " Consecrated Virgins Living in the World", Consecrated Virgins.org; http://www.consecratedvirgins.org/welcome.html, 3 November, 2010.

29 Catechism of the Catholic Church, (New York: An Image Book, Doubleday, 1995), No. 924.

CHAPTER TWELVE

1 David M.Martin, Geraldine Cassidy, Farooq Ahmad, and Mary S. Martin, "Women With Learning Disabilities and Menopause", Journal of Intellectual Disabilities (2001, Vol. 5): 122.

2. Ibid.

3 Ann Taylor, "Systemic Adversities of Ovarian Failure", Journal of the Society for Gynecologic Investigation (2001, Vol. 8, No. 7): 58.

4 Lynnette Leidy Sievert, Menopause a Bio-Cultural Perspective (New Jersey: Rutgers University Press, 2006), 35. You might also be interested in these additional facts. Just "prior to ovulation the primordial follicle(s) advance to the preantral stage and then onto the antral state where the follicles are protected by granulosa and theca cellular envelopes; they also produce the necessary hormones for ovulation. The size of the "maturing" follicle increases as it matures from a primordial follicle to the pre-ovulatory state. For instance, a primordial follicle it is only about 0.5 mm in diameter, the preantral stage follicle is about 2 mm in size, the antral stage follicle is about 5 mm in diameter, and, finally the pre-ovulatory stage follicle has grown to roughly 20 mm in size.

5 Ibid.

6 A. Stuart Mason (MD; F.R.C.P), "The Events of the Menopause", The Journal of the Royal Society for the Promotion of Health (1976, Vol. 96): 70.

7 G.C.Lasiuk and K.M. Hegadoren, "The Effects of Estradiol in Central Serotonergic Systems and its Relationship to Mood in Women", Biological Research for Nursing (2007, Vol. 9): 151.

8 Ibid.

9   Lynnette Leidy Sievert, Menopause a Bio-Cultural Perspective (New Jersey: Rutgers University Press, 2006), 35.

10   Andrew Kaunitz, "Hormonal Contraception in Women of Older Reproductive Age", New England Journal of Medicine (2008, Vol. 358):1262.

11   Christopher Longcope, "Endocrine Function of the Postmenopausal Ovary", Journal of the Society for Gynecologic Investigation (2001, Vol. 1, No. 8):1.

12   World Health Organization, "WHO Technical Report: Research on the Menopause in the 1990's", Series 866 (1996): 31.

13   Anders Svensson, Mark Connolly, Frederico Gallo, and Leif Hagglund, "Long Term Fiscal Implications of Subsidizing In Vitro Fertilization in Sweden: a Lifetime Tax Perspective", Scandinavian Journal of Public Health (2008): 841.

14   Rene Almeling, "Selling Genes, Selling Gender, Egg Agencies, Sperm Banks and the Medical Market in Genetic Material", American Sociological Review (2007): 320.

15   Toby L. Schonfeld, "Smart Men, Beautiful Women: Social Values and Gamete Commodification", Bulletin of Science Technology and Society (2003): 169.

16   Katherine H. Shelton, Jacky Boivin, Dale Hay, Marianne, B.M. van den Bree, Francis J Rice, Gordon T. Harold, Anita Thapar, "Examining Differences in Psychological Adjustment Problems Among Children Conceived by Assisted Reproductive Technologies", International Journal of Behavioral Development (2009): 385.

17   Toby L. Schonfeld, "Smart Men, Beautiful Women: Social Values and Gamete Commodification", Bulletin of Science Technology and Society (2003):170 -171.

18   Rene Almeling, "Selling Genes, Selling Gender, Egg Agencies, Sperm Banks and the Medical Market in Genetic Material", American Sociological Review (2007): 320.

19   Dr. Jack Burnham, Teaching Notes of the Couple to Couple League for Natural Family Planning, (Jan. 1, 2008): R-4.

20   USCCB Committee on Laity, Marriage, Family Life, and Youth, Marriage, Love and Life in the Divine Plan: A Pastoral Letter - abridged version, (Washington, DC, Feb. 2010, Publication No. 7-113), 21.

21   P. Frank- Hermann, J. Heil, D. Gnoth, "The Effectiveness of a Fertility Based Method to Avoid Pregnancy in Relation to a Couple's Sexual Behavior During the Fertile Time; a Prospective Longitudinal Study", Human Reproduction (2007): 10.

22   Cristina Alarconis, "An Ecological Blindspot? Contraceptives are polluting women's bodies and the environment, but who cares?", Mercator.net, Nov.. 15, 2010, http://www.mercatornet.com/articles/view/an_ecological_blind_spot/Contraceptives are polluting women's bodies and the environment, but who cares?, 18 November, 2010. Cristina Alarconis, pharmacist and writer holds a Masters in Bioethics; she lives in Vancouver, BC. Her articles are posted regularly on Mercator.net.
Each of the points below this reference point was also obtained from this source.

23   Linda Kracht, "What's in Your Water? ", Fortifying Families of Faith.com, http://fortifyingfamiliesoffaith.blogspot.com/search/label/drinking%20water: Nov. 4, 2010.

24   Ibid.

25   Ibid.

26   Pope Paul VI, "HUMANAE VITAE: On The Regulation Of Birth", (1968): No. 21.

27   Bill Turrentine's served with me on the Board of Directors for the Couple to Couple League. The statement was recorded at a Board meeting in Feb. 2010.

28   Ibid.

Conclusion

1   Carl Anderson and Jose' Granados, Called to Love (New York: Doubleday Publishing Group, 2009). 35

2   U.S. Census Bureau, US and World Population Clocks, http://www.census.gov/main/www/popclock.html (15 November, 2010, 18.41 UTC)

3   The two comments listed in quotation marks are extracts from Gaudium et Spes, an encyclical written December 7, 1965 by the late Pope Paul VI.

4   Proverbs 1:8; 6:20-24

The Female and Male Reproductive System

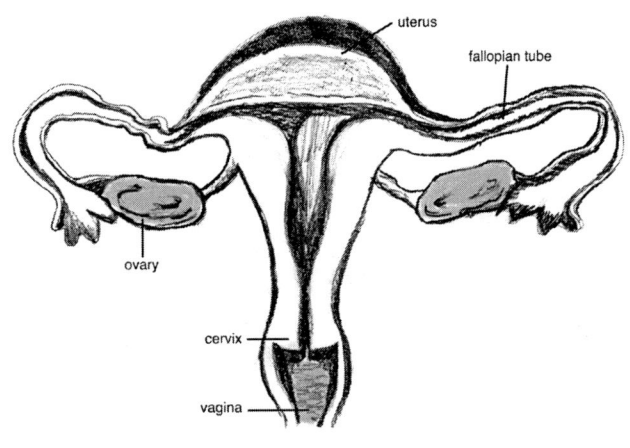

FEMALE REPRODUCTIVE SYSTEM

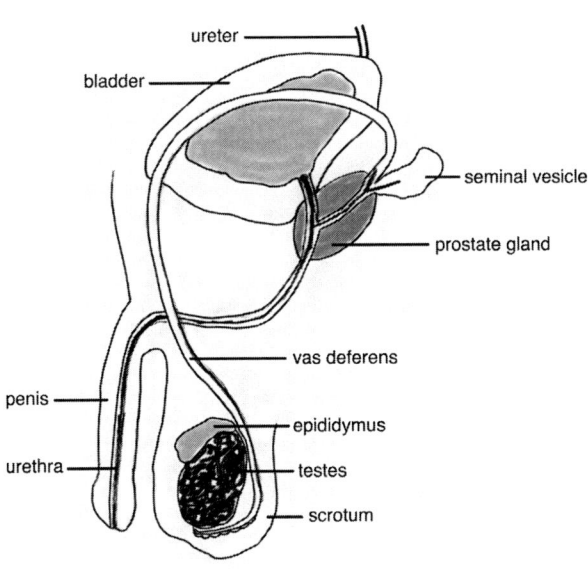

MALE REPRODUCTIVE SYSTEM